W9-BWD-423

How
to Peel
a Peach

How to Peel a Peach

AND 1,001 OTHER THINGS EVERY

GOOD COOK NEEDS TO KNOW

Perla Meyers

WILEY

JOHN WILEY & SONS, INC.

To Claude and Peggy who are blessed wth the gift of curiosity in and out of the kitchen

This book is printed on acid-free paper.

Copyright © 2004 by Perla Meyers. All rights reserved

Published by John Wiley & Sons, Inc., Hoboken, New Jersey
Published simultaneously in Canada

No part of this publication may be reproduced, stored in a retrieval system, or transmitted in any form or by any means, electronic, mechanical, photocopying, recording, scanning, or otherwise, except as permitted under Section 107 or 108 of the 1976 United States Copyright Act, without either the prior written permission of the Publisher, or authorization through payment of the appropriate per-copy fee to the Copyright Clearance Center, Inc., 222 Rosewood Drive, Danvers, MA 01923, (978) 750-8400, fax (978) 750-4470, or on the web at www.copyright.com. Requests to the Publisher for permission should be addressed to the Permissions Department, John Wiley & Sons, Inc., 111 River Street, Hoboken, NJ 07030, (201) 748-6011, fax (201) 748-6008, e-mail: permcoordinator@wiley.com.

Limit of Liability/Disclaimer of Warranty: While the publisher and author have used their best efforts in preparing this book, they make no representations or warranties with respect to the accuracy or completeness of the contents of this book and specifically disclaim any implied warranties of merchantability or fitness for a particular purpose. No warranty may be created or extended by sales representatives or written sales materials. The advice and strategies contained herein may not be suitable for your situation. You should consult with a professional where appropriate. Neither the publisher nor author shall be liable for any loss of profit or any other commercial damages, including but not limited to special, incidental, consequential, or other damages.

For general information on our other products and services or for technical support, please contact our Customer Care Department within the United States at 800-762-2974, outside the United States at (317) 572-3993 or fax (317) 572-4002.

Wiley also publishes its books in a variety of electronic formats. Some content that appears in print may not be available in electronic books.

LIBRARY OF CONGRESS CATALOGING-IN-PUBLICATION DATA:

Meyers, Perla.
   How to peel a peach : and 1001 things every good
cook needs to know / Perla Meyers.
     p. cm.
   ISBN 0-471-22123-6 (Cloth)
1. Cookery--Miscellanea. I. Title.
TX652.M473 2004
641.5--dc22   2003019728

Printed in the United States of America

10 9 8 7 6 5 4 3

Contents

This book has been years in the making, and I am grateful to the many people who have helped me acquire the ingredients, refine the formula, and finally bring the finished product to the table.

First of all, a special thanks to Jane Dystel, my intrepid literary agent, whose support has been unwavering throughout.

And to Carolyn Niedhammer, whose extraordinary editorial expertise has been invaluable to my shaping and defining of such an expansive subject.

To JoAnn Pappano, whose organizational skills and endless patience kept me on track.

To my editor, Susan Wyler, for her unflagging enthusiasm and commitment, and for her editorial guidance. To senior production editor, Andrea Johnson, for her attention to detail and for keeping track of all the pieces. And to art director, Jeff Faust, for coordinating all the creative impulses that became the jacket design.

I also want to thank Alice Medrich, Norman Weinstein, Jeremy Marshall, Susan Purdy, Arianne Daguin and Karen Lee for sharing their knowledge and patiently answering my questions.

My gratitude, too, to the thousands of students all over the country who have attended my classes and whose questions both inspired and formed the basis for this book. Their inquisitiveness continues to fuel my own endless curiosity about the world of food, its ingredients, and its preparation.

To my husband Robert whose cooking questions over the past 35 years contributed greatly to this project.

And, finally, loving thanks to my mother who has always shared and supported my love for food.

Whenever I put together the menus for a series of workshops, I always focus on dishes that raise questions, because, to me, that is the main reason why a cooking class makes sense and why many people feel that they need to take them. Most cooking classes tend to be recipe driven, with basic ingredients and simple techniques taken for granted. This is frustrating for me as a teacher because I am never sure of how much my students really know about food, how their interest in food has developed, and how much I can assume they know.

My best classes are those where we start at the beginning—by taking a field trip to a local grocery store, specialty store, or farmers' market. We break up into groups, and each group shops for one of the recipes that will be made in class that day, with the option of picking up additional ingredients for a vegetable dish of their choice. When we meet again, we go over how each group has gone about the task of marketing, with the group's notes and questions. To me, this is where cooking begins—with the intimate knowledge of one's ingredients, how to shop for them, store them, and cook with them.

I still remember my first day at the École Hôtelière, in Lausanne, Switzerland, where I first studied cooking. The chef started the class by saying, "The quality of your cooking more often than not depends on the choices you make before you begin." This has been my motto ever since I started to cook 35 years ago.

Today, few people grow up learning to cook at the side of their grandmother or mother. At a time when mothers hold full-time jobs and grandmothers live hundreds of miles away, we don't learn to cook instinctively, knowing how to peel a tomato, roast a chicken, or make a simple vinaigrette. At the same time, many of us are exposed to better and better restaurants, food magazines that tempt us to try something new for supper, and cookbooks with recipes for dishes that range from Arborio rice and truffle soup to zabaglione. We have access to specialty shops that introduce us to unusual ingredients from around the world. We are curious. We travel, we taste, and we read about food.

It is at this point that many people decide to make use of their own kitchens and see what it would be like to put together a meal. An aspiring cook might start with a cookbook or two. The photographs look great, and they make you feel inspired, but the fact is that none of the books tells you where to start. Yes, you know you need some utensils and some pots. Of course, you have some basic equipment, but then what?

The first trip to the market can be a dizzying experience. Why buy that big box of kosher salt when you have perfectly good salt around? And olive oil—virgin? Extra virgin? Light? Does that mean less fat? What is the difference between the bottle of balsamic vinegar that costs four dollars and the one for twenty-eight dollars? Your recipe calls for whole Italian plum tomatoes, but getting the crushed ones would eliminate a whole step, so wouldn't it make sense to get the crushed?

You plan to grill and your shopping list calls for skirt steak, but the meat department carries only flank. Are they interchangeable? Your grocery store does not carry either fresh thyme or fresh basil. Is dry okay? The pears feel like rocks, the lemons like golf balls, but the market is running a special on oranges. Should you change the menu? You soon realize that you have more questions than answers.

It all seemed so simple when you read the recipes, but now how important is it that you stick to them? Where can you improvise? These are the normal questions that all cooks have, whether beginners, chefs, or seasoned home cooks. The fact is that cooking is not hard if you are curious and flexible. But an intimate knowledge of ingredients is a must. No matter how creative a cook you are, you will always be handicapped by mediocre ingredients, whether the pantry basics, produce, meat, or seafood.

It is essential to understand that all meals start at the grocery store, a farm stand, or a green market, and that shopping for food is the single most important step in the preparation of any dish. Although the art of buying food carefully is familiar to most Europeans, particularly in countries where real markets still thrive, selective marketing is not part of the American shopping tradition today. This is partly due to lack of time, but it is also caused by inexperience.

I am always surprised to hear how many people are actually intimidated by the idea of shopping in a small specialty store. They prefer the anonymity of a supermarket. Perhaps they feel that they will be expected to buy something if they walk into a small shop, or they don't really know what they want and hesitate to talk to the shopkeeper. But small-business people, particularly those who deal in food, know their merchandise and are usually flattered to be asked questions, as they are eager to share their knowledge. Even if you do most of your shopping in supermarkets, occasionally make time to stop by a small meat shop, fish store, or produce market. Talking to the shopkeeper and forging an ongoing relationship can be a valuable learning experience. The same goes for farmers' markets, where you are likely to connect with people who care about their produce, meat, fish, poultry, and cheese and where you can get a real sense of seasonality and freshness.

Personally, I never think of marketing as a quick one-stop, because this is where the creative process begins. But it makes sense to start off with some knowledge, and that is what this book is about. The more you understand about an ingredient, the easier shopping will be.

You will find that the largest chapter of this book focuses on produce because buying good fruits and vegetables is such an important part of cooking. I still remember asking my mother what kind of potatoes she used for making her wonderful mashed potatoes.

"There are only two types of potatoes," was her answer. "Good ones and bad ones. I use the good ones."

These days it is not that simple. Most markets carry three or four types of potatoes—the same goes for onions and greens. What I try to do in this book is work through the hype and

help you make the right choices when you go shopping for food. Once you get back in your kitchen with the best you can buy, it is important that you pay attention to proper technique, even if it is something as simple as roasting some carrots or sautéing a chicken breast.

To learn to cook well and gain confidence, you need to cook frequently. Cooking is about timing, about tasting, and most of all about feeling that it is worthwhile. It is not about a state-of-the-art kitchen or the best possible equipment. It is about loving to cook, not once a month or twice a year, not just to entertain or to impress a few friends, but because you like doing it. Creating a dish out of a few simple ingredients is ultimately extremely satisfying. That is why you should cook and that is why you should read this book.

I am often told that I am fortunate to be doing something that I really love to do, and it is true. Learning more and more about food, testing a new recipe, working with a new mushroom or fruit, cooking and savoring a new dish or one I have loved since childhood is a wonderful part of my life. I hope that by answering some of your questions, by being able to inspire you with my passion for good ingredients and the way to prepare them, I can make cooking a greater part of yours as well.

On a recent visit to a friend's house in New Mexico, I offered to make dinner. As we sat by the pool on a glorious spring day, we mapped out the menu. Asparagus risotto to start sounded like a good idea, followed by braised veal shanks with fresh peas and spring onions. Creamy mashed potatoes were also voted in. And to keep things rich, I convinced my friend that a marsala sabayon would make the ideal topping for local strawberries.

With an equipment list in hand, I decided to check out the kitchen before embarking on my shopping trip. What the kitchen cabinets revealed forced us to rethink everything. A couple of lightweight Revere Ware saucepans canceled the risotto, braising the veal shanks in a nonstick skillet seemed difficult at best, and attempting to make a sabayon in a makeshift glass double boiler would probably be a disaster.

Going back to square one, we decided on a nice salad and roast chicken accompanied by sautéed vegetables and roasted potatoes, which could be cooked in disposable foil pans. All that was kept of the original menu were the strawberries, but they would now be tossed in fresh orange juice, giving my hostess a chance to use her new toys: a juicer and a microplane zester.

The need to change the menu proved once again that without the right utensils, you are limited in what you can do. This does not mean that you need to invest in what the French call a *batterie de cuisine* to make a good meal. You can do wonders in a well-seasoned cast-iron skillet, and entire cuisines are based on grilling over small hibachis. Many a professional cook would laugh at the tables full of useless kitchen gadgets sold in cook shops and specialty stores these days.

When I left home for college in Switzerland in the early sixties, I raided my mother's kitchen for some cookware and tools. I did not plan to do very serious cooking, but by that time I was already hooked on the pleasures of preparing my own food and could not imagine relying on the school cafeteria. I remember settling on a couple of well-worn Le Creuset casseroles and a deep, cast-iron chicken fryer, some wooden spoons, and a few other odds and ends. The only thing I bought were two good knives, which I kept sharp by handing them over to my butcher every couple of weeks. All seemed well, and I coasted along, making some pretty tasty dishes that made me quite popular among my college friends.

Then I started cooking school and suddenly a world opened up to me. The right balloon whisk, rubber spatula, copper bowl, pepper mill, food mill, and best of all, mandoline— these were classic utensils that made all the difference. At the time we cooked in heavy tin-lined copper cookware, which had to be polished daily. Everything was done by hand—be it whisking a mayonnaise or beating egg whites or making a puree in a food mill.

All these tasks taught me the value of well-crafted kitchen utensils. The chef checked the edges of my knives daily, and my station had to be impeccably clean and organized, with chopped ingredients placed in bowls in order of

use. Gadgets were kept at a minimum and had to be placed in their exact place in the drawer, to be taken out only when needed.

At the beginning, it all seemed overwhelming and difficult, but I soon learned that the discipline would serve me well and that by learning to cook efficiently and by being organized, I was able to cooked more creatively. I learned that I did not need a drawer full of gadgets and bowls of all sizes, shapes, and materials; that flimsy saucepans were not worth whatever they cost; and that a good piece of cookware was worth the investment.

Soon I started to put together my own kitchen batterie, keeping my own style of cooking in mind. No need for various soufflé dishes or terrines, no need for individual quiche pans or copper molds, since I was not going to make soufflés or quiches or terrines. On my twenty-sixth birthday, however, my parents gave me a fabulous copper roasting pan and a 2-quart copper *faittout,* which means "does everything" and is, indeed, an all-purpose saucepan. (Thirty-five years later, these two pieces of cookware have traveled and moved with me and are still in constant use in my kitchen.) Slowly I put together the kitchen essentials I would need, adding and modernizing my equipment as time went on. My carbon steel knives gave way to stainless steel. Copper pots were replaced by enameled cast-iron and stainless steel saucepans, and old-fashioned iron skillets by some with a nonstick finish.

I can't stress enough that buying flimsy pots, pans, and other equipment is a waste of money. You really do not need that much, especially if you do not cook frequently, but buy the best there is, or at least the best you can afford. In some cases, if you feel that you can't handle the cost of a good piece of cookware at the time, wait until you can. When you settle for less quality, you will end up regretting it.

This does not mean that you need to waste money on "designer" tools. A simple well-crafted perforated spoon will do the same job as one imported from Italy or Switzerland. You do not need a state-of-the-art pasta pot or half a dozen food processor blades that you will never use. Do not buy knives or cookware in sets, but rather buy what you need and always keep in mind your own style of cooking. What is the point of investing in a beautiful copper bowl when all you will ever beat are 4 to 6 egg whites, which can be done perfectly well in a stainless steel bowl? And what is the point of buying an exquisitely crafted Japanese knife when you are never going to learn how to cut fish for sushi?

I'll confess that my kitchen has more whisks than I will ever need, more spatulas, and more gadgets—proof that I am a consummate consumer and that when you love to cook, it is almost impossible to pass a cookware shop or specialty store without being drawn in to purchase something that for the moment you cannot live without. But more and more I am actually streamlining my kitchen, getting rid of such excess items as a strawberry peeler or a clever but useless garlic press. At the same time, I am looking for new, useful tools. An Omega vegetable juicer suddenly makes sense, and I have replaced my old, rather heavy immersion blender with an updated lighter one. I recently discovered a wonderful All-Clad saucepan that has become my new risotto pot.

In the following Q & A's I try to answer some of the questions many of my students have asked me over the years. I am aware that cooks and bakers have different needs, and since baking is not on top of my list, I do not address in detail the needs of the "baking kitchen."

You'll find that your essential kitchen will change from year to year. As your cooking evolves, so will your needs and interest in cooking equipment. A cook who loves to experiment with dishes from the Far East will not need the same equipment as one who specializes in Italian dishes. You'll soon discover that acquiring new tools and learning to use them is part of the fun of cooking.

Equipment

■■■

Cutting Boards

I can never find a cutting board that feels good. What do you recommend?

I am very partial to wood, even though the days of wood in the kitchen are almost over. I hear all the arguments against wood, because if not cleaned properly, wood breeds bacteria. However, if you do take care of your chopping boards and clean them thoroughly, wood is still the very best surface to chop on and will not harm your knives. My choice is the J.K. Adams cutting board made of solid New England maple. It will not warp, but its drawback is that at six pounds, it is heavy and hard to maneuver back and forth to the stove. If you want a lighter board, choose one made of wood composite. I find the best way to clean cutting boards is with a light detergent, scrubbing well with a scraper to remove all food residue. When a cutting board is in need of serious cleaning, sprinkle it with kosher salt and leave overnight. Then use half a lemon from which you have already extracted the juice to scrub and remove stains.

TIP Remember to oil wood cutting boards once every six months with mineral or almond oil to prevent them from splitting.

Knives

What should I look for in a good knife?

First, it should be made of top-quality, no-stain high-carbon steel. Second, it should have a full-tang handle. The tang is the part of the blade that extends into and forms part of the handle. When the tang is the same length and shape of the handle and you can actually see it, that is called a full tang. When you pick up the knife, it should have good balance, and the grip should feel comfortable.

I know that good knives are a must, but how many do I need?

You do not need a lot of knives. The ones you do buy should be of top quality. Although it may save you some money, do not buy knives in a set. Instead, buy the following knives:

Three 3- to 4-inch paring knives. It is very tempting to buy inexpensive paring knives, since they are available in every hardware store.

But a cheap knife with a poor blade and uncomfortable handle is of little use. Paring knives must not be too flimsy, and you must be able to sharpen them. A dull paring knife is a dangerous tool. Companies such as Henckels make rather inexpensive paring knives with plastic handles that have good blades. They sharpen easily, and I highly recommend them.

An 8-inch chef's knife and possibly a 10-inch one, if your hand is large. This is the most important knife in the kitchen. It should be made of high-carbon steel with a full tang and a plastic-impregnated handle. If all of this sounds complicated, just stick to the top brands such as Wusthof or Henckels or one of the other companies that make excellent knives. The key is to buy them from a reputable source who will guide you through the maze of knives available without trying to sell you the store.

A 10-inch slicer. This may not be a knife you will use daily, but even if you roast a turkey or a leg of lamb only a couple of times a year, this knife will come in very handy. Be sure not to use it for daily chores, since the blade does not lend itself well to chopping or mincing.

A serrated knife. This is a good knife to have on hand for slicing tomatoes, cucumbers, and even small loaves of bread. I find that I use it a lot. The best one on the market is made by Wenger, a Swiss company. It is carried by many good specialty shops.

A bread knife. Here you do not need to spend much money, so choose one that feels good in your hand and is not too heavy.

A cleaver. This can be made of either stainless steel or carbon steel. Cleavers must be heavy. Remember that their main function is to go through bones. Always select a heavier cleaver than you think you need. At the end of the day you will be glad you did.

Is there an easy way to keep my knives sharp?

The best way to sharpen a knife is with a sharpening steel. However, I find that while this is a key kitchen gadget, most people do not know how to use it properly. I therefore recommend two tools:

1. **A kitchen honing device.** The concept is similar to that of an electric knife sharpener, but it is inexpensive. If you get the Chantry-Victor, which I consider to be the best one on the market, you can run your knives through it every day and keep a nice sharp edge on them for a very long time. Be sure, however, to change the blade on the Chantry about twice a year. You can order replacements through the Internet. Companies such as Henckels and Wusthof also make this device, but the Chantry-Victor is by far the sturdiest and best one on the market.

2. **An electric knife sharpener.** This is an expensive tool, but one that I recommend very highly. Two small hardened steels are placed at the correct angle for treating both sides of the blade at the same time. As you draw the blade through it, the knife edge is realigned, ensuring a sharp cutting edge. The best one on the market is Chef's Choice.

TIP Save an old paring knife for removing the plastic and metal bands on bottles and jars and cutting the plastic around wine bottles.

Miscellaneous Kitchen Tools

With all the peelers on the market, is there one that does the job better than others?

The most inexpensive and easy-to-clean peelers are U-shaped and come in a variety of colors. These peelers tend to remove more than just a thin layer of the peel, so I usually do not use them for delicate vegetables such as asparagus. I very much like the old-fashioned Marvel Peeler, a combination peeler, grater, and corer, which you can still find in hardware stores. The ever popular Oxo brand makes a most attractive and sturdy peeler as well. Most people love that heavy black rubber handle, though I find it too space consuming.

TIP Remember that peelers dull just like knives and since they cannot be sharpened, should be replaced once a year.

I notice that you travel with your own pepper mill. Do cooks get attached to a mill as they do to their own knives? Do you have a favorite?

The key to a good mill is its mechanism, and its function is to grind pepper evenly. When you find a mill that will do that, it is worth traveling with. I like two mills; both happen to be French. First, the Perfex, which could also be called "the perfect." This is a stainless steel mill that holds almost two tablespoons of peppercorns. I like the design of this mill, with its pull-out chute, and its adjustable tension knob that allows you change the coarseness of the grind. The Perfex is sturdy and functional and will probably never need replacing. Another great classic is the Peugeot wooden pepper mill. The mechanism of this mill is probably the best one made and because of its durability, it is used by other pepper mill manufacturers as well. I like the beechwood finish but also recommend buying the dark wood one if you plan to have two mills, one for black and one for white peppercorns.

I have an old-fashioned ball-bearing rolling pin but now see many other types. Which do you recommend?

When it comes to rolling pins, I am pretty old-fashioned and like a wooden pin rather than those made out of marble or glass. Many good cookware stores now carry the French style, a straight pin with tapered ends made out of maple or beechwood. These are both ideal for rolling out a pie crust dough.

Which spatula is better for glazing a cake— one that is straight or one that has the blade set at an angle?

They are both the same. Just be sure that the spatula has enough flexibility to evenly coat the cake.

I am a serious gadget consumer and find myself with tons of stuff, but I never seem to find the right gadget when I need it. What are the must-haves?

Here is my "almost basic" list with a few tips:

1. **Garlic press.** Be sure to buy a good sturdy one. The most reliable is still the Susi, from Zyliss of Switzerland. What makes it so user friendly is that you do not need to peel the cloves and it is easy to clean. Another one that is high on my list is the Henckels stainless steel model, which also has a ginger press attachment. Stainless steel is considered the very best material, since it does not discolor or change the taste of garlic.

2. **Whisks.** Do not buy a whisk in a hardware store or the average supermarket. The whisk is one of the most important tools in the kitchen, almost right up there with your knives. So invest in quality. You will need two sauce whisks, such as the ones made by Best. These are elongated in shape with either wood or stainless steel handles. You will also need an egg white whisk. Personally, I much prefer the wood handle. The longer the handle, the better, since it allows you more freedom to move your hand up and down when you are whisking whites.

3. **Salad spinner.** In this age of constant spraying of lettuce in supermarkets, the spinner has become an essential kitchen tool to remove all that moisture. You can also use it for other greens, especially spinach and escarole. It is worth investing in a good one such as the Swiss Zyliss or the Oxo, which do an excellent job.

4. **Corer.** The only time you really need a corer is when you make a baked apple and want to fill the center with some butter, nuts, and spices. It is then you reach for this particular tool, and there is really nothing else that will do the job. Corers do not do a perfect job of coring an apple, and chances are that you will still have some seeds and bits of the core in the apple no matter which gadget you use.

5. **Melon ball cutters.** These gadgets come in many sizes and can produce both rounds and ovals. Once available only to professionals, they are now sold in good

cook shops. I highly recommend them because they are fun and can turn certain vegetables into decorative shapes. These may not be everyday gadgets and do not need to be top of your list, but if you do see them and wonder what to do with them, think twice and you will come up with many interesting ideas that can really change the appearance of a dish. Think of a round tiny zucchini or potato ball or an oval carrot ball.

So many recipes refer to a mandoline these days. Does it do anything that the food processor can't do?

The principle behind the mandoline is that you slide food over the blade, which allows you to slice it as finely and evenly as you like. This device is mostly used by restaurants for cutting vegetables and fruit into slices or strips. Although the manufacturers of food processors claim that you can do this well in a food processor, the results are not the same, and a mandoline is a great tool well worth investing in. You can now get an inexpensive mandoline made out of plastic that will do a very good job of slicing. But once you get beyond this and into serious cooking, you may want to invest in either the classic stainless steel French mandoline made by Bron or the new one by Matfer, also from France. This mandoline is easier to use and great fun. I highly recommend it.

TIP **Mandolines come with guards, which I find hard and cumbersome to use. Instead, I use a kitchen towel to hold the food in place. Also it is key to remember to keep your hand flat to avoid cutting your knuckles on the blade!**

Pots and Skillets

Which cookware set do you recommend?

It is tempting to buy a multiple-piece set of cookware. There are fewer decisions to make and you can save quite a bit of money. But there are large disadvantages. In many sets, one or several of the pieces duplicate the function of other pieces, and quite frankly, there is no culinary rationale for having matching pots and pans because no single kind of cookware does the best job for every kind of cooking. For a well-equipped kitchen, you should capitalize on the best features of each kind of cookware, even if the pots and pans are not matching. Of course, if you are starting from scratch, buy a small set of no more than five pieces plus lids, composed mostly of saucepans and possibly including an omelet pan. Supplement these pieces with cookware made of solid materials, such as cast iron or heavy-gauge stainless steel, suitable for specific purposes.

What size saucepans should I have? How heavy do they need to be?

I like to use easy-to-clean, medium-gauge stainless steel or anodized saucepans such as Cuisinart or All-Clad.

For starters, get three sizes: 1-, 2-, and 3-quart pans with lids. Now you are pretty much covered if you want to do anything from boiling water to cooking vegetables. When you get into the more serious cooking, the 3- and 4-quart heavy enameled saucepans from Le Creuset are a must. With these you can make more complicated sauces, risottos, and pilafs, and every kind of soup. If you plan to work with chocolate, sugar, or very delicate sauces, you should invest in one tin or stainless steel–lined copper saucepan with cast-iron handles. This is an expensive piece of cookware that is extremely high maintenance, but I wouldn't be without it because it heats up and cools down quickly and evenly, giving you complete control.

TIP Avoid flimsy light saucepans, since even water will burn in them. Also, as you are cooking, you will get a better idea of what size you use the most and you can build from there.

Is it necessary to have both a pasta pot and a stockpot?

A good-quality, heavy-gauge 8-quart stockpot can easily double as a pasta pot and I use mine all the time. The advantage of a pasta pot is the steamer insert, which is very helpful in draining pasta. However, if I had to choose one or the other, I would go with a quality stockpot such as the Calphalon commercial hard anodized nonstick stockpot or the Chantal enamel stockpot.

Are there some pots that are better suited for cooking on an electric stove?

Yes, the heavier stainless steel saucepans in which the steel or aluminum core is sealed between two layers of stainless steel are the best saucepans. They are also expensive. Another good choice is aluminum saucepans with a gray anodized coating that is guaranteed for life. I find them most useful because the handles stay cool.

What shall I look for in a skillet?

A heavy black cast-iron skillet is the best and most versatile piece of cookware I know. It can be used for anything, including oven-roasting. Cast iron needs getting used to, since it retains heat and does not cool quickly. Also, it is heavy, and the handle does get hot, but it is such a great piece of cookware that you will soon be willing to overlook these small inconveniences.

TIP For vegetable sautéing, pan-searing of fish, and egg cookery, I like heavy aluminum pans with a nonstick coating. All nonstick coating scratches and wears off, but the heavier skillets are better balanced with handles that do not heat up and overall are extremely forgiving. My favorite brand is All-Clad.

What size skillets do I need?

I recommend two 10-inch and one 12-inch skillet rather than 14-inch skillets. Larger skillets are hard to maneuver and they will never cook food evenly, especially if you are cooking on electric heat.

For the more serious cooks and those who cook with gas, the best sauté pan, or deep skillet, is made of heavy copper lined with either tin or stainless steel and with an iron handle. This fabulous piece of equipment is heavy but will do a great job on anything from slow-braising vegetables to cooking a cut-up chicken to perfection on top of the stove. The best size for the home cook is a 3-quart pan, about 10 inches in diameter.

For quick sautéing of small quantities, you should have at least two 8-inch skillets, preferably with nonstick coating. For specialty cooking such as stir-frying and crepe making, it is good to have a carbon steel flat-bottomed wok and a traditional black steel crepe pan.

My mother gave me her favorite cast-iron skillet. How can I use it so that food doesn't stick?

It needs to be seasoned properly, which you should do by covering the bottom with a thick layer of kosher salt, then adding ½ inch cooking oil. Place the pan on top of the stove. Heat the oil until it is almost smoking, then pour it out into a dry metal container. With a large ball of paper towel to protect your hand, wipe the surface of the skillet clean. Your pan is now perfectly seasoned. It will be practically maintenance free and can be used for anything, including oven-roasting. Its only drawback is that it should not come in contact with any acid foods such as tomatoes, lemons, or wine.

TIP Once a cast-iron skillet has been seasoned, never wash it with soap and never scrub it with anything but a soft sponge. If food gets stuck in it, treat the area again with a little coarse salt, rubbing it with a paper towel. Never soak in water and remember to reseason every 6 to 8 months or whenever food starts to stick.

I love to stir-fry but do not have a gas stove. Can you recommend a good pan to stir-fry in?
My favorite stir-fry pan is the original flat-bottomed wok by Joyce Chen. It is made out of carbon steel, which unfortunately cuts down on heat and makes the food steam slightly, but the flat bottom enables you to use it on any cooking surface. Also, the domed cover is a terrific asset, since it allows you to use the pan as a steamer. The pan comes in various sizes; I recommend the 12-inch size.

Do you recommend buying a double boiler?
I have a wonderful old aluminum double boiler that my mother-in-law gave me years ago and I use it often. But with the advantages of the microwave, you rarely need a double boiler. As for stovetop cooking, you can use a good saucepan with a heavy stainless steel bowl that

fits snugly into it. If you are tempted to get a double boiler, do not buy a glass one, since they are poor conductors of heat.

Bowls

Mixing bowls come in glass, ceramic, and metal. Which are the most versatile?
Take your cue from restaurants that use only stainless steel with an occasional ceramic bowl for fruit salads, mixed salad, or dough. Heavy-duty stainless steel bowls are the best, but the only time weight really matters is when you are going to use them as the top part of a double boiler for making a custard or keeping something warm, such as a potato puree or a puree of vegetables. Otherwise, inexpensive stainless steel bowls are fine. The nesting glass bowl sets are very popular, but I am not much of a fan of glass.

TIP It is not a good idea to whip cream or egg whites in a glass bowl because it is hard to chill the bowl properly and evenly.

Do you recommend a copper bowl for beating egg whites?
I use my copper bowl all the time. A copper bowl is still the best tool for beating the perfect egg white because of the alchemy that takes place between copper and the protein in the egg whites and makes the foam more stable. Egg whites beaten in copper will also expand more when heated. Don't buy an expensive copper bowl, because they all do the same trick. Twelve inches in diameter is ideal.

Try this recipe for Sherry Citrus Sabayon In a bowl, combine ¾ cup cream sherry with 5 egg yolks and ½ cup sugar. Add 2 teaspoons orange zest and I teaspoon lemon rind and whisk the mixture until well blended. **Transfer to a copper bowl set over simmering water and whisk the mixture constantly until thick and smooth. Remove and transfer to a bowl. Chill until set. Whip I cup heavy cream until it forms soft peaks and fold into the mixture. Chill until ready to serve. Serve with poached pears, sliced strawberries, or raspberries.**

TIP **Before using your copper bowl, make sure that it is spotless by cleaning it with white vinegar and then rinsing it with soapy water. If there is even a speck of grease in the bowl, it will keep your whites from foaming.**

Roasting Pans, Baking Dishes, and Casseroles

I still have my old roasting pan that came with my oven, but I am ready for a new one. What do you recommend?

The most important feature of a roasting pan is weight, so look for a heavy roasting pan in which you can easily roast a large turkey, a leg of lamb, or a ham. My favorite pans are the enameled cast iron by Le Creuset and the All-Clad stainless steel roasting pan. Choose a pan 13 to 14 inches long, about 10 inches wide, and no more than 2 inches high. If the sides of a roasting pan are too high, the food will steam rather than roast. Make sure that the handles of the pan are comfortable, since you will have to handle the pan several times during cooking to baste your roast and check the pan juices.

When heavy roasting pans are full of food they become difficult to lift. Are there lighter versions that will do the job?

Roasting pans are meant to hold heavy ingredients and to be moved from the oven to the top of the stove for last-minute cooking such as deglazing or reducing a sauce. This cannot be done with a lightweight pan. Several companies such as Calphalon make lighter nonstick roasting pans but I do not recommend them, since I find them too flimsy. Nonstick is not a good choice when it comes to roasting pans, since the pan juices do not caramelize.

TIP **You must use the right size roasting pan for the amount of food you are cooking. If you use a large roasting pan for making a small roast or a single chicken, the pan juices will burn. On the other hand, if you use a pan that is too small for the size roast you are making, the food will steam rather than roast.**

Can I use a 12-inch black cast-iron skillet for roasting?

Absolutely. I do it all the time. A cast-iron skillet is perfect for roasting a chicken or half a leg of lamb. Because cast iron retains heat, you will have to watch your roast carefully and baste often so as not to burn the pan juices. Also remember that the handle will be very hot, so be sure to keep a couple of pot holders on hand.

What is the difference between a roasting pan and a baking dish?

The difference is only a matter of size and material. You need a roasting pan of a certain size for a turkey, leg of lamb, or brisket or if you are roasting more than one duck. But many foods such as potato gratin, roasted vegetables, pudding, or braised vegetables are cooked in a baking dish. You should invest in at least two or three baking dishes of various sizes.

There seems to be an endless choice of baking dishes. Which are the best sizes and which is the best material?

For best results, choose baking dishes that are shallow to allow the heat to circulate around the ingredients. Avoid glass, which is a poor conductor of heat. The best choice is porcelain, followed by glazed earthenware. I also like enameled cast iron, which is heavy and sturdy and perfect for roasting vegetables and a single chicken. Always check the handles; they should be practical and easy to handle. My favorite sizes are 9 by 11 inches (5 quarts) or 9 by 13 inches (6 quarts). Another good size is a rectangular 10-quart dish that measures 12 by 10 inches by 2¼ inches deep. These are standard sizes and easy to find in good cook shops in a variety of materials. They should be microwave proof and able to stand low direct heat.

There are so many casseroles to choose from these days. Which do you recommend and what are the best sizes?

My favorite casserole and one that I always recommend is the cast-iron one by Le Creuset. Yes, it is heavy, but it is a great piece of cookware that will last you a lifetime. The best sizes are the 4½- and 6-quart round casseroles. If you like to make short ribs, lamb shanks, or stew for a large number of people, then the 9-quart oval is also a good piece to have.

Electric Appliances

I am just starting to equip my kitchen and have limited space. Which appliances shall I start with?

I would start with a hand-held electric mixer that will mix, whip, and blend, and an immersion blender. Combined, these will do the same jobs as a food processor and take up less space, provided that you are willing to use your knives for cutting and slicing and a four-sided grater for shredding. The immersion blender is the best tool for pureeing soups right in the pot and for making vinaigrettes and mayonnaise-based sauces.

My old electric hand mixer has finally given up. Which one do you recommend?

My two favorite hand mixers are the KitchenAid and the Cuisinart. The KitchenAid is strong and sturdy but not too heavy. It is also quieter than the old-fashioned mixers. The beaters are easy to clean, and I especially like the soft-start feature that eliminates splattering the dough or whipped cream all over the place. What is more, it comes in a variety of colors. Another equally good choice is the Cuisinart, which is designed for both left- and right-handed cooks. Its best feature is a balloon whisk that beats whites better than any hand mixer I have ever had.

Do you recommend the KitchenAid heavy-duty mixer? Many of my friends have it.

The KitchenAid is a favorite classic that many serious cooks rely on. It is great for baking and eases the task of making a double batch of cookies, making bread dough, or beating more than 6 egg whites. It also has the advantage of supporting attachments such as a pasta maker, citrus juicer, and meat grinder. However, it is not on my list for beginner cooks or those who are not interested in baking.

One of my wedding presents, a Crockpot, is still in the box. What is the best use for it?

Crockpots are great for cooking beans at a slow, even temperature with no worry about the

KITCHEN TOOLS

THE BASICS

2-cup glass measure

1-cup glass measure

1 set heavy, stainless steel dry measuring cups

2 sets measuring spoons, preferably stainless steel

Instant-read thermometer, preferably Taylor

Nutmeg grater

2 metal turner spatulas

Cake spatula with flexible stainless steel blade and wooden handle

2 flexible rubber scrapers

Soup ladle

Four-sided grater

Potato ricer or masher

Long-handled fork

Bulb baster, preferably glass rather than plastic

Bottle opener

Corkscrew

Food mill, either plastic or stainless steel

Basic can opener, not electric

2 stainless steel slotted spoons

2 stainless steel long-handled spoons

2 kitchen tongs, 1 short, 1 long

Vegetable peeler

Kitchen timer

Salad spinner, preferably Oxo or Zyliss

Wooden or metal pasta fork

3 to 4 wooden spoons

Balloon whisk

Sauce whisk

Reamer

Zester

Garlic press

Colander

2 sieves, 1 large, 1 small

Ice cream scoop

Kitchen shears

BAKING EQUIPMENT

2 9-inch round cake pans, heavy-duty aluminum or heavy-gauge steel with nonstick coating by Chicago Metallic

9-inch springform pan

2 standard 8½ by 4½-inch bread pans

4 nonstick 6 by 3-inch loaf pans

Bundt pan

8-inch pie pan

9-inch pie pan

2 baking sheets, preferably rimless, shiny heavy-duty aluminum

Jellyroll pan, preferably with a matte uncoated aluminum finish by Chicago Metallic

Flour sifter

2 10-inch quiche pans, preferably porcelain

Pastry brush with boar bristles

ELECTRIC APPLIANCES

Food processor

Blender

Electric hand mixer

Immersion blender

Toaster

Coffee grinders, one for coffee, one for spices

POTS AND SKILLETS

1½- to 2-quart saucepans

8-quart stockpot

Pasta pot with steamer insert

8-inch nonstick skillet

10-inch cast-iron skillet

10-inch nonstick skillet

12-inch heavy-gauge sauté pan

6-quart casserole

½- to 6-quart Dutch oven or braising pan

Roasting pan

2 baking dishes

Double boiler, optional

water boiling away and the beans burning. You can also use it for soups. Look for models in which the cooking pot is removable for easier cleaning.

I still have my very first food processor, but the blade is not sharp and the motor is finally giving out. What shall I buy to replace it?

Cuisinart, the pioneer of the food processor, still continues to make some of the best machines. The 14-cup-capacity basic machine would be my choice. The good news is that it now comes with an easy-to-handle cover that eliminates the need of using the rather complicated feed tube when you are not slicing or shredding. If you are looking for something smaller, Cuisinart also makes an 11-cup version ideal for smaller kitchen spaces or if you are not cooking large quantities. Another excellent choice is the KitchenAid Professional food processor, which features a top of the line blade made by Sabatier and comes with a small 3-cup bowl and blade that is perfect for chopping small amounts of ingredients such as parsley, a few cloves of garlic, or cheese. Although this machine comes with only two extra blades, they are really all you need. You can buy an additional five-disk set that includes a French fry cutter and a julienne disk.

I use my food processor all the time, but many recipes call for a blender. What is the difference? Do I need both?

The food processor is a terrific tool, but when it comes to a very fine puree or a homemade mayonnaise, the blender does a better and smoother job. The new blenders are much more powerful than they used to be, so if you want to make a summer smoothie, a gazpacho, or an herb mayonnaise, I would definitely invest in a blender such as the Kitchen Aid Ultra Power blender or the Waring professional blender.

To make blender mayonnaise Combine 1 whole egg, 1 egg yolk, 1 teaspoon Dijon mustard, 1 tea-spoon red wine vinegar or 2 teaspoons lemon juice, and a pinch of salt in the container of the blender. With the machine running, add $\frac{2}{3}$ cup oil (half grapeseed, half olive oil) in a very slow drizzle and blend until the mixture is thick. Correct the seasoning. Transfer to a container and chill. This makes 1 cup of mayonnaise that will keep for 4 to 6 days. For herb mayonnaise, add 2 tablespoons chives, parsley, dill, cilantro, tarragon, or basil or use a combination of herbs, such as chives and parsley, dill and chives, tarragon and parsley, or cilantro and parsley.

A friend gave me an immersion blender, and I have yet to use it. What exactly is it good for?

The immersion blender has been a household basic in kitchens throughout Europe for over twenty years. Its advantage is that it takes up little space and allows you to puree soups and vegetables right in the pot—no need to transfer foods to the container of a food processor, less cleaning up, and more counter space. I use mine all the time. The immersion blender makes great mayonnaise in seconds and is excellent for whipping cream as well.

No matter whether you are a beginner cook or a chef, a well-stocked pantry is the key to even the most basic cooking. Salt and pepper, oil and vinegar, herbs and spices, butter and eggs, flour and chocolate are just some of the ingredients that can make a significant difference in the results of any recipe. Knowing how to buy them and use them is important.

Smart shopping is fundamental to good cooking. Before you set out to make a dish, whether a simple salad or a complex ragout, you should learn to make smart choices about ingredients. Always ask yourself, why? What is the difference between kosher salt and fine salt? Do you need both? Should you use ground spices or whole? And which brand of, say, canned tomatoes should you buy?

Your pantry should contain all the right everyday ingredients needed to create good, flavorful food. But exactly what it should be stocked with has much to do with personal preference and the kind of cooking you plan to do. Because our food cupboards reflect our lifestyles and habits, no two are alike; no two contain exactly the same items. If you like to dabble in Chinese or Indian cooking, then an Asian ingredient shelf is a must. If, on the other hand, you prefer Mexican food, then several types of dried chiles are an important part of your pantry. And for those who like to bake, two or three types of flour, three kinds of sugar, nuts, vanilla beans, cocoa, dried fruit and a couple of types of chocolate are all key staples.

Because I love Italian and Spanish food and cook it often, I keep at least three kinds of pasta, excellent extra virgin olive oil, whole canned tomatoes, dried porcini mushrooms, and three types of rice in my pantry. Your pantry, on the other hand, may reflect your fascination with Thai or Indian cooking, your penchant for spur-of-the-moment salads, or your husband's love for peanut butter and preserves.

To keep a well-stocked pantry that feels "fresh," you need to shop carefully and often with a thorough understanding of ingredients. Personally, I follow no set schedule for restocking. Since I love to shop spontaneously and enjoy even a large supermarket, I am constantly replenishing my pantry shelves.

There are, I believe, certain guidelines for shopping wisely for the kinds of basics needed for everyday cooking. They can help us steer clear of trendy, overpriced, and out-of-season foods that don't deliver. While it is fun to browse through a good gourmet shop and check out the new items on the shelf, I try to focus on how I would use them. White truffle honey sounds great, but would it fit into my cooking repertoire? And how would I really use the beautifully bottled currant vinegar? If I feel that this will be an item that could just gather dust in my cabinet, I opt instead for a quality mustard or excellent peppercorns that I know I will use frequently.

I divide my pantry into a basic shelf, an ethnic shelf, and the refrigerator for perishable ingredients. It goes without saying that real basics like dried herbs, spices, dried beans, good oils, canned tomatoes, condiments, potatoes, garlic, and onions create the backbone of everyday

cooking. But because our repertoire has expanded to include a wide variety of international and regional dishes, what used to be considered an exotic ingredient has likely become a pantry staple. Now fresh ginger, soy sauce, toasted sesame oil, coconut milk, and rice vinegar share the ethnic shelf with porcini mushrooms, truffle oil, and balsamic vinegar.

Your refrigerator should include fresh milk, yogurt, unsalted butter, and eggs. Add sour cream or crème fraiche if you use them frequently. Think of your freezer as part of the pantry, too, and use it for supplies like stock, frozen berries, nuts, ice cream, and pastry dough.

Since you will be spending time and effort on purchasing excellent ingredients, you will want them to be in top condition when you are ready to cook with them. The most important aspect of extending shelf life and maintaining quality is proper storage.

It is easy to recommend that you store spices, oils, potatoes, and other basics in a cool dark place. In a perfect world we would all have cool, dark basements, but the reality is that we keep things stored in the kitchen, which tends to be hot. That is why—short of ripe tomatoes and semi-ripe fruit—your best bet is to refrigerate everything you do not use on a constant basis. This includes rice, dried beans, nuts, fruity oils, and most spices. I keep my olive oil in the refrigerator.

For me, the best invention is the zippered plastic bag, which I use for everything, including the basic vegetables, which I try to shop for at least once a week. Do not let the vegetable bin become a catchall. Use produce while it is fresh and tasty, and keep it organized. Don't buy six lemons or limes if they are going to end up shriveled in the back of the bin. Buy what you need and use them, then buy more.

Be sure to buy a refrigerator thermometer and check the temperature often. If you are going to take up cooking seriously and want to be prepared to react spontaneously to a craving for your favorite dish, you'll need to keep your pantry up to date. Stale ingredients won't give you the results you want. Perla's rule: If it is out of date or out of taste, throw it out!

Admit to yourself that you'll never, ever use the rest of those pickled cactus pads you bought after that trip to Mexico five years ago.

Ask yourself why you seem to have an irrational, emotional attachment to that half bottle of rose water you used for a Moroccan recipe once. Admit that although you loved the food in Hungary, that can of paprika you bought there went flat two years ago. Throw it out!

And if you look in my pantry, please, don't ask me what I'm still doing with that enormous jar of miso mayonnaise, Aunt Sue's pear balsamic vinegar, the tiny bottles of fruit extract with pretty hand-painted labels, and the homemade jar of pickled asparagus that seems to have turned an unappetizing shade of chartreuse!

The Basic Pantry

■■

Anchovies

What should I look for when buying anchovies?

I always buy flat anchovies, since rolled ones are usually more expensive. The best anchovies are those packed in olive oil and imported from either Portugal or Spain. Avoid those imported from Taiwan, since they tend to be mushy and overly salty. Jarred Italian anchovies are more expensive than canned, but they are far more meaty and flavorful. Look for them in high-end grocery stores and specialty markets.

Is there an easy way to remove some of the saltiness of anchovies?

You can make anchovies less salty by soaking them in a little milk to cover for 10 to 15 minutes, then draining them well before adding to a dish.

Do anchovies give meat dishes a fishy flavor?

When mashed with a little garlic and fresh herbs, anchovies add a wonderful piquant flavor to a leg of lamb, a roasted chicken, or veal roast. In fact, used judiciously, anchovies act more like MSG—that is, enhancing flavor rather than adding a fishy taste.

Once I open a can of anchovies, I usually do not use the whole can. What is the best way to store them?

Anchovies will keep well in the refrigerator for several weeks. Just transfer them to a jar and cover with olive oil.

What is anchovy paste? How and when do you use it?

Anchovy paste is a mixture of pounded anchovies, vinegar, and spices. When all you need is a teaspoon or two, it offers a good alternative to canned anchovies. I often use anchovy paste to enhance the flavor of a mayonnaise, vinaigrette, or marinade. It is also mixed with soft butter for canapés and as a topping for grilled steaks.

Bouillon

When you can't make a homemade stock, which is better, bouillon cubes or canned stock?

I much prefer bouillon cubes or powder. But quite truthfully, I don't think either is good unless you boost its flavor. When using store-bought stock, simmer it for 20 to 30 minutes with some aromatic vegetables. I am a great believer in the extra flavor boost provided by a few extra chicken wings, which I keep in my freezer at all times. This will increase the cooking time to about 40 minutes, and, yes, it takes longer than opening a can but is still not as time consuming as making a big batch of stock from scratch.

Caperberries

Recently I sampled a wonderful dish of braised fish with olives and caperberries, which I had never tasted before. What exactly are caperberries and where can I get them?

A caperberry is the olive-sized fruit of the caper bush (rather than a bud, which is what a caper is). They are becoming very popular, but I have seen them for sale only in specialty stores, where they are stocked alongside capers and other condiments. You might try mail-ordering them from Zingerman's (see Sources, page 399).

Capers

What kind of capers are best? The salted ones or the ones in vinegar?

I much prefer the "meatier" salted capers. They are flavor packed and easy to handle. Simply rinse off the salt and use. For vinaigrettes and salads, I do use capers packed in vinegar. Your market may carry only the vinegar-packed variety, which in the end are really fine.

What's a nonpareil caper?

The small, young variety of caper called nonpareil is considered the most delicate. There are also larger capers available—some common ones are superfine, fine, and Capuchin. I find them less flavorful, but they are used extensively in Italian cooking, so I suppose it is really a matter of taste. Nonpareil capers are carried in grocery stores everywhere, so you should have no trouble finding them.

Cornichons

What are cornichons? Are they the same as gherkins?

Gherkins are small, young green cucumbers, used mainly for pickling, but they are also delicious raw. The smallest gherkins are called cornichons, which are harvested when very young and pickled. You may be most familiar with them as the tiny, tangy pickles traditionally served with a country pâté or sausages. I always add some diced cornichons to a tuna, egg, or chicken salad.

Cornmeal

I've seen blue cornmeal in specialty shops. Is it really derived from blue corn or is the coloring added later? Can I use it in place of yellow or white cornmeal?

Blue corn has been around for centuries and is grown and eaten by various Native American tribes for ceremonial use. Hybrids are now being cultivated to make the most of both yellow and blue corn. The blue color is actually purple pigment in the skin of the kernel, and the corn tastes much like yellow corn, depending on the variety. You can use blue cornmeal in recipes for cornbread, but add a pinch of baking soda to the batter to keep the blue looking blue, not murky. If you use blue cornmeal as breading, take care not to turn the oven heat too high. It tends to overbrown at temperatures higher than 350°F.

Mustards

There are so many different kinds of mustards in the grocery story. Which ones do I need?
If you are a mustard fan, one kind of mustard won't do. You should have on hand one good-quality Dijon mustard, a can of Coleman's dry mustard, and possibly a honey mustard if you like that taste. Other good choices are green peppercorn mustard and herb mustard. Mustard's affinity for meat and practically all salad dressings makes it an indispensable pantry basic.

What is the difference between Dijon mustard and other mustards?
The method of making Dijon mustard is quite different from methods used for other mustards. Traditionally, this mustard is made from seeds of a specific mustard plant called *Sinaplis alba* and is mixed with white wine. Dijon mustard has been made in the city of Dijon since the eighteenth century. The region is considered to grow the very best mustard seeds, and the variety *moutarde Blanc de Dijon* is stronger than other French mustards. I highly recommend Maille mustard, which is imported from France and when fresh has the right pungency and depth of flavor. If you can, avoid Grey Poupon Dijon mustard, which is made in California and has little flavor.

When do you use dry mustard?
A little dry mustard reconstituted with water goes a long way. I often add it to prepared Dijon mustard to kick up the flavor. Certain vegetables—especially carrots, greens beans, and celery root—need that extra punch, so whenever you make a mustard dressing to go with these vegetables, be sure to add some reconstituted dry mustard to the dressing.

If a recipe calls for Chinese mustard, can I substitute other mustard if I don't have any?
Chinese dry mustard is reconstituted for the mustard sauce that accompanies spareribs, dumplings, and other Chinese dishes. You can use Coleman's dry mustard.

Do I need to refrigerate mustard once the jar is opened? How long does it keep?
Once it's opened, definitely refrigerate mustard and even then try to use it within a few weeks. I consider myself a compulsive mustard buyer and never pass up an opportunity to buy it when I am in Canada or France. But I find that often the mustard does not hold up for more than a couple of months.

I recently opened a jar of mustard and it had a really off taste. How do you tell good mustard from bad?
Look at the jar and be sure to buy mustard only at a grocery store that sells a lot of it. If the mustard has separated and has even a tiny layer of oil at the very top, pass on it. Mustard has a limited shelf life and also loses taste and pungency if it has gone through extreme climate

changes, as it does in the winter months. I recommend buying it at a market, not necessarily a specialty store, with a large turnover. Do not hesitate to return it if the taste is off.

Olive Oil

There are so many different brands of olive oil. Which do you recommend?

For everyday use other than in salads, Bertolli, Colavita, and DeCecco virgin or extra virgin oil are good all-around choices. These are mass-produced oils and none, in my opinion, is good enough to be used in salad dressings. But they are fine for sautéing vegetable and tomato-based sauces. For salad dressings, I particularly like the Spanish L'Estornell, the French Nicolas Alziari, and the Tuscan Antinori, which are full bodied and fruity.

Pure olive oil has been chemically refined. This strips it of most of its flavor and aroma. The result is a rather tasteless, colorless oil. Sometimes you may see pure olive oil with a slightly greenish tinge, which means that a little extra virgin olive oil has been added to give it some flavor. It is fine for cooking but does not hold up in salads where a good olive oil shines.

What is the difference between virgin and extra virgin olive oil?

Extra virgin olive oil is made from the first pressing of the olives. It is essentially the juice of the olive and to qualify as extra virgin it must be of low acidity, less than 1 percent. The percentage is always printed on the label.

Virgin oil is made with olives that have already gone through the first pressing. This means that the oil has a much higher acidity level and is less flavorful.

There is such a price difference in olive oils. Why is that?

When you buy an olive oil, check the label to see if it tells you where the olives have been harvested. Many less expensive oils are labeled "Product of Italy," but the olives actually come from various parts of the world and are machine processed in Lucca, Italy, resulting in an oil with no distinctive flavor or quality. First-press extra virgin olive oil requires a lot of hand labor; hence the high price.

When it comes to picking an expensive high-quality olive oil, much depends on how much you like an intensely flavored oil. I would start with a small bottle of very good oil from either France, Spain, or Italy and use it in a simple vinaigrette. Then decide if you think the price is worth it.

What exactly is light olive oil? Is it lower in calories?

Light olive oil is a marketing gimmick. It has nothing to do with calories and everything to do with lack of taste. There is really little point in using it except for certain baking.

Can you tell a good olive oil by its color?

The color of olive oil depends on the type of olives and where they come from. The color can range from a golden yellow to a deep green. Olives from each of the great growing regions—Tuscany, Puglia, Catalonia, Crete, and Provence—have their own flavor and color characteristics. The only way to learn and choose your favorite oil is by tasting oils from different regions.

I understand that olive oil is extremely high in fat. Can I use less or can I use another oil instead?

All oil is close to 100 percent fat and should be consumed in moderation. Some oils are better for you than others, however. Olive oil is the essential oil in the Mediterranean diet, and many studies have shown that this monounsaturated fat may be beneficial in reducing "bad" serum cholesterol.

What exactly does the term "fruity" mean when applied to olive oil?

This is a lovely way to describe an olive oil, because when you taste really good oil, it can remind you of freshly cut grass, apples, pears, and even melons.

I now see organic olive oils on the market. Are they better or safer? They seem expensive.

Because of the extensive use of pesticides on olive trees, organic olive oil is gaining popularity, and I buy it whenever I see it in my grocery store. Look for L'Estornell, a medium-priced, excellent extra virgin olive oil from Catalonia. Two excellent sources for organic olive oils are Zingerman's and Williams-Sonoma (see Sources, page 397).

I have been using the same extra virgin olive oil from Tuscany for years, and there seems to be a difference in taste from one bottle to another. Why is that?

This happens often. Olive oil is an agricultural product and much as with wine, its flavor is influenced by weather, climate, vintage, and so on. However, proper storage and handling also play a major role. If the oil tastes "off," return it to the store and exchange it for another brand.

Quite honestly I do not have much experience with olive oil. How can you tell a bad olive oil?

Bad oil will taste musty, rancid, and even bitter. It may leave you with a sharp unpleasant taste in the back of your throat.

What is the best way to keep olive oil?

All you need is a cool dark place in your kitchen or pantry. If this is not possible, then refrigerate the oil and allow 5 minutes for it to warm up and decongeal before you use it.

Vegetable Oil

Are there certain types of cooking oils that should I keep on hand?

In addition to olive oil, you will need corn, canola, or peanut oil and possibly grapeseed oil. Corn and peanut oil have more flavor, but canola oil, like olive oil, is monounsaturated. All three are also similar in the sense that they have a rather high smoking point and are, therefore, good for sautéing. Grapeseed is the least flavorful but has an even higher smoking point. It is also becoming increasingly popular for use in salads because it is high in linoleic acid, an essential fatty acid that is good at lowering cholesterol.

Specialty stores carry unusual oils that look so appealing. How do you use the citrus-, herb-, and nut-flavored oils?

Specialty oils are a wonderful addition to the pantry but should be bought, used, and stored carefully. Nut oils are best used in salad dressings with greens that complement them. Be sure to use mild vinegar so as not to overwhelm the nuttiness of the oil. Sesame oil is an excellent flavor addition to Asian foods. Citrus oils are excellent with cooked shellfish and in marinades. I am not a great fan of herb oils, since they are so specific in their taste and not versatile enough for daily use. Rather, make your own herb oil as needed.

To make an herb oil Bring a large quantity of salted water to a boil. Fill a bowl with ice water and set aside. Add 1 heaping cup flat-leaf parsley, basil, or cilantro leaves to the boiling water and blanch for 20 seconds. Drain and immediately transfer to the ice water. When cool, drain and squeeze out as much water as possible. Transfer to a blender and add 2 cups canola oil in a thin steady stream. Blend for 3 to 4 minutes. Transfer to a jar and refrigerate.

TIP Nut oils have a very short shelf life, so be sure to refrigerate them as soon as they are opened. In fact, these oils will go rancid even when they have not been opened, so use them as soon as possible after purchasing them.

How long can I store cooking oil? Does it need to be refrigerated?

Cooking oils should be fine for up to 2 months, but they need to be stored in a cool, dark place. Refrigerating oils is definitely a good idea. Keep in mind that different oils have different shelf lives. In particular, olive and peanut oils, which are high in monosaturated fat, are best kept refrigerated.

Olives

Is there a good brand of canned or jarred olives?

I cannot recommend any brand of canned olives. They are simply tasteless. When it comes to jarred olives, choose green olives imported from Spain. Jarred black oil-cured olives are not a good choice, since they are quite bitter and very salty.

What kind of olives can I keep in my pantry as a snack?

The green pimiento- or anchovy-stuffed olives from Spain are excellent. Taste various brands and choose those with the most flavor and a crisp texture. But I prefer to buy loose olives and store them in the fridge. They keep for several weeks.

How long do olives keep?

It depends on whether they are brined or packed in oil. As long as the olives are covered in brine, they will keep for several weeks. You can add olive oil to oil-cured olives to extend their shelf life.

I love spicy olives and have tasted really good ones in various restaurants but cannot find them in my grocery store. Can I make my own?

You can flavor your own olives very easily. Just add a finely sliced jalapeño pepper, 1 or 2 sliced garlic cloves, and some fruity olive oil to your olives and let them marinate for 2 or 3 days. Get a crusty loaf of bread and a nice, slightly aged goat cheese and enjoy!

Peppercorns

What is the difference between black, white, green, and red peppercorns? How is each used?

Black and white peppers grow as berries on the pepper shrub. White pepper is the seed of the fully ripe berry. Black pepper results when the pepper berries are picked not quite fully ripe. Green peppercorns are the underripe berry of the *Piper nigrum* and are available dried and preserved in brine. Pink peppercorns, which are pungent and slightly sweet, are the dried berries from the Baies rose plant.

Black peppercorns are the most widely used, in salads, pasta dishes, marinades, rubs, and overall seasoning. White peppercorns are generally used with light-colored sauces where the dark-colored pepper would stand out. They are also used extensively Scandinavian cooking. Green peppercorns are used in a French butter sauce as well as the classic green peppercorn sauce that accompanies a steak. Pink peppercorns are more of a novelty item, but you may still see them used in vinaigrettes and light fish sauces.

TIP You can now find a peppercorn blend that includes Sichuan, pink, green, black, and white peppercorns. It is always best to toast this blend before transferring it to a mill; toast only as much as you think you will use at a time.

Specialty food catalogs offer all kinds of black peppercorns. Which do you recommend?
By far the best but also the most expensive peppercorns are Tellicherry, imported from the Malabar Coast of India. These are large and have a robust flavor, first hot, then with a sweet aftertaste. The Lampong from Indonesia are also excellent. They are smaller and have a sharper bite. Another good choice is Sarawak, from Malaysia. It is quite acceptable, but nothing comes close to the fruity and well-rounded taste of Tellicherry.

If you want to really understand the difference, get several types of whole black peppercorns and try them, freshly ground, with a salad or a pasta dish. You will soon be able to tell the difference.

TIP Peppercorns that are not labeled by variety or point of origin are most likely imported from Brazil and are of inferior quality. Avoid them if you can.

My grocery store carries peppercorns in various grinds—fine, medium, and coarse. Is it okay to use these instead of whole peppercorns?
There is a world of difference between freshly ground pepper and the ground spice you get at the grocery store. But if a recipe such as a marinade calls for as much as 1 tablespoon of ground pepper, or when you prepare a "rub" for a turkey, then using a medium or coarse grind of pepper makes sense.

Porcini

What exactly is a porcini mushroom?
Porcini is a fabulous-tasting fall mushroom that is rarely available fresh in markets in the United States. However, dry porcini, which have a rich woodsy aroma and a wonderful concentrated taste, are now available in gourmet shops everywhere. They are sometimes sold by their French name, *cèpes*. Make sure to choose those that are tan to pale brown and avoid those that look crumbly, a sure sign that the porcini are not "fresh."

I recently bought dry mushrooms and they were gritty even after several washings. Is there a secret to washing these mushrooms?
You probably bought the imported mushrooms from Chile that come in plastic containers

simply labeled "imported dry mushrooms." These mushrooms, which are much less expensive than the Italian porcini, have an intense smoky flavor. I use them often for soups and risottos as well as in pasta dishes. They usually come with their stems attached, which contain a lot of grit.

To remove it, you will need to soak the mushrooms in warm water for 15 minutes. Once they are reconstituted, be sure to strain the mushroom broth through a double layer of cheesecloth.

I bought a large bag of porcini while I was in Italy, but by the time I wanted to use them, they were all broken. What is the best way to store dry mushrooms, and how long do they keep?

Dry mushrooms keep best in the fridge for as long as 6 months.

Salt

Is iodized salt better than plain?

I buy only salt that has not been iodized. Iodized salt is supposedly better for you because it has had various minerals added to it, but the result is a salt with a rather unpleasant taste that can easily change the flavor of a dish. People who eat fish regularly get enough iodine in their diet and do not need to use iodized salt.

What is the difference between coarse and kosher salt?

There is no difference. Mineral or rock salt is the common salt used in the United States and many other countries. It comes three ways: fine, iodized, and coarse, which is also called kosher salt. The two best-known kosher salts are Morton's and Diamond Crystal.

TIP When a recipe calls for 1 teaspoon salt, you need 1½ teaspoons coarse or kosher salt.

I find many recipes are confusing when it comes to salt. Many call for just salt, some call for coarse salt, and others call for sea salt. Is it necessary to have all three salts?

I use kosher salt in cooking and fine salt for last-minute flavoring, but I much prefer sea salt in salads. If you want to use just one kind of salt for everything, use sea salt, which has a less salty, sweeter taste than mineral salt.

What exactly is sea salt?

Sea salt is the mineral extracted by evaporating seawater. Mineral salt is extracted from mineral deposits in the earth.

The only sea salt I can find comes in large granules. How shall I use it?

The only way to use the granular sea salt is in a salt mill, which looks very much like a pepper mill. However, in cooking, it is far more practical to use fine sea salt, which is becoming increasingly available in gourmet shops everywhere.

Which is the best kind of sea salt?

This is really a matter of taste. I am a great fan of French sea salt from the Mediterranean and the coast of Brittany. Sea salt from Sicily has a wonderful taste as well and can be found in many good specialty stores. French Mediterranean sea salt in granular form is available in many upscale supermarkets around the country.

TIP When buying a salt mill, look for one with a good mechanism, such as the French Peugeot, and avoid the "see-through" plastic ones.

I recently saw several kinds of very expensive salt listed in a fancy food catalog. Which do you recommend?

The finest sea salt is the type raked by hand from the salt beds on the Atlantic coasts of Brittany and Dover, called *fleur de sel* in France and Malton salt in England. These salts are used on the table as condiments rather than in cooking. All you need are 3 or 4 grains of these salts to "up" the flavor of a grilled steak, a roasted piece of fish, or a salad. They are never used in cooking because they are so costly and also because of their intense salty flavor. However, it is fun to have some *fleur de sel* around. Nothing is more delicious than a super-fresh radish dipped in a little sweet butter with 1 or 2 grains of this salt. The same goes for a hard-boiled egg or leftover roasted turkey. *Fleur de sel* should be used coarse, and should be ground in a salt mill.

TIP Remember to use a pinch of salt in all cakes, muffins, and tarts. Salt makes sweet things taste sweet and gives them a complexity of flavor that makes all the difference.

Which is the best seasoned salt?

Seasoned salts are not a good idea. They are usually flavored with onion, garlic, and celery seeds and will change the flavor of any dish.

Spices

I have a cupboard full of spices but seem to have little use for many of them. What are the essential seasonings I need to keep on hand?

Here is my list of must-have spices:

■ **Caraway seeds** Besides being synonymous with rye bread, caraway seeds are a must in a goulash or a Viennese Goulash Soup (page 237), braised sauerkraut, and Ukrainian and Russian borscht. I also like the flavor of caraway seeds in a pork roast and roasted duck.

■ **Cardamom** Here is a spice that is a must in Indian cooking. It has a sweet floral aroma that enhances curry and is delicious in a rice pudding. It is also a key ingredient in garam masala, the Indian spice mix.

■ **Cayenne, red pepper flakes, whole chiles** A pinch of cayenne goes a long way to add a little bite to bland food. I usually add a pinch of cayenne to all egg-based dishes, especially scrambled eggs, omelets, and frittatas. A pinch of cayenne also perks up a potato salad, a slaw, or a tomato sauce.

When you are looking for real heat, you can use a teaspoon of red pepper flakes at the beginning of a preparation, but I prefer whole chiles, since you can regulate their heat. If you use them whole and remove once they darken in the oil, you get a light-to medium-spicy dish; if you break them up, you will get real heat. Try to find the Thai dried chile peppers, which come in small cellophane bags, rather than the Chinese ones that are larger and less seedy, and, therefore, less hot.

■ **Cinnamon, ground; cinnamon sticks** This is probably America's favorite spice. It is good when paired with apples, peaches, pears, and bananas in fruit desserts and also in quick breads and cakes. Ground cinnamon is also a good addition to Tex-Mex chili and to Greek lamb stews. Cinnamon sticks add great flavor to fruit compotes, homemade apple sauce, curries, and rice puddings, and are a must in the Indian spice mix garam masala.

TIP **Be sure to look for Ceylon cinnamon sticks rather than the cassia variety, which is what you get in the average grocery store. You will probably have to stop at a specialty shop or good cook shop for Ceylon cinnamon. It is also widely available by mail-order.**

- **Coriander seeds** The whole seeds are best when lightly toasted. The somewhat soft seeds can be crushed in a mortar and pestle or placed between layers of paper towels and crushed with a heavy pan or rolling pin. Besides using them in Indian and Asian dishes, I like to sprinkle them over pan-seared salmon or tuna.
- **Coriander, ground** I like to add ground coriander to curry in Indian preparations and to flavor a yogurt marinade.
- **Cumin, ground** Ground cumin is a must in an all-American chili, in Mexican dishes, and in Indian marinades, especially those based on yogurt. I also like to use ground cumin in a honey-ginger vinaigrette and as part of a rub.
- **Cumin seeds, whole** The seeds are best toasted before using, then must be ground in a spice grinder. I use cumin seeds extensively in marinades in Indian-type stews, and many Middle Eastern dishes. I also sprinkle some into a cucumber salad.
- **Fennel seeds and Anise seeds** I put these together because they are so closely related. Both have a slight licorice taste and are good in many Middle Eastern and Indian dishes. I use fennel seeds more than anise—the seeds are softer and can be used whole in all dishes

made with fresh fennel, since they enhance the flavor of the vegetable. Both seeds can be used whole in a marinade for a whole fish, lamb chops, and pork tenderloins. Anise seed is better toasted; it adds an interesting flavor to a tomato sauce, to a Mediterranean seafood and tomato stew, and to biscotti and some cookies.

- **Ginger, ground** I use ground ginger mainly in a cobbler topping, quick bread, and yogurt marinade. It is not interchangeable with fresh ginger.
- **Juniper berries** Although I may only use juniper berries, which contribute an herbal, "gin" taste, a few times a year, I still find that I like to have them on hand for a flavorful sauerkraut and the occasional red wine marinade for a boned leg of lamb.
- **Nutmeg, whole** Whole nutmegs are the olive-shaped hard seeds of the nutmeg tree. I much prefer to use freshly grated nutmeg rather than the ground spice, which has a short shelf life and is never as rich and aromatic as when you grind it fresh.

TIP **An inexpensive nutmeg grater is a rather clumsy gadget. I always feel that I am about to grate off the tip of my finger with it. Now you can get several nicely designed nutmeg graters that make grating nutmeg quick and easy.**

- **Paprika** Paprika is one of my favorite and most frequently used spices. I use two kinds: the imported sweet Hungarian paprika (see page 32) that comes in a small can and Spanish smoked paprika (Pimentón de la Vera) that also comes in small cans but is not widely available. Do not purchase bottled paprika or even the one that comes in cans if it does not specifically say "Sweet Hungarian Paprika." All paprika should be refrigerated once it is opened.

■ **Peppercorns** Peppercorns are the most important kitchen spice. The best come from India, and you should look for ones labeled Tellicherry, Lampong, or Sarawak. Tellicherry is the very best. Chances are that you will not get any of these in the average grocery store and will have to stop at a specialty store or buy the peppercorns by mail. (See also pages 26–27.)

What is the difference between using whole and ground spices?

There is a world of difference in taste between a ground spice and one that you grind yourself. However, it is generally more practical to use a ground spice, and as long as it is fresh, it is fine. It is important to follow the recipe; if it calls for a whole spice, do as it suggests. For example, when making a sugar syrup, you should use a cinnamon stick rather than ground cinnamon.

How long do ground spices keep?

Much depends on the quality of the spices and how they are stored. Generally, I keep ground spices for only 4 to 6 months and then replace them. If the jars are tightly closed each time after you use the spice, that will help to keep them fresh. Curry and chili powder must be refrigerated as soon as they are opened.

TIP Sniff a ground spice and rub a little between two fingers. If it is highly aromatic, it is fresh.

Is it better to buy spices in jars or cans?

I buy them only in jars, since I usually opt for Spice Island, Wagner's, or Vanns, which come only in jars. I do not recommend buying spices in small cellophane bags or loose because they are less likely to be fresh.

How long can you keep whole spices?

If stored in a cool dry place, they should last for at least 2 or 3 years. When in doubt whether a spice has retained its flavor, toast a little in a skillet. If the spice is fragrant, it is fresh.

What is the best way to grind whole spices?

I suggest that you get an inexpensive coffee grinder and use it only for that purpose.

What is the best way to use garlic and onion powder in cooking?

I do not suggest you use either of them. Both impart a bitter taste to food and are hard to digest. When it comes to garlic, it is easy to mash a whole clove and add it to your seasoning. A couple of whole unpeeled onions cut in half will add the flavor you look for in a pan juice. You can also grate some raw onions into a spice mixture.

How long do bay leaves last? I rarely use them and am not sure if they are still good.

Whole bay leaves will last indefinitely if stored in a well-sealed container. Be sure to buy only Turkish bay leaves. They do not look as pretty as the California variety, which are slender and pointed, but they are much more flavorful. Make sure to remove the bay leaf before serving a dish because its sharp edges can get stuck in the throat, and people have been known to choke on them.

Why is saffron so expensive?

Saffron comes from the stigmas of a small purple crocus. An ounce of saffron contains 14,000 of these stigmas, each of which must be laboriously hand-picked and then dried.

When a recipe calls for saffron, is there another spice I can use instead?

For a similar color, you can use turmeric, but the unique taste of saffron cannot be replaced by another spice.

I bought some saffron a couple of years ago. How can I tell if it is still good?

If the saffron has become a very dark red, chances are it is not fresh. Another good way to tell is to toast a tiny bit in a skillet, shaking it until the saffron becomes fragrant.

What is the difference between ground chiles and chili powder?

Pure ground chiles are exactly that, while chili powder usually has cumin added to it.

What exactly is Hungarian paprika?

There are various types of paprika available from different parts of the world, with Hungarian considered the best. Hungarian paprika is made out of special kinds of red peppers that have a unique, slightly sweet flavor. It comes both sweet and hot, but I prefer to buy it sweet and add heat with a small chile pepper. Be sure to buy Hungarian paprika only in cans labeled "Sweet Hungarian Paprika." I also like the smoked paprika now imported from Spain. It is not widely available but is worth looking for.

Curry powders differ widely in flavor—some seem too hot, others too bland. Which do you recommend?

Curry powder is actually a very complex spice consisting of up to twenty different spices, herbs, and seeds. It varies from region to region and according to the taste of the cook. A good supermarket choice is the Madras curry im-ported by Sun Company that comes in cans. It should be refrigerated after opening.

If a soup recipe calls for fresh herbs, is it okay to use dried herbs instead?

The taste of dried herbs generally is too aggressive and can easily overwhelm the milder flavors in the soup. Make sure you add fresh herbs only at the very end of cooking, because the heat will kill their distinctive yet delicate flavor.

Tomatoes, Canned

Many recipes call for whole canned tomatoes, but since I only use them for sauces and soups, doesn't it make sense to buy them crushed instead?

I really do not recommend buying crushed or chopped tomatoes. The best tomatoes are usually processed whole. Those that are packed crushed or chopped usually contain a fair amount of tomato paste, which gives the tomato an unpleasant taste and texture.

Is there a difference in taste between round and plum tomatoes?

The best canned tomatoes are plum tomatoes. They are fleshier. I find that once you drain a can of round tomatoes, you are left with little tomato pulp and tons of juice. One of my favorite brands of tomatoes, however, is Muir Glen, which is a round organically grown tomato that is packed with flavor and has very good consistency. Unfortunately, they are not widely available outside the West Coast, so you may have to search for them.

Many recipes call for a 2-pound can of plum tomatoes, drained, or 2 cups, but often I do not get 2 cups of tomato pulp out of a can.

Is there a brand that really yields 2 cups of drained tomato pulp?

As long as you buy top brands of Italian plum tomatoes, preferably those imported from the San Marzano area, you will get plenty of tomato pulp. The worst offenders are brands such as Progresso and Vitello that contain tomatoes of inferior quality, with little pulp and lots of juice. Even the imported Italian tomatoes vary in quality. Some of my favorites are the organic Muir Glen from California and the Italian Lavalle, but these may not necessarily be available in your area. Try different brands, and you are bound to find a good one. You may have to seek them out at gourmet grocery stores rather than your local supermarket, which may carry only the large name brands.

What is the best way to store leftover canned tomatoes? Should I freeze them or just refrigerate them?

You can simply refrigerate them in a jar, and they will keep for as long as a week. If you have drained the tomatoes and are left with some pulp, you can add a sliced clove of garlic, some shredded basil leaves, and a few tablespoons good extra virgin olive oil. This adds wonderful taste and adds shelf life as well.

Can I make really good tomato soup with canned tomatoes?

You can make an acceptable soup with canned tomatoes, but unfortunately, it's almost impossible to duplicate the flavor of fresh, ripe tomatoes. I suggest making tomato soup when tomatoes are in season. If you don't have enough, supplement them with either organically grown canned tomatoes or those imported from the San Marzano region of Italy.

Tuna, Canned

What brands of canned tuna do you recommend?

Look for Progresso light tuna packed in olive oil. It is an excellent brand that is widely available. I think the flavor of the light tuna is more interesting than white albacore. Although it is called light, it is in fact rather dark in color and very juicy. If you are watching your fat intake, tuna packed in spring water is a good choice.

Is there a difference between tuna packed in vegetable oil and tuna packed in olive oil? It seems so much more expensive.

Olive oil adds more flavor to tuna, but if you can't get tuna packed in olive oil, you can buy it packed in vegetable oil. Once drained, cover it with virgin olive oil and let the tuna marinate in the oil for several days.

I have a terrific recipe for a niçoise salad that calls for freshly grilled tuna. Can I use canned tuna instead?

The traditional Provençal salade niçoise is always made with canned tuna, which gives the salad its special characteristics.

Vinegar

What kind of vinegar is best for salads?

Different salads require different vinegar, and much depends on the types of greens you use. With mild, buttery greens such as bibb and Boston lettuce, I usually use a milder vinegar like balsamic or Champagne vinegar, while romaine, frisée, and radicchio need a more assertive vinegar such as sherry or a wood barrel–aged red wine vinegar.

My supermarket carries a large selection of vinegar. How do I go about choosing one or two?

This is good news, because most supermarkets have very poor selections of vinegar. So check it carefully. If you like salads as much as I do, then I would start with three key vinegar varieties: a good wood barrel–aged red wine vinegar, preferably from France or the West Coast wine country, a Spanish sherry vinegar, and a balsamic vinegar. I also keep in my pantry some Japanese rice vinegar and a French Champagne vinegar, but these are not as important.

Besides the generic red wine vinegar by Heinz, I see red wine vinegar from Spain, Italy, and France. Which do you recommend?

The country of origin is not as important as the quality of the vinegar. Read the label carefully. For openers, it should state what kind of grapes were used and the percent of acidity. Pass on anything you generally see on the supermarket shelf, which is usually industrially made vinegar.

Should vinegar be very acidic or mild and sweet?

The usual acidity in vinegar is between 6 and 7 percent, and I always check the bottle before buying it. However, this is not a criterion you can apply to all vinegar, because so much depends on the way the vinegar is made, how it was bottled, and so forth. A poor-quality balsamic vinegar can be harsh in spite of being low in acidity, while a sherry vinegar may have a higher acidity yet taste smooth and mellow.

I cannot seem to get good vinegar and find the labels very confusing. Can you recommend a source for good vinegar?

Buying good vinegar can be more confusing than buying good olive oil. You'll find a thorough discussion in Ari Weinzweig's *Zingerman's Guide to Good Vinegar,* available from the Zingerman's catalog (see Sources, page 399). Other than aged balsamic and sherry vinegar, most vinegar is inexpensive, and it is well worth trying a few kinds to see what you like.

What exactly is sherry vinegar? Which one do you recommend?

I am extremely partial to sherry vinegar, since I grew up in Spain, but the truth is that good sherry vinegar is a fabulous product that will enhance anything from a sliced ripe tomato to the pan juices of a roasted chicken (see Provençal Chicken with a Sherry Vinegar–Garlic Essence and Concassé of Tomatoes, page 206). Quality sherry vinegar is made in the sherry-producing region of Jerez in southwest Spain. The most widely available brand is Sanchez Romate. Williams-Sonoma carries another excellent brand called De Soto. Some of the smaller lesser-known brands, such as Santa Maria, are available in different parts of the country.

I keep experimenting and believe that you should try various brands until you find one that really appeals to you.

I have seen balsamic vinegar at five dollars a bottle, at fifteen dollars, and even much more. What is the reason for the price difference?

In balsamic vinegar, there are no bargains. What you pay for is what you get. Making real balsamic is a very long process. Just think, a moderate-quality balsamic vinegar has to age for fourteen years. Add to this another forty to fifty years for great-quality vinegar, and you have the reason for the price difference. I would definitely stay away from the five-dollar bottles. The stuff is only balsamic by name and its age is about the time that it takes for it to get from Italy to your grocery store. A medium-priced balsamic should cost twelve to fourteen dollars, at which point you should be able to get some real flavor. The best way to determine if you are getting something worthwhile is to taste it.

Good specialty stores are now conducting tastings, and it is really important that you get to taste several vinegars before settling on one.

What should good balsamic vinegar taste like?
What you should look for is a complex, mellow, sweet and sour taste. A good balsamic has character. It should not be overly sweet or too acidic.

Ethnic Ingredients

Coconut Milk

Is there a difference between coconut milk and coconut cream?
Unsweetened coconut milk is used in many Southeast Asian dishes. It is made by soaking the grated coconut meat in water and straining the results. Coconut milk is available canned and frozen, or you can make it yourself from a fresh coconut. Coconut milk separates in the can with the thicker coconut cream rising to the top. If you need the cream for your recipe, skim this off. If your recipe calls for thick coconut milk, shake the can vigorously to mix the two together. Coco Lopez is sweetened coconut cream and is used for desserts. "Light" coconut milk is the same liquid with less of the fatty cream, but it also has less of the distinctive flavor and fragrance.

Does cooking with coconut milk require any special techniques?
After adding coconut milk or cream to your dish, heat the mixture gently, never letting it boil, or it will curdle. A bit of cornstarch will also help prevent curdling. If you open a can of coconut milk and find oil floating on top, discard it. This is an indication that the product was overheated during shipping. You can store opened coconut milk in the refrigerator for a few days, but do not let it sit at room temperature because it spoils easily.

Edamame

What are the salted pea pods served in Japanese restaurants? How do you prepare them?
They are fresh soybean pods, called *edamame*. Although you can find them fresh seasonally in Japanese grocery stores, your best bet is to buy them frozen, in which case they have already been steamed. All you have to do is to pop them into boiling water for 2 or 3 minutes, then refresh them in ice water and serve sprinkled with coarse salt.

Fish Sauce

Is fish sauce made from fish or for fish? How is it used?
Fish sauce is called *nuoc mam* in Vietnam, *nam pla* in Thailand, and sometimes fish gravy in

China. It is made from salted fish and is used in place of salt. Thai and Vietnamese brands are the best.

Garam Masala

What is garam masala? Where can I get it?
Good-quality garam masala is a sweet and often spicy blend of several spices that you can make yourself. The basic combination usually includes cumin seed, cardamom, black pepper, cloves, cinnamon, and occasionally hot pepper. You will find recipes for excellent garam masala In Julie Sahni's *Classic Indian Cooking* and in Madhur Jaffrey's *Indian Cooking*. You can buy prepared garam masala in good specialty stores or order it by mail from Kalustyan's (see Sources, page 402). Be sure to store the spice mix in a tightly covered jar and refrigerate it. As with all ground spices, the shelf life of garam masala is relatively short.

Ginger

What should I look for in fresh ginger, and is it a seasonal ingredient?
Always look for large ginger knobs that are unwrinkled, have a smooth skin, and are golden-beige in color. The best will have a yellowish-green interior and will smell spicy and gingery as you break off a piece. This is called winter ginger. Fresh stem ginger, also called spring or baby ginger, can be found during the spring in Asian grocery stores. It has a thinner skin and is milder than winter ginger.

Ginger will keep uncovered in the refrigerator bin for 4 to 6 weeks. I often buy a large piece, scrape off the peel with a spoon and then slice it with a paring knife or a mandoline and place it in a jar with rice vinegar to cover. Refrigerated, the ginger will keep indefinitely.

TIP For a delicious drink, combine 2 cups of water with 2 slices of ginger. Simmer for 5 minutes, strain, and serve. I find this to be great for colds and sore throats.

Can I substitute dry ginger for fresh ginger?
Powdered ginger does not add the snappy fresh flavor of knob ginger. Instead, it can easily overwhelm a dish with its spiciness, so be careful when using the powdered spice.

How do you juice ginger?
To make ginger juice, peel and slice the ginger root, then crush it with the side of a cleaver or a large chef's knife. Use a garlic press to squeeze the crushed slices. You can also use a ginger grater, which releases the ginger juice. These little graters are now available in cook shops everywhere.

Lemongrass

Some Asian recipes call for lemongrass. What does it look like and is there any substitute?
Fresh lemongrass looks like a long woody stalk with coarse leaves. It is pale yellow-green and cannot be eaten raw. When you add fresh lemongrass to a recipe, use only the bulb, 4 to 5 inches above the stem end; discard the tops. This softer part of the stem can be coarsely chopped or bruised with the side of a cleaver or a chef's knife and added to hot and sour Thai soups and to coconut milk–based and curry-flavored dishes.

Remember that lemongrass, just like bay leaf, is not eaten and is only used to flavor. If you cannot get fresh lemongrass, use the juice of a large lime and some lime zest rather than lemon.

TIP I have recently seen lemongrass sold in small packages containing 4 to 6 pieces. Stored in the crisper of the refrigerator, these will keep for several weeks.

Mirin

What is the difference between mirin and rice wine?

Mirin is a Japanese rice wine made from fermented rice and water. It is now widely available in Asian stores and many supermarkets. Unfortunately, most commercial mirin contains corn syrup, which masks its authentic flavor. For pure mirin, I usually go to a health food store or a good Asian market.

Chinese rice wine is also made from fermented rice but is aged for at least 10 years. It has a much drier flavor, with an alcohol content similar to a dry sherry. In fact, you can substitute Amontillado or Dry Sack sherry in recipes that call for Chinese rice wine. I often use Chinese rice wine in marinades and in deglazing a pan, while mirin is a lovely addition to sautéed vegetables that have a natural sweetness, such as snow peas, carrots, and beets.

What Asian sauces should I keep on hand for a quick stir-fry?

In addition to soy sauce I keep oyster and hoisin sauces, which are very flavorful additions to stir-fried vegetables, shellfish, and noodle dishes.

Rice Vinegar

Does rice vinegar differ greatly from other vinegars?

Both Chinese and Japanese rice vinegar are milder and less acidic than other standard vinegars you might have on your shelf. Japanese rice vinegar is pale to golden yellow and also comes seasoned with sugar. I use rice vinegar in a salad dressing to which I add sugar, sesame oil, and some grapeseed oil and toss it in a cabbage salad or with mixed greens. Pearl River Bridge is a good brand.

Sichuan Peppercorns

How important is it to use Sichuan peppercorns in recipes that call for them?

Sichuan peppercorns are not really pepper but rather small berries with a sharp spicy taste. They add an interesting flavor to highly seasoned marinades. I also like to mix them with coarse salt as a dipping salt for deep-fried quail or the Fried Cornish Hens "al Ajillo" on page 211. Just like cumin seeds, Sichuan peppercorns have to be toasted before being ground in a spice grinder or by mortar and pestle. You can also smash the peppercorns with a heavy iron skillet. Place the peppercorns in a small dry skillet and toast them over medium heat until very fragrant. Be sure to store the peppercorns in a vacuum-sealed bag to retain their fresh taste.

Soy Sauce

The Asian market where I buy soy sauce has many varieties. Are some better than others?

Selecting soy sauce has much to do with what you are going to use it for. For Chinese preparations, especially stir-fry, it is best to use a Chinese soy sauce that contains molasses and lends a touch of sweetness and gloss to the food.

In Japanese-inspired dishes, a good choice is Kikkoman, which is light in color and not too assertive. Tamari, the darkest of the soy sauces, has a strong flavor that can overwhelm delicate foods.

Are mushroom soy and superior soy better than ordinary soy sauce?

Superior, a soy sauce that contains molasses, is sweet and thicker than other brands. I sometimes use it in a marinade and for a last-minute coating for grilled fish steak or baby back ribs. But you must be careful not to use too much, particularly when it comes to grilling, since the sugar level in the sauce can easily make food burn.

Mushroom soy is infused with shiitake or straw mushroom extract; you can substitute it in any recipe that calls for plain soy sauce. If you are interested in the different flavors of soy sauce, buy one of each and experiment to see what you like best. Remember that soy sauce has an almost indefinite shelf life.

Is light soy sauce less salty?

Unfortunately not. Light means that the soy sauce is more delicate and lighter in color, but the salt content is pretty much the same. Kikkoman makes a "lite" version of its soy sauce with 40 percent less sodium.

Wasabi

I have not had much luck making wasabi from powder. It is always too runny and does not have the same texture as that served in restaurants. Is it possible to buy prepared wasabi?

You can now find prepared wasabi paste in every Japanese grocery store and many supermarkets, but I find the powder to be stronger, more flavorful, and less expensive. The key to a thick paste is to add water gradually drop by drop. Let it develop flavor for at least 10 minutes before serving.

The Baking Shelf

Chocolate

I asked Alice Medrich, author of *Extraordinary Chocolate Desserts*, to contribute some of her expertise on chocolate.

What is the best way to melt chocolate?

Several methods work well, so long as you pay enough attention to remove the chocolate from the heat while it is warm to the touch, rather than hot. Chop the chocolate into pieces about the size of almonds or smaller, then melt the chocolate in one of three ways: microwave at 50 percent power (use 30 percent for milk and white chocolates), using short increments of time. You can also use a double boiler with barely simmering water, or, and this is my favorite method of all, put the chocolate in a heatproof bowl set directly in a wide skillet of barely simmering water. In any and all cases, use perfectly dry containers and utensils, do not cover the chocolate, stir frequently, and try to remove the chocolate from the heat source before it is entirely melted, then stir to finish the melting.

How and for how long should chocolate be stored?

Store chocolate well wrapped in a cool, dry, odor-free environment. Refrigeration (or freezing) is not necessary unless you live in a very hot climate, in which case, let cold or frozen chocolate return to room temperature before you unwrap it; this prevents moisture from forming on the surface of the chocolate. Chocolate absorbs moisture and odor like a sponge. No matter how well you wrap it, do not store chocolate in the spice cupboard or in a closet with mothballs—it will absorb those and any other strong odors and flavors.

Dark chocolates (semisweet, bittersweet, and unsweetened), unless they contain some milk solids, have natural antioxidants that prevent spoilage. Properly wrapped and stored, these chocolates can keep for a year or more. Milk chocolate and white chocolate are stored similarly, but for a shorter period of time. The milk content of these chocolates turns sour, rancid, or just plain stale-tasting more quickly. Buy only what you will use within 2 to 3 months. To tell whether chocolate is still good, taste it.

How should chocolate be chosen for recipes?

The simpler the recipe, the less sugar it has in it and the more it will show off the flavors and quality of the chocolate that you use. Squares of ordinary cooking chocolate from the supermarket are fine when you are baking brownies for the soccer team, but when it comes to fine cooking and discerning company, your chocolate tortes, mousses, truffles, soufflés, and custards will taste even better with great chocolate—choose the same quality chocolate that you love to eat. For best results, however, stick to the type (unsweetened or semisweet or bittersweet) of chocolate called for in the recipe.

What are your favorite brands of chocolate?

I like Scharffen Berger, Valrhona, El Rey, and Callebaut chocolates.

Are there any other quick tips for buying, using, and storing chocolate?

Chop or cut chocolate with a heavy chef's knife or a knife with a serrated blade, or use the heavy-duty multipronged ice picks that are now being sold especially to break chocolate.

Make a point of tasting and enjoying some of the better-quality, stronger chocolates available. The labels on many premium imported and some domestic semisweet and bittersweet chocolates tell us what percentage of the bar, by weight, contains chocolate liquor (ground cocoa beans). The higher the percentage, the more intense the chocolate flavor and the less sweetness the chocolate can be expected to have. It is not uncommon to see imported chocolates labeled with percentages from 61 percent to over 70 percent, compared with standard American semisweet and bittersweet chocolates, which usually contain 50 to 55 percent chocolate liquor, although they are not so labeled. Stronger chocolates deliver strong chocolate impact and are delicious to eat. In recipes that do not call for strong chocolate, you may compensate by using less chocolate and adding a little extra sugar. If you want to substitute the stronger chocolate ounce for ounce in recipes, you will have to make some adjustments, such as adding extra liquid to sauces and glazes, baking cakes and tortes for a shorter period of time, or adding extra sugar to suit your taste.

Cocoa

What kind of cocoa powder do you recommend?

I use only Dutch process cocoa. Droste and Van Houten are two excellent brands. Droste is now available in most grocery stores so you should have no problem getting it.

What is "Dutch process" cocoa?

Cocoa that has been treated with alkali is called "Dutch" because the process was developed in Holland. The alkali removes some of the bitterness of the unrefined cocoa and neutralizes its natural acidity. Dutch process cocoa is darker and milder in flavor.

What is the best way to store cocoa?

I store cocoa in its box in a zippered plastic bag in the fridge. It keeps for more than a year.

I have cocoa around all the time. Can I substitute it for chocolate in cakes?

You can use cocoa as a substitute for chocolate in many recipes. Three tablespoons cocoa plus 1 tablespoon butter equals 1 ounce chocolate. Do not use instant cocoa, which contains sugar and is unsuitable for anything but a delicious hot drink.

Flour

I asked Susan Purdy, author of *Let Them Eat Cake* and *The Perfect Cake,* to contribute some of her expertise on flour.

Is it better to use bleached or unbleached all-purpose flour?

Whether labeled bleached or unbleached, most commercially milled American flour (with the exception of the King Arthur brand) is both bleached and conditioned. This process gives the flour a slightly different chemistry to produce a softer, more delicate crumb. Unbleached flour is often thought to be more nutritious, because some of the wheat bran is retained during milling and refining. Because of this, it is also slightly heavier than bleached flour. I use unbleached most often for pie crust, coffee cake, muffins, and cookies. To make the most delicate cakes, I always prefer to use bleached all-purpose flour unless the recipe calls for cake flour.

What is the difference between cake, pastry, and bread flour?

Each type of flour is milled for a specific use. All wheat flour contains gluten and gliadin as part of the wheat protein. When wheat flour is mixed with liquid and stirred or kneaded, the gluten and gliadin develop into stretchy stands that give dough both elasticity and strength. For tender, flaky pie crust or delicate pastries, soft-wheat, low-gluten flour, such as pastry flour, is desirable. For perfect pie crusts, I like to blend pastry flour half and half with bleached or unbleached all-purpose flour.

Cake flour is low-gluten flour that has been bleached to slightly increase its acidity, enhancing its ability to help cakes set faster, absorb liquid quickly, and retain moisture during baking. It makes cakes with a very delicate crumb; however, I find layer cakes with a more substantial, moist crumb do best with an all-purpose flour.

Bread flour is best for bread making because it is milled from high-gluten hard wheat. It has the greater elasticity needed to support the gases from the yeast.

How can I adjust a recipe to use self-rising cake flour?

Self-rising cake flour contains a mixture of baking powder, baking soda, and salt. I prefer not to adjust a recipe for self-rising cake flour. Use a recipe designed for this type of flour.

What is instant flour?

Instant flour is made to blend easily with water to make gravy without lumps. Sprinkle 2 teaspoons instant flour directly into the pan juices of a turkey or a roast chicken and whisk until the sauce thickens. Add 2 tablespoons butter for enrichment and you will have a beautifully textured sauce.

Is there a foolproof way of making a good pie crust?

Here are tips to keep pie crust light and flaky: keep all ingredients ice cold; add a minimum of moisture and a minimum of extra flour; handle the dough lightly; and add a little acidity, such as 1 tablespoon lemon juice or vinegar, to inhibit gluten development and keep the dough tender.

What is the reason for chilling pie dough?

Chilling dough causes the gluten to relax and ensures a tender crust. Gluten is the elastic portion of the protein in wheat flour; cold inhibits its development or relaxes it once it is developed, thus preventing dough from becoming tough.

Does flour always need to be sifted before use?

Follow the recipe. If the recipe calls for "1 cup sifted flour," you should sift before measuring. If the recipe says "1 cup flour, sifted," measure before sifting. Never count on flour to be pre-sifted, even though labeled as such. Before using flour that will not be sifted, stir it first to lighten and aerate it, spoon it into the cup, then sweep off the top with the back of a knife to level it. Don't tap the measuring cup; compacting the contents can cause a cup to hold up to 2 tablespoons more flour than needed, and this can toughen your baked goods.

Is it a good idea to store flour in the refrigerator?

I store bulk flour in the freezer and small amounts in the refrigerator. This prevents infestation, and flour is best used when cold because cold is an inhibitor of gluten development. The less gluten developed, the more tender the cake, pie crust, or pastry. For bread baking, bring flour to room temperature because bread dough needs warmth for good gluten development.

Gelatin

The last time I made my favorite gelatin dessert, which has always been reliable, it did not gel. What could have gone wrong?

Your gelatin may have been too old. Gelatin has a limited shelf life and should have a sell-by date, which unfortunately it doesn't. If you can't remember when you bought it, it is probably time for a new package.

I now see recipes calling for leaf gelatin. What is it and how do I use it?

Leaf gelatin is popular all over Europe and is now readily available here. Five sheets of leaf gelatin equal 1 package of powdered. The sheets have to be softened in a bowl of cold water, which may take up to a minute or two, then are added to whatever liquid you are using. The mixture needs to be heated to the point of melting the gelatin. The advantage of gelatin leaves is that they have practically an unlimited shelf life, and they will result in dishes with a much better texture than powdered gelatin would give.

TIP Always measure the packet of powdered gelatin—it is supposed to contain 1 tablespoon but may contain more or less.

I understand that gelatin contains animal products. I am a vegetarian. Is there any substitute?

Agar-agar is a flavorless dry seaweed that can be substituted for gelatin. It is available at Asian markets and natural food stores. Be careful of your recipe because you need to use much less of this product than of gelatin.

Leavening

What is the difference between baking powder and baking soda? Are they interchangeable?

Baking powder and baking soda are leavening agents that cause batter to rise through a chemical reaction that produces tiny bubbles of carbon dioxide. The two products are not interchangeable, because recipes for baked goods using them are more precise formulas than other recipes in which you can exercise your creativity by adding or subtracting a little of this or that. Baking soda produces the leavening gas when mixed with an acid, so it must be combined with acidic ingredients such as lemon juice, buttermilk, honey, molasses, or chocolate. It starts working as soon as it comes in contact with a liquid, so if your recipe calls for baking soda, have your oven preheated and mix the ingredients quickly. Baking powder is baking soda combined with one or more dry acids. The most widely available product in the United States is double acting baking powder that has one acid that begins working as soon as the liquid is added and another that doesn't begin to leaven until the batter is heated.

Some recipes rely on a more complex mixture of both baking powder and baking soda. Both of these products can lose their potency over time. If you don't bake regularly, check the expiration date on the container or test ½ teaspoon in ¼ cup warm water. If it fizzes, you can use it.

If you find yourself without baking powder and you're willing to take a little risk, substitute 2 teaspoons cream of tartar, 1 teaspoon baking soda, and 1 teaspoon salt per cup of flour in your recipe.

Seeds

I love the taste of sesame seeds and add them to many dishes, but they seem to lose their flavor. How can I get the nice toasty sesame flavor I am looking for?

Sesame seeds are best when toasted in a dry skillet until they turn a light brown and have a lovely, fragrant aroma. The best way to get that nice toasty taste is to use the seeds only as a garnish and not to cook with them.

What are black sesame seeds? Do they taste different from the white ones?

Sesame seeds come in both white and black. White sesame seeds have a lovely sweet nutty flavor; the black seeds are more bitter. Both should be toasted to bring out their flavor before they are added to a dish.

Are poppy seeds used in cooking? I like them on my bagels but never seem to see them anywhere else.

Poppyseed cake is an old-fashioned favorite. The seeds give a slightly crunchy texture to the cake.

Sugar

I store sugar in a plastic container but it always cakes. Is it better to keep the sugar in the original box?

Sugar cakes in humid surroundings whether it is stored in its box or a sealed container, but it can easily be mashed. For a small amount, use a fork; for larger amounts, I put the sugar in a zippered plastic bag and pound it with a rolling pin. You can also use a food processor or blender to break it up.

Try to find an airtight container. If you use the ones with a rubber gasket in the lid, chances are that your sugar will not cake.

What is the difference between powdered and confectioners' sugar?

Both names refer to the same product, which is refined granulated sugar that has been pulverized. Commercial bakers can choose from a range of textures, but the average consumer can usually get only the ones labeled XXXX or XXX, which is less fine. All powdered sugar contains 3 percent cornstarch to keep it from lumping, but to be on the safe side, sift powdered sugar before using.

What is icing sugar?

Confectioners' sugar is called icing sugar in Britain because it dissolves so easily and is often used to make icings and candy.

What is the difference between dark brown and light brown sugar?

Brown sugar is white sugar combined with molasses. The more molasses, the darker the sugar and the more intense the flavor. They are generally interchangeable.

TIP To prevent dark brown sugar from caking, place it in a container with a heel of rye bread; it will keep almost indefinitely.

I now see many types of gourmet sugars in my market, such as Demerara sugar and turbinado sugar. What kind of sugars are these and what are they used in?

Demarara sugar is a wonderfully delicate light brown raw sugar from the Demerara area in Guyana. It does not contain molasses and is delicious with cereals and as a topping for grapefruit. Turbinado sugar is raw sugar that has been steam-cleaned. It has a lovely blond color and a slight molasses flavor. It, too, can be used as a sweetener for bananas and grapefruit as well as a topping for cereals. I prefer it to brown sugar in crisps and cobblers.

Is it true that brown sugar is less fattening than white sugar?

Unfortunately, brown sugar has more calories than white sugar: white sugar has 770 calories per cup while brown sugar has about 820 per cup, but brown sugar is rather rich in calcium and potassium.

How do you make a sugar syrup?

A simple sugar syrup is made by combining 3 cups water with 1 cup sugar in a saucepan.

Bring to a simmer and cook for 2 or 3 minutes or until the sugar is dissolved. You can now store the syrup indefinitely.

If you plan to use the syrup for fruit, add a 2-inch piece of vanilla bean and leave it in the syrup. You can also add a cinnamon stick and a large piece of lemon rind. Be sure to remove the cinnamon stick and rind after 2 or 3 days.

What do you use a sugar syrup for?

Sugar syrup is used for freezing fruits, making sherbets, and stewing fruit (see Three-Berry Coulis with Nectarines, page 323). It is also used for sweetening lemonade and iced tea.

What is the difference between a sugar syrup and a caramel syrup?

A simple sugar syrup is nothing but a combination of sugar and water that is simmered until the sugar is dissolved. A caramel syrup is quite different: Here you combine 1 cup sugar with 3 tablespoons water and cook the mixture over high heat until it turns a hazelnut brown. Remove the pan from the heat and add ½ cup hot water, stirring the mixture until the caramel is dissolved. You now have a caramel syrup that keeps indefinitely. This syrup makes a great topping for ice cream and fresh fruit.

Many recipes call for superfine sugar, which I cannot get at my grocery store. Can I use regular sugar instead?

In many cases you can use regular sugar, or you can easily pulverize regular sugar in a blender.

Vanilla

What should I look for when buying vanilla beans?

Good vanilla beans should have a strong vanilla scent and be slightly oily. Depending on the variety, they may vary in length and thickness. Mexican beans and Bourbon beans from Madagascar are similar. Beans from Tahiti are shorter and plumper with a fruitier aroma. Always buy vanilla beans in glass vials so that you can judge the bean's quality.

Why are vanilla beans so expensive?

Vanilla beans are extremely costly to grow. First the beans must ripen on the vine for 9 months. Once they are harvested, they are put out to dry in ovens until they have shrunk by 400 percent, which can take months. It can take as long as four years for them to reach your grocery store. When you think that it takes about 5 pounds of uncured vanilla beans to yield 1 pound of cured beans, it is easy to understand their high cost.

How long can I store vanilla beans?

If kept sealed, vanilla beans will keep indefinitely. Even if they dry out, they can be used in a sugar syrup.

I am never quite sure how to use vanilla beans. Should they be kept whole or diced?

The best way to use a vanilla bean is to slit it open with a sharp paring knife and scrape out the seeds for use, as the seeds contain most of the flavor. Most recipes do not require more than a 2- to 3-inch piece of vanilla bean. Once the pod has been used for poaching fruit, it can be dried carefully with paper towels and re-used. I usually bury a large piece of vanilla bean in my sugar container for several weeks. The sugar absorbs the taste of the vanilla bean, giving you an extra bonus when making any kind of dessert.

Is there a difference in taste between a vanilla bean and vanilla extract?

When a recipe calls for a vanilla bean, it is best to follow it, such as in sugar syrup or in flavoring cream or milk for a pudding. Vanilla extract is best used in cakes and pastry cream.

The Refrigerator

Butter

Is there an important difference between salted and unsalted butter when it comes to cooking?

I use only unsalted butter in cooking and recommend that you do the same. Salt burns at low temperatures, which means that if you use it to sauté, it can easily burn your food. Salt acts as a preservative as well as a flavoring. The amount of salt added to butter differs from brand to brand, so you can never be sure how the salt in the butter will affect the taste of your food.

My family loves the taste of whipped butter. Can I use it in cooking as well?

Whipped butter is perfectly good for eating, but I do not recommend it for cooking, since it is full of bubbles and you would have to measure it by weight, which is a nuisance.

My market now carries several brands of European butter. Are they worth the extra expense?

I find that imported butter is well worth the extra you have to pay for it. European butter, with 90 percent butterfat versus 80 percent in American brands, is more suitable for sautéing, since there is less splattering and the butter can be heated to a higher temperature. It is also better for baking, especially in pastry used for tarts, where the higher fat content causes less shrinkage.

Does freezing butter change its texture or taste?

Once butter has been frozen, it will be slightly more watery and cause splattering when heated, but the taste will not be affected.

How should I store butter?

Butter is very delicate and will absorb refrigerator smells quickly. Put an opened bar of butter into a zippered plastic bag and then store it in the butter compartment of the refrigerator, never in the cold cut and cheese drawer.

What is ghee?

Ghee is clarified butter (page 384) that has been taken a step further by letting the butter turn a light hazelnut brown, which gives it a slightly nutty taste. Ghee has a higher smoking point than even clarified butter. It is used primarily in Indian cooking, in which spices are first fried over high heat.

GOAT CHEESE

I love goat cheese but am not sure which one to buy. Can you recommend any?

Buying good goat cheese can be a challenge because most supermarkets usually stock only the vacuum-packed logs. Most of these are made with powdered milk and frozen curd and usually taste chalky or just bland. If you have access to a good cheese store, look for imported farm goat cheeses or some of the domestic ones, such as Coach Farms or Laura Chenel, both of which are made with fresh goat's milk and are properly aged. Depending on where you live, you may find goat cheeses made by small local producers. These are well worth seeking out because, while they will be more expensive than the imported vacuum-packed ones, they are fresh and usually better tasting.

Is it true that goat cheese has much less fat than any other cheese?

Unfortunately, goat cheese is as high in fat as cow's milk cheese, but much depends on the aging of the cheese. When cheese is aged and the moisture evaporates, the fat gets concentrated, so fresh goat cheese is lower in fat than the aged varieties.

TIP If you can, try to avoid vacuum-packed goat cheeses, since these are never as fresh as the ones wrapped in paper.

MASCARPONE

So many recipes call for mascarpone these days. What exactly is that?

Mascarpone is an Italian cheese from the Lombardy region. Made from cow's milk, it is buttery rich and has the consistency of clotted cream or very soft butter. Good-quality mascarpone is now produced in Wisconsin and should become more readily available.

I now see mascarpone in the cheese department of my supermarket. What do you use mascarpone for?

Mascarpone is very similar in taste to very rich heavy cream. It is wonderful served with berries or fruit tarts. I like to enrich a risotto with 2 or 3 tablespoons of mascarpone. It is the key ingredient in a tiramisù, the very popular Italian dessert that is made with coffee-soaked ladyfingers and layers of sweetened mascarpone.

TIP Even though mascarpone usually has a sell-by date, be sure to taste it before using it. If the taste is not that of very sweet cream, it is not fresh. Once opened, mascarpone has to be used within a day or two, so turn it into a quick and delicious mousse by sweetening it and flavoring it with either instant coffee, vanilla, or an orange liqueur.

PARMESAN

My grocery store carries several kinds of Parmesan cheese. They vary greatly in price. What is the difference between them?

True Parmigiano-Reggiano is produced in the region of Emilia-Romagna, in Italy, and the words "Parmigiano-Reggiano" are always stenciled on the rind. There is also another import called Grana Padano, which is made in the style of Parmesan but is aged for only 4 months and is produced all over Italy. It makes a good grating cheese but overall lacks the flavor of real Parmesan. Still, if it is nice and moist, it makes for a good nibbling cheese with sliced apples and grapes.

Parmesan cheese is also produced in Argentina, Australia, and the United States. To me these products taste like sawdust and are too salty. You can tell domestic Parmesan by its rind, which is usually black. When you taste it, you will notice immediately that it lacks the characteristics of real Parmesan.

Sometimes the Parmesan I buy is mellow and lovely tasting and other times it is quite bitter. What exactly should I look for when buying Parmesan?

Always check the rind of the cheese. It should be cream-colored and there should only be a slight color difference between the rind and the cheese itself. Also, the cheese should have a crumbly texture. If the cheese is hard with a deep-colored rind, it has gone through major temperature changes and will have developed a bitter flavor.

Is it okay to buy grated Parmesan if I plan to use it as a topping for pasta?

I don't recommend it. Good Parmesan never comes grated, because the cheese loses its subtle wonderful taste within hours of being grated. Instead, buy a piece and grate it yourself. It is a cinch to do in the food processor. Don't even bother with any special blade—just use the steel blade and grate only enough for your dish.

What is the best way to store Parmesan?

The best way to keep Parmesan fresh is to wrap it loosely with a damp piece of cheesecloth or 2-ply paper towel and then loosely in foil. Do not wrap the foil too tightly around the cheese or the Parmesan will become moldy within days.

I recently bought a rather large piece of Parmesan and a few weeks later it was covered with mold. Can the cheese still be used?

Surface mold does not affect the taste of Parmesan. Simply scrape it away, but next time buy less if you find that you do not use the cheese often.

TIP Parmesan cheese is relatively low in fat, since it is made from partially skimmed milk.

Is there a way to use Parmesan other than on pasta?

Parmigiano-Reggiano is a superb eating cheese that goes well with a number of fruits, especially pears, apples, figs, and melons. It is also lovely served in fine slivers as a topping for salads. Greens such as arugula, Belgian endive, and romaine have a particular affinity for Parmesan. Don't forget that grated Parmesan is perfect as a topping for a risotto and various soups, especially hearty bean soups and the classic minestrone.

TIP If you do not have a cheese slicer, you can use a vegetable peeler to make fine slivers of Parmesan.

RICOTTA

I have tasted wonderful fresh ricotta in Italy and the taste was totally different from what I get in my market. Is there anything I can do to improve its taste?

American ricotta is made from whole or partially skimmed cow's milk rather than the whey of sheep's milk. It is much blander, moister, and creamier and actually not very flavorful. Draining the cheese improves its consistency but not its flavor.

You can now get imported ricotta in some

specialty food markets but be sure to taste it before buying it. If it has a sharp prickly taste, pass on it because the cheese is no longer fresh.

What is the difference between ricotta and ricotta salata?

Ricotta salata is a dry pressed cheese. It is made out of lightly salted sheep's milk curd aged a minimum of 3 months. Good ricotta salata should have a sweet milky flavor. Be sure to taste it before buying it because it is often salty. I like to use ricotta salata grated on fresh pasta or as a topping for grilled or steamed vegetables.

Cream

HEAVY CREAM

Can I use light cream in recipes that call for heavy cream?

Light cream is not a substitute for heavy cream, since it contains only 18 to 30 percent milk fat, while heavy cream contains at least 36 percent. The high level of fat is important because it allows the cream to be boiled without separating and to be whipped. This is especially important when making custards and pastry creams. When air is beaten into heavy cream, the fat globules stick together and support the air bubbles, which in turn create whipped cream.

What is the difference between light whipping cream and heavy whipping cream?

Heavy whipping cream, also simply called heavy cream, has a fat content between 36 percent and 40 percent. It will double in volume when whipped. Light whipping cream has 30 percent to 35 percent fat. It sometimes contains stabilizers and emulsifiers to help it maintain volume.

I now see bottled heavy cream in the grocery store that is more expensive than the ultra-pasteurized cream in cartons. Is it worth the extra money?

The return of old-fashioned heavy cream that is not ultra-pasturized is great news and well worth the extra cost. Ultra-pasteurized cream is a product that has been heated at high temperatures to give it a longer shelf life, resulting in a major loss of flavor and a gummy texture. It also does not whip as well as regular heavy cream and you cannot use it to make crème fraîche.

Can I freeze leftover cream?

Freezing alters the taste and texture of heavy cream. However, ultra-pasteurized cream will keep for several weeks in the fridge.

TIP Madeleine Kamman in her book *The Making of a Cook* suggests stabilizing whipped cream by adding 2 level measuring spoons nonfat dry milk to each cup of plain cream before whipping.

When a soup recipe calls for cream, is yogurt an acceptable substitute?

Hot soups cannot be enriched with yogurt, which curdles when heated. Unfortunately, you really cannot beat the flavor and silkiness you get from cream. If you don't want to use it, simply omit it. It is delicious but not essential.

SOUR CREAM

Can I use light sour cream in recipes that call for full-fat sour cream?

You can use light sour cream if you add herbs and other flavorings to it. Otherwise, the taste is quite chalky and not too pleasant.

Can I substitute yogurt for sour cream in recipes?

I often use yogurt in Middle Eastern cooking and potato salad but always drain it first. A combination of yogurt and sour cream makes for a richer taste. Neither should be used in hot preparations, since both will curdle the sauce. That said, many Greek dishes call for yogurt in hot dishes with delicious though curdled results.

I recently added sour cream to enrich a sauce and it curdled. What did I do wrong?

If you have a choice, it is better to use crème fraîche rather than sour cream, since it does not curdle. If you can't get it, however, be sure to mix 2 teaspoons flour into the sour cream before adding it to a sauce.

CRÈME FRAÎCHE

So many recipes call for crème fraîche but my market does not carry it. Can I make my own?

Making your own is very easy. In a bowl combine 2 cups heavy cream with 4 tablespoons buttermilk. Whisk the mixture until well combined and transfer to a jar. Keep at room temperature for 12 to 24 hours or until very thick. Refrigerate and use the crème fraîche within 10 days.

I tried to make crème fraîche but the mixture remained liquid and never set. What did I do wrong?

To get crème fraîche to set you must use cream that has not been ultra-pasteurized. Unfortunately, this is not easy to get in certain parts of the country. In this case, you need to double the amount of buttermilk to 4 tablespoons per cup. Also, it is best to make it in a porcelain or ceramic jar, which holds the temperature evenly, rather than in glass or plastic, which are uneven heat conductors.

My recipe calls for crème fraîche to sit on the counter for 24 hours. Is there a quicker way to get it done?

Unfortunately, there is no quick method to make real crème fraîche. But for a quick way to get the same flavor, you can add a dollop of sour cream to whipped cream, which will give you the light sour taste of crème fraîche. This makes a delicious topping for fresh fruit but cannot be used in cooking the way crème fraîche can.

What brand of commercial crème fraîche do you recommend? How long does it keep?

Vermont Butter & Cheese Company crème fraîche is an excellent brand. All crème fraîche has a sell-by date and will be good for a week to 10 days after that.

Eggs

How do I know if the eggs I am buying at the supermarket are fresh?

The difficulty in shopping for really fresh eggs is that they are dated from the time they are packed rather than from the time they are laid. Your best bet is to buy AA or A graded eggs, which are the freshest. If the eggs in your market are not dated, then check the code that pertains to the date the eggs were packed. I try to buy my eggs either at a health food store that carries local farm eggs or at a supermarket that has a large turnover. You cannot always assume that farmers' markets carry fresher eggs. It is often not the case.

Is there a difference in taste between brown and white eggs? Which do you prefer?

There is no taste difference between white and brown eggs. The color of the shell has to do with the breed of the chicken. I prefer brown eggs because they have a more "country" look and because of their thicker shells.

Some of the eggs I buy have pale yolks while in others the yolk is golden. What does that mean?

The color of an egg yolk depends entirely on what the chicken is fed; the color does not affect its taste. Canadian eggs have pale yolks, which Canadians prefer. In the United States, we prefer deep yellow yolks, so most of our eggs come this way. Both kinds of yolks contain 34 percent fat and 16 percent protein, the rest being water.

Are organic eggs worth the extra money?

It really depends on taste and freshness. The very best-tasting eggs come from free-range chickens, those that stroll around freely pecking and scratching here and there for their food and living a normal chicken life. But these chickens lay very few eggs, so there are few free-range chickens out there. Organic eggs do not taste that much different from nonorganic ones, and therefore I do not feel that they are worth the extra cost. If you can find truly fresh eggs instead, they are definitely worth the high price.

I often lose count of when I bought the last batch of eggs. Is there a way to tell if they are still good?

The first thing to do is to check if the eggs are heavy for their size; the heavier the egg, the fresher it is. Then proceed to do the water test.

Place the eggs in a bowl of cold water. If the eggs remain horizontal, they are fresh; those that float almost vertically are not. The very best way to tell if an egg is fresh is to crack one open. The yolk should be centered in a dense, cohesive white. An older egg has a thinner white, is more watery, and the yolk may be off center. After 3 weeks the yolk will probably lie flat and the white will be watery. This egg is still considered fresh, but its taste and appearance do not compare to a truly fresh egg.

Food magazines suggest that eggs should be stored in their cartons. Why?

The shell of an egg is porous and can pick up refrigerator odors easily. Storing eggs in their carton protects them and keeps them fresh. In many refrigerators the egg rack in the refrigerator is in the door, an area that is too warm and unprotected.

TIP Store eggs with their broad rounded ends up. The rounded end of the egg is slightly less delicate and less likely to break when bumped accidentally.

Why is it sometimes so hard to peel a hard-boiled egg?

Believe it or not, a very fresh egg is harder to peel than one that is 1 to 2 weeks old. By that time the white has shrunk away from the shell slightly, making it easier to peel. On the other hand, only a very fresh egg will poach perfectly without the yolk breaking away from the white.

How do you keep hard-boiled or soft-boiled eggs from cracking during the cooking process?

Cold eggs crack more easily than eggs at room temperature. It is best to start to hard-boil eggs in cold water. When the water comes to a simmer, count 10 minutes, and the eggs will be done perfectly. Be sure to bring the eggs to room temperature before cooking soft-boiled eggs. Ease the eggs with a large spoon into lightly simmering water and then count 3 to 5 minutes, depending on how you like your eggs done.

The yolks of my hard-boiled eggs are often surrounded by a greenish tinge. What does this mean?

The greenish color is simply the sign of an overcooked egg. Be sure to time your eggs. A perfectly hard-boiled egg needs only 10 minutes from the time the water has come back to a simmer.

TIP Cold eggs separate better than warm ones because the egg white is more viscous. When using eggs for baking, always separate one egg at a time because even the tiniest speck of yolk will keep the white from whipping and absorbing air.

Is it necessary to stick to the size of eggs called for in a recipe?

Large eggs are the standard called for in most cookbooks. For many recipes, such as scrambled eggs, quiches, and custards, you can use any size egg. When it comes to baking, however, you need to measure the volume of the eggs according to this chart:

1 large egg, beaten = 3¼ tablespoons

2 large eggs, beaten = 6½ tablespoons

3 large eggs, beaten = 9⅔ tablespoons or ½ cup plus 1½ tablespoons

4 large eggs, beaten = 12¾ tablespoons or ¾ cup plus 1 teaspoon

5 large eggs, beaten = 1 cup

I often find myself with a lot of leftover eggs. Can I freeze them for later use?

Eggs freeze quite well. To do so, break them into a container. (I usually use 5 large eggs, which equals 1 cup.) With a fork, pierce the yolks and stir slowly to mix them. Be sure not to whip up any foam because the air bubbles will dry out the eggs as they freeze.

If you have any leftover yolks, you can freeze them, too. Be sure to add a large pinch of salt to the eggs you plan to use for cooking and a teaspoon of sugar to those you will use for baking.

Leftover whites can easily be frozen, and once thawed will whip beautifully.

Dried Fruit

How should I store dried fruit?

I store my dried fruit in zippered plastic bags in the fridge. When kept on a pantry shelf, dried fruit gets hard and leathery.

Any tips for buying dates?

Some dates are treated with corn syrup, which I find unnecessary, since dates are one of the sweetest foods I know. I buy only untreated dates, usually in a health food store or at a green market. If you have a choice of varieties, the Medjool is softer and creamier than the more common Deglet Noor.

PRUNES

Is it better to buy prunes pitted or unpitted?

Unpitted prunes are always my first choice, and the larger the better. They have much better flavor and they do not fall apart in cooking. Of course, if you serve a dish with unpitted prunes, be sure to warn your guests or family.

TIP **Prune puree, which is available in most grocery stores, can be used instead of butter in baked goods. It adds the right moisture and an interesting flavor.**

I know dried fruit is high in fiber, so I'd like to eat more of it, but except for adding raisins to my oatmeal cookies, I'm at a loss. Do you know some good ways to use dried fruit?

You're right, dried fruit is a terrific and delicious source of fiber. The highest-fiber dried fruits are dates and prunes, followed closely by apricots and raisins. One great way to use dried fruit is to make a compote.

In a saucepan, cover the fruit with water. Add a little sugar, a cinnamon stick, and a 3-inch piece of vanilla bean, and simmer for 25 to 35 minutes or until the fruit is very tender. Refrigerate in the poaching liquid.

You can also simmer dried apricots this way, puree them, then serve the resulting sauce over ice cream.

I see all kinds of dried fruits in the market these days: cranberries, sour cherries, even strawberries. What do you use them for other than a snack?

I usually use sour cherries and cranberries in muffins, quick breads, and especially in rice pudding, where they add a delicious chewy texture.

RAISINS

When a recipe calls for raisins, which ones should I buy?

It really depends on what you are going to make. I use golden raisins in some preparations and dark raisins in others. I also like currants. Now that you can get Muscat raisins, be sure to try them. It is a good idea to have a box of various kinds of raisins, since they also make wonderful healthy snacks. Make sure to refrigerate them if you do not use them regularly.

TIP **If you find yourself with raisins that have dried out, just simmer them in water to cover until they plump up. If they don't, and stay crumbly, you will have to get a fresh batch.**

What is the difference between a currant and a sultana raisin?

Sultanas are golden raisins, made from yellow sultana grapes (and sometimes, especially in the United States, from Thompson seedless yellow grapes). Currants are made from the tiny Zante grape, much smaller than raisins and sultanas.

Nuts

Nuts sold in cellophane packages are sometimes not as fresh as they should be. How can I ensure that I'm getting really fresh nuts?

Buying nuts can be most frustrating, because—contrary to European custom—we do not date our nuts. That means you have no idea how fresh they really are. If you buy nuts in bulk in a health food store you can, of course, taste them, which is an advantage. Canned nuts are usually more expensive, but vacuum packing keeps them fresher than the cellophane-packed varieties.

Which nuts do you always keep on hand and how do you store them?

Except for pine nuts, walnuts, and pecans, I try to buy nuts as I need them, and I highly recommend that you do the same. The best way to store nuts is to keep them in the freezer and toast them lightly before using. The exception to this rule is pine nuts, which I keep in the refrigerator, because I use them on a regular basis. Nuts contain natural oils that can eventually go bad when the nuts are not properly stored.

What's the best way to get the skins off nuts like almonds and hazelnuts? Is this really necessary?

You really should remove the skins from nuts such as almonds and hazelnuts because the skins get tough during baking. This is quite easy to do. Just place the nuts on a cookie sheet and toast them in a 200°F oven for about 10 minutes, or until the nuts are nice and golden. You should be able to smell a distinct nutty aroma but not a burned one. Then transfer the nuts to a clean kitchen towel and rub until most of the skin comes off.

When a recipe calls for blanched almonds and I cannot find them in the store, can I blanch them myself?

Blanching almonds is very easy; in fact, it's a good idea to buy almonds in their skins and to blanch them yourself, since this way you will get a fresher almond. To do this, put the almonds in a saucepan with water to cover and cook for 2 to 3 minutes. Drain and rub off the skins with some paper towels. Spread the blanched almonds on a cookie sheet to dry at room temperature, or pop them into a 200°F oven for 5 minutes. Be sure to keep an eye on them—what you want is blanched almonds, not toasted ones.

TIP When a recipe calls for ground almonds, use slivered ones and be sure to add a little sugar to them before grinding them up in the food processor. The sugar will keep the nuts fluffy and dry.

I recently bought peanuts and they did not taste "peanuty." Are there different kinds of peanuts I should look for?

Peanuts come two ways, either roasted or raw. Raw peanuts do not have the familiar "peanutty" taste, so look for roasted unsalted peanuts for everyday cooking.

I love to buy unshelled peanuts, but they sometimes taste dry and even rancid. Is there a way to tell really fresh peanuts?

The first thing to do is taste as many peanuts in the markets as you can. That is usually a pretty good test, but most important is that the peanuts have clean unbroken shells and that the nuts do not rattle when shaken; the rattle is a sign that the nuts are not fresh. Consume peanuts quickly because they are high in fat and become rancid quickly.

When a recipe calls for ground peanuts as in a Thai peanut sauce, can I use peanut butter instead?

In some cases you can, but in many Thai recipes, it is the coarseness of the ground peanut that gives the dish an extra dimension. I usually prefer using ground whole unsalted peanuts rather than peanut butter.

What kind of nuts should I use to make pesto?

Classic pesto is always made with pine nuts, although there are versions of this wonderful sauce that call for walnuts. You can call me a traditionalist, but to me pine nuts, fresh garden-grown basil, excellent olive oil, and top-quality Parmesan are the four "must-have" ingredients for good pesto.

What are pignoli?

Pignoli is the Italian name for pine nuts, the most important ingredient in pesto. Unfortunately, most of the pine nuts you now see in grocery stores come from China and their quality is inferior to that of the Mediterranean variety. However, Chinese pine nuts are perfectly acceptable when toasted and added to rice dishes or used to garnish grilled vegetables. Mediterranean pine nuts are elongated in shape and have a nuttier, less oily flavor. It is easy to tell which is which, since real pignoli are twice as expensive as the Chinese nuts.

What is the best way to buy prepared chestnuts?

The best chestnuts now come vacuum-packed in either small or large jars and are available in markets everywhere. You can also order them by mail through specialty stores such as Zingerman's and Dean & DeLuca (see Sources, page 398). You will notice them more around Thanksgiving, when markets stock up on them. The jarred nuts keep for at least a year.

Olives

My market has just put in an olive bar, but I find choosing olives very confusing. Which olives do you recommend?

The nice thing about an olive bar is that it allows you to taste various olives. Generally, green olives are firmer with a sharper flavor than black olives. They are also less oily, since green olives are the unripe fruit. On the other hand, the flesh of black olives is softer and their flavor more delicate. Once you get hooked on olives, you are likely to choose more than one variety.

Most black olives seem to be very salty. Are some saltier than others?

The most common black olives carried by grocery stores are the black kalamata olives from Greece. These are quite fleshy, often large, and very salty. I prefer the smaller Italian black olives, especially the gaeta and the French niçoise olives. However, when a recipe calls for olives, I find that the pitted kalamata olives are quite acceptable. To remove their saltiness, just simmer in water for 2 or 3 minutes.

How long do olives keep?

It depends on whether they are brined or packed in oil. As long as the olives are covered in brine, they will keep for several weeks. You can add olive oil to oil-cured olives to extend their shelf life.

I love spicy olives and have tasted really good ones in various restaurants but cannot find them in my grocery store. Can I make my own?

You can flavor your own olives very easily. Just add a finely sliced jalapeño pepper, 1 or 2 sliced garlic cloves, and some fruity olive oil to your olives and let them marinate for 2 or 3 days. Then get a crusty loaf of bread and a nice slightly aged goat cheese and enjoy!

Is there a taste difference between green and black olives? Which are better suited for cooking?

There is a very definite taste difference between green and black olives, as well as texture differences. There is also a large flavor difference between various kinds of green olives and the many kinds of black ones. It is a matter of tasting as many kinds as you can and settling on the ones you enjoy. You can use both black and green olives in a variety of dishes. I personally prefer black ones because of their softer texture and milder flavor.

■ **Cream of Asparagus and Spring Onion Soup** ■ **Avocado Salad in Ginger-Lime Vinaigrette** ■ **Roasted Beet, Watermelon, and Mango Salad** ■ **Pan-Seared Baby Bok Choy with Red Bell Peppers and Oyster Sauce** ■ **Skillet-Braised Broccoli with Garlic** ■ **Sauté of Brussels Sprouts with Bacon, Pine Nuts, and Sour Cream** ■ **Braised Red Cabbage with Orange Zest and Grenadine** ■ **Skillet Braised Carrots with Pine Nuts And Raisins** ■ **Puree of Celery Root, Potatoes, and Sweet Garlic** ■ **Creamy Celery and Stilton Cheese Soup** ■ **Corn and Chive Fritters with Smoked Salmon Sauce** ■ **Spicy Corn and Ginger Relish** ■ **Sauté of Cucumbers in Chive and Dill Cream** ■ **Fricassee of Roasted Eggplant and Two Mushrooms** ■ **Charcoal-Grilled Eggplant with Lemon-Scallion Mayonnaise** ■ **Skillet-Braised Belgian Endives** ■ **Ragout of Fennel, Tomatoes, and Potatoes** ■ **Sauté of Green Beans with Tuna, Tomatoes, and Red Onion** ■ **Kale, Potato, and Butternut Squash Chowder** ■ **Braised Leeks with Shiitake Mushrooms and Crème Fraîche** ■ **Portobello Mushrooms in Tarragon-Lime Butter** ■ **Wild Mushroom, Scallion, and Gruyère Bread Pudding** ■ **Bruschetta of Roasted Sweet Onions** ■ **Roasted Vidalia Onions with Garlic and Rosemary** ■ **Sugar Snap Pea Soup** ■ **Curried Bell Pepper and Zucchini Ragout** ■ **Mascarpone and Chive Mashed Potatoes** ■ **Gratin of Russet Potatoes and Sweet Onions** ■ **New Potato Salad in Mustard, Shallot, and Caper Vinaigrette** ■ **Puree of Sweet Potatoes and Carrots** ■ **Puree of Rutabaga and Potato with Crispy Shallots** ■ **Shallot and Cassis Marmalade** ■ **Sauté of Spinach with Scallions, Dill, and Yogurt** ■ **Acorn Squash, Apple, and Wild Mushroom Soup** ■ **Wild Mushroom and Parmesan Timbales**

In 1973 my first book, *The Seasonal Kitchen*, was voted best cookbook of the year. The concept then seemed new, refreshing, and different from that of other cookbooks. Here was a book defined not just by recipes but by menus that focused on seasonality and freshness. It was about the way I grew up, the way I felt about raw materials, the way I thought about food, and the way I cook.

At the time I was often asked what type of cuisine I wrote about. I had to explain repeatedly that the seasonal kitchen was not a cuisine but a philosophy, and that every type of cooking fits into it. It was and continues to be what peasant and regional cooking is all about around the world. For millions of cooks, whether in Europe, the Middle East, or Southeast Asia, seasonal produce is the basis of most dishes because it is simply tastier and more economical. To this day, you can visit markets in France, Spain, Italy, or Istanbul, and even if you are not a gardener or a cook, you can tell what is in season simply by looking around you.

For Americans in the seventies, the concept seemed almost radical. After all, don't we live in a country where everything is available no matter the season? Is there a time when you cannot get apples or raspberries or tomatoes? They may have been grown in a hothouse, or lost taste and texture while being kept for months in cold storage, or picked green so they can be shipped from thousands of miles away, but they are on produce shelves everywhere. In the months after the book came out, I traveled across the country, conducting workshops and trying to make my point. At times I would make the same soup with frozen vegetables and with fresh ones to demonstrate the difference.

Americans do know what fresh produce tastes like. People all over the country have always loved farm stands. Everyone agrees that fresh vegetables bought at a local farm stand taste much better than grocery store produce.

Why, then, do so many consumers forget about seasonality the minute the weather turns cold? Why would anyone buy corn in a grocery store in the middle of the winter? Why bother with out-of-season tomatoes, melons, or asparagus? Why don't we think winter squash and greens, parsnips, mushrooms, and celery root deserve as much attention as the summer classics and are equally satisfying when fresh and in season? So, just as with your wardrobe, change your meals to include the many varieties of root vegetables, broccoli rabe, earthy spinach, and kale.

Seasons can change as often as month to month or even week to week, so be sure to plan your menus after you've done your produce shopping, rather than before. It is a waste of effort to build even a simple menu around a particular vegetable or fruit only to find that it is unripe, limp, or just not fresh. Instead, start with the best produce available. And you can be sure that you will find a recipe for it.

Often a perfect experience can come in simple ways. On a recent Sunday in the country, I made a Greek salad. The tomatoes were juicy and flavorful, the cucumbers crisp, the lettuce tasty, and the radishes crunchy. I had bought some delicious, not too salty feta cheese and excellent olives. These simple ingredients combined with a fruity olive oil made it all happen. Here was a salad for which there was no need for a recipe, and it was memorable.

It reminded me of my Greek friends who, whenever they make this classic salad, always enjoy it as if it were their first time. Why? Because the raw materials can change daily, and the way each cook uses them influences the result.

Just because a vegetable or a fruit is in season, it doesn't mean it is worth buying. It never ceases to amaze me when shoppers opt for less than perfect lettuce, bagged carrots, and fruit that will never ripen no matter how much time it spends in a bowl. You may have to look beyond your all-purpose market for the best produce. For example, if the carrots in your supermarket look limp and tired, if the radishes only come packaged, or if the cilantro or basil comes in small cellophane containers, try another market where the turnover is greater.

You'll find it worth your time to search out the best. What is the point of spending precious time and money working with produce in which the odds are against you from the start? Why put effort into a dish that cannot possibly deliver?

The reason for this chapter is to help you learn to buy the best produce by answering many of the fruit and vegetable questions I have heard over the years—questions such as "How do you tell a good celery root or parsnip?" And "Is it really worth buying carrots with their tops if you are going to discard them anyway?"

Another major concern today is the importance of shopping for food that has been grown organically. On a recent visit to the Berkeley

Bowl, one of the most exciting stores in northern California, I was thrilled to see the abundance of organically grown produce and to taste the difference between a commercially grown strawberry and an organically grown one.

There was a time when organic produce did not look as appealing as commercially grown varieties. Today the quality is far superior, and while you may not find absolutely perfect-looking fruits and vegetables, what you give up in looks, you will gain in taste.

Storage has become a big issue with the increasingly popular use of misting to keep vegetables looking fresh. Unfortunately for the consumer, supermarkets are ignoring the fact that all this moisture causes quick decay once these misted vegetables are bagged. I have now adopted the habit of shaking a bunch of parsley or lettuce several times before bagging it, often resulting in angry looks from a nearby shopper who was not anticipating a damp shower.

Because produce shopping is expensive and time consuming, allow yourself the time once you arrive home to store your vegetables properly. It is very frustrating to reach for what you thought was going to be fresh parsley or a bunch of arugula, only to find it rotten in its bag, or to find your leeks, celery, or carrots looking limp in the bottom of the crisper because you did not take the extra time to bag them.

A recipe for a fruit or vegetable dish is only a recipe; it is the quality of the produce that will greatly affect the outcome of your dish. Below you'll find many tips on how to keep your fruits and vegetables fresh and tasty. Then it is up to you to buy the freshest and to learn to distinguish the best from the merely acceptable.

Artichokes

■■

Is there a secret to picking a good artichoke?
Choose an artichoke that feels heavy for its size. Lift a few off the pile and compare them to determine if they are firm and see if the leaves are tightly bound. Neither brown tips nor black streaks are signs of rotting but rather of frost damage that only affects the outer leaves. Artichoke growers call these "winter kisses."

What is the best season for artichokes?
The spring, starting in March and going through June, is the best time. September and October are a secondary season.

How do I clean an artichoke and prepare it for cooking?
Before you start, fill a large bowl with cold water and squeeze half a lemon into it to make acidulated water. Cut off the artichoke's stem and remove two or three layers of the bottom leaves. With a sharp knife, cut ½ inch off the top of the artichoke. Then, with a pair of sharp kitchen scissors, trim about ¼ inch off each leaf. Drop the artichokes into the acidulated water until ready to cook.

I love the taste of artichoke but have never cooked one. How do you cook and serve an artichoke?
The American globe artichoke, which is the most common variety that you will find in the

market, is best cooked whole in plenty of acidulated, slightly salted water.

Simmer it until the stem can be pierced easily with the tip of a sharp knife and an inner leaf comes out easily when it's pulled. This may take as long as 30 to 40 minutes. Be sure to drain the artichoke upside down on a double layer of paper towels or a large plate. Serve it warm with melted butter or a garlic-flavored butter.

What is the difference between the heart and the bottom of the artichoke? What is the fond?

The artichoke heart is the tender, meaty bottom of the artichoke, from which all the leaves and the fuzzy choke have been removed. The resulting flat disk is called the heart or bottom here, while in France and Spain it is called the fond.

How can I get to the heart, or bottom, of the artichoke in the easiest way?

First, choose the largest artichokes you can find. Break the stems off close to the base of the artichoke and then pull off three or four layers of leaves until you reach pale yellow-green leaves that fold inward. Slice off these leaves just above the heart and plunge the trimmed artichokes into acidulated water while you prepare the rest of the artichokes.

Cook in plenty of lightly salted water until the hearts, or bottoms, are easy to pierce with the tip of a sharp knife. Allow to cool in the water, drain, and gently scoop out the fuzz with a grapefruit spoon. Trim any remaining leaf ends.

Is there any use for the artichoke leaves when the recipes call only for the bottoms?

Unfortunately the leaves are of no particular value so I usually discard them.

Can artichokes be cooked successfully in the microwave?

A single artichoke microwaves beautifully. Trim the leaves and the stem end and then rinse the artichoke under cool tap water. Wrap the damp artichoke in plastic and microwave for about 10 minutes or until softened and an inside leaf pulls out easily when tugged. If you have a large microwave, you can cook two artichokes at a time by increasing the cooking time by a few minutes. If you want to cook more, it's easier to cook them in plenty of boiling water on top of the stove.

Is there a special method for cooking those baby artichokes sometimes available in the market?

Baby artichokes are wonderful braised. Trim the artichokes and cut ½ inch off the tops. Cut the chokes in half lengthwise and reserve. In a large cast-iron skillet, heat 3 tablespoons olive oil, place the sliced artichokes cut side down in the pan, season with a sprinkling of salt, and add 2 or 3 finely sliced garlic cloves and about 1½ cups water. Cover the skillet and simmer the artichokes for 15 minutes or until tender. Serve warm or at room temperature.

How long do cooked artichokes keep?

They'll store well for as long as a week if you put them in a covered container or sealed plastic bag and refrigerate. They also freeze well.

Asparagus

■■■

Is it better to buy thick or thin asparagus?

Thick stalks are more flavorful. Thin asparagus look pretty but not only are they harder to peel than thick stalks, they actually take longer to cook and can be quite stringy.

How can I tell if asparagus is fresh?

Check the bottoms of the stalks. They should be firm and moist, never dry or woody. The tips of the asparagus should have purplish-green, tightly closed clusters.

What is the best way to store fresh asparagus?

To store asparagus for more than 2 or 3 days, fill a quart-sized plastic container with one to two inches of water. Place the asparagus upright in the water and cover the tips with a double layer of slightly dampened paper towels, and keep them in the refrigerator. If you'll be cooking the asparagus within a day or two, simply store in the vegetable bin in a perforated plastic bag.

Is it really necessary to peel asparagus? The spears look so much nicer unpeeled.

Peeled asparagus spears cook more evenly. You can make them look attractive by using a swivel peeler that doesn't take off too much of the stalk. Make sure to rotate the asparagus as you peel to maintain their round shape. Otherwise, the stalks will look square.

TIP The best way to peel asparagus neatly is to place the stalks over a small, inverted stainless mixing bowl and rotate the stalks as you peel them.

When I prepare asparagus for cooking, how much of the stalk should I remove?

Cut 1 to 1½ inches off the bottom of the stalks. The best way to tell how much is to bend one of the stalks; it will snap at the point where the woody stem turns into a juicy stalk. This will give you an approximate idea of how much to cut off all the stalks.

My market bundles asparagus spears of different sizes, some thin, some thick. When cooking several bunches at one time, how can I make sure that some spears won't be overcooked while others are underdone?

Start with plenty of lightly salted, boiling water. Using ordinary kitchen string, tie same-sized spears together in bundles of 6 to 8 stalks—and leave one stalk of each size separate for testing. The bundles are easy to pull from the water when the test spear is done. Once the asparagus spears are cooked, spread them out on a double layer of paper towels. This keeps them from discoloring. If you plan to serve the asparagus at room temperature, it is best to shock them in a bowl of ice water to keep them bright and green. You can also steam asparagus, but it usually takes longer than boiling and the vegetable stays too crisp for my taste.

I like the idea of grilled asparagus but have had little luck with it. Can you help?

I find that uncooked asparagus does not lend itself well to grilling, and I suggest blanching the stalks in simmering water for 2 or 3 minutes until they are crisp-tender. Run them under cold water to stop further cooking. Dry on paper towels and then brush them with a little olive oil before putting them on a medium-hot grill. Grill the asparagus for 3 minutes, turning them once or twice until you can see grill marks. Use a large spatula to remove them from the grill and season with coarse salt and freshly ground pepper. The Emerald Mayonnaise that follows is an excellent accompaniment.

Emerald Mayonnaise

SERVES 6

3 tablespoons minced flat-leaf parsley

3 tablespoons minced scallions

2 large garlic cloves, crushed

4 flat anchovy fillets, drained

1 cup mayonnaise

½ cup crème fraîche or sour cream

Juice of 1 large lemon

Salt and freshly ground black pepper

Combine the parsley, scallions, garlic, and anchovies in a food processor or blender. Add the mayonnaise, crème fraîche, and lemon juice and process until smooth. Season with salt and a large grinding of black pepper, and chill for 4 to 6 hours or overnight.

Avocados

■■

What are the marks of a good avocado?

Avocados should be evenly ripe or evenly unripe. The best way to tell is by cradling the fruit in the palm of your hand and squeezing it lightly. If ripe, it should be somewhat soft to the touch. Depending on where you live, it may not be easy to buy a ripe fruit or, worse, an evenly ripe one. If the fruit is soft in some places and hard in others, you had better pass on it, since it will never ripen evenly. Unripe avocados usually take 2 or 3 days to ripen. Simply place the fruit in a warm place in an earthenware or porcelain bowl. To hasten the ripening, put it in a brown paper bag with a banana.

Some avocados are large and smooth, others smaller with a pebbly skin. Is there a difference in taste?

There are, in fact, many varieties of avocados that come into the markets at various times of the year. They vary in taste from nutty and slightly bitter to sweet and buttery. The Hass avocado, which has a tough, hardy, and pebbly skin and turns almost black when ripe, is by far your best bet. It does not bruise easily, has lots of delicious pulp, and, when ripe, will keep well in the fridge for 2 to 3 days.

What is the best way to slice an avocado?

First, cut through the skin lengthwise, then give the fruit a light twist to separate the halves. Then (this I learned from the guacamole chef at Rosa Mexicana), hit the pit with the edge of a sharp knife, twist lightly, and the pit will come right out. Of course, the avocado must be perfectly ripe, which is not always the case. You can spoon the avocado out, but I find it equally easy to cut it in quarters and remove the peel with my fingers.

Is there any trick that will keep an avocado from turning dark?

Although many people, including chefs, believe that leaving the pit in the cut fruit or propping it in the middle of a bowl of guacamole slows down the darkening process, I am not sure that it really helps. Sprinkling the fruit with fresh lemon or lime juice does delay discoloration. Plan to use the entire avocado at one time, and try to use it as soon as possible after slicing into it.

I love avocados, especially in guacamole. Is there any other simple preparation that is as good but has a different twist?

Good guacamole is hard to beat, but the Avocado Salad in Ginger-Lime Vinaigrette (page 109) is right up there with my favorite avocado recipes.

Beans

■■■

Is there a difference between snap beans, green beans, and string beans?

Snap, green, and string beans are really all the same bean. "Green beans" is the old-style name for them, which gave way to "string beans" (a misnomer, since new varieties of beans rarely need stringing). To avoid confusion, I refer to them as green beans, with the exception of wax beans. "Snap beans" to me are those grown in the garden or purchased at a farm stand that are picked even before reaching pencil-thin size. Test these by snapping one in half. If it breaks with a nice, clear sound, chances are the beans are fresh.

I see haricots verts in recipes and on restaurant menus. What are they?

Haricots verts simply means "green beans" in French but the term is used to indicate a slender type of bean that, while very popular in France, is just starting to be cultivated in the United States on a commercial basis. You can find them in specialty stores practically year-round, since they are imported and are quite expensive. Depending on the season and the turnover, haricots verts can be delicious and cook quickly and evenly, while at other times they take forever to cook and are quite tasteless. To make sure they stay green, "shock" them as soon as they are done (see below).

Recipes in food magazines suggest "shocking" vegetables. How do you do that and what does it do?

Shocking green vegetables is a restaurant technique that is well worth trying. Before blanching broccoli, asparagus, or green beans, place a large bowl of ice water next to the stove. As soon as the green vegetable is done, drain it in a colander and transfer to the ice water. This will help the vegetable retain its lovely green color. To heat, melt a little butter and olive oil in a skillet, add the green vegetable, season with salt and pepper, and toss gently in the butter just until heated through.

What is really the best way to prepare green beans for cooking? Should I snap off both tails and tips?

I usually snap off the tail only and leave the tip on, which I find looks pretty. Always make sure that the beans are not stringy. If they are, pull the string down along with the tail as you clean them. Haricots verts need to have only their tails removed.

TIP **The best way to speed up bean preparation is to line up a few at a time and cut off the ends all at once.**

What are Roma beans?

Roma or flat beans are wide, long, and meaty green beans that are unfortunately seldom available in the average supermarket. They are extremely popular in Mediterranean countries, particularly Spain and Italy. Roma beans do need stringing and are best when cut into 1-inch pieces, cooked until very tender, and then buttered.

What is the best method for cooking beans? Do you recommend blanching or steaming?

Personally I do not like to steam beans, since it takes longer and the result is usually a rather crunchy bean. To me, the best method is to drop the beans into plenty of lightly salted water and cook at a rapid boil, testing several times for doneness (tender with a slight bite). Run the beans under cold water to stop further cooking and they are ready for a number of preparations, even something as simple as a little fresh butter, a drizzle of good olive oil, or a nicely flavored vinaigrette.

Beets

I thought beets were always red, but sometimes I see yellow ones and even pink-and-white-striped ones. Are these true beets?

Several varieties of beets are available today—they are all true beets but have different colors and somewhat different flavors. You're probably familiar with the standard round, red beet *(Beta vulgaris)*, which has been grown for over two thousand years. It's sweet and tender when cooked properly. The Chioggia, or candy-striped beet, has a bright red exterior and a wonderful ringed red-and-white interior. It's slightly mellower than the standard beet. The golden beet is deep yellow and slightly more oval in shape than the standard beet, with a denser texture and flavor. And, believe it or not, there is a white beet! It looks like a turnip and has a highly concentrated super-sweet flavor. While you can certainly use all these beets interchangeably, the

Chioggia lends itself to raw dishes because of its amazing and surprising colors, the golden is best roasted and combined with other roasted root vegetables, and the white beet . . . best as a conversation piece, perhaps!

Is there any way to peel a beet without making a huge mess?

Garnet-colored beet juice does go everywhere. Always peel beets after they're cooked, as it's much easier to do at that stage. Here's my method for minimizing mess and cleanup: place raw scrubbed beets in the middle of a piece of heavy aluminum foil. Rub the beets with olive oil, seal the foil, and bake until a fork easily pulls out of the center of one of the beets. Let them cool slightly and then use a dry paper towel to rub off the skin. The oil makes the peel slip right off and the paper towel keeps your hands relatively beet-juice free. Another option is to wear rubber gloves.

Why do some beets cook in almost no time and others seem to take forever? Would peeling help?

Beets are a seasonal vegetable. They are at their best and freshest in spring and summer, and at that time of year beets cook in less than 30 minutes. Mature older beets can take up to an hour or more, so if you want young tender beets, stay seasonal. Peeling beets is not a good idea, since they will bleed their color into the cooking water and you end up with pink rather than deep ruby-red beets. Always cook them unpeeled, and be sure to leave about an inch of their tops so as not to cut into the beet, which also causes bleeding.

So many recipes call for roasted beets these days. What method do you prefer?

If you are cooking beets in cool weather, oven-roasting them at 350°F is a good idea. Be sure to wrap each beet in aluminum foil and place on a cookie sheet. Test the beets for doneness after about 45 minutes with the tip of a sharp knife;

do not pierce all over, since the beets will start losing their juices. I prefer cooking young beets on top of the stove in plenty of water, since doing so does not require using an oven and goes rather quickly. Both baked and cooked beets will keep well refrigerated for several days.

Can beets be eaten raw?

Raw beets really show off their sweet, earthy flavor, and they are certainly striking. You can grate them right into a salad.

Whenever I try cooking the greens from my beets I get a stringy mess. What's the deal?

I cook only the leafy tops of very young beets, mostly those that I pull out of the garden when I'm thinning my crop. You can, of course, find young beets at farmers' markets during the spring and summer. Make sure the greens are tender and crisp. For best results, simply stir-fry the beet greens with a couple of sliced garlic cloves in a little olive oil and season with a generous grinding of black pepper. A cupful of diced or julienned cooked beets is a nice addition to the greens, as is a spoonful of sour cream or crème fraîche.

Broccoli

I love broccoli and so does my family, but all I do is steam it. Do you have any other interesting suggestions for cooking broccoli?

One of my favorite methods is to skillet-braise it. See the recipe for Skillet-Braised Broccoli with Garlic, page 112.

Try adding other vegetables to the braised broccoli, such as a julienne of red peppers and shitake mushrooms.

When I serve raw broccoli with other raw vegetables as part of an appetizer spread, the broccoli often loses color, goes limp,

and remains uneaten. Do you have any tricks to liven up broccoli when it is served as a crudité?

I often pass on raw broccoli at parties for this very reason. To keep the broccoli bright green, drop the florets in a saucepan of hot but not boiling water for 2 minutes and then stop the cooking process by either running the drained broccoli under cold water or placing it in a bowl of water filled with ice cubes. This blanching and water-bath method really keeps the green color vibrant long after the party is over.

I see a variety of broccoli-like greens in my produce department. What are they?

There are several relatively new hybrids well worth including in your cooking repertoire. Broccolini is considered "baby broccoli." It is very flavorful and doesn't take as long to cook. Prepare it the same way you would broccoli with shorter cooking times. Broccoflower (a trademarked brand name) is another hybrid—a combination, as the name indicates, of cauliflower and broccoli. It looks and tastes much more like cauliflower than broccoli, and I find it to be just a novelty.

When I cook broccoli, the florets are too soft by the time the stalks are done. What am I doing wrong?

Try keeping the florets aside and cooking the stalks first, then adding the florets 2 or 3 minutes later. Also, be sure to scrape the stalks with a vegetable peeler or sharp paring knife and cut them into even sizes. The thinner and more uniform in size the stalks are, the more evenly they will cook, and the less likely you are to overcook them.

TIP When stir-frying broccoli, slice the florets in half to allow more of the floret to come into contact with the heated surface of the wok or skillet.

Can I microwave broccoli if I'm in a hurry?

Yes, as a matter of fact, broccoli is one vegetable that does very well in the microwave. Place the broccoli in a microwaveable bowl with about 1 inch of water. Cover the bowl with either plastic wrap or a damp paper towel and microwave on full power for 3 minutes for florets, 6 minutes for stems, and 8 minutes for a full head. Be sure to allow the broccoli to rest for about 1 minute before carefully removing the covering. Pierce with a knife to see if it's done and return it to the microwave for another minute if it is not fully cooked.

I have plenty of recipes for florets, but I often end up just throwing broccoli stems away. Do you have any suggestions for using them?

It's a shame to toss out perfectly good, tender broccoli stems. Raw, they make a nice crunchy addition to salads, but be sure to peel them with a vegetable peeler and then slice them finely. Toss with a well-seasoned vinaigrette, possibly made with a touch of sesame oil.

What is the difference between broccoli and broccoli rabe?

The names confuse a lot of people, but these are two totally different vegetables—one is a cruciferous vegetable and the other is a type of bitter green. (The name broccoli rabe derives from the flowers at the tips of the greens, which resemble small broccoli florets.) Broccoli can be prepared in a variety of ways, but broccoli rabe, like all bitter greens, is best when sautéed simply in some olive oil with garlic. Broccoli rabe also sometimes goes by the names broccoli rapini or rape.

I am not sure how to prepare broccoli rabe. Do I remove all the leaves or cut off most of the stalk as with other greens?

I remove most of the stalk and some of the coarse leaves. Don't remove all the leaves or you will be left with hardly any greens.

I tried stir-frying broccoli rabe, but it was so bitter I could hardly swallow it. Is there any way to mellow the taste?

You can mellow the greens by blanching them in salted water for 2 minutes. Once they're drained, I usually like to sauté them in some virgin olive oil with a couple of finely sliced garlic cloves. Be sure to season the broccoli rabe with plenty of fresh cracked pepper.

Brussels Sprouts and Cabbage

I have seen tiny little Brussels sprouts at Pike's Market in Seattle, but the ones I get at my grocery store are large and packed in cartons. Can I use frozen sprouts instead of the larger ones?

The fresh Brussels sprouts sold in most supermarkets are often a real disappointment, but the frozen sprouts are not a good substitute. You will do better quartering large sprouts or breaking them up into leaves and then sautéing them with some butter and broth. They are delicious this way. See Sauté of Brussels Sprouts with Bacon, Pine Nuts, and Sour Cream, page 113.

Whenever I cook Brussels sprouts, my whole kitchen smells like cabbage. Is there a way around it?

Only overcooked sprouts have that smell. Blanch the sprouts in water to cover for exactly

8 minutes. Drain and oven-braise, covered, seasoned with butter, salt, and pepper, for 25 minutes. You will get wonderful-tasting sprouts this way and your kitchen will not have that nose-wrinkling odor.

Do white and red cabbage taste different?

In their raw state, the cabbages taste similar. However, since they are usually prepared very differently, in a sense they have become two distinct cabbages. For example, red cabbage is traditionally teamed with beets in borscht or prepared in a sweet and sour sauce with red wine and vinegar (see Braised Red Cabbage with Orange Zest and Grenadine, page 114). Green cabbage can be braised in butter with leeks, shredded in a slaw, and added to a variety of hearty soups. It is more versatile, since it doesn't discolor other ingredients the way red cabbage does.

Should I buy a large or small head of cabbage?

Size is of little importance when it comes to cabbage; freshness is the key. Summer cabbages tend to be smaller with heads weighing 1 to 2 pounds, while winter cabbage is larger and can weigh as much as 3 pounds or more.

How can I tell a really fresh cabbage?

Very fresh cabbages still have their outer leaves attached and the leaves look green or dark red. As the cabbage ages, the outer leaves are trimmed off by the grocery store, or fall off, and the remaining leaves lose pigment, so that green cabbages look almost white and red cabbage is rosy white rather than that lovely deep red color of the fresh vegetable.

Does the age of the cabbage have anything to do with how much it smells when it's cooked? Are fresher cabbages milder?

The fresher the cabbage, the milder the taste, and I honestly think that cabbage has gotten a bad rap. Unless it's overcooked, cabbage is a mild vegetable that does not have a strong aroma.

I recently sampled the most wonderful, mild-tasting cabbage dish and was told it was made with Savoy cabbage. What is that?

This is indeed my favorite cabbage. Look for it in your market toward the end of summer. The heads have lovely ruffled green leaves, which are perfect for stuffing, and the inner leaves can be prepared in many interesting ways. Keep an eye out for the fresh heads of Savoy cabbage, which show up in markets during the winter months every once in a while. The only recipe for which Savoy is not suitable is American-style coleslaw. Otherwise, it is the king of cabbages.

What is mustard cabbage?

Mustard greens sometimes are called mustard cabbage. You will see them most frequently in the South, or in Chinese grocery stores, although I recently bought lovely fresh mustard greens in a Connecticut market in July. The leaves of this green are ruffled and bright green. They taste tangy, but the larger, mature leaves can be too strong for most tastes. Stick to very young mustard greens with leaves that are not full of holes. Use them in stir-fries the way you would other braising greens.

What is the difference between Chinese and Napa cabbage?

The terms are used interchangeably. There are actually two types of Napa, or Chinese, cabbage. One is football-shaped with a tightly packed head and green ruffled leaves. The other, less popular variety has long stems with compact leaves. Both are extremely mild and delicious in soups or stir-fries. I generally add some finely sliced garlic or a hot chile to this cabbage to enhance its taste. Napa cabbage keeps in the refrigerator for as long as 3 weeks and is good to have around for a quick vegetable.

I hear about bok choy all the time. Isn't it just another name for Chinese cabbage?

Bok choy is a leafy green Chinese vegetable that is a member of the cabbage family. It has dark green, spoon-shaped leaves and bright white stalks that come together at the root. It tastes something like very mild cabbage, but it is more about texture than taste.

Bok choy goes by many names: pak choi, "Chinese white" cabbage, white-mustard cabbage, celery mustard, and so on. It is not Chinese cabbage (which is also called Napa cabbage), although it is often mislabeled as such. Bok choy will keep for about 4 days in the refrigerator in a plastic bag.

Whenever I cook bok choy, it seems to shrink so much. How much do I need to serve four to six people?

Like all leafy greens, bok choy shrinks when cooked by releasing much of the moisture in its leaves. A 1½-pound head of bok choy will yield 4 scanty side-dish servings.

How should I cook bok choy? Are the yellow flowers edible?

To prepare bok choy for cooking, detach the stalks from the cluster at the base and then cut the leaves from the stalks. Cut the stems in 1½-inch pieces and stir-fry quickly in olive oil with some sliced garlic cloves until just tender. Add the cut-up leaves and continue sautéing until just wilted.

The lovely yellow flowers of bok choy are edible and look very pretty when scattered over the stir-fry.

Sometimes I see tiny bok choy in my market. How do you prepare it?

There are many different varieties of bok choy, although they all taste pretty much the same and respond well to the same cooking methods. Baby bok choy, sometimes called Shanghai cabbage, can be steamed whole either in a skillet on top of the stove or in the microwave. Plan on one to two per person. If you plan to chop it for a stir-fry, I would not spend the extra money for the baby variety, since it is more expensive. See Pan-Seared Baby Bok Choy with Red Bell Peppers and Oyster Sauce, page 111.

Carrots

■■

Is there any great difference between bunches of carrots sold with their tops and those bagged without them?

Other than carrots just dug from the garden, the best, sweetest carrots are those sold in bunches with their tops. If the tops look crisp and bright, you can be assured the carrots are fresh. Chop the greens off the carrots before storing them, leaving about 2 inches of stem—if you leave the greens attached, they will rob the carrots of some of their moisture and they will go limp in a day or two. Store carrots in a plastic bag and refrigerate them for up to 2 weeks.

Many recipes call for fresh carrots with their tops, but these are not always available in my market and are quite expensive. Can I use bagged carrots instead?

Bagged carrots are fine for stock and soups, and I always have a bag of these in my crisper, but fresh carrots with their tops attached are a much better and a fresher choice if you plan to eat them raw or as a cooked vegetable on their own.

Do you recommend the bags of baby carrots that are so popular these days?

Don't be fooled into thinking that these are really baby carrots—they are large carrots cut by machine to resemble baby carrots. To me, they are tasteless and uninteresting, so what you are paying for is appearance and not taste.

TIP To crisp flabby raw carrots, peel and put them in very cold water for about 20 minutes. They will perk right up and will be nice and crisp, ready for nibbling.

I live in New England and have been growing carrots for years, but truthfully the fresh carrots I buy in the market seem sweeter. Is this possible?

The further west you go, the sweeter the carrots. Carrots grown in the Northwest and California are the sweetest, followed by those coming from Florida and Arizona. Unfortunately, the soil in the Northeast does not produce a very sweet carrot.

For a good vegetable stock Start with 12 cups water, add 3 to 4 celery stalks with tops, 2 or 3 leeks, 3 to 4 carrots, a bunch of flat-leaf parsley, and a little salt. Cover the pot and bring to a boil. Reduce the heat and simmer for 45 minutes to an hour. Remove the stock from the heat and let the vegetables sit in the liquid for 2 or 3 hours. Strain the stock and discard the vegetables. The flavor of vegetable stocks is intensified when the vegetables sit in the broth for several hours after cooking. Use the vegetable stock right after it's strained, or refrigerate it for no longer than 3 days. If you plan to store it for longer than that, you can freeze it for several months. After a stock has been refrigerated for 2 or 3 days and you decide to freeze it, make sure you bring it to a boil first to kill any bacteria. Leave it uncovered to cool completely before freezing.

Some recipes call for carrots to be cored, others do not. When is it important to core a carrot?

Unless you use carrots for stocks or roasting, it is always a good idea to core them, especially if they are large and the core is very developed. Here is how you do it.

Peel the carrot. Cut it into 2-inch pieces crosswise and then quarter it lengthwise. Remove the core with a sharp knife, then cut the carrot into cubes. It is now ready for cooking or braising.

Is it always necessary to peel carrots before eating or cooking?

The only time I do not peel carrots is when I use them in stocks or when they are very young, right out of the garden. Be sure you don't remove too much of the peel, because most of the nutrients lie close to the skin. Small baby carrots, however, only need a thorough rinsing and possibly a light scrubbing.

Do you have any suggestions for carrot recipes that I can make in advance?

When I was growing up in Spain, one of my mother's best dishes was the Skillet-Braised Carrots with Pine Nuts and Raisins, page 116. This can be made up a day or two in advance. Another great make-ahead carrot recipe is the Puree of Sweet Potatoes and Carrots, page 143. This is my favorite side dish for a roast turkey, a chicken, or a pork roast.

Celery

■■

My market carries celery in loose bunches and in plastic packages. Which is the best way to buy it?

Buy celery only in bunches. It is less expensive and has the added bonus of the celery leaves—the most flavorful part of the celery stalk and a must for stocks and many soups.

Does the color of celery make a difference in taste? I see dark green bunches as well as many that are very pale.

There are two kinds of celery. Golden heart is bleached white and is therefore very light in color and has a very mild taste. Pascal celery has darker stalks and a more assertive flavor. Both are equally tasty. If you like milder celery, reserve the outer stalks for cooking and use the lighter-colored inner stalks for salads and snacks.

Celery seems to go limp in 2 or 3 days. How can I keep it crisp?

If properly stored, celery keeps well for 2 or 3 weeks. As soon as you buy it, cut about 3 inches off the leafy tops. Store these separately in plastic bags in the crisper and use the leaves to flavor stocks, soups, and stews. You may have to remove 2 or 3 of the outer stalks after a few days if they develop brown spots. Although I rarely freeze celery, you can do so. Cube it and store it in a zippered plastic freezer bag. The celery will lose its crunch but will still add good flavor to soups and stews.

My celery often freezes in the refrigerator and loses its crisp texture. Why does this happen?

Celery has a very high water content. If your refrigerator is cold, especially in the back, it will freeze rather quickly. Make sure you keep it away from the coldest section in the back of the refrigerator and store it in the crisper. If the bunch does not fit, cut it in half crosswise and store it in two separate bags.

I find I use celery only in chicken and tuna salad and for soup flavoring. This leaves me with lots of leftover celery. What can I do with it?

I like to use celery in creamy celery soup spiked with some blue cheese, for which celery has a great affinity. Try it in the recipe for Creamy Celery and Stilton Cheese Soup, page 118. It also makes a wonderful cooked vegetable that is worth trying.

Is it true that celery is high in sodium and not very healthful?

Celery is high in sodium, but it is also high in vitamins A and C and very low in calories. A large stalk has only 7 calories and ½ cup cooked celery can have as little as 11 calories. This makes celery a favorite with dieters.

Is there a difference between celery root and celeriac? What does celeriac look like?

Celery root, celeriac, and knob celery are names given to a wonderful, rather peculiar-looking vegetable. It is a cousin of the run-of-the-mill celery plant. The "knob" resembles an unwashed bumpy horseradish root about the size of a baseball and is covered with lumps and grooves. But don't be fooled. Under its unglamorous outer shell lies flavorful, crisp, cream-colored flesh that tastes somewhat like the finest celery but has a texture similar to a potato. If you're not familiar with this knobby root, it's definitely worth seeking out.

What should I look for when I buy celery root?

If you see celery roots with their tops, buy them. They usually come in bunches of 3 medium-sized roots. Unfortunately, particularly in winter and spring, the roots, which range from large to very large, are apt to be topless. But as long as they are really firm and crisp looking, they should be all right.

Also, look for roots with a distinct celery aroma. I cannot stress this enough. More than any other vegetable, celery root can be most disappointing if it is not truly fresh, because it will be hollow, stringy, and dry. As demand grows for this outstanding vegetable, you will have better luck buying it.

How long can I store fresh celery root?

Celery root keeps for at least 2 weeks. Leave the root uncovered or store it in a plastic bag and put it in the vegetable bin. As soon as you have the chance, make the Puree of Celery Root, Potatoes, and Sweet Garlic, page 117. You will be hooked on this vegetable for life.

Can celery root be eaten raw like celery?

Yes and no. You cannot nibble on celery root the way you can on other celery. On the other hand, the most popular way to serve celery root is grated raw and tossed in a very mustardy mayonnaise. Celeri-rave, or celeri rémoulade, is a classic French salad that is sold in many take-out shops in France. This wonderful salad is easy to make using the grating attachment for the food processor. By far my favorite version is in Julia Child's *Mastering the Art of French Cooking*, volume 1.

TIP Once peeled, drop celery root into acidulated water or toss with some fresh lemon juice to keep it from turning brown. To keep the root ivory-colored during cooking, add a couple of tablespoons of milk or 1 tablespoon of flour to the cooking water.

Chiles

Southwestern recipes call for types of hot peppers not available in my local market. Can I substitute one hot pepper for another?

There are numerous varieties of hot peppers, also called chiles. Believed to be the world's second most popular seasoning, topped only by salt, these are usually judged by their spiciness rather than flavor.

As a general rule, you can substitute one hot pepper for another, but some are hotter than others. Small, pointy chiles tend to be hottest, while larger, rounded ones are mild. Usually, you find that the smaller the chile, the hotter it is. This is because the seeds and ribs, which contain most of the heat-producing capsaicin, are most abundant and confined in the smaller varieties. A pepper's heat is also affected by growing conditions such as rainfall, temperature, soil conditions, and other variables, so one is not always identical to another.

Let taste be your guide. Buy a few different varieties and give them a try. But take care when you experiment—these fiery little pods are potent.

TIP If you love chiles, acquaint yourself with the Scoville scale, which rates them according to their amount of capsaicin. Pure capsaicin would be 16,000,000 Scoville units. A cayenne chile—the common thin red pepper—is 30,000 to 50,000 units, and a jalapeño is 2,500 to 5,000 units.

Is it just me, or do jalapeño peppers seem milder than they once were?

It's not your imagination. According to restaurateur and Mexican-food expert Rick Bayless, jalapeños are being grown for American palates, which are not as accustomed to heat as those of our southern neighbors. Some jalapeños are no hotter than green bell peppers, while others are richer tasting and offer only medium heat. In general, smaller jalapeños, called serranos, are hotter.

My market carries only serrano and jalapeño peppers. Will these substitute for poblano, Scotch bonnet, and others?

The only time you need to adhere to a certain pepper variety is when you are cooking a specific Mexican or New Mexican dish. Even then, you can make substitutions. But know that jalapeños and serranos, while hot, are not as hot as some other chiles. If you have tasted the dish made with a fiery Scotch bonnet (considered by some to be the hottest chile), you

may be disappointed. On the other hand, if the dish calls for mild poblanos and you substitute jalapeños, the dish will taste spicier than expected.

If fresh chiles aren't available, will the bottled ones do? What about dried chiles?

Keep in mind that the bottled and canned kind are usually pickled. Rinse them well before using them. If you are after heat alone, dried hot peppers are a good choice—especially the small Thai ones. But do use the whole ones rather than the flakes, because if you taste the dish and it is getting too spicy, it will be easy to remove the chile.

Is there a difference between ground chile and chili powder?

Ground chile is the pure ground dry chile pod minus the seeds. Chili powder is a combination of ground mild and hot chiles, oregano, and cumin. Sometimes garlic and salt are also added.

TIP If you don't have fresh chiles on hand when a recipe calls for them, use a small dried chile. You won't get exactly the same flavor, but you will get plenty of heat.

A jar of chili powder has been in my cupboard for a while and it's getting lumpy. Shall I toss it out?

That lumpiness is probably the result of natural oils in the chili powder, which is a sign of freshness. Chili powder should have a strong, spicy smell, and if you rub a pinch between two fingers it should leave a stain (it's those natural oils again). Chili powder keeps as long as two years when stored in an airtight container in the refrigerator, although it will lose some potency as it ages.

What's the best way to handle chiles so that my eyes don't sting for hours?

The volatile oils in chiles are capable of burning skin, especially the tender membranes around your nostrils, lips, and eyes. Many cookbooks suggest wearing rubber gloves when working with them. I don't, but I make sure to wash my hands with soap and warm water afterward. A vigorous scrub won't remove all the oils, but it helps. If you choose not to wear gloves, be careful not to touch your eyes, blow your nose (the oils soak right through a tissue), or touch any other sensitive skin tissue.

I am not a great fan of very spicy foods. Is there a way to tone down hot peppers?

The best way to reduce a fresh pepper's heat is always to start by removing the seeds and membranes. Once you have tasted the pepper itself, you can judge how spicy it is and add a few seeds at a time to adjust the spiciness.

Corn

■■■

What's the best way to select an ear of corn? Even local farm stands won't allow you to strip the ears back to look at the kernels.

I share your frustration, but I understand the farmers' need to protect their produce. Lots of shoppers strip back the husk of every ear of corn and discard those they don't want, which leaves the exposed kernels to dry out in the sun and air.

The key is to look for ears that are cool to the touch and have tight green husks and moist, green-tinged tassels. Avoid soft or shriveled ears with spots of decay or visible worm damage. Don't buy corn that has been sitting out in the sun all day. If you feel the need, peel back just enough of the husk to check if the kernels look plump and juicy and are packed tightly on the cob. Make sure to smooth the husk back into place if you decide to reject it. Also, pass on supermarket corn that's already been husked and wrapped in plastic. It is just not worth the trouble.

My market carries corn all year long, brought in from different parts of the country. Is it better from one state or another?

Some states, such as New Jersey, Pennsylvania, and places in the Midwest, are famous for their wonderful corn. But the secret to good-tasting corn is its freshness, not its origin. Corn that was grown just a mile from your house will be better than the very best corn shipped from another state. Unfortunately, supermarkets rarely buy from local growers, so the vegetable always has to go through some kind of storage, which at that point does not make it worth buying.

Is there a difference in flavor between yellow, white, and bicolor corn on the cob?

It's all a matter of personal preference. Some people like the super-sweet taste of crunchy white kernels, called Silver Queen in some regions. Others prefer the creamy texture and buttery flavor of yellow corn, which may be called Golden Bantam, or the in-between flavor of white-and-yellow corn, often called Sweet Sue. Names vary throughout the country, but every corn lover agrees that the fresher the corn, the better it tastes. When sweet corn is at its peak in midsummer, it's fabulous. Some people even eat it raw right off the cob or cut the tender kernels off the cob to add to a salad.

What is baby corn?

Those wee little ears you see either in the gourmet area of the produce section or packed in jars on the supermarket shelves are just standard ears in a dwarfed stage. They're grown close together so the ears have room to mature but never achieve their normal size. You can pickle them or use them in stir-fries, but be prepared to pay dearly for them. I think they're more about looks than taste.

If I can't get fresh corn for a recipe, do you suggest using canned or frozen corn?

Canned corn is almost a vegetable in its own right and is superior to frozen corn. Mind you, opinions differ here. Some cooks prefer using frozen corn when fresh is not available, while I prefer using canned. In the dead of winter when wonderful fresh corn is just a memory, use canned corn to make cornbread, a pudding, or fritters. See Corn and Chive Fritters with Smoked Salmon Sauce, page 120.

If I buy corn still in the husk, can I hold it in the refrigerator for a few days?

If you asked a farmer how to store corn, he'd tell you not to do it that way! As soon as corn is picked, the natural sugar in the kernels begins converting to starch, so the sooner you cook it, the better it tastes. However, on the more practical side, if you can't eat corn right away, wrap the unhusked ears in damp paper towels, put them in a plastic bag, and keep in the refrigerator for no longer than a day. Alternatively, you can husk the ears, boil them for 5 minutes, cool, and then slice the kernels from the cobs. Refrigerate the corn kernels for up to 2 days or freeze them.

What's the best way to cook fresh corn on the cob?

Drop the husked ears in enough rapidly boiling water to cover them, put a lid on the pot, then boil for 3 minutes. Remove the pot from the heat and let the corn stand in the hot water, still covered, for 5 minutes. Drain and serve the corn right away with butter and salt.

You can also microwave the unhusked ears for 5 minutes (for 2 ears) or 8 minutes (for 3 or 4). Let them stand for 5 minutes before husking. Use great care, as they will be very hot and emit quite a bit of steam.

I've heard about adding either salt or sugar to the corn water before cooking. What does this do?

Adding salt to the water will toughen the kernels, so I don't advise it. Some cooks suggest that a teaspoon or so of sugar will sweeten the corn, but if the corn is fresh, there is no need for the sugar; if the corn is starchy, no amount of sugar will help.

If a recipe calls for fresh cooked corn kernels, should I take the corn off the cob when it is raw or after it is cooked?

I usually take the corn kernels off the cobs after cooking. It is much less messy.

TIP To cut fresh kernels off a raw ear of corn, stand the ear upright in a shallow bowl. Use a sharp knife to cut the kernels off the cob. They will fall into the bowl along with any corn milk, or juice. After the kernels are stripped, run the dull side of the blade along the cob to release any remaining pulp and corn milk.

I've tried to grill corn and find I end up burning it much of the time. Are there any tricks to it?

I bow to the advice of John Willoughby, co-author of *The Thrill of the Grill*. He says to peel the husks back without detaching them from the ears. Remove the inner silk and then pull the husks up back around the corncob. Soak the corn in water for at least 15 minutes and then put it on the grill for about 15 minutes. You can serve the corn at this time, or, if you prefer, pull the husks off the corn, brush the ears with melted butter, and season with salt and pepper. Let the ears come into contact with the grill for a few minutes to give them a nice golden, toasted look and taste.

Cucumbers

Should I buy fat or thin cucumbers?

When you have a choice, definitely buy slimmer, medium-sized cukes. Large, fat cucumbers are full of seeds, and by the time you remove them and the watery flesh, you're left with very little.

What is the difference between a burpless, a gourmet, and an English cucumber?

There is no difference at all, but your confusion is understandable. These names and more are given to the slender, long green cucumber, often sold in plastic shrink-wrap. It is an English hybrid that has also been called European. Its advantage is that it never needs peeling and has so few seeds that it is often called "seedless." However, they usually still need seeding.

I noticed that the gourmets, or seedless cucumbers, are more expensive than the more common ones. Are they better?

During the winter months, you're better off paying the extra money for the seedless cukes. For shape and color, I think they rate a "10," although they have somewhat less flavor than good summer cukes. They are my first choice for hot, cooked cucumber dishes, because they retain their shape and crunchy texture. See Sauté of Cucumbers in Chive and Dill Cream, page 123.

Many recipes call for seeded cucumbers. How do you seed a cucumber, and is it necessary?

Cucumbers are much more appetizing without their seeds, and removing them is easy. First, rinse the cuke well, peel it if you like, and cut it in half lengthwise. Next, scrape out the seeds and the watery flesh with a grapefruit spoon or the tip of a sharp knife. The seeds will pop right out and leave a hollowed-out, fleshy shell. Salt the cucumber lightly to draw out moisture and let it drain in a colander for about 30 minutes. Then rinse it under cool, running water and pat dry with paper or cloth towels.

Do all cucumbers have to be peeled, or only the waxed ones?

Unless you have a garden-fresh cucumber or a Kirby, peel the cucumbers that you intend to use in salads. The peel can be bitter, which can ruin a salad. For an attractive presentation, Kirbys and seedless cucumbers can be scored with the tines of a fork or peeled in alternating strips. In the wintertime, when waxed cucumbers are the only game in town, be sure to peel them.

What's a pickling cucumber?

Pickling cucumbers are also called Kirbys, my favorites! They are pale green and 4 to 5 inches long, which makes them a little larger than gherkins. Their skin is naturally bumpy and their shape irregular, but they have tons of flavor and plenty of delicious crunch. Because their seeds are so tiny, I rarely bother removing them, nor do I peel them when they are fresh and in season—especially if I buy them at a local farmers' market or roadside stand.

I also love using Kirbys in salads and for a quick, refreshing refrigerator sweet-and-sour pickle that takes absolutely no time to make.

To pickle Kirbys Layer 2 sliced medium-sized onions with 8 to 12 quartered Kirbys in a glass bowl. In a saucepan, combine 1 cup distilled white vinegar with 1 cup sugar, 4 tablespoons pickling spice, 1 teaspoon mustard seeds, and 1 tablespoon salt. Simmer until the sugar dissolves. Add a pinch of cream of tartar, stir, and pour over the vegetables. Cover and refrigerate for 24 hours, stirring from time to time. Serve chilled.

TIP Do not store cucumbers in plastic bags. Leave them loose in the crisper and be sure to use them within 2 or 3 days of purchase, especially if they are unwaxed.

Eggplant

Can you tell me how to choose a good eggplant?

A good seedless eggplant will be light in relation to its size, not heavy as most cookbooks suggest. The lighter the eggplant the fewer seeds it will have. Eggplants must have firm glossy skins without cuts or blemishes, and the stem should be green or at least greenish brown and not dark. The size of the eggplant does not matter. Some varieties are enormous while others are slim and tapered, but both can be delicious if really fresh.

The small and nearly seedless eggplants so common in Italy and Spain don't seem to be available in the States. Can I get the same delicious taste from large eggplants?

Unfortunately, the small varieties found in southern Europe are not grown in this country. During the early spring, you may be able to buy pricey baby eggplants imported from Holland. A little later in the spring, they will come from Mexico and will be far less expensive. These are tasty, but you can get the same flavorful results with larger eggplant, as long as it is quite fresh.

TIP Always choose eggplants that weigh about 1 pound and pick those that are light for their size. The lighter the fruit, the less likely it is to be seedy.

Are certain eggplants better for some dishes than others?

The common large purple eggplant is the one I use most often. It is ideal for grilling, sautéing, and roasting. It is the only eggplant you can use for classic dishes such as a ratatouille or Italian caponata. Asian eggplants, also called Japanese eggplants, are about the size and shape of a zucchini. They are less seedy with a creamier texture. They are good stir-fried, quickly sautéed, or grilled.

Is it necessary to peel eggplant?

Generally there is no need to peel eggplant because the skin is so flavorful, Plus, the peel keeps the vegetable from falling apart during cooking. Wash it well, dry it thoroughly, and then trim the stem and blossom ends before proceeding with the recipe.

If a recipe calls for peeled eggplant, a vegetable peeler does the trick. Make sure to peel it just before cooking or the flesh will darken.

Many recipes require salting and weighting eggplant slices before cooking. Is this step necessary?

This process does work, but I prefer submerging slices of eggplant in cold, salted water for an hour. This removes the bitterness and is far easier than using weights. Be sure to dry the slices well with an absorbent cloth towel—paper towels are not absorbent enough—before baking

or sautéing. Plant breeders are working on producing eggplant that is less bitter and does not need salting or soaking.

TIP Test the freshness of an eggplant by pressing down on the flesh with your finger. If the indentation remains, the eggplant is not as fresh as it should be and may be pulpy and bitter.

Eggplant seems to absorb an astonishing amount of oil during cooking, usually more than the recipe calls for. How can I avoid this?

When you fry eggplant, it does absorb great quantities of oil, especially if the eggplant slices have not been salted and weighted or submerged in salted water and thoroughly patted dry. The good news is that the eggplant releases the oil within 15 minutes of cooking, so let the cooked slices drain on a double layer of paper towels for 15 minutes before continuing with the recipe. You can also brush eggplant slices lightly with olive oil and bake them in a 350°F oven until done. They will not brown as nicely or be as tasty as when they are fried, but this is a good way to cut down on fat.

I love the taste of the roasted eggplant dish called baba ghanoush. Can I make this at home?

It is easy to make this classic, Middle Eastern dish at home either by charring the eggplant on a grill or roasting the whole vegetable over a medium-high gas flame while keeping a close watch on it. Turn the eggplant with tongs so it chars evenly on all sides. Do not prick the skin as you turn it, or all the delicious juices will escape. I've even roasted the eggplant directly over the coils of an electric stove with excellent results. In fact, the only technique I don't recommend is broiling—the eggplant will char, but you won't get the desired smoky flavor. See Charcoal-Grilled Eggplants with Lemon-Scallion Mayonnaise, page 126.

Do you have any new and unusual ways to serve eggplant?

Try filling hollowed-out fresh tomatoes with roasted eggplant pulp mixed with a touch of mayonnaise; serve it as a starter.

Endive

■ ■

Is there any way to tell which heads of Belgian endive are likely to be bitter?

Belgian endive needs to be kept in the dark. Good markets keep it in its original shipping box, wrapped in paper to protect it from light, which causes it to turn green and bitter. Avoid endive that is wrapped in plastic and make sure it is almost all white with just a tinge of yellow.

TIP To remove all traces of bitterness from endive, cut out its core with a paring knife. If you plan to cook the endive, add the heel of a loaf of stale bread to the cooking liquid, which will remove all bitterness.

Is there any way to serve endive other than raw in salads?

When cooked, endive is buttery soft and sweet. It can be braised in a skillet, oven-roasted, or blanched and served with brown butter. It is a perfect companion for sautéed sea scallops, salmon, chicken breasts, and all cuts of veal (see Skillet-Braised Belgian Endives, page 127).

Fennel

■ ■

What is Florence fennel? Is it different from the fennel used for fennel seeds?

Florence fennel—also called bulb fennel, or finocchio in Italy—is a crisp, anise-flavored vegetable that looks a little bit like celery only with a more swollen base and feathery fronds. It has become quite popular in recent years, with both home cooks and chefs, and has nothing to do with the feathery herb that produces the anise-flavored fennel seeds used in cooking and baking.

Is there a difference in taste between large and small fennel bulbs?

There is no difference in taste, but smaller fennel bulbs slice more evenly.

What is the best way to store fennel?

I chop off all the feathery leaves, right down to the bulb, before I store the fennel in the crisper in perforated plastic bags. You may want to keep some of the feathery greens in a separate bag to use for garnish.

TIP If fennel bulbs show brown spots after a few days in the refrigerator, just peel off the outer layer.

How do you prepare fennel for cooking?

First, remove the stalks where they join the bulb and then remove the white, outer leaves encasing the bulb, which tend to be stringy and tough. Depending on its size, cut it into quarters or eighths. Use a vegetable peeler to remove strings and any brown spots. Instead of pushing the peeler away from your body, hold the fennel and work the peeler toward you. If you're not going to cook the fennel right away, put the bulb in a bowl of cold water. I save the stalks to add to soup later, and the wispy fronds can be minced and used as a garnish.

TIP When preparing fennel, don't cut too much off the flat end or the bulb will fall apart.

Can I serve fennel raw in a salad?

It is delicious in a salad, especially when mixed with arugula and Belgian endive, as the Italians do. It's also wonderful on its own, sliced and tossed with olive oil, pepper, and coarse salt. Make sure to slice it super thin—the best way to do this is with a mandoline, a kitchen tool described on page 11.

What are some simple ways to cook fennel?

My favorite way to prepare fennel is to roast it in the oven. It is also excellent braised. For a simple and tasty dish, blanch it for 3 to 4 minutes until the fennel is almost tender. Then sauté it on top of the stove in some butter and olive oil until nicely browned, or oven-roast it for 10 minutes.

What's the best way to prepare fennel to maximize its licorice flavor?

When I want that pronounced licorice taste, I add a teaspoon of fennel seeds to the dish before cooking, or I finish the dish with a few drops of Pernod, an anise-flavored liqueur imported from France.

Garlic

I have seen both purplish-pink and pure white heads of garlic in the markets. Is there a difference between the two?

White garlic, which is rather mild, is the most common kind. It is grown primarily in California and, for my taste, is not nearly pungent enough. The pink variety is a Mexican garlic known as Spanish roja. It's smaller than the California garlic, but has plumper cloves and more flavor. Unfortunately, it's not available year-round, so your choice may be limited to white heads.

Either way, just make sure you select large, firm cloves that appear to be bursting out of their skins. These will be the freshest and easiest to peel. Whatever you do, do not buy the small, packaged garlic usually sold two to a box. These heads generally are not very fresh and have tiny cloves that are extremely hard to peel.

What is elephant garlic?

Heads of elephant garlic are two to three times larger than other varieties and look like a garlic lover's dream. But looks are deceiving. These gentle giants are so mild you might as well not use garlic at all—unless you want extremely mild garlic flavor for a salad dressing or marinade. Besides being nearly tasteless, elephant garlic is about three times more expensive than regular garlic. Recently I attended a press dinner at which the chef braised the oversized cloves in butter and cream and served them as a side dish to roast duck. No one at the table could identify the taste and we concluded we were eating a new, rare vegetable from another hemisphere.

TIP To keep garlic from sticking to the knife when mincing, sprinkle the garlic with coarse salt. This also heightens the flavor of the garlic.

I store garlic in one of those pots with little holes on the side, but it still dries out and shrivels. Is there a better way to store it?

Regardless of what every professional chef and cookbook author recommends, I find garlic does quite well stored in the refrigerator's crisper. Yes, it must be kept loose and not bagged, but the cloves keep for a long time this way. I also store whole heads in a shallow plastic bowl in the refrigerator with success. Just make sure it stays dry and your garlic will keep for at least 2 months.

Sometimes garlic cloves get little green sprouts in the middle. Are these edible?

That little green shoot is a sure sign that the garlic is mature and most likely will have a slight bitter flavor. If the sprout is tiny, as is often the case, either leave it or simply remove it with the tip of a sharp paring knife.

My market carries jarred peeled garlic cloves that look like a good idea. Is there much of a difference in flavor between these and fresh, unpeeled cloves?

I find there is an enormous difference. The peeled, prepared cloves taste strong and slightly bitter but lack the subtlety of fresh garlic. Since fresh garlic is available all year, I see no reason to use jarred garlic. However, if you are in a big hurry and need large quantities of peeled cloves, you can improve the flavor by blanching them for 2 or 3 minutes before adding them to the recipe.

What's the best way to peel garlic?

There are all kinds of clever devices on the market to help with this chore, but it's very easy to accomplish with nothing more than a chef's knife and cutting board. Place a few cloves on the cutting board, hold the flat side of a chef's knife over them, and give the knife surface a quick smack with the heel of your hand. Do this hard enough to crack the skin but not so hard you smash the clove. The skin slips right off. When a recipe calls for whole peeled cloves, blanch them for 2 or 3 minutes, drain, and then peel the loosened skin by hand.

How can I tone down the sharp taste of garlic?

One of the nicest ways to ensure that you get a delicate garlic taste is to blanch the whole cloves twice. Simmer the cloves in water to cover for

2 to 3 minutes, drain them, then simmer again in fresh water. Some cooks recommend blanching the cloves in a mixture of water and milk to keep the cloves white and tender. If you are looking for very mild garlic flavor in a salad dressing or marinade, try elephant garlic.

Do you recommend using a garlic press? Is there another way to get the same result?

Using a garlic press is just fine. I use mine constantly, especially when I want a strong garlic flavor. Make sure to use the garlic within 30 minutes of pressing, or it may develop a bitter, metallic taste. I recommend using a stainless steel garlic press rather than a plastic or aluminum one because it doesn't alter the taste of garlic as quickly.

Another way to mash garlic is to lay the cloves on a cutting board, sprinkle them with coarse salt, and then use a small sharp paring knife to shave each garlic clove until you have a smooth paste. This may sound time consuming, but it is really extremely easy and quick to do. The salt softens the clove and mashing it this way produces an intense garlic taste. Using a mortar and pestle is another good way to get a garlic paste. Put sliced cloves and some coarse salt in a mortar and work into a paste with the pestle. Or, use the side of a chef's knife to work the salt into the garlic until it becomes smooth and creamy.

I grow garlic chives in my garden. Can I use these in place of garlic cloves in recipes?

Garlic chives have a pleasing, mild flavor and are great as a tasty garnish. I love adding them to stir-fries or mincing them very fine and stir-ring them into sauces, but they are not a substitute for the real thing. They are more like pungent chives than garlic.

Is it possible to prepare whole roasted heads of garlic in the microwave?

You can microwave garlic, but for that sweet, creamy, nutty flavor you're after, I recommend using the oven.

Slice off the top of the head to expose the tips of the cloves. Arrange the tips facing up in an ovenproof dish. Pour a little olive oil over them, cover tightly with foil, and bake in a preheated 375°F oven for about 1 hour, or until the garlic is soft. When the heads are cool enough to handle, separate the cloves and squeeze the softened garlic out of the skin. This roasted garlic pulp is wonderful squeezed directly onto grilled or toasted peasant bread. Or put it in a small bowl and cover it with a thin layer of olive oil, and serve it with bread.

When you're short on time, microwaving is fine.

Trim the stem ends to expose the cloves. Put one head in a 2-cup measuring cup, add ¼ cup chicken broth and 1 tablespoon olive oil, cover tightly with plastic wrap, and microwave on high for 7 minutes. Remove from the microwave and let the garlic rest for about 5 minutes before using as described above.

TIP To remove the odor of garlic from your hands, hold them under running water and gently rub your hands along the flat side of a stainless steel knife or spoon. Rubbing the cut side of a lemon over your hands works well, too.

Greens, Leafy

In summer, the markets seem to be full of interesting greens that I am not familiar with. Which do you recommend?

My favorite summer green is Swiss chard. It's both a vegetable and a green because the ribs can and should be cooked separately and have a beetlike flavor. At many farm stands you can find both the white-ribbed Swiss chard and the red-ribbed variety. They are both delicious.

You may also find beet greens and sorrel in the summertime. These are more often found in farmers' markets than the supermarket. I simply steam the beet greens or stir-fry them with some sliced garlic and minced dill. Sorrel can be used in several wonderful soups and also in a creamy sauce to serve with pan-seared salmon fillets or grilled bass.

More and more you can now find a mix called braising greens, which, like the mesclun salad mix, is a combination of young greens.

These can be quickly stir-fried in a touch of extra virgin olive oil with 1 or 2 garlic cloves and minced fresh ginger.

Can you recommend interesting winter greens?

For my money, kale is the most interesting winter green. It's fabulous in soups, such as the Kale, Potato, and Butternut Squash Chowder, page 130, or sautéed with some pine nuts and finely diced smoked ham. Make sure the kale looks crisp and fresh and has dark glossy green leaves with a bluish tint.

If you live in the South, chances are you can find wonderful collard greens. These should be young, crisp, and velvety. Unfortunately, due to lack of turnover, impeccably fresh collard greens are hard to come by outside the Southeast or in other areas where they are popular.

Herbs

I often buy pretty herbs in the supermarket, but they seem to lack the flavor of the farm stand herbs I get in the summer. I wonder why?

Hothouse herbs are meeker than field-grown herbs, so if you're making a dish with supermarket herbs, you may have to double or even triple the amount called for in the recipe. This is especially true of cilantro, dill, and basil. A

way around this is not to chop these herbs finely but rather to snip them with scissors or, if the leaves are small, keep them whole to achieve the same flavor level. Since fresh herbs stand out most when added just before serving, you may want to try reserving about half of any fresh herb that the recipe asks you to incorporate during cooking and adding it at the end.

The flavors of my home-grown sage, thyme, and tarragon seem different from what is served in restaurants. Is it my imagination?

Most likely you are tasting varieties of these herbs different from the ones you grow at home. There are many types of thyme available to the gardener and at least three types of tarragon. The list of sage varieties is considerable as well. The "generic" types of these herbs are common sage, French thyme, and French tarragon, so you probably want to look for those names when buying seeds or plants. Sometimes recipes get more specific and call for lemon thyme, Mexican tarragon, or pepper sage, but you can always use the more common form of the herb.

TIP Be most careful when purchasing a tarragon plant for your garden if what you want is French tarragon and not the Mexican variety. Because the leaves are similar, you will have to taste them to be able to tell the difference.

What does fines herbes mean? Is it just a fancy French way of saying fine herbs?

Fines herbes is a family of herbs that includes chives, chervil, parsley, and tarragon. These complement each other and are key to many French preparations. A classic fines herbes mixture consists of 1 part tarragon; 2 parts chervil; 8 parts parsley; 1 part chives. Many recipes call for fines herbes to be chopped. In that case, you should chop the first three together, then snip the chives separately (to keep from mashing them) and combine all four. You can adjust these proportions to suit your own taste and the availability of certain herbs. For example, if you can't find chervil, just use more tarragon or fennel tops to make up for it.

Marjoram and oregano taste pretty much the same to me. Are they interchangeable?

It is fine to substitute these herbs for each other. Marjoram and oregano are very similar, although marjoram's flavor is much less assertive. Traditionally, oregano is used in Mediterranean dishes, while the cuisines of central Europe rely heavily on marjoram.

Some recipes call for flat-leaf parsley, some just for parsley. Is there a difference?

You will probably find two types of parsley in your grocery store, flat-leaf and curly. Curly has smaller leaves and tends to be rough in texture. I use flat-leaf parsley, sometimes called Italian parsley, almost exclusively.

Which herbs can be substituted for each other?

That's a complicated question. Some herbs, particularly parsley and chives, have an affinity for just about all foods, but others work only in specific dishes. When you're making a classic preparation, you should stick to the standard. For example, ravioli are traditionally served in a sage and butter sauce, and they taste heavenly that way, so there's no reason to replace the sage with cilantro, for example. A béarnaise sauce would not be the same if not made with fresh tarragon, but a cucumber or beet salad, on the other hand, is delicious when made with either dill or mint or a combination of herbs. So as long as you learn the tastes of herbs and which ingredients they complement, you can have fun and be creative cooking with them.

TIP Some herbs "marry" particularly well. You might want to try the following herb combinations:

---

dill, parsley, chives, and chervil

tarragon, parsley, chives, and chervil

basil, parsley, chives, and chervil

sage, parsley, and chives

rosemary, thyme, and parsley

oregano (or marjoram), thyme, and parsley

cilantro, mint, parsley, and chives

TIP There are two basic categories of herbs: character herbs and accent herbs. Character herbs are usually added to a dish during cooking or at the beginning and don't have any trouble asserting their flavors. Accent herbs are more delicate and are usually incorporated just before serving.

CHARACTER HERBS

bay leaves, marjoram, oregano, rosemary, sage, tarragon, thyme

ACCENT HERBS

basil, chervil, chives, cilantro, dill, mint, parsley

Within days after purchase, my fresh cilantro and basil turn into bags of rotten leaves. Can you suggest a way to keep these herbs fresh for a longer period of time?

Both basil and cilantro are delicate. The trick is to keep them dry and sealed in their bags. If you buy the herbs pre-washed in sealed bags, leave them in the bags until you're ready to use them. If you buy loose bunches, shake out any moisture, then remove the leaves and place them in a single layer on a paper towel. Top with another paper towel and continue to layer leaves and paper towels, ending with a sheet of paper towel on top. Roll up this stack and place in a plastic bag with a zipper closure. Seal the bag

carefully, expelling all air. They should keep for several days this way.

Should I keep fresh herbs in a glass of water or in a plastic bag in the vegetable bin?

The first thing to do is to shake the herbs vigorously to remove the excess water accumulated during all that misting in the supermarket. Then wrap the herbs loosely in paper towels and store them in a perforated baggy. I have not found the glass method to be too effective and only use it when I plan to use the herb as a garnish on the day I buy it fresh.

What's the best way to clean herbs to remove all the grit?

Some herbs are particularly sandy. With the leaves still on their stems, swish them in a bowl of water. Hold still for a moment to allow the dirt to fall to the bottom of the bowl, then pull out the herbs, rinse the bowl, and repeat until absolutely no sand appears in the bottom of the bowl. Then rinse one more time, just to be sure. Dry herbs thoroughly, either with paper towels or a dish towel. If you are using a large quantity of herbs, you may want to dry them in a salad spinner. Wet leaves are impossible to chop and quickly turn into mush.

My supermarket carries basil practically year-round. Is it worth the bother to grow my own?

Garden-grown basil has a stronger, cleaner flavor than hothouse basil. If you don't have a garden but live in the Northeast or Midwest, during the summer and well into the fall look for delicious field-grown basil at farm stands, which usually sell it in large bunches and at low prices. In Florida and California you may find it as early as February.

It would be easy to grow basil on my sunny patio, but there are so many different kinds. Which is best?

The best basil to grow on a patio is the all-purpose basil called fino verde. Its sweet, somewhat pungent flavor is ideal for all recipes calling for this popular herb. If you want to assemble a small basil garden, try a few of the tiny-leafed globe basil plants, plus a pot or two of purple basil, which is quite beautiful. You might want to try some ruffle basil too—its leaves are milder in flavor and can be added raw to salads.

Is there any way to freeze basil leaves without their turning black?

As a rule, herbs don't freeze well. If you want to save some basil for later use, grind the leaves to a paste and mix them with some olive oil. Cover the basil paste with a thin layer of olive oil before freezing.

What exactly is pesto?

Pesto is a basil paste from the Italian city of Genoa, used primarily as a sauce on pasta.

To make a traditional pesto

>   3 to 4 cups basil leaves, loosely packed
>   2 to 3 garlic cloves, crushed
>   2 to 3 tablespoons pine nuts
>   About ½ cup freshly grated Parmesan cheese
>   About ¾ cup extra virgin olive oil

Purée everything except the olive oil in a blender (or crush in a mortar and pestle, if you're a traditionalist). Drizzle in the olive oil with the blender running. You can store pesto, covered, in the refrigerator for 2 or 3 days. If you're planning to do that, omit the garlic and add it just before serving, and drizzle a thin layer of oil over the paste before you put it in the refrigerator to keep the basil from turning black.

TIP When is a pesto not a pesto? Classic pesto consists only of basil, garlic, pine nuts, cheese, and olive oil. Phrases like "cilantro-walnut pesto" or "tarragon pesto," often seen on restaurant menus, simply refer to herb pastes.

Do you have any suggestions for using pesto other than as a pasta sauce?

Pesto is wonderful stirred into soup (see White Bean and Chorizo Soup, page 292). You can also drizzle pesto over grilled vegetables or oven-roasted tomatoes, and it adds punch to rice pilaf when added just before serving. For an unusual potato salad, toss pesto with boiled, sliced potatoes while they're still warm, then serve at room temperature.

My large rosemary plant looks beautiful and smells great, but sometimes the flavor of the leaves is a little overwhelming. Any ideas for subduing it a bit?

Rosemary can be powerful, almost pungent. To avoid overpowering dishes with rosemary flavor, I use only the very young and tender rosemary leaves in most dishes. The older, needlelike leaves serve best to stuff a chicken or whole fish and are also good for marinades. Most herbs lose their flavor when finely minced, but rosemary becomes even more powerful, so if you're after delicate flavor, use minced rosemary sparingly.

Do those tiny thyme leaves really have to be stripped off their stems? The stems are so brittle that they break.

This is a necessary kitchen chore, as thyme stems are woody and unpleasant to eat. You can add whole sprigs to soups and sauces for flavor, as long as you remove them before serving. Try pinching the end of a thyme sprig with one hand and pulling straight down with the thumb and index finger of your other hand to scrape off the leaves. Also, if both the leaves and your hands are dry, you'll find the job easier.

My chive plants grow pretty purple flowers. Is there a use for them?

Chive blossoms are edible and make a lovely addition to a salad. Make sure that you cut the blossoms back two or three times a year to stimulate growth.

How are Chinese chives used?

These flat-leaf chives have a stronger flavor and less delicate texture. Unlike regular chives, they are best when lightly sautéed or incorporated into stir-fries. They are also nice added to an egg mixture for an omelet.

What are giant chives?

This recently introduced variety is sturdy and excellent for cooking, but it is rarely available in stores. Giant chives grow very successfully in window boxes.

Is there a difference between cilantro, Chinese parsley, and coriander?

Those are three names for the same thing—an herb that looks somewhat like flat-leaf parsley but has saw-toothed ridges around the edges of the leaves. This herb is used in cooking both Chinese dishes (hence Chinese parsley) and Mexican foods (hence cilantro, its Spanish name). Coriander usually refers to the dried version or the seeds of this plant.

Cilantro is one of my favorite herbs, but my family says it tastes like soap and refuses to

touch it. Any suggestions for how to please myself and the rest of the family?

Isn't it amazing that an herb can provoke such intense emotions? Everyone's got an opinion about cilantro. The solution is simple: use whole leaves as a garnish rather than incorporating them into your dishes. That way you can sprinkle the cilantro on your own portion only. If you still want to try to sneak it into something, keep in mind that cilantro's particular flavor grows milder when the leaves are minced.

All of a sudden, so many recipes call for chervil. What exactly is it?

Chervil is a delicious herb that has long been used in French cooking and has recently experienced a boom in popularity here. It has feathery, delicate leaves and makes a nice addition to creamy sauces as well as to salads. Many commercial mesclun mixes include some chervil. Chervil's flavor—mild, with a hint of anise—is impossible to duplicate, so there is no real substitute for it. However, since chervil is often used as an element in fines herbes (see page 84), if I can't find any, I use the feathery tops of fennel to make up for its absence. Like dill, chervil thrives in cool places, so if you live somewhere that's not too warm, you may want to grow your own.

Are dill seeds a good substitute for fresh dill?

You would not be happy with the result. Dill seeds are best used for pickling and have none of the delicacy of dill fronds.

When a recipe calls for mint, does that mean peppermint or spearmint?

Peppermint is my first choice and spearmint my second, although you are more likely to find spearmint in the grocery store. I also like apple mint, especially for mint sauce. If you are interested in growing your own mint, remember that mint is a bully that will take over your entire garden if you let it, so it should be isolated in one flower bed.

When fresh herbs are not available in the supermarket, can the same herb be used in dried form?

Bay leaf, marjoram, oregano, and thyme can be used in cooking in dry form as long as you add them at the start of preparation. In other words, don't use dried herbs to flavor a finished dish, or in a vinaigrette or marinade. All other herbs should be used fresh, especially chervil, parsley, cilantro, basil, and tarragon, which lose their flavor when dried. If you can't find fresh rosemary, use fresh thyme.

Do dried herbs last longer if refrigerated?

They don't need to be refrigerated, but do date them and replace them twice a year. Dried herbs tend to have a short shelf life, so be sure to close their jars tightly and store them in a cool, dark place.

TIP You can use this quick test to check whether your dried herbs are still fresh. Place a small amount of the herb in the palm of one hand and rub it with your fingers. You should immediately detect the distinct aroma of that herb. If it doesn't have a smell, it won't have any taste either.

Jerusalem Artichokes

What are Jerusalem artichokes?

Jerusalem artichokes are root vegetables that look something like smooth pieces of ginger. While they are not related to globe artichokes, they taste enough like artichokes to make you notice. Jerusalem artichokes, also called sunchokes, are not as popular as they should be, and you may have trouble finding them. Their season runs from early fall to early winter. You'll have the best luck finding them in good specialty markets and farm stands, but more and more now you can find them in quality supermarkets.

What is the best way to store Jerusalem artichokes?

If you store them in a perforated plastic bag in the refrigerator, they will keep well for up to 10 days, after which they start to shrivel. It's best to cook them within 3 or 4 days of purchase.

My recipe for Jerusalem artichokes says to cook them for 20 minutes but they turn out mushy. What is the right way to cook this vegetable?

Jerusalem artichokes can be frustrating to cook because one minute they feel undercooked and the next they're overcooked. The best way to handle them is to pan-braise them in some butter with a touch of broth and seasoning. Cook them covered over low heat for 5 to 7 minutes or until just tender.

Jicama

My market carries jicama in all sizes. Does the size have anything to do with the taste?

The size of jicama has nothing to do with its taste. I prefer to buy a medium-sized jicama and use it up within 2 or 3 days. Large jicamas are harder to store and there is just so much jicama you can eat unless you really love it or are serving a crowd.

I have had some delicious, crisp jicama and some have a woody texture. Is there a way to tell a good jicama?

Look for jicama with relatively smooth, thin skin. Thick skin usually indicates a starchy jicama, instead of sweet, juicy flesh.

The only way I know to serve jicama is cut up as a snack or for a crudité platter. It's refreshing and crunchy this way, but do you have any other suggestions?

Jicama is delicious quickly stir-fried with snow peas or finely sliced red and yellow bell peppers.

Lettuce

The ready-made salad mixes are quite expensive. How can I make my own?

The key is to choose a selection of greens that go well together, keeping in mind that different lettuces have different characteristics. Some are buttery and mild while others are acid and bitter. As a rule, combine greens of different textures, flavor, and color. A nicely balanced mix would be bibb lettuce, arugula, Belgian endive, and raddichio.

What is the best way to store salad greens?

It is a real challenge to keep greens fresh these days because the constant misting in the market keeps them too wet and almost soggy. The key is to store them as dry as possible. The best way to do this is to wrap them unwashed in a double layer of paper towels and store them in a perforated plastic bag. The greens will keep this way for 3 to 4 days.

Which salad greens keep best?

The best-keeping green is, of course, iceberg lettuce, but it is not the most flavorful. Romaine has great flavor, plenty of crunch, and sturdy leaves. Before storing romaine, cut 1½ inches off the top and remove any wilted outer leaves. Store in a perforated baggie in the vegetable bin.

Lettuce from the farm stand is so gritty that it is practically impossible to clean. Is there a secret to getting rid of the dirt?

The best way to do this is to separate the leaves and soak them in plenty of warm rather than cold water, swish the lettuce gently, and then transfer to a bowl of very cold water. Lift it out gently and roll it in a kitchen towel or spin it dry. If there is any grit remaining in the lettuce when you serve it, you can always claim that the crunch is coming from freshly ground peppercorns!

Leeks

■■

Recipes frequently call for thin leeks, but all I ever see in the market are fat ones. Is there any difference in taste?

The smaller leeks are more tender, but there is no difference in taste between the two. It's a good idea to avoid leeks that are too large, though, especially in the spring, when they have a fibrous core that must be removed. Thin leeks are terrific for braising and serving whole, but they're only available in the fall, unless you live in the Northwest, where because of the climate they are available much of the year. Still, many specialty markets carry thin leeks, so when you see them, buy them. They're worth the expense if you plan to braise them. Either way, fresh leeks with dark green, crisp tops and white root ends are excellent for all recipes that call for diced or sliced leeks.

TIP Before you start to cook a green vegetable—snow peas, green beans, or asparagus—fill a large bowl with ice water. As soon as you drain the vegetables, pop them in the ice water. This will stop any further cooking and allow the vegetable to retain its beautiful green color.

Leeks tend to go limp after a couple of days in the refrigerator. Is there a way to keep them fresher longer?

Leeks will stay fresh much longer if you cut 3 inches off their tops. This also keeps precious nutrients from leaching back into the leaves during storage. Put the leeks in plastic bags and refrigerate them for up to 2 weeks. But don't discard the green tops. I keep the inner light green leaves in a separate bag and use them to flavor soups and stocks.

No matter how well I rinse leeks, some grit always remains. Is there a way to clean them thoroughly?

Leeks are really easy to clean once you know the secret. Begin by removing all but the first 2 inches of the green tops. Dice or slice the leeks lengthwise and rinse them in a colander under warm (not cold!) water for several minutes. Drain well. You'll have nice, clean leeks every time.

Can I treat leeks like other members of the onion family and serve them raw?

Even young leeks are too strongly flavored to eat raw. Even if you like strong onions, you'll find raw leeks too harsh tasting.

I use leeks most often in soups. Is there another way to cook them?

When leeks are poached, cooled, and dressed with a mustard vinaigrette, they make a great first course. You can always braise diced leeks in butter and broth and serve them alongside seafood, veal, or chicken (see Braised Leeks with Shiitake Mushrooms and Crème Fraîche, page 131).

Mushrooms

Recipes frequently call for wild mushrooms, but I never see any in the market. Do I have to pick them myself?

Generally, recipes that call for wild mushrooms do not refer to true wild varieties, but rather wild mushrooms that are now being cultivated. These include enoki, oyster, portobello, shiitake, and cremini, which are also called brown mushrooms. You can easily find these in most supermarkets. Be sure to experiment with them to see which ones you like, since some are much more flavorful than others.

As for picking them yourself, that is definitely an activity best left to the experts, since amateur mushroom hunters can easily mistake toxic mushrooms for the edible varieties.

Are any true wild mushrooms available commercially?

The only true wild varieties available commercially are chanterelles, trumpet mushrooms, and the more costly morels, which are available in better markets at different times of the year. While most wild mushrooms appear in the fall, there are some spring varieties. Weather plays a major role in their availability. Also, keep in mind that since wild mushrooms are extremely perishable and generally do not travel well, you may not see a good assortment in your area. While you can get fabulous fresh chanterelles in the Northwest, the same mushrooms may never show up in a Northeastern market. Find out what kind of mushrooms grow in your area and seek out a market or farm stand that may carry them.

Are white button mushrooms a suitable substitute for wild ones?

Different mushrooms have different flavors and textures. Comparing them is like comparing zucchini to cucumbers. They belong to the same vegetable group and are somewhat similar in texture, but in fact are very different vegetables. So, while the white, all-purpose buttons are certainly pretty enough, they're very mild and unassertive compared to other mushrooms and won't give you the flavor that the wild varieties will.

I always see white mushrooms sold loose in a basket right next to the plastic-wrapped ones in a carton. Which is the better choice?

You'll notice that loose mushrooms are more expensive than packaged. That's because you can choose and pick each one individually according to its size and appearance, eliminating those that aren't in the best condition. But as long as the packaged containers are labeled "all natural," which means they haven't been treated with a chemical, they are basically the same.

Which of the grocery store mushrooms do you consider the most flavorful?

I'm particularly fond of the brown cremini mushrooms. They have a lovely, earthy taste and are not watery. The portobello, which is actually cremini's big brother, is also a flavor-packed mushroom that is good roasted at a low temperature (Portobello Mushrooms in Tarragon-Lime Butter, page 132) and even grilled. Shiitakes that are large and spongy are wonderful sautéed and served as a topping for a salad or julienned and added to stir-fries.

■■

Black trumpets Delicate texture, outstanding flavor, but better when dried, then reconstituted.

Button mushrooms Commercial mushrooms available fresh all year. Their taste is rather bland but you can mix with other "wild" mushrooms for a wonderful flavor.

Cèpes Also called porcini. Grow wild and are sometimes available fresh in the fall. Very perishable.

Chanterelles Resemble a curved trumpet or vase. Bright orange or apricot with an apricot-like aroma. These are very delicate, so clean gently with a damp towel. Fresh chanterelles require a longer cooking time than most other mushrooms.

Enoki Cultivated and available fresh all year. Resemble bean sprouts, slender and snow white. Very mild flavor.

Morels Grow wild and are available fresh in the early spring. Easily recognized by their conical shape and honeycomb markings. Should be heavy for their size and spongy to the touch. Have a meaty, intense flavor, wonderful sautéed in butter.

Oyster mushrooms Grow wild and also cultivated. Mild, buttery-tasting mushrooms with large, fanlike leaf and stem that somewhat resemble the shape of an oyster.

Shiitakes One of the best-flavored commercial mushrooms available. Stems are tough and inedible but caps have a great smoky flavor.

■■

What is a porcini mushroom? I always see them dried but never sold fresh.

The porcini is a huge, fabulous-tasting, wild fall mushroom that looks like a giant brown common mushroom. But its meaty, silky texture is anything but common. Unfortunately, they're extremely perishable, so they're rarely seen fresh in markets and are very expensive. However, dry porcini, which have a rich, woodsy aroma and a marvelous concentrated flavor, are far from second best and are now available in gourmet shops everywhere. They're often sold by their French name, *cèpes*, or the Latin, *Boletus edulis*.

What exactly should I look for in shiitake and oyster mushrooms? Should they be large or small?

When buying shiitakes, try to pick the ones that are about 2 inches or less across the top. This is important because you eat only the caps, and if you're paying by the pound, you don't want any of the heavy, nonusable stems loading up the scale. The caps are slightly spongy in texture and have a pleasantly smoky flavor. Oyster mushrooms also have a wonderful silky texture, and you can use the entire mushroom.

Are black trumpet mushrooms safe to eat?

Yes, and they are wonderful. Despite its ominous name, this mushroom is excellent, although very delicate in texture. Black trumpets have an outstanding buttery flavor that is revealed only after they are dried and reconstituted.

What's the best way to clean mushrooms?

You can rinse mushrooms quickly, but never soak them, because they'll act like a sponge. The best way to clean the white ones is with a damp towel. Other mushrooms, such as shi-itakes or portobellos, need only a quick rinsing; once you remove the stems, they are essentially ready to be cooked. In fact, mushrooms arrive in markets quite clean, since they're grown in peat instead of dirt. Don't bother with one of those fancy little mushroom brushes. You'll probably use it one time and then relegate it to the gadget drawer. Morels, on the other hand, need a thorough cleaning under running water, since there are so many nooks and crannies where dirt can hide.

TIP If you don't have access to good wild mushrooms, next time you make risotto, try this fool-the-eye trick. Remove and discard the gills from the bottom of a clean portobello and mince the mushroom. Sprinkle the raw portobello on top of the risotto, then drizzle with a bit of truffle oil. See if your guests can tell the difference.

What can I do with mushroom stems? I hate to throw them away.

The stems lend terrific flavor to soups and stocks. If you're not going to use them right away, trim them but do not rinse, and store in a paper bag in the refrigerator. Make sure to use them within a few days.

Onions

■ ■

Is there a difference between yellow, white, and red onions?

Bulb onions, which come in yellow, white, and red, are the most readily available onions, and these are the ones we have to rely on through the winter months. All three types are actually similar in flavor, but depending on the time of year and where they're grown, there can be a distinct flavor difference. Some onions may be quite sweet, while others taste sharp. For most recipes, you can use yellow and white inter-changeably. Both are pretty potent and have plenty of kick even after a few hours in a stew pot. You can also use red onions in many dishes that call for yellow ones, although the color will change the appearance of the dish.

What is the difference between thick-skinned onions and thin-skinned ones? I find the very thin-skinned onions hard to peel.

Like most other vegetables, onions are sea-sonal, and even though they're available in markets year-round, they vary quite dramatically. From April through August you'll generally find flat onions with paper-thin skins. These are called "new" onions, and even though they are quite sweet, they're hard to peel. New onions are very perishable, so I usually buy only a few days' supply and store them in a cool dark place or refrigerate. The onions that you'll find in the fall and throughout the cool-weather months are considered "old" or "storage" onions, since they have gone through a cool storage period.

These are round with thick skins. Stored properly in a cool well-ventilated place, these will last for 6 to 8 months, but their flavor will be sharp and more pronounced.

How do I tell which onions are sweet?

Sweet onions have a thinner, lighter-colored skin than the storage ones and tend to be more fragile. Signs in produce sections usually differentiate between the two and most producers also put stickers on each individual onion, such as "Texas 1015 Super Sweet," "Sweet Imperials," "Vidalia," etc. Another indication is price—sweet onions are premium products and prices are higher than for the regular bulb varieties with thicker skin.

What is the difference between a Bermuda onion and a Spanish onion?

There is no difference, and don't be fooled by the names. Neither the Bermuda nor the Spanish onion comes from its namesake country. Instead, both varieties are U.S. grown. The Spanish variety has a large, spherical shape and a mild, sweet flavor. I find it to be crisper than regular yellow storage onions. At one time Bermuda did actually grow a fabulous large, sweet yellow onion that you could occasionally get here, but that variety died out years ago. These days people regard the red onion as the "Bermuda," but they are mistaken.

What is the best onion to use in salads?

If you like a very mild fresh taste, use the green part of the scallion; otherwise, my first choice is always the red onion (also called Creole onion). The best red onions are imported from Italy and are available from the end of August through the fall and early winter. During the spring and summer, all red onions are grown in Texas. These are large and flat and have a very sharp taste. For a spring salad, try Florida or local spring onions that come with their greens attached, or the Georgia-grown Vidalia.

What makes Vidalia onions so popular? Is there a way to prepare them other than raw in salads and sandwiches?

Vidalia onions have enjoyed some great public relations. After peaches, Vidalia onions are one of Georgia's premier crops. For a while, they were hard to come by and rather expensive, making them the "in" thing. Now, because of proper storage, their spring season has been extended into summer and there are a lot more Vidalias available. They're still quite pricey and perishable and should be used within a few days of purchase. My favorite way to use them is to gently braise them in olive oil with a touch of rosemary and minced garlic and serve them as a side to roast chicken or steak. (See recipe, page 136.) You can also roast them in a slow oven and drizzle with a mustard vinaigrette before serving.

What is a Walla Walla onion?

The Walla Walla is to the Northwest what the Vidalia is to Georgia. It is basically the same onion, just grown in different locales. Both are large, sweet, seasonal onions, available from spring through summer, and are wonderful eaten raw with just a seasoning of salt and pepper and possibly a drizzle of olive oil. Another sweet onion that western chefs love to use if they can get it is the Maui onion from Hawaii. Eating this onion is truly a memorable experience, since it is so sweet you can almost eat it like an apple. If you see Mauis in the market, grab one (or two). Texas Super Sweets and Oso Sweets, the newest onion on the block from Chile, are also nice and live up to their names, but the Maui is magic.

ONIONS AT A GLANCE

SWEET ONIONS

Texas Sweets, Spring Sweets, and Texas 1015s Spring Sweets are the first spring sweet onions in the marketplace, arriving in March. The 1015s (named for the suggested planting date, October 15) arrive in mid-April. Both last through mid-June.

Vidalia From Vidalia, Georgia. Slightly squashed looking, thin-skinned with more water than storage onions. Their season is short, from April to June, but you may still see some as late as August, when the flavor becomes more sharp. Best in salads and sandwiches; make great onion rings.

Walla Walla From the Northwest. Available mid-June through late August.

Maui Available mid-February through late April. Hard to find in most markets east of the Rockies.

Sweet Imperial From California. Available late April through August.

Oso Sweet From Chile. Newest onion on the block. Available November through March.

BULB ONIONS

Yellow onion Known as the all-purpose onion, holds up well when cooked. Has a strong flavor, great in soups and stews.

Spanish Sweet A large, spherical yellow onion with a mild, sweet flavor. Crisper than regular yellow storage onions.

White onion Has a sharp taste but still milder and crisper than a yellow storage onion.

Red onion Similar in taste to the Spanish Sweet. Loses its bright color when cooked. Flavor ranges from mild to very strong. Usually at its best in salads or used raw in cold dishes.

Pearl onion Any bulb onion that measures no larger than $1\frac{1}{2}$ inches in diameter is considered a pearl onion. Great in soups, stews. Sweeter than the larger bulbs.

Cippoline From Italy. A small, flat yellow onion found in many specialty markets. Mild.

When a recipe calls for "pearl onions," what does that mean? Can I use them in more than just soups and stews?

Most people think of pearl onions as only being white, but in fact, the tiny yellow ones and red ones now marketed in small mesh bags cook faster and are even sweeter than the white ones. All three colors are available in markets throughout the country. I love to braise them to use them as an accompaniment to roasted meats and chicken.

To braise pearl onions sauté $\frac{1}{2}$ pound diced onions with $\frac{1}{4}$ cup diced bacon until lightly browned. Add 2 tablespoons brown sugar, $\frac{1}{4}$ cup chicken stock, $\frac{1}{4}$ cup red wine, and $\frac{1}{2}$ cup raisins. Sprinkle with salt and pepper and cook over low heat until the onions caramelize and the liquid cooks down to a syrupy glaze, about 30 minutes. Cool and store tightly covered in the refrigerator. They will keep for weeks.

TIP When you can't find super-sweet onions, you can "tame" regular bulb onions, especially red ones, by soaking them in ice water for 30 minutes. Drain, then use raw or in your recipe. The onions will be crisp and less sharp tasting.

Pearl onions seem to take forever to peel. Is there a trick to peeling them faster?

You can speed up the process by dropping the unpeeled onions in boiling water for about 20 seconds, draining them, and then transferring them to a cold-water bath. When cool enough to handle, trim the root end with a sharp paring knife and gently squeeze the onion toward the stem, and the onion will pop out unblemished.

Peas

■■■

Are snow peas and sugar snap peas interchangeable?

Snow peas have flat, tender pods with tiny undeveloped peas and are completely edible. Sugar snaps are also completely edible, but they look like old-fashioned peas with fully developed peas popping through.

Snow peas and sugar snaps cannot be used interchangeably in every preparation. Both are good steamed, but snow peas are actually more interesting stir-fried. On the other hand, you can make a great Sugar Snap Pea Soup (page 137), which you cannot do with snow peas.

My market has just started to carry sugar snap peas. How do you prepare them and how long do they keep?

The simpler the preparation the better. I usually simply cook them in salted water for 3 to 4 minutes, then drain and butter them. I also like to add a sprinkling of dill, mint, parsley, or chives. Both sugar snaps and snow peas keep much better than old-fashioned peas—up to a week or more, depending on how fresh they are when you get them.

Fresh peas are almost impossible to find in my area. Can I use frozen peas instead?

There is no substitute for truly fresh peas, but here is the problem: peas, like corn, start to deteriorate and their natural sugars start converting to starch as soon as they are picked. By the time they get to the grocery store, they are several days or even weeks old. On the other hand, frozen peas are processed soon after harvest and flash frozen, which halts the deterioration. Another reason so many people prefer frozen peas is that no one has the time or patience to shell a bag full of peas—1 pound yields only 1 cup. Still, good fresh peas are in a league of their own.

Is it really necessary to string snow peas?

I usually string and trim the stems of both snow and sugar peas, since the fiber that runs along the spine of the pod is unpleasant to chew on. The good news is that more and more often snow peas come string-free, a nice bonus.

TIP Buy snow peas at a market with a large turnover. Pass on those that come packaged or that are limp and soft.

Food magazines occasionally feature a lovely garnish described as "pea shoots." Are they edible?

Pea shoots have a lovely delicate taste, and you will start seeing more and more of this "new" green in stores as their popularity increases.

Right now, you are most likely to find pea shoots at Asian grocery stores or at farmers' markets during the spring.

Peppers, Bell

What is the difference between green bell peppers and the red, orange, and yellow ones?

All are varieties of bell peppers, but with some taste difference. Red peppers are fully ripened green peppers and taste much sweeter. Green peppers are fleshier and firmer and are my first choice for stuffed peppers. Yellow and orange peppers are thin-skinned and more perishable than red peppers, but their taste is similar and I use them more for color than flavor.

Why can't I get good green peppers in the supermarket? Is there a particular season for really flavorful green peppers?

Green peppers are available year-round in supermarkets everywhere, but in the fall and winter you'll find a thick-walled variety that is not particularly flavorful. The best green peppers are those that appear in markets during the spring and summer, when you get a smaller, thin-walled pepper that is juicy and delicately flavored. These peppers are ideal for stuffing and for eating raw in salads.

Why are red peppers so much more expensive than green peppers? Is there a time of year when they are less pricey?

For much of the year, red bell peppers are imported from Holland and are therefore pricey.

About mid-August, the domestic crop is harvested and prices come way down. Domestic red peppers are thin-walled and are a little harder to roast or grill, but I find that they are tastier than Holland peppers.

Can green peppers be used when a recipe calls for red or yellow peppers?

Green and red peppers have very different flavors and are not interchangeable. The taste of green peppers is very distinct when cooked and tends to dominate a dish. While green peppers are delicious stuffed and stir-fried, they are not good in pasta dishes or soups. Red peppers, on the other hand, can be used in innumerable dishes, both raw and cooked.

Is there an easy way to roast and peel bell peppers?

Roasting a pepper over a gas flame or a charcoal fire is still the very best way, and once you taste that delicious, smoky flesh, it's worth the trouble. You can pop peppers into the broiler, but this method cooks the peppers instead of roasting them and leaves them soft instead of crisp. When evenly charred over a flame or hot coals and wrapped in a damp paper towel for a few minutes, peppers are easy to peel. The skin will slip off once the stem separates from the flesh, or you can hold the peppers under cool running water and rub the skin away. Don't worry about removing every last bit of skin—little charred flecks are not the end of the world and give the pepper a rustic look.

Can peppers be roasted ahead of time and stored?

Cut the roasted peppers in wide strips, put them in a glass container, then add a thick layer of olive oil. Covered with a tight lid, they will keep for up to 2 weeks. Use them for quick appetizers, in salads and pasta dishes, or to top pizza.

What kinds of peppers are used for a stir-fry of peppers and onions like street vendors make?

There is no better aroma than that of peppers and onions cooking on a flattop. Urban street vendors serve this dish tucked into a hard roll with Italian sausage. The best peppers for this dish are the elongated, pale green frying peppers with thin skin, sometimes called sweet or Italian peppers. They cook quickly and have a mild sweetness that melds beautifully with onions. I often quickly grill them and serve them skin and all with a drizzle of olive oil as part of an antipasti table.

Potatoes

■■■

What are new potatoes? Should they be red or white?

A new potato is one that goes directly from the field to the market after harvesting in the spring, with no time in storage. There has been no time for its sugars to convert to starch, and consequently it is waxier and moister than other potatoes. Because new potatoes are not a variety, they can be white- or red-skinned, although most people prefer them red. They may arrive in the market as early as February, when Florida, Texas, and California ship their spring crops.

New potatoes do not mash well but are wonderful simply cooked in their jackets and served with a touch of butter. You can also use them in potato salad. Depending on the recipe, you don't have to bother removing their very thin skins.

Cookbooks say that the season for new potatoes is spring and summer. So what are the potatoes I see in my market during the winter months that are called "new potatoes"?

Calling small-sized potatoes that have been in storage for months "new" potatoes is a marketing gimmick. Some wholesalers call all red-skinned potatoes new potatoes, regardless of their size or age. Just to confuse the issue a little more, the Red Bliss potato, which is grown in the Midwest and harvested in the fall, also masquerades as a new potato. A true new potato will be moist and fresh tasting, but it's hard to know the difference until you taste one.

What is the difference between an Idaho and a russet potato?

There is no difference. Idaho is the largest producing region for russet baking potatoes. A large, Idaho-grown russet is considered the best of the lot. It has a fluffy, mealy texture that is perfect for baking. Other states also produce excellent russet potatoes. While they may be smaller, they are equally good and often much less expensive.

I am always confused as to which potato to use for which purpose.

Russet potatoes are oblong in shape with darkish brown skins and are best for baking. They can also be used in gratins and for French fries. Yukon Gold potatoes are my choice for mashing and potato salads, and red-skinned potatoes are good for just about everything else, such as in soups, sliced and fried, or cooked and turned into hash browns. All-purpose white potatoes bake just as well as russets. In fact, my favorite baking potato is the white-skinned variety grown in California, known as White Rose or Schafter White.

TIP Do not wrap potatoes in foil before baking. Because the foil keeps the moisture in the potatoes, they turn out soggy instead of dry and fluffy. Steak houses and other restaurants follow this practice simply because it's easy, not because it's good.

What potatoes should I use for mashing?

There is nothing better than the texture of mashed Yukon Gold potatoes to which you have added some butter and a touch of milk or sour cream. With their silky texture and fabulous flavor, they already taste buttery. Until recently these potatoes were considered gourmet items and were not widely available. Now you can get them anywhere, and you do not have to pay their weight in gold anymore, either.

Is there a specific kind of potato that is best for roasting?

New potatoes, red or white, and Red Bliss are my first choices for roasted potatoes. They retain a buttery fluffy texture inside, while the outside crisps up nicely.

What potato do you recommend for potato salads?

Red and white new potatoes are great for salads. Red Bliss potatoes are good as well, but my all-time favorite salad potatoes are fingerlings and very small Yukon Golds, which have now become widely available. Look for the ones bagged by Dole.

TIP Do not buy assorted fingerling potatoes. Although they look nice and colorful, they require different cooking times and do not mix successfully.

What is the best potato for making home fries?

Home fries are best when made with red-skinned potatoes; Red Bliss and Yukon Gold are excellent choices as well.

I now see blue potatoes in my grocery store. What is the best way to use them?

These vibrantly colored potatoes, which range from pale blue to deep purple, are just one example of the "heirloom" potatoes that have become popular in recent years. They are not particularly interesting, since they are rather dry and turn grayish when cooked. However, they will retain their blue color when deep-fried.

How are sweet potatoes related to other potatoes?

Botanically, they're not related at all. In the market, the tubers labeled sweet potatoes have yellowish or brown skin and yellowish or light orange flesh. Those labeled yams have coppery or purple skin and dark reddish-orange flesh. The two varieties are closely related and are best baked or pureed.

True yams are large starchy tubers with brown skin and white flesh which grow in the tropics. They can be boiled or baked and when mashed become gummy, a quality considered desirable by some African cultures in which they are a staple.

Shallots

What are shallots?

Shallots are a member of the onion family and look rather like small, elongated onions with dark tan, papery skin. They often have double attached bulbs. If you can, buy them loose or in small mesh bags. Avoid those packed in cellophane-wrapped packages.

How are shallots different from onions?

Shallots have a much more distinctive and complex flavor, with a hint of garlic. Although they belong to the onion family and can be quite pungent, they actually sweeten fish stocks and tomato sauces and are essential in many preparations. Classic French preparations such as a beurre blanc and a sauce béarnaise simply would not be the same without shallots.

What can I use as a substitute for shallots if I don't have any on hand?

When they're not available, go ahead and substitute some finely minced scallions. Depending on the size, you can use the white parts of 6 to 8 scallions to equal one shallot.

TIP Keep minced or sliced shallots covered with white wine in a jar in the refrigerator. They will remain fresh for weeks.

When a recipe calls for a shallot, do I use the whole bulb or just a single clove?

The shallot grows as a small, single bulb or as a cluster of several cloves gathered into a bulb, a lot like garlic. Each single clove is considered to be one shallot.

How do you roast shallots?

Roasted shallots make a wonderful accompaniment to a pan-seared steak or added to the pan juices of a rib roast, pork roast, or roasted chicken. Another wonderful way to serve shallots is to sprinkle them with balsamic vinegar and a large grinding of black pepper and use as a topping for a well-seasoned salad.

To roast shallots Preheat the oven to 400°F. Toss 18 medium-sized unpeeled shallots with 3 tablespoons olive oil in a large bowl. Place snugly in a single layer in an ovenproof dish. Add ½ cup water, cover the dish tightly with foil, and place in the center of the oven. Roast the shallots for 40 minutes.

When done, the shallots will slip right out of their skin. Store the shallots covered with a layer of olive oil.

Spinach

■■■

Sometimes fresh spinach has a wonderful, full flavor and other times it is bland and characterless. Are there different kinds of spinach?

There are basically two types of spinach widely available: the curly, crinkly variety, also called Savoy, and the flat-leafed variety, called New Zealand spinach (but grown in California).

Crinkly Savoy spinach has a far more assertive, true spinach flavor and is at its best and most available during cool-weather months. If you live in the Western states, and California in particular, chances are you will find only New Zealand (flat-leaf) spinach, which is very good in salads, but not particularly interesting when cooked.

Is it better to buy spinach in bunches or bagged?

You can buy very good bagged spinach as long as you know what to look for. The bag must feel bouncy, never soggy or wet, and the spinach should look dry and richly green. If it looks dark, wet, or yellow, pass on it. In theory, bagged spinach has fewer stems and is pre-washed. However, I find that it still needs a thorough rinsing. Flat-leaf New Zealand spinach is sold only in bunches. It is usually much less gritty than the curly variety and easier to clean.

How do you get the dirt out of spinach? Even after rinsing in the colander, it remains gritty.

For starters, use warm water instead of cold. Fill a very large bowl with warm water, immerse the spinach, and swish it around briefly. Let it sit for a few minutes to give the sand and grit time to settle on the bottom of the bowl. Lift out the spinach and pour out the water.

For bagged spinach, you will need one or at the most two rinsings. Loose spinach will require as many as three to four. Flat-leaf spinach is easily cleaned in one rinsing.

What is the best way to cook spinach?

My favorite way is to blanch spinach in plenty of lightly salted boiling water for about 2 minutes, drain, and run it under cold water so it keeps its color. Sauté the spinach in a skillet over low heat in some butter and season it with plenty of freshly ground pepper and a pinch of freshly grated nutmeg. Pine nuts, raisins, finely sliced garlic, yogurt, and diced smoked ham all go well with sautéed spinach.

Another nice method that is particularly suitable for flat-leaf New Zealand spinach is to dry it thoroughly in a salad spinner once it's washed and then stir-fry it in some fruity olive oil with a couple of sliced garlic cloves. The spinach will wilt quickly and be ready in a couple of minutes. Season carefully and serve with seafood, poultry, or veal.

Blanched spinach keeps better than the raw, as much as 3 or 4 days in the refrigerator. You can also freeze it in a zippered plastic bag for several weeks.

Squash

■■

Summer Squash

Is there a difference between yellow squash and yellow zucchini? Are they interchangeable?

The pale yellow crookneck or straightneck squash are rather watery and mild flavored, while yellow zucchini have a lovely nutty taste and retain great texture when cooked. Unfortunately, yellow zucchini are not very plentiful, so if you can't find them, go right ahead and use yellow squash.

Which is the best summer squash for grilling?

They all work well, but yellow and green zucchini and pattypan squash do best, since they are less seedy and more flavorful than yellow crookneck squash. Cut the zucchini on the diagonal and make the slices a little thicker than you would for sautéing.

Baby squash are so attractive on a plate, but are they really worth the extra money?

I don't think so. They often taste bitter because they are picked prematurely to qualify as "baby." Also, unless your market has a large turnover, the tiny squashes are probably not as fresh as the average zucchini.

TIP All the flavor of the green zucchini is in the peel. To get the best taste when sautéing or otherwise cooking zucchini, use the skin and a small amount of flesh. To do this, cut the zucchini into logs $1\frac{1}{2}$ to 2 inches long. Lay the logs vertically on a cutting board and slice the skin off with about a quarter inch of flesh. Put these zucchini rectangles flat on the board and cut them into strips or "batonnets," which will look like thin French fries.

What's the best way to prepare zucchini blossoms?

Delicate, deep-fried squash blossoms are one of the great treats of summer and are best eaten the same day they're picked. You can fry batter-dipped blooms plain or stuffed with smoked mozzarella and a bit of anchovy, as they do in Tuscany and Puglia, Italy. If you are fortunate enough to have a garden or access to a good farmers' market, zucchini blossoms will be easy to come by. Otherwise, seek them out where and when you can.

To make Fried Zucchini Blossoms Combine 1 cup milk with 1 cup all-purpose flour and 1 large egg. Whisk to mix very lightly until just blended. Season with salt and a pinch of cayenne. Stir lightly; do not overmix. Pour vegetable oil into a pot to a depth of 2 to 3 inches and heat until very hot and simmering. Dip the blossoms in the batter and then deep-fry for 2 to 5 minutes until crisp and brown. Remove with a slotted spoon, drain on paper towels, and serve immediately with a little salt. This is enough for about 12 blossoms.

What's the best way to cook scalloped patty-pan squash? They have such an odd shape.

Choose small specimens, quarter them, and cut the quarters into slices about ⅛ inch thick. They are delicious simply sautéed or oven-roasted in a little butter and olive oil and then sprinkled with a little lemon juice and minced parsley or basil. If you are grilling, place the cut-up patty-pan squash on a large piece of foil and sprinkle with some fresh herbs, a drizzle of good olive oil, and a grinding of pepper. Wrap the foil into a package and cook the squash right along with your steak. The vegetable steams on the grill and tastes absolutely delicious.

Winter Squash

Recently more varieties of winter squash have been showing up at the farmers' market and grocery store, but it's hard to know which ones are worth experimenting with. Can you help?

I often experiment with different types of squash but always come back to my favorites: acorn squash, butternut, spaghetti squash, and buttercup. However, each region in this country has its own types of winter squashes and it is worthwhile experimenting.

Is there a difference between butternut and buttercup squash?

Butternut squash has a lovely buttery, nutty taste. It peels easily and has flesh tender enough to dice or slice. Its consistency is very different from that of buttercup, which is very sweet but stringy.

What is the mark of a good acorn squash? Is bigger better?

Both dark green and bright orange acorn squash are good choices. Look for those tinged with yellowish orange, an indication that they are ripe and sweet. Also, when it comes to acorn squash, large is better than small, and heavy is better than light. The lighter the squash, the more dehydrated and fibrous it is, so go for the heavyweight every time.

It is so hard to cut a raw acorn squash in half. Would it help to microwave it first?

I always bake the squash first for 35 to 40 minutes in a 350°F oven until it can easily be pierced with the tip of a sharp knife. You can also microwave it, but baking the squash does a more even job. At this point it is very easy to cut the squash in half and finish baking it with the seasoning of your choice. Remember that plenty of butter and brown sugar make for a delicious-tasting squash. This is one of my favorite ways to prepare acorn squash: Bake a medium-sized acorn squash until it is soft, let it cool a little, halve it, and scrape out the seeds with a grapefruit spoon. Put 1 tablespoon of unsalted butter and 1 tablespoon of brown sugar in each half, and season with salt and pepper. Return to the oven and bake for another 10 to 15 minutes, or until browned and fragrant. Serve half a squash per person.

Can all pumpkins be used for cooking?

Those grown for jack-o'-lanterns or other decorations are quite flavorless. Look for small, heavy pumpkins labeled Sugar Pies, Cheese, or Baby Bear pumpkins when you want to make a pie.

Is there a big taste difference between fresh and canned pumpkin?

Canned pumpkin is fine for pies, especially since you are going to add the usual spices. But be sure to begin with plain pumpkin puree, not those sold as pie fillings that are already spiced. You will want to add your own seasoning.

How do you prepare spaghetti squash?

You can handle spaghetti squash one of two ways. Either boil it in a large pot of water until tender, cut it open, and scoop out the pasta-like strands, or bake it. Baking is my preferred method, since it concentrates the squash's mild taste—and eliminates the boiling pot. Put the squash directly on the oven rack in a 350°F oven for about 1 hour, or until it can easily be pierced with a fork. Cool slightly and then cut in half. Scoop out the seeds, then pull out the fibrous flesh with a fork to separate the strands.

What kind of pasta sauce goes well with spaghetti squash?

Despite its name—which refers to the spaghetti-like strands of flesh inside the squash—spaghetti squash is not pasta, and I do not find that it marries well with tomato or any other full-flavored sauces. Instead, I treat it like winter squash rather than pasta and either braise it in butter and seasonings or toss the cooked strands in a butter and cream sauce flavored with mild goat cheese.

Here is a lovely side dish for roast turkey, duck, or pork tenderloin Combine 1 medium-sized cooked spaghetti squash with ½ cup heavy cream, 3 tablespoons unsalted butter cut into pieces, 2 tablespoons brown sugar, a pinch of nutmeg, salt, and pepper. Pour the mixture into a baking dish, cover tightly with foil, and bake at 350°F for 25 to 30 minutes. Serve hot.

Tomatoes

Is there a major difference in taste between round tomatoes and the oval ones called plum or Roma tomatoes? Are they interchangeable in recipes?

When perfectly ripe, both round and plum tomatoes deliver great taste, and for many recipes, either can be used. The plum tomato is meatier, less watery, and more suitable for tomato sauce. I also like a good, ripe plum tomato in salads, especially Greek salads. Some people object to the relatively thick skin of plum tomatoes. In general, a good tomato with distinct aroma and true freshness is the best bet, no matter what its shape.

TIP When you can't get good ripe tomatoes, switch to cherry tomatoes. They tend to be more flavorful and more easily available than vine-ripened tomatoes.

What are heirloom tomatoes?

The word "heirloom" does not refer to a variety but is a term to describe old-fashioned varieties of fruits and vegetables that have, for one reason or another, fallen out of favor but are now being "rediscovered." Tomatoes are the most popular heirloom, although you can find heirloom potatoes, apples, and other produce.

Heirloom tomatoes may be green, pink, yellow, or striped as well as red.

It's usually the most dedicated farmers who seek out heirloom seeds, so most of the heirloom tomatoes I've run across have been at farmers' markets. As a whole, their quality is very high. Brandywine tomatoes are my favorite heirlooms; they're extra juicy and spectacularly flavorful.

Do yellow and orange tomatoes have a distinct taste or are they mainly cultivated for visual appeal?

Yellow and orange tomatoes actually taste sweeter and less acidic than the regular red varieties, and they are very appealing when combined with red tomatoes in a refreshing sliced tomato platter drizzled with virgin olive oil and sprinkled with some herbs.

What are pear tomatoes? Are they the same as grape tomatoes?

Both these tomatoes are a little smaller than cherry tomatoes but can be used in precisely the same ways. Pear tomatoes bell out at the bottom to become pear shaped. They may seem new, but they have been popular for years in Italy. The pear-shaped Vesuvio tomatoes that grow near Naples, Italy, are particularly well known. Grape tomatoes are the shape of large grapes and taste incredibly sweet. These tomatoes have a slightly thicker skin than regular cherry tomatoes, which means they hold their shape better when sautéed. They also have a longer shelf life.

TIP For a quick hors d'oeuvre, serve a bowl of cherry or tiny pear or grape tomatoes alongside a small dish of vodka and a dish of coarse salt. Dip the tomato in the vodka first, then in the salt for an exciting nibble.

Can cherry tomatoes be used in recipes that call for all-purpose tomatoes?

It depends on the recipe. Cherry tomatoes can't be peeled or seeded and so are not recommended for any recipe that calls for peeled, seeded tomatoes such as a tomato fondue or sauce. They work perfectly in many other preparations, especially quick sautés, vegetable medleys, and many pasta dishes. The best news is that they provide more flavor than most other tomatoes.

What varieties of tomatoes do you recommend for growing in pots on my patio?

My favorite is the Carmello, which I consider to be the finest all-purpose variety. Besides being delicious, it's easy to grow and bears a lot of fruit. Early Girl is another good all-purpose tomato. The heirloom Brandywine, both red and yellow, is another good choice. The red ripens to a pretty pink and is big, meaty, and mild, while the yellow is very sweet with a creamy texture. For cherry tomatoes, try the Juliet Santa and the Sungold—a rich, juicy jewel that turns an intense golden orange and is as beautiful on the vine as in the mouth.

Will tomatoes ripen more quickly on a sunny windowsill?

Tomatoes ripen best in a dark, cool corner of the kitchen or when placed on a baking sheet, covered with newspaper, and stored under the bed. I do this often with the green tomatoes at the end of the summer growing season and it really works. In a sunny spot, they'll just get soft without ripening. Whatever you do, don't refrigerate tomatoes. It makes them woolly and tasteless and doesn't increase their shelf life.

Is there a trick to peeling and seeding tomatoes?

Peeling tomatoes can be quite simple if you cut a cross into the base of each tomato with a paring knife, then immerse them in boiling water for 30 seconds. The hot water causes the peel to unfurl from the body of the tomato, and you can lift it right off. Cut the peeled tomato in half crosswise to expose the neat little seed pockets. Use your fingers to dig them out and the job is done.

How important is it to peel and seed the tomatoes when making homemade tomato sauce?

There are some preparations that absolutely require peeled, seeded tomatoes, but these rarely call for more than 3 or 4 tomatoes. If you are cooking a large batch of sauce, just cut up the unpeeled tomatoes and once they are cooked run the mixture through a food mill. This will give you a nice smooth sauce which, if too thin, can be cooked down to a thicker consistency.

TIP Add a pinch of sugar to tomato-based sauces before cooking. The sugar counterbalances the acidity.

What's the best way to use sun-dried tomatoes? Are they a good substitute for fresh?

Sun-dried tomatoes have a wonderfully intense flavor but are not a substitute for fresh ones. They come packed in oil or dried. Drain the oil-packed tomatoes before chopping; reconstitute the dried in warm water. Use them as an accent, like olives, or try them on a salad or pizza with crumbled goat cheese.

What is tomato confit? How is it made and used?

The term confit usually describes a particular method of using duck, goose, or pork fat to preserve certain foods, but in the past few years, the word has been co-opted for other foods. Today, it's common to see the term applied to dishes with tomatoes and other vegetables such as turnips and Belgian endive. Tomato confit is lovely served over crusty peasant bread, in pastas, as a filling for an omelet, or as a garnish for pan-seared seafood.

To make a Tomato Confit Cut ripe plum tomatoes in half lengthwise, gently squeeze to remove some of the seeds, and place cut side down on a baking sheet. Drizzle lightly with olive oil and season with coarse salt, freshly ground pepper, and a sprinkling of sugar. Bake in a preheated 275°F oven for 6 to 8 hours, or until the tomatoes have shrunk to half their size. Once cool, pack the confit in a large jar, cover with a thin layer of olive oil, and refrigerate.

Turnips

■■■

What is the difference between white and yellow turnips?

White turnips are delicate, mild-tasting spring root vegetables that keep well for as long as 10 days. Make sure to look for white turnips with a deep purple band about the root end. When they are fresh and young, white turnips can be eaten raw, much like radishes.

Yellow turnips, also called rutabagas, are large globes that mature in the early fall and are available through the winter. They are often sold waxed to increase their shelf life, and so will keep for up to 2 months in the refrigerator. Peel off the waxy skin before cooking.

What are Swedish turnips?

Recipes in old cookbooks, particularly those featuring Scandinavian recipes, refer to rutabagas as "Swedish turnips." This is because of the popularity of this hardy vegetable in Scandinavia, where turnips are a staple during the winter. Oddly, I saw big rutabagas called Swedish turnips in the southern state of Georgia.

What is the mark of good turnips? So many seem to be woody and have a sharp unpleasant flavor.

Turnips are a wonderful delicate root vegetable when they are really fresh. Unfortunately, because of lack of turnover in many parts of the country, the tops are removed to increase their shelf life. Even without their leafy tops, fresh turnips are easy to spot by their deep purple band and white skin. The lighter the band, the older the vegetable. Stay away from dull-looking turnips.

Are turnips and rutabagas interchangeable in recipes?

White turnips, with their delicate flavor, taste lovely combined with carrots, leeks, and potatoes, added to stew, or roasted alongside a plump chicken. On the other hand, rutabagas have a much more assertive taste and are best served on their own or in combination with potatoes, as in the Puree of Rutabaga and Potato with Crispy Shallots, page 144.

TIP If you have access to a good farmers' market where you can find unwaxed small rutabagas, you can substitute them for white turnips in soups and stews.

Cream of Asparagus and Spring Onion Soup

The marriage of asparagus and spring onions is heavenly, especially in this full-flavored soup. If you cannot get the Texas or Florida spring onions, you can use two bunches of scallions instead. A homemade chicken stock does make a difference in this delicate soup, but if you do not have the time to make it, a good-quality bouillon will do. Serve the soup hot or at room temperature accompanied by crusty bread and good butter.

SERVES 6

4 tablespoons unsalted butter

2 medium spring onions, all but 1 inch of
 green parts trimmed, diced

8 cups chicken stock or bouillon

3 tablespoons all-purpose flour

1½ pounds asparagus, trimmed, stalks peeled,
 asparagus cut into 1-inch pieces, stalks and
 tips separated

½ cup heavy cream

Salt and freshly ground white pepper

2 tablespoons minced fresh dill or chives

1. Melt the butter in a heavy 3-quart saucepan over low heat. Add the spring onions together with a couple of tablespoons of the stock and simmer, covered, until tender.

2. Add the flour and cook, stirring constantly, for 1 to 2 minutes without browning. Add the remaining chicken stock and whisk until well blended. Bring to a boil, reduce the heat, add the asparagus stalks, and simmer, partially covered, for 30 minutes.

3. Strain the soup and return the stock to the saucepan. Puree the vegetables in a food processor until smooth. Add the puree to the stock and whisk until well blended.

4. Add the asparagus tips and cream and simmer until just tender. Taste and correct the seasoning with salt and pepper and serve the soup hot or at room temperature, garnished with a sprinkling of dill or chives.

Avocado Salad in Ginger-Lime Vinaigrette

Here is an East meets West avocado salad that I simply adore. I like to serve fine slices of top-quality raw tuna interspersed among the avocado slices, or I garnish the salad with a large sprinkling of rock shrimp. A crumbling of aged goat cheese or finely sliced black gaeta olives or both is another nice variation.

SERVES 4 TO 5

Juice of 1 large lime

½ cup extra virgin olive oil

1 tablespoon soy sauce or more to taste

1 to 2 large garlic cloves, mashed

1 tablespoon grated fresh ginger

3 tablespoons minced scallions or chives

2 ripe Hass avocados, cut crosswise into fine
  slices

Tiny whole cilantro leaves

1. In a small bowl, combine the lime juice together with the olive oil and whisk the mixture until it emulsifies. Add the soy sauce, garlic, ginger, and scallions and whisk until well blended. Add a dash more soy if you like a saltier dressing. You may also add another clove of garlic.

2. Place the sliced avocados on a round serving platter and spoon the sauce over the slices. Sprinkle with the cilantro and serve at room temperature or lightly chilled.

Roasted Beet, Watermelon, and Mango Salad

When I first sampled a watermelon and roasted beet salad in a café on Venice Beach in California, I expected it to be gimmicky. It turned out to be amazingly tasty and refreshing, and I could see that the idea had some possibilities. I have since come up with this version, which includes mango, blue cheese, and pecans.

SERVES 4 TO 5

1 tablespoon sherry vinegar

1 tablespoon balsamic vinegar

¼ cup plus 2 tablespoons grapeseed oil

1 teaspoon Thai chili sauce, optional

Coarse salt and freshly ground black pepper

4 cups baby arugula, mâche, or mesclun greens

3 cups watermelon, cut into ¾-inch cubes

2 cups roasted beets, cut into ¾-inch cubes

1 mango, cut into fine julienne

4 tablespoons diced Maytag blue cheese

½ cup coarsely chopped pecans

Sprigs of mint

1. In a bowl, combine the two vinegars with the oil and the chili sauce. Season with salt and pepper and whisk the dressing until well blended. Taste and correct the seasoning.

2. Pour half the dressing into a large salad bowl. Add the greens and toss gently.

3. In another bowl, combine the watermelon, beets, and mango. Add the remaining salad dressing and toss gently. Season lightly with salt and pepper.

4. Divide the greens among individual dinner plates. Top each serving with some of the fruit and beet mixture. Sprinkle each serving with some of the cheese and pecans and add another grinding of black pepper. Garnish with the mint and serve immediately.

Pan-Seared Baby Bok Choy with Red Bell Peppers and Oyster Sauce

Until recently, the leafy mild-flavored bok choy was available only in Asian markets, greatly limiting its use. Now this lovely green, especially refreshing in its "baby" form, can be purchased in most grocery stores. I like to serve this quick stir-fry with anything grilled, such as a flank steak, shish kebabs, or fish steaks.

SERVES 4 TO 5

1/4 cup olive oil

2 large garlic cloves, finely sliced

1/2 tablespoon finely sliced peeled fresh ginger

2 pounds baby bok choy, cut crosswise into 1-inch pieces

2 medium red bell peppers, stemmed, quartered, ribs removed, and finely sliced

Salt and freshly ground black pepper

3 tablespoons oyster sauce

1. In a large skillet, heat the olive oil together with the garlic and ginger. Immediately add the bok choy. (You may to have to do this in stages, waiting until one batch wilts to add more to the pan.) Add the bell peppers, season with salt and pepper, and cook over medium heat until the peppers are slightly soft and the bok choy wilted.

2. Add the oyster sauce and gently stir it into the vegetable mixture. Taste and correct the seasoning.

3. Transfer to a serving dish and serve hot.

Skillet-Braised Broccoli with Garlic

Broccoli is a wonderful year-round vegetable that we seem to take for granted, giving it little chance to shine. For a change of pace try it this way. Here the broccoli is skillet-braised with good olive oil and some garlic. For a variation, add 2 tablespoons sautéed pine nuts or a roasted pepper cut into fine julienne. Serve as an appetizer topped with some freshly grated Parmesan or as an accompaniment to a simple veal roast, pan-seared lamb chops, or the slow-braised chicken breasts on page 204.

SERVES 4 TO 6

1 large bunch of broccoli (about 1½ pounds)
3 tablespoons extra virgin olive oil
2 large garlic cloves, finely sliced
⅓ cup chicken stock or bouillon
Salt and freshly ground black pepper

1. Trim the broccoli stalks, removing all the leaves. Peel the stalks with a vegetable peeler and cut crosswise into ½-inch slices. Separate the tops into florets.

2. In a large heavy skillet, heat the olive oil over medium heat. Add the broccoli stems together with the garlic and cook for 1 to 2 minutes, stirring often. Add the florets and the stock; season with salt and pepper, and simmer, covered, for 10 minutes or until just tender. Taste and correct the seasoning. Serve hot.

VARIATION Core, seed, and finely slice a large red bell pepper and add it to the skillet in Step 2. Continue with the recipe.

Sauté of Brussels Sprouts with Bacon, Pine Nuts, and Sour Cream

Brussels sprouts can be prepared in the simplest of ways, but they must never be either undercooked or overcooked. The secret is to blanch them first before baking or sautéing to remove that cabbage taste. Here I team them with diced smoked bacon, but you can use smoked turkey or ham instead. Serve the sprouts as a side dish to a pork roast or pan-seared veal chops.

SERVES 4

3 tablespoons olive oil

$\frac{1}{2}$ cup slab bacon cut into $\frac{1}{4}$-inch dice and blanched

3 tablespoons pine nuts

2 pints Brussels sprouts (1$\frac{1}{2}$ pounds), trimmed and cut into $\frac{1}{4}$-inch slices

$\frac{3}{4}$ cup chicken stock or bouillon

Salt and freshly ground black pepper

$\frac{1}{2}$ cup sour cream, optional

1 large garlic clove, mashed

1. Heat the olive oil in a cast-iron skillet over medium-low heat, add the bacon and pine nuts, and sauté until lightly browned. Add the sprouts together with $\frac{1}{2}$ cup of the stock, season with salt and pepper and simmer, partially covered, for 6 to 8 minutes or until the sprouts are crisp-tender. Add the remaining $\frac{1}{4}$ cup stock if necessary to cook the sprouts.

2. Fold in the sour cream and the garlic, and cook until reduced to a glaze. Taste and correct the seasoning and serve hot.

Braised Red Cabbage with Orange Zest and Grenadine

Everyone has favorite holiday dishes and this is one of mine—although I am not quite sure which holiday I mean, since I try to make this dish as soon as the cool weather sets in and am still serving it by Memorial Day. Red cabbage braised with wine, grenadine liqueur, and plenty of orange zest develops a mellow sweet flavor that is a lovely accompaniment to roasted duck, pork, and venison.

SERVES 6

2 tablespoons butter

3 tablespoons peanut oil

2 medium onions, finely diced

3 tablespoons dark brown sugar

$\frac{1}{2}$ cup sherry vinegar

1 medium red cabbage, finely sliced
   (5 to 7 cups)

Zest of 1 large orange, cut into fine strips

Coarse salt and freshly ground black pepper

2 cups red wine

$\frac{1}{2}$ cup grenadine

1 tablespoon flour

1. Preheat the oven to 350°F.

2. In a large heavy flameproof casserole, heat the butter and 1 tablespoon of the oil. Add the onions and cook over medium heat until soft but not browned. Add the brown sugar and sherry vinegar. Bring to a simmer, reduce the heat, and cook until most of the vinegar has evaporated. Add the cabbage and orange zest. Season with salt and pepper. Add the wine and grenadine. Bring to a boil, reduce the heat, cover, and transfer the casserole to the oven. Braise the cabbage for 1½ to 2 hours, checking it every once in a while to be sure the juices do not run dry.

3. When the cabbage is very tender, remove from the oven and set aside.

4. In a small skillet, heat the remaining 2 tablespoons oil. Add the flour and cook over low heat for 1 or 2 minutes, stirring constantly, until the flour turns a hazelnut brown. Do not let the flour burn. Immediately add the flour mixture to the cabbage and stir well to blend thoroughly. Reheat the cabbage over low heat and correct the seasoning. Serve hot.

REMARKS This cabbage is best when made a day ahead of time. It will keep refrigerated for up to a week.

Skillet-Braised Carrots with Pine Nuts and Raisins

Carrots are one of the vegetables that we tend to take for granted and do not make enough use of. For me, they are a basic pantry vegetable that I reach for whenever I want to make a quick side to a roasted chicken, sautéed chicken breasts, or a stew. You can make the dish hours ahead of time and reheat it right in the skillet just before serving.

SERVES 4 TO 5

8 large carrots, peeled
1½ tablespoons olive oil
3 tablespoons pine nuts
3 tablespoons butter
1 teaspoon sugar
Salt and freshly ground black pepper
½ to ¾ cup chicken stock or bouillon
⅓ cup blanched raisins
Minced cilantro or flat-leaf parsley

1. Peel the carrots. Cut them in half lengthwise and then crosswise, to make 4 even pieces from each carrot.

2. In a small skillet, heat 1 tablespoon of the olive oil. Add the pine nuts and sauté for 1 minute, or until they are nicely browned. Do not burn. Set aside.

3. In a large heavy skillet, heat the butter and the remaining ½ tablespoon olive oil. Add the carrots, sprinkle with sugar, and season with salt and a large grinding of black pepper. Sauté over medium heat until the carrots are lightly browned. Add the stock, reduce the heat, and simmer, covered, for 8 to 10 minutes, or until just tender. Add the raisins and continue to cook for another 2 to 3 minutes, adding a little stock if necessary.

4. When the carrots are done, transfer to a serving dish and sprinkle with minced cilantro or parsley. Serve hot.

Puree of Celery Root, Potatoes, and Sweet Garlic

This creamy puree that combines the wonderful taste of celery root with potatoes and a touch of sour cream is addictive. Serve the puree as a side to a pork roast, braised lamb, or nice homey stew.

SERVES 6

1 cup low-fat milk

1 large celery root (about 1½ pounds), peeled and cut into 2-inch pieces

8 large garlic cloves, peeled

1 pound Yukon Gold or all-purpose potatoes, peeled and cubed

2 to 3 tablespoons butter

⅓ cup sour cream

Salt and freshly ground black pepper

1. In a large saucepan, bring 2½ quarts salted water to a boil. Add the milk, celery root, and garlic. Bring to a boil, reduce the heat, and cook for 10 minutes, or until the celery root is almost tender.

2. Add the potatoes and continue to cook until they are very tender.

3. Drain the vegetables. Puree with the butter and 2 tablespoons of the sour cream in the food processor until smooth. You may need a little more sour cream. Add salt and pepper to taste.

REMARKS The puree can be made well ahead of time and reheated in the microwave. Leftovers can be refrigerated and will keep well for several days.

Creamy Celery and Stilton Cheese Soup

I first had this delicious soup many years ago in a restaurant in Devon and was surprised to find out that it is an English classic. To many, its taste comes as a surprise because most of us do not associate celery with anything but salads or a raw snack. Here, with the addition of a creamy mild Stilton, celery has a chance to shine. It is best to make the soup a day ahead of time and reheat it just before serving.

SERVES 6

8 ounces Stilton cheese

4 tablespoons unsalted butter

6 large celery stalks, diced (about 3 cups)

1 large onion, minced

2 tablespoons all-purpose flour

6 to 7 cups chicken stock or bouillon

1 medium leek, white part only, cut into fine julienne

1 medium carrot, peeled and cut into fine julienne

1 large celery stalk, cut into fine julienne

1¼ cups heavy cream

Salt and freshly ground white pepper

1. Trim the Stilton cheese of its outer yellow-brown crust and use only the center. You should have about 6 ounces. Crumble the cheese.

2. In a large heavy saucepan, melt the butter over medium heat. Add the diced celery and onion, and cook, partially covered, until the onion is soft but not brown.

3. Add the flour, blend well into the vegetables, and cook for 1 minute. Add the stock all at once, bring to a boil, reduce the heat, and simmer, covered, for 25 minutes, or until the vegetables are very tender. Strain the soup through a colander set over a large bowl, reserving the vegetables and stock separately.

4. Transfer the strained vegetables to a food processor with ½ cup of the stock and process until very smooth. Whisk the pureed vegetables into the bowl containing the remaining stock and return the soup to the pan.

5. Add the julienned vegetables to the soup and simmer for 5 to 8 minutes, or until the vegetables are just tender.

6. In a food processor, combine the cream and Stilton cheese and process until smooth. Add the Stilton mixture to the soup, whisk until well blended, and just heat through. Do not bring the soup back to a boil. Add salt to taste and a large grinding of pepper, and serve hot.

Corn and Chive Fritters with Smoked Salmon Sauce

Corn is an ideal candidate for fritters. You can, of course, use fresh corn in season, but canned corn works just as well. Served with the delicious smoked salmon sauce, the fritters make an elegant appetizer, but I often serve them as an accompaniment to pan-seared scallops, shrimp, and salmon. You can vary the fritters by adding minced jalapeño and minced cilantro instead of chives.

SERVES 8 TO 10

One 11-ounce can corn kernels, drained
(about 1½ cups)

½ cup whole milk

⅓ cup all-purpose flour

⅓ cup yellow cornmeal

½ teaspoon baking powder

2 extra large eggs

2 extra large egg yolks

4 tablespoons unsalted butter, melted

¼ cup minced fresh chives

¾ teaspoon salt or more to taste

Freshly ground black pepper

Corn or peanut oil or clarified butter
(see page 384) for frying

Sprigs of fresh dill and chives

1. Combine the corn and milk in a food processor and process until smooth. Transfer to a large bowl, add the remaining ingredients except for the oil and the dill and chives, and whisk until well blended.

2. Cook the fritters in several batches of 4 to 6 fritters per batch. For each batch, heat 2 teaspoons oil or clarified butter in a large nonstick skillet over medium heat. For each fritter, add 1½ to 2 tablespoons of the batter to the hot oil, without crowding the skillet, and cook for 1 to 2 minutes per side or until lightly browned. Serve warm, garnished with a dollop of smoked salmon sauce and sprigs of dill and chives.

Smoked Salmon Sauce

MAKES ABOUT 1½ CUPS

2 teaspoons finely grated raw onion

1 cup crème fraîche

½ cup mayonnaise

Juice of ½ lemon

3 ounces smoked salmon

Salt and freshly ground white pepper

In a food processor, combine all the ingredients and process until very smooth. Season with salt and pepper.

Spicy Corn and Ginger Relish

Here is a wonderful piquant relish that I make with leftover fresh corn as soon as corn season begins. I usually double and triple the recipe because the relish keeps well refrigerated for 2 to 3 weeks. Serve the relish as a side with all grilled meats, especially a juicy burger or fish or chicken. It also complements a nice summer sandwich of finely sliced leftover flank steak or chicken breast.

SERVES 6

4 ears of fresh corn, cooked

¾ cup rice vinegar

¾ cup sugar

½ cup very finely diced red pepper

3 tablespoons very finely diced red onion

1 tablespoon minced fresh ginger

1 small fresh cayenne or jalapeño pepper, finely diced

⅓ cup grapeseed or peanut oil

Coarse salt and freshly ground black pepper

Small leaves of fresh cilantro or basil

1. Cut off the corn kernels from the cooked cobs and transfer to a bowl.

2. Combine the vinegar and sugar in a small saucepan and simmer until the sugar is dissolved and the mixture reduces to ½ cup and becomes syrupy.

3. Pour the vinegar mixture over the corn kernels. Add the remaining ingredients except the cilantro to the bowl, and let stand at room temperature for 4 to 6 hours before serving. Garnish with cilantro or basil and serve at room temperature as an accompaniment to grilled meats or fish.

Sauté of Cucumbers in Chive and Dill Cream

The large seedless cucumbers make a wonderful hot vegetable that takes minutes to prepare and is the perfect accompaniment to grilled or sautéed chicken breasts and every salmon preparation. I purposely do not peel the cucumbers because the peel contains so much taste and also allows the cucumbers to retain their shape.

SERVES 4

> 2 large seedless cucumbers
> 3 tablespoons unsalted butter
> 1½ teaspoons sugar
> ½ cup chicken stock or bouillon
> Salt and freshly ground white pepper
> ½ cup crème fraîche
> Minced fresh dill and chives

1. Cut the cucumbers lengthwise in half. Scoop out the seeds with a grapefruit spoon and discard. Cut the cucumbers crosswise into ¼-inch slices (half moons).

2. In a large skillet, melt the butter over medium heat. Add the cucumbers and sugar and sauté for 2 minutes, tossing constantly. Add the stock and season with salt and pepper. Bring to a simmer, reduce the heat, and cook, covered, for 5 minutes or until just tender. Remove the cover, raise the heat, and cook until all the moisture has evaporated and the cucumbers are nicely glazed. Stir in the dill and chives and correct the seasoning.

Fricassee of Roasted Eggplants and Two Mushrooms

The first time I had this dish was as part of an antipasti table in northern Italy. The fricassee had been made with local wild mushrooms and the taste was amazing. Even though I cannot duplicate that mushroom taste, I still love to make this dish toward the end of summer and serve it at room temperature, garnished with slivers of Parmesan and a drizzle of truffle oil.

SERVES 5 TO 6

2 medium eggplants, trimmed but not peeled and cut into $^3/_4$-inch cubes

4 to 5 tablespoons olive oil

2 shallots, minced

2 large garlic cloves, minced

$^1/_2$ pound cremini mushrooms, stems removed, caps cubed

Coarse salt and freshly ground black pepper

6 large fresh shiitake mushrooms, stemmed

3 to 4 tablespoons minced fresh parsley, preferably flat-leaf

1. Preheat the oven to 400°F.

2. Place the eggplant cubes in a single layer on a nonstick baking sheet. Drizzle with 1½ tablespoons of the olive oil and set the sheet in the center of the oven. Roast for 20 minutes or until tender and lightly browned.

3. Meanwhile, heat 2 tablespoons of the oil in a large heavy skillet. Add the shallots and half the garlic together with the cremini mushrooms. Season with salt and pepper and sauté over medium-high heat until the mushrooms are soft and lightly browned. Set aside.

4. When the eggplant is done, remove from the oven, transfer to a dish, and season with salt and pepper. Add the shiitakes to the baking sheet, drizzle with the remaining 1 tablespoon oil, season with salt and pepper, and roast for 10 to 15 minutes or until tender and lightly browned.

5. When the shiitakes are done, remove from the oven and quarter. Add the shiitakes together with the eggplant to the pan containing the cremini mushrooms. Add the remaining garlic and the parsley and cook the fricassee for 2 or 3 minutes, or until just reheated. Correct the seasoning and serve hot or at room temperature.

Charcoal-Grilled Eggplants with Lemon-Scallion Mayonnaise

Here is a variation of baba ghanoush, a popular Lebanese appetizer that is traditionally made by combining the flesh of smoked grilled eggplant with tahini, a Middle Eastern sesame paste, and garlic and plenty of lemon juice. This lighter and simpler version makes a delicious accompaniment to grilled shish kebabs, lamb chops, and marinated flank steak. It is best served slightly warm or at room temperature.

SERVES 4

2 medium eggplants

Juice of ½ lemon or more to taste

½ to ¾ cup mayonnaise

1 large garlic clove, mashed

¼ cup minced scallions

Salt and freshly ground black pepper

Small black oil-cured olives and ripe cherry or
    grape tomatoes, halved

1. Prepare a charcoal grill.

2. When the coals are very hot, place the eggplants directly on the coals and grill until the skin is charred all over and the eggplants are quite tender.

3. Carefully transfer the eggplants to a cutting surface and, with a sharp knife, cut in half lengthwise. Scoop out the pulp, cut into cubes, and place the pulp in a shallow serving dish. Add the lemon juice, mayonnaise, garlic, and scallions, season with salt and pepper, and mix well. Taste and correct the seasoning, adding more lemon juice if necessary, and serve garnished with the olives and tomatoes.

Skillet-Braised Belgian Endives

Most people consider endives a green rather than a vegetable to be added to a salad. In fact, Belgian endives are delicious served hot, either skillet braised or roasted. Since they are available year-round and keep well in the fridge for a week or more, I consider them a basic that I reach for when I am looking for a flavorful and quick vegetable side dish. Serve the endives with pan-seared veal chops, roasted chicken, or sautéed salmon fillets.

SERVES 4 TO 6

3 tablespoons butter
2 tablespoons peanut oil
6 to 8 Belgian endives, cut in half
Salt and freshly ground black pepper
2 teaspoons sugar
½ to ¾ cup chicken or beef stock or bouillon
Minced flat-leaf parsley, optional

1. Heat the butter and oil in a large cast-iron skillet over medium heat. Add the endives, season with salt, pepper, and sugar, and cook until nicely browned. Add the stock and braise, covered, until tender and caramelized, 10 to 15 minutes.

2. Transfer the endives to a serving dish, garnish with the parsley, and serve at room temperature.

Ragout of Fennel, Tomatoes, and Potatoes

Fennel is fast becoming a staple on the fresh produce scene, and its affinity for fish preparations makes it one of my favorite vegetables. Gently braised in olive oil with potatoes and tomatoes, it is the perfect accompaniment to sautéed scallops, pan-seared bass or snapper, or oven-roasted mahi mahi. This vegetable ragout can be made up to a day ahead of time and reheated on top of the stove.

SERVES 4

1 large fennel bulb, trimmed

3 tablespoons olive oil

2 large garlic cloves, finely sliced

Coarse salt and freshly ground black pepper

½ teaspoon fennel seeds

2 ripe tomatoes, cubed

2 medium red potatoes, peeled and cubed

1 cup chicken stock or bouillon or water

2 tablespoons minced fennel tops

Freshly grated Parmesan, optional

1 tablespoon fruity extra virgin olive oil

1. Quarter the fennel bulb and cut crosswise into ¼-inch slices.

2. In a large heavy skillet, heat the olive oil. Add the fennel and garlic and sauté for 2 or 3 minutes or until lightly brown. Season with salt and pepper. Add the fennel seeds and tomatoes and bring to a simmer. Cook for 2 or 3 minutes, or until the tomatoes have released most of their juices.

3. Add the potatoes and stock and lower the heat. Cover the skillet and simmer the mixture until the potatoes are very tender, 20 to 30 minutes. Uncover, taste and correct the seasoning. If the ragout is still a little soupy, simmer, uncovered, for a few minutes.

4. Transfer the ragout to a serving dish, garnish with the fennel tops and Parmesan, and drizzle with the oil.

Sauté of Green Beans with Tuna, Tomatoes, and Red Onion

Here is a typical Niçoise appetizer that you can find in simple restaurants all over the South of France. Its flavorful simplicity is based on the freshness of the beans and the ripeness of the tomatoes.

SERVES 4

> 1 pound green beans, trimmed
>
> 3 tablespoons extra virgin olive oil
>
> 1 medium red onion, quartered and finely sliced
>
> 2 large garlic cloves, minced
>
> 6 ripe plum tomatoes, quartered
>
> Salt and freshly ground black pepper
>
> One 6-ounce can light oil-packed tuna, drained and flaked
>
> 2 to 3 tablespoons fresh basil, cut into fine julienne
>
> Pitted small black oil-cured olives, cut in half, optional

1. In a large pot of boiling salted water, cook the green beans until tender, 5 to 7 minutes. Drain and rinse under cold running water; drain well. Cut the beans into 1½-inch lengths.

2. In a large heavy skillet, heat the olive oil over medium heat, add the onion and garlic, and cook until soft but not browned, about 10 minutes. Add the tomatoes, season with salt and pepper, and cook until most of the tomato juices have evaporated, stirring often. The tomatoes should still retain their shape.

3. Add the green beans and tuna and just heat through. Fold in the basil and correct the seasoning. Garnish with the olives and serve hot, directly from the skillet, or at room temperature.

REMARKS You may also omit the tuna and serve this as a vegetable side dish.

Kale, Potato, and Butternut Squash Chowder

Kale is a gutsy winter green that is wonderful in soups. Here it is teamed with potatoes, winter squash, and plenty of garlic. Diced chorizo or other smoked sausage adds character. I like to serve this soup for a Sunday lunch or simple supper, accompanied by crusty bread and good sweet butter.

SERVES 5 TO 6

3 tablespoons olive oil

5 large garlic cloves, minced

1 pound kale, stemmed, washed, dried, and torn into 1½-inch pieces

2 tablespoons unsalted butter

1 large onion, minced

Salt and freshly ground black pepper

2 cups butternut squash, cut into ¾-inch cubes

7 to 8 cups chicken stock or bouillon

3 medium all-purpose potatoes, peeled and cut into ¾-inch cubes

½ cup heavy cream, optional

2 cups diced smoked turkey sausage, or 1 cup diced chorizo

1. In a 4-quart saucepan, heat the olive oil over medium heat. Add the garlic and sauté until soft but not browned. Add the kale, tossing with the oil and garlic until just wilted. Remove the mixture from the pan and set aside.

2. Melt the butter in the pan, add the onion, and cook until soft but not brown. Return the kale-garlic mixture to the casserole and season with salt and pepper. Add the butternut squash, stock, and potatoes. Bring to a boil, reduce the heat, and simmer, covered, for 25 to 30 minutes, or until the vegetables are tender.

3. Add the cream and the sausage and bring to a simmer. Taste and correct the seasoning. Serve the soup hot.

Braised Leeks with Shiitake Mushrooms and Crème Fraîche

Tender buttery braised leeks are one of my favorite side dishes to all kinds of fish preparations, whether pan-seared or oven-roasted. The shiitakes add an interesting texture and flavor to this simple and flavorful vegetable dish. If you cannot get shiitakes, you can use cremini mushrooms instead, and for a variation add a sprinkling of dill or fresh tarragon. Serve as a side dish to a pan-seared fillet of salmon, grilled veal chops, or chicken breasts.

SERVES 4

4 medium leeks, all but 2 inches of green
parts removed

4 tablespoons (½ stick) butter

2 teaspoons olive oil

½ pound shiitake mushrooms, stems
removed, caps finely sliced

⅓ to ½ cup chicken stock or bouillon

Salt and freshly ground black pepper

2 tablespoons crème fraîche or heavy cream

2 tablespoons minced chives or flat-leaf
parsley

1. Cut the leeks in half lengthwise and then crosswise into ¼-inch slices. Rinse thoroughly under warm water to remove all grit.

2. In a large heavy skillet, heat half the butter and the olive oil. Add the mushrooms and sauté until nicely browned. Remove with a slotted spoon to a dish.

3. Add the remaining butter to the pan. When it's hot, add the leeks and ⅓ cup stock. Season with salt and pepper. Cover the skillet and simmer for 4 to 5 minutes or until the leeks are just tender.

4. Add the mushrooms and crème fraîche or heavy cream. Simmer, uncovered, for 2 or three minutes. You may need to add a little more stock. Correct the seasoning. Add the chives or parsley and serve hot.

Portobello Mushrooms in Tarragon-Lime Butter

Until recently, I never thought of portobello mushrooms as being particularly interesting and found them rather leathery tasting, especially when grilled. Once I started slow-roasting them, I began to enjoy cooking them, especially in this simple preparation, which I serve as an appetizer or as a side dish to pan-seared salmon fillets or chicken breasts.

SERVES 6

8 tablespoons (1 stick) butter, softened
Juice of 1 lime
2 tablespoons minced fresh tarragon
Coarse salt and freshly ground black pepper
6 medium portobello mushrooms
2 tablespoons olive oil

1. Preheat the oven to 300°F. In a small bowl, combine 6 tablespoons of the butter with the lime juice and tarragon. Season the butter with salt and pepper and blend thoroughly.

2. Butter a large baking sheet with the remaining 2 tablespoons butter. Season the mushrooms with salt and pepper and drizzle with the olive oil. Place the mushrooms on the baking sheet and cover with foil. Roast the mushrooms for 25 minutes.

3. Remove the mushrooms from the oven. Top with bits of the tarragon butter and return the pan to the oven, uncovered. Roast for another 2 to 3 minutes or until the herb butter is just melted. Transfer the mushrooms to a serving platter and drizzle with the buttery pan juices. Serve hot.

Wild Mushroom, Scallion, and Gruyère Bread Pudding

I love all kinds of mushrooms, and now that you can get several types all year, it is fun to experiment with them. Here I use both porcini and cremini in a savory bread pudding that makes a delicious and elegant accompaniment to a roasted turkey, chicken, or pork. The pudding can be made a day ahead of time and reheated in a low oven.

SERVES 6 TO 8

3½ tablespoons butter

½ pound cremini mushrooms, finely diced

1½ cups finely sliced scallions, green tops included

Coarse salt and freshly ground black pepper

8 slices day-old Tuscan or other day-old peasant bread, sliced

4 cups milk

4 whole eggs

Pinch of cayenne

½ cups grated Gruyère cheese

1. Preheat the oven to 375°F.

2. In a large skillet, heat 3 tablespoons of the butter. Add the mushrooms and sauté until soft. Add the scallions, season with salt and pepper, and continue to cook until the scallions are just wilted.

3. Place the bread in a large bowl. Add the milk and soak the bread for a few minutes, pushing it down to submerge it. Remove the bread from the milk, squeezing it lightly to remove most of the milk, and tear the bread into bite-sized pieces and set aside.

4. Add the eggs to the milk. Season with salt, pepper, and cayenne and whisk the mixture until it is well blended.

5. Butter a 9 by 12-inch baking dish. Scatter half the bread on the bottom of the dish and top with the mushroom-scallion mixture, sprinkle with half the cheese, and top with the remaining bread. Add the egg mixture and the remaining cheese.

6. Place the dish in a larger baking dish. Pour enough hot water into the larger dish to come halfway up the sides of the smaller dish. Bake the pudding for 35 to 40 minutes or until a knife inserted in the center comes out clean. Serve hot or warm, directly out of the baking dish.

REMARKS If the bread is thoroughly dry, you may cube it prior to soaking it in the milk. A nice airy bread such as Tuscan bread is ideal for this recipe. Do not use a sourdough bread.

Bruschetta of Roasted Sweet Onions

When Vidalia onions are slow-roasted it brings out their wonderful sweet flavor. I usually do a batch whenever I plan to spend some time in the kitchen and the oven is available. You can store the onions for days and use them in many ways. I like to add a couple of spoonfuls to mashed potatoes or to the pan juices of a roasted chicken or turkey. They also make a wonderful topping for pan-seared salmon or swordfish steaks, or they can be used as part of an antipasti table. Place the onions in a jar, cover with a thin layer of olive oil, and refrigerate until ready to use.

SERVES 4 TO 8

4 to 5 large Vidalia or other sweet onions
5 tablespoons fruity olive oil
Coarse salt and freshly ground black pepper
2 to 3 large garlic cloves, quartered
8 slices day-old peasant bread
8 pitted Kalamata olives, diced
Coarsely chopped basil or flat-leaf parsley
8 flat fillets of anchovies, optional

1. Preheat the oven to 325°F. Slice the onions crosswise into ¼-inch slices. Place in a single layer on a large cookie sheet. Drizzle with the olive oil. Season with salt and pepper and roast the onions for 2 hours or until they are lightly browned and very soft. Turn with a spatula two to three times during baking.

2. When the onions are done, transfer them to a colander set over a bowl and let the oil drain out of them for 30 minutes.

3. Turn the oven to broil.

4. Mash the garlic in a garlic press and rub a little into each bread slice. Drizzle each slice with a little of the onion oil.

5. Place the bread on a cookie sheet and broil until nicely browned. Watch the bread carefully so it does not burn.

6. Remove the bruschetta to a serving platter. Top each slice with some of the onions, sprinkle with olives, basil, or parsley, and top each slice with an anchovy fillet.

Roasted Vidalia Onions with Garlic and Rosemary

The season for Vidalia onions is becoming longer and longer, so I am now looking for interesting ways to use them. You can roast them with a variety of herbs, especially fresh oregano, marjoram, or, as here, rosemary. I usually double and triple the recipe, since the onions keep for several days and I like to serve them with practically everything, but especially with grilled meats and fish.

SERVES 4 TO 5

4 large Vidalia onions, cut into thick rounds

½ cup olive oil

2 teaspoons sugar

2 tablespoons minced rosemary

Coarse salt and freshly ground black pepper

1 large garlic clove, minced

¼ cup minced flat-leaf parsley

1 tablespoon balsamic vinegar, or more
  to taste

1. Preheat oven to 325°F.

2. In a large baking pan, combine the onions with the olive oil and toss gently. Spread the onions evenly in the pan and sprinkle with the sugar, rosemary, salt, and pepper. Add ½ cup water to the pan and set in the center of the oven. Bake for 3 hours, turning the onions once or twice to make sure they are roasting evenly.

3. When the onions are very tender, remove from the oven and transfer to a serving dish. Sprinkle with the garlic, parsley, and vinegar and toss gently. Taste and correct the seasoning, adding a little more vinegar to taste.

Sugar Snap Pea Soup

At the first sign of spring, heaps of fresh peas would appear at every market in Barcelona, and shelling peas at the kitchen table was part of my daily chores when I was growing up. It was well worth it because these jewels of the spring were used in many of my favorite dishes. I loved them simply cooked with bits of diced ham or in my mother's intensely flavored, superb pea soup.

Unfortunately, fresh peas are not easy to come by in this country, so I decided to try making the soup with sugar snaps, with the most delicious results. Be sure to make the soup a day ahead to allow it to develop full flavor, and whisk in some fresh butter just before serving.

SERVES 6

3 tablespoons butter

1 large bunch of scallions, diced (all but 2 inches of greens removed)

2 tablespoons flour

1½ pounds sugar snap peas

3 large sprigs of mint

8 cups chicken stock or bouillon

Salt and freshly ground black pepper

½ cup heavy cream or crème fraîche

2 tablespoons minced mint

1. In a large heavy saucepan, heat the butter. Add the scallions and 2 tablespoons water. Cook the scallions until very soft.

2. Add the flour and, with a wooden spoon, blend it thoroughly into the mixture. Add the sugar snaps, sprigs of mint, and chicken stock. Season with salt and a large grinding of black pepper. Bring to a boil, reduce the heat, and simmer until the sugar snaps are very tender.

3. Discard the mint and transfer the soup to a food processor. Puree until smooth and return to the saucepan. Add the cream or crème fraîche. Taste and correct the seasoning. Serve the soup either warm or at room temperature, garnished with a sprinkling of mint.

Curried Bell Pepper and Zucchini Ragout

I love curried vegetable stews, especially in the summer, when the green peppers are thin skinned and the zucchini is young and flavorful. Serve this delicious ragout either hot or at room temperature. You can vary it by adding ¼ cup blanched raisins to it and/or 2 to 3 tablespoons sautéed pine nuts.

SERVES 5 TO 6

¼ cup fruity olive oil

2 or 3 small zucchini, cut into ¾-inch cubes

Salt and freshly ground black pepper

2 large garlic cloves, mashed

1 tablespoon minced jalapeño pepper

2 teaspoons curry powder

2 medium onions, sliced

2 large green bell peppers, quartered, seeded, and finely sliced

2 red bell peppers, seeded, quartered, and finely sliced

4 plum tomatoes, diced, or 1 can Italian plum tomatoes, thoroughly drained and chopped

½ cup chicken stock or water, optional

Small cilantro leaves

1. In a large heavy skillet, heat 2 tablespoons of the olive oil. Add the zucchini and sauté until nicely browned. Season with salt and pepper. Remove with a slotted spoon to a side dish.

2. Add a little more oil to the skillet. Add the garlic, jalapeño, and curry. Cook for a minute, stirring constantly. Do not let the curry burn.

3. Add the onions and bell peppers and cook over low heat for 15 minutes, or until the mixture is soft and lightly browned. You may need a little more oil.

4. Add the tomatoes. Bring the mixture to a simmer and cook until the tomato liquid is mostly evaporated.

5. Return the zucchini to the pan and simmer for another 5 minutes. Correct the seasoning. Add the stock or water if more liquid is desired. Serve the ragout hot or at room temperature, garnished with the cilantro.

Mascarpone and Chive Mashed Potatoes

The good news is that mashed potatoes, that wonderful homey dish, is back in vogue. Not only can you make them at home but you can also now sample a variety of interpretations in many restaurants on both sides of the Atlantic. The bad news is that mashed potatoes taste good only when enriched with butter, sour cream, or mascarpone, and the more the better. Is it worth it? To me it is. Serve this version with just about any main course in this book. Also remember to double the recipe and have leftovers. The potatoes heat up beautifully in a low oven or the microwave.

SERVES 4

> 5 medium Yukon gold (about 1½ pounds),
>   peeled and cut into eighths
>
> Salt
>
> 4 tablespoons unsalted butter
>
> 2 tablespoons sour cream
>
> ¼ cup mascarpone
>
> 2 to 3 tablespoons minced chives
>
> Freshly ground black pepper

1. Drop the potatoes into salted boiling water and cook until tender. Drain, pass through a food mill, and transfer to the top of a double boiler.

2. Add the remaining ingredients and mix well. Season with salt and pepper and serve hot.

Gratin of Russet Potatoes and Sweet Onions

You really can't beat the marriage of flavors of these two simple vegetables. They work together in many combinations, from an onion and potato soup to a zesty potato and onion salad. Here they take almost equal billing. Serve the gratin as a side dish to roast beef, grilled flank steak, or roasted leg of lamb.

SERVES 4 TO 6

4 tablespoons butter

2 to 3 tablespoons corn or peanut oil

2 large Spanish onions, quartered and finely sliced

Salt and freshly ground black pepper

4 large Russet potatoes, peeled and finely sliced

2 tablespoons finely minced fresh thyme, or 1 teaspoon dried thyme

1½ cups chicken stock or bouillon

2 tablespoons freshly grated Parmesan or Gruyère cheese

1. Preheat the oven to 350°F. In a large skillet, heat half the butter and the oil. Add the onions, season with salt and pepper, and cook over medium-high heat until lightly browned, 5 to 7 minutes. Lower the heat and continue cooking the onions for 40 minutes, stirring several times, until they are very soft and nicely browned. Do not let the onions burn; add more oil if needed.

2. Place a layer of potatoes, slightly overlapping, in a well-buttered baking dish and season with salt and pepper. Top with a layer of onions and some of the thyme. Make another layer of potatoes, onions, and thyme, finishing with a layer of potatoes. Season again with salt and pepper.

3. Add the stock. Cover the dish and place in the center of the oven. Bake for 50 to 60 minutes, or until the potatoes are tender and all the stock has been absorbed.

4. Sprinkle the cheese evenly over the potatoes and bake, uncovered, for another 10 minutes, or until the cheese is melted and browned. Serve directly out of the baking dish.

REMARKS The gratin can be made a day ahead of time and re-heated. Leftovers are delicious when reheated either in the oven or in the microwave. For a variation, use a mixture of fresh herbs such as thyme, rosemary, and parsley. For best results, cut the potatoes on a mandoline (see page 11). Not only will the potatoes cook more evenly, but the gratin will look much more attractive.

New Potato Salad in Mustard, Shallot, and Caper Vinaigrette

I love a good potato salad, but for years I rarely made it because I could not find the right potatoes. Now that fingerling potatoes are widely available, this zesty salad is tops on my list. Serve it often as an accompaniment to grilled or sautéed sausages or grilled chicken.

SERVES 5 TO 6

1½ pounds new potatoes, preferably Yukon
  Gold or fingerlings

1½ tablespoons sherry vinegar

6 tablespoons peanut or olive oil

1 tablespoon Dijon mustard

1 large garlic clove, mashed

Salt and freshly ground black pepper

1 large shallot, minced (about ¼ cup)

1 dill gherkin, finely diced

½ cup finely diced green or red bell pepper or
  a mixture of both

2 tablespoons tiny capers

1 to 2 tablespoons sour cream or mayonnaise,
  optional

1. In a large saucepan, combine the potatoes with water to cover. Cook for 20 minutes over medium heat until the potatoes are just tender. Do not overcook. Drain and cool completely. Peel, slice, and place in a large bowl.

2. In a small bowl, combine the vinegar, oil, mustard, and garlic; whisk the dressing until well blended. Season with salt and pepper and pour over the potatoes.

3. Add the shallot, gherkin, bell pepper, and capers to the bowl; toss the salad gently with a wooden spoon so as not to break the potatoes. Taste and correct the seasoning. Add the sour cream or mayonnaise if you like a creamier salad, and chill the salad for at least 2 to 4 hours or overnight. Bring the potato salad back to room temperature before serving.

Puree of Sweet Potatoes and Carrots

Sweet potatoes and carrots have a marvelous affinity for one another. Come fall, this puree becomes one my favorite sides. It makes the perfect accompaniment to a roasted turkey, pan-seared duck breasts, or a ragout of pork. For a variation, I often add grated ginger or season the puree with toasted cumin seeds and minced cilantro.

SERVES 6

> 3 large sweet potatoes (about 2 pounds),
>   peeled and cut into 1-inch pieces
>
> 3 to 4 large carrots (about 1¼ pounds), peeled
>   and cut into 1-inch pieces
>
> 3 tablespoons sour cream
>
> 2 to 4 tablespoons unsalted butter
>
> 2 tablespoons dark brown sugar
>
> Salt and freshly ground black pepper

1. Combine the potatoes and carrots in a large saucepan with plenty of salted water to cover, and simmer until very tender.

2. Drain well and transfer to a food processor together with the sour cream, butter, and brown sugar; combine. Season with salt and pepper. Serve hot.

REMARKS You may keep the puree warm, covered, in a double boiler until serving.

Puree of Rutabaga and Potato with Crispy Shallots

Rutabaga is not a vegetable one likes at first taste, but when teamed with potatoes, sour cream, and butter in a delicious puree, it is a winner. The crispy fried shallots add texture to the puree, but they are not a must. You can also use small white onions cut into thick rounds instead of shallots. The puree can be made a day or two ahead of time and reheated either in the microwave or in a double boiler. Serve as an accompaniment to grilled, sautéed, or roasted meats and duck.

SERVES 6

> 2 medium rutabagas (about 3 pounds), peeled and cut into 2-inch pieces
>
> 1 medium all-purpose potato, peeled and cut into 1½-inch pieces
>
> 4 tablespoons unsalted butter
>
> 3 tablespoons sour cream
>
> Salt and freshly ground white pepper
>
> 1½ tablespoons peanut oil
>
> 3 large shallots, finely sliced

1. Preheat the oven to 200°F.

2. In a large saucepan, bring plenty of salted water to a boil, add the rutabagas and potato, and cook until very tender.

3. Drain the vegetables and transfer to a food processor. Add 3 tablespoons of the butter and the sour cream; season with salt and pepper and process until smooth. Transfer to an ovenproof dish, cover, and set in the center of the oven to keep warm.

4. In a heavy medium skillet, melt the remaining 1 tablespoon butter together with the oil over medium-high heat; add the shallots and sauté until they are nicely browned and crisp-tender, 4 to 5 minutes. Fold the shallots into the vegetable puree and correct the seasoning. Serve hot.

Shallot and Cassis Marmalade

I first had a taste of this delicious "marmalade" in the city of Tours in the Loire region, known for its superb goat cheeses. It was served as an accompaniment to warm goat cheese toasts and a simple salad. I like to serve the jam this way, but it also goes well with grilled salmon fillets, pan-seared tenderloin steaks, and sautéed calves liver. Caramelized shallots can be made in quantity and stored in a jar; they will keep for weeks. Sliced small pearl onions can be prepared in the same manner, but the subtle, more delicate taste of the shallot produces more interesting results.

SERVES 6

6 tablespoons unsalted butter
2 pounds shallots, finely sliced
$\frac{1}{4}$ cup sugar
3 cups dry red wine
$\frac{1}{4}$ cup cassis
$1\frac{1}{2}$ tablespoons sherry vinegar
Salt and freshly ground black pepper

1. In a large cast-iron skillet, melt the butter over medium heat. Add the shallots and sugar and cook until the sugar has melted and the shallots begin to brown.

2. Reduce the heat, add the red wine, cassis, and vinegar, and cook for 25 to 30 minutes, or until all the liquid has evaporated and shallots are soft and nicely caramelized. Season with salt and pepper, and serve as an accompaniment to grilled or pan-seared fish.

REMARKS You may add $\frac{1}{3}$ cup plumped currants and $\frac{1}{4}$ cup pine nuts, sautéed in a little olive oil, to the marmalade for a more unusual taste and texture.

Sauté of Spinach with Scallions, Dill, and Yogurt

Sautéed vegetables are often served as appetizers in Spain, and sautéed spinach is an especially popular starter in Catalonia. I like serving it this way, particularly in the spring, when spinach is at its best. If possible, use the curly variety, which is far more flavorful than the flat-leaf type of spinach. Serve as a side dish to pan-seared lamb chops, pork chops, or grilled or sautéed shrimp.

SERVES 6 TO 8

1 cup plain yogurt

2 bags (10 ounces each) spinach, stemmed and washed

2 tablespoons butter

1 tablespoons virgin olive oil

3 scallions (white and 2 inches of green), chopped

1 large garlic clove, crushed

Salt and freshly ground black pepper

4 tablespoons minced fresh dill

2 to 3 tablespoons finely diced feta cheese, optional

1. Place the yogurt in a fine sieve placed over a bowl and drain for 1 to 2 hours or overnight.

2. In a large saucepan, bring salted water to a boil. Add the spinach and cook for 2 minutes. Drain and run under cold water to stop the cooking.

3. In a large nonstick skillet, heat the butter and olive oil. Add the scallions and garlic and cook for 1 to 2 minutes, or until soft but not browned. Immediately add the spinach. Season with salt and pepper and cook for 2 to 3 minutes. Add the dill and yogurt and stir with a wooden spoon to thoroughly blend the mixture. Taste and correct the seasoning, adding a large grinding of black pepper. Add the feta and transfer the spinach to a serving bowl. Serve.

REMARKS If you can get imported Greek sheep's milk yogurt, be sure to use it, since it adds a special tart taste to the spinach and is especially good with feta. If you do use feta, season the spinach carefully, since feta is usually quite salty. Also, if you have the choice, use the French rather than the Greek or Bulgarian feta.

Acorn Squash, Apple, and Wild Mushroom Soup

Soups should be seasonal, and acorn squash, apple, and mushroom soup is just that. It spells fall, crisp cool weather, and an appetite for something hearty and full flavored. I like to serve this soup at Thanksgiving, but you don't need a holiday to enjoy it. Serve with crusty bread and some sweet butter.

SERVES 4 TO 5

2 medium acorn squash (about 1 pound each)

5 tablespoons unsalted butter

2 Golden Delicious apples, peeled, cored, and cubed

1 teaspoon granulated sugar

1 large onion, minced

2 tablespoons dark brown sugar

$\frac{1}{2}$ teaspoon ground ginger

$\frac{1}{4}$ teaspoon ground coriander

$\frac{1}{4}$ teaspoon ground cardamom

Large pinch of freshly grated nutmeg

8 to 9 cups chicken stock or bouillon

$\frac{1}{3}$ cup heavy cream, optional

$\frac{1}{4}$ pound fresh chanterelle or shiitake mushrooms, stemmed and cut into $\frac{1}{4}$-inch slices (if using shiitakes, discard the stems)

Salt and freshly ground white pepper

1. Preheat the oven to 400°F.

2. Place the acorn squash in the center of the oven and bake for 45 to 60 minutes, or until very tender when pierced with the tip of a sharp knife.

3. Remove the squash from the oven, peel, and remove the seeds. Dice the pulp coarsely and set aside.

4. In a large cast-iron skillet, melt 2 tablespoons of the butter over medium-high heat. Add the apples and sauté until lightly browned. Add the granulated sugar and continue to sauté until the apple slices are caramelized and very well browned. Remove from the heat and reserve.

5. In a 3½- or 4-quart saucepan, melt 2 tablespoons of the butter over low heat. Add the onion and cook until soft and lightly browned. Add the brown sugar and spices and continue to sauté for 2 minutes without letting the sugar burn.

6. Immediately add the acorn squash and stock. Bring to a boil, reduce the heat, and simmer the soup, partially covered, for 20 minutes. Add the apples and continue to simmer for another 15 minutes. Cool the soup slightly and then puree in batches in the food processor. Return the soup to the casserole and stir in the cream.

7. In a small heavy skillet, heat the remaining 1 tablespoon butter over medium-high heat. Add the mushrooms and sauté quickly for 1 to 2 minutes, or until the mushrooms are lightly browned. Season with salt and pepper. Add the mushrooms to the soup, and correct the seasoning. If the soup is too thick, thin it out with additional stock. Serve hot.

Wild Mushroom and Parmesan Timbales

Here is a lovely mushroom flan that can be served either as an appetizer or as a side to roasted chicken, veal chops, or a pan-seared steak. Instead of using ramekins, you can make the dish in a loaf pan and serve it sliced at room temperature over a bed of well-seasoned spinach greens.

SERVES 6 TO 8

4 tablespoons butter

1 large shallot, minced

4 garlic cloves, minced

1½ pounds cremini mushrooms, stems removed, caps minced

Salt and freshly ground black pepper

¼ cup minced flat-leaf parsley

2 tablespoons minced fresh thyme, optional

3 extra large egg yolks

1 cup heavy cream

½ cup finely grated Parmesan cheese

1. Preheat the oven to 375°F. Butter 6 to 8 ramekins.

2. In a large heavy skillet, heat the butter, add the shallot and garlic, and cook for 1 minute without browning. Add the mushrooms and continue to cook until the mushrooms are soft and all of their water has evaporated. Season with salt and pepper and add the parsley and thyme. Taste and correct the seasoning.

3. In a bowl, combine the egg yolks, cream, and Parmesan. Whisk thoroughly and season with a pinch of salt and pepper.

4. Add the mushroom mixture and blend well. Taste and correct the seasoning.

5. Spoon the mushroom custard into the prepared ramekins and place in a baking dish. Add enough hot water to reach halfway up the sides of the ramekins and place the dish in the oven. Bake for 25 to 35 minutes, or until the timbales are set and the tip of a knife inserted in the middle of the custard comes out clean.

6. Remove the ramekins from the baking dish and set aside for 5 minutes. Run a knife around each one and unmold onto a serving platter or individual serving plates. Serve hot.

■ **Pan-Seared Arctic Char with Lemon-Chive Essence** ■ **Brook Trout en Papillote with Asparagus, Snow Peas, and Dill Butter** ■ **Stir-Fry of Calamari, Red Peppers, and Lemon** ■ **Fillets of Lemon Sole in a Lime, Jalapeno, and Caper Butter** ■ **Oven-Roasted Mackerel with Caper, Lemon, and Anchovy Butter** ■ **Steamed Mussels in Basil-Garlic Cream** ■ **Pan-Seared Red Snapper Fillets with Sweet and Spicy Asian Syrup** ■ **Pan-Seared Skate with Red Onion, Tomato Jam, and Brown Caper Butter** ■ **Roasted Sea Bass with a Fricassee of Fennel and Potatoes** ■ **Sauté of Swordfish with Shrimp, Snow Peas, and Three Bell Peppers** ■ **Sautéed Scallops with Red Bell Pepper and Chili Sauce** ■ **Spicy Shrimp and Ginger Fritters with a Ginger-Tamari Dipping Sauce** ■ **Fillets of Salmon in Teriyaki Marinade with Gingered Carrots** ■ **Tuna Tartare**

No matter where I find myself shopping for seafood—in one of Barcelona's many fish markets, at the port in Nice, along the varied displays in New York's Chinatown, or even at my local seafood market—I find the amazing diversity of fish is one of the most exhilarating food experiences I know. And given the exceptional importance of freshness in relation to the seafood, it is also one of the most challenging.

I admit that buying top-quality fish is difficult for many shoppers. The distribution system is not ideal, and the flavor of farm-raised fish is a far cry from that of the wild species. But in spite of the fact that most Americans live far from an ocean and have to rely on local supermarkets for their fish, the consumption of seafood is growing.

The questions I am most often asked are "Where can I get good fish?" and "How can I tell when fish is fresh?" Buying fresh fish is not as simple as buying good beef or chicken, even for someone like me living in New York City, which has a fair share of good seafood markets and a bustling, lively Chinatown. The challenge becomes more difficult the farther you get from the ocean. Often in cities where I conduct workshops, the smell of ammonia and spoiled seafood hits me the moment I walk into the store. The fish look dead, with opaque flesh and dull skin. These are times when I want to change my menu to chicken or pasta. How frustrating not to have the choice of good fish and to have to make do with inferior quality.

The good news is that supermarkets around the country are rising to the challenge. I am often pleasantly surprised by fish counters that display lively-looking shrimp, fresh clams, and excellent salmon, laid out on beds of ice. I have found such a supermarket quite a long distance from my house, where the fish counter looks clean and inviting. Here the turnover is terrific, and I am always certain to find an excellent assortment of fish. As I approach the counter, I can almost smell the sea, with fish that look alive, sporting beautifully translucent flesh and shiny silvery skins.

It is at this kind of supermarket that you should try to build a relationship with the fishmonger, letting him or her know that you care about the quality of the fish you buy. Never ask the question "Is this fish fresh?" but rather, "What do you recommend today?" or "When did the scallops come in?"

I have learned to be spontaneous and try never to go with a specific recipe in mind. Instead, I choose the freshest-looking fish with the knowledge that cooking it is the easiest part of the meal. On days that the selection is particularly good, my creative juices start to flow, and I end up with way too much fish.

There is nothing better than finding yourself in a small coastal seafood market when the dayboats come in with fresh scallops or a beautiful line-caught cod. This is when you should be flexible. It is rare that you cannot substitute one fish for another in a given recipe, as long as you understand the texture differences. For instance, when a recipe calls for tuna, you can substitute swordfish, mako shark, or halibut steaks with equally good results. The same goes for recipes that call for striped bass, where sea bass, snapper, or grouper would work as well.

I have also learned that fish can't wait. As soon as I get home, I unwrap the fish and place it in a glass or porcelain baking dish surrounded with plenty of ice cubes, and store it in the bottom part of the fridge where it is coldest. If I can't cook it the day of purchase, then I know the following day is a must.

I am often asked whether freshly frozen fish is not a better choice than fish that is not truly fresh. If the fish has been frozen right on the boat as soon as it has been caught, chances are that you can get good results, but much depends on how it has been defrosted. Frozen fish tends to exude water, so the fish can't brown and is often dry and mealy. So unless I am dealing with shrimp or squid, I much prefer buying fresh fish or fish that is still frozen and looks as if it has been properly handled.

What makes fish an ideal food for today's busy cook is that it cooks quickly and marries beautifully with a wonderful variety of herbs and vegetables. When you need dinner in 30 minutes or less, think seafood. Since fish is naturally tender, all you need is a good nonstick skillet, preferably one that can be placed in the oven, and some practice to tell when fish is done.

When it comes to preparing fish, it is good to remember that just as with a good steak, less is more. Keep it simple, and keep it fresh. That is what all cooks who know their fish will tell you. I realize that this may sound simple, but, in fact, if you have never cooked a swordfish steak or a fillet of salmon, just remember that every type of fish can be pan-seared in just a little olive oil or butter. If the steak is thick, finish cooking it in a medium-hot oven; if it is a thin fillet, simply turn it over with a large spatula and finish cooking it on top of the stove, lightly covered.

For an even easier method, you can simply butter and season the fish of your choice, place it in a well-buttered dish covered with foil, and roast in a 350° to 400°F oven. If you want to be creative, you can always add a little white wine to the skillet, as well as a few pieces of chopped tomatoes and some herbs.

Most types of fish like the company of fresh vegetables, and some matches are especially delicious. Try salmon with beets, dill, or cucumbers; sea bass with tomatoes, oregano, and shallots; or pan-seared skate with a drizzle of brown butter, lemon, and capers. If you are planning a more elaborate sauce, make it first, since even a thick fish steak will not take longer than 12 to 14 minutes to cook.

I cannot think of any foods other than fruits and vegetables that offer as much variety, taste, and enjoyment as seafood with the added bonus of being low in fat and presenting a healthful alternative to meat. And, with more and more restaurants serving creative fish preparations, it is easy to be inspired and to duplicate them at home for a fraction of the price.

Fish

■■■

How can you tell if a whole fish is really fresh?
The key is aroma. Very fresh fish smells clean, just the way the salty air at the beach does. There should be no smell of iodine. A whole fish should not look bruised in any way. Its skin should be firm, glossy, and shiny, not dull. Also, it must have its gills, which should be bright red and moist looking. Finally, the flesh of a fresh whole fish will adhere closely to the bones. If possible, press lightly on the flesh. It should be firm and return to its original shape. If a gentle nudge creates a permanent indentation, pass on the fish.

My market sells fish only in fillets and steaks. Is there any easy way to spot fresh fish when you cannot see the whole fish?
As long as the skin is still on, you should have no trouble telling if the fish is fresh. Inspect the fish carefully. Its skin should be smooth and unbroken, with an appealing silvery glint. Always ask to see it up close, since many fish counters have slightly rosy lights that make both the flesh and the skin look brighter. The flesh should not be flaky or separating and must have translucent, even coloring. Press gently on the flesh: If it leaves a dent, the fish is not truly fresh.

I often buy flounder that seems very fresh but has a strong iodine aroma. Is that okay?
Although in most fish that smell is a no-no, in flounder and skate you may detect a slight hint of iodine. That's due to their diet and will not affect their taste; however, it should never be an off-putting smell.

Cookbooks always say that you should look a fish in the eye to judge its freshness, but what exactly does that mean?
The eyes of a fresh fish are clear, bright, and flush with the surface of its head. Don't buy a fish with dull, cloudy, or sunken eyes; that's a sign of decay. When viewing a fresh fish and

a not-so-fresh fish side by side you will be able to tell the difference in an instant.

Are there any types of fish that are less fishy tasting?

Swordfish, mako, halibut, and very fresh tuna have a meatier mouthfeel and an unfishy taste. Tuna in particular can almost pass for a meaty steak.

Does fish benefit from marinating?

There are two very distinct cooking techniques that may both be referred to as "marinating." One is marinating the fish to give it more flavor before you grill or sauté it, in which case you want to let it marinate for only 30 minutes or less, because the acidity in a marinade "cooks" the fish. The other method is curing the fish in a salt, pepper, and herb mixture (see my book *Spur of the Moment Cook*, Morrow, 1996). In this case, you can cure it anywhere from 24 to 48 hours, depending on the recipe.

Cooking fish seems to smell up the entire house for days. Any suggestions for avoiding this?

Pan-searing with skin on is the worst offender in this department, as are oily fish such as salmon, mackerel, and bluefish. But there are wonderful odorless methods for cooking fish such as roasting, poaching, or baking in foil.

My husband does a lot of fishing and comes home with whole fish all the time. What's the best method for cooking a whole fish?

For small fish (up to 3 pounds), roasting or grilling will give you great results. When it comes to larger fish, and when we are talking about the freshest possible fish that has been caught that day, all pros agree that poaching is the number-one method. Old fishermen in Provence were famous for putting napkins over their heads to eat freshly poached fish because that way the aroma of the sea and that of the fish would mingle in those little tents, and they could enjoy the experience fully. All that a freshly poached fish needs is a sprinkling of salt, a grinding of pepper, a drizzle of olive oil, and a wedge of fresh lemon. Another great method for preparing a whole fish is roasting it in foil with some fresh herbs, seasoning, plenty of butter, and a sprinkling of lemon juice.

Is there really a simple way to tell when a whole fish is done?

Many cookbooks recommend measuring the fish at its thickest part and counting 8 minutes per inch. This is rather confusing and not accurate. To oven-roast a whole fish, heat the oven to 450°F and figure about 12 minutes per pound. Check the progress by making a small slit just behind the center bone. The flesh should be white and slightly flaky; if it is still translucent, it is not done. Alternatively, use an instant-read thermometer and cook the fish to between 140° and 145°F. This is still on the rare side, but it will continue to cook after you remove it from the oven. Many cookbooks will suggest cooking a fish up to 165°F, but at that point it is overcooked.

TIP When weighing a fish to decide how long to cook it, be sure to take the size of the head into consideration. A fish with a large head, such as a red snapper or sea bass, will weigh more than a branzino or mackerel.

When fish fillets are cooked with the skin on, they tend to curl up. Is there any way around that?

Try scoring the skin side of the fillets on the diagonal with a sharp paring knife. That way the skin doesn't tighten as the fish cooks, and the fillets remain flat.

What does cooking fish "en papillote" mean?
Fish cooked en papillote is enfolded in a parchment paper envelope together with herbs, butter, seasoning, and sometimes finely sliced or diced vegetables and a little wine, then baked in the oven, where it steams in its own moisture. Many chefs now use aluminum foil instead of the traditional parchment paper, with excellent results.

Is it a good idea to cook fish in the microwave?
The microwave might seem like a timesaver, but oven-braising produces a moister, more evenly cooked piece of fish, and the time difference is negligible.

Catfish

My market carries very fresh catfish, and I would like to know more about it.
Not so long ago, catfish was caught wild in rivers and lakes. It was an interesting fish that in spite of its sometimes muddy flavor had good taste. I often used it for fried fish. Now catfish is farmed on a major scale in the Mississippi River and has little character. Still, it is quite delicious fried in a light batter, and also takes well to a spicy rub or marinade, after which it can be simply broiled.

Grouper

I have had the most wonderful grouper in Florida but cannot find it in any market where I live. Can I use another fish instead?
Grouper is a distant relative of sea bass, which you can use instead. However, the texture of grouper is firmer and the flesh whiter. It also has a more lobster-like texture. Some fish markets sell grouper under names such as red grouper or black grouper, which may have a slightly different taste, but as long as the fillets are pearly white and fresh they are a good choice.

Halibut

I live in the Northwest and see wonderful halibut in the markets. How do you suggest using it? Can I substitute it in salmon recipes?
Halibut, which is at its best from March to September, is an extremely versatile fish, although personally I find it a little too mild flavored. Be sure to buy the fish very, very fresh. The flesh should not look opaque or cloudy, but rather translucent. When halibut is available only cut in steaks, I usually cube them for shish kebabs or pickle them to make a great dish.

And yes, you can use halibut for all preparations that call for salmon.

I recently pan-seared halibut, and it gave off a lot of liquid and would not brown. Is that the wrong preparation for this fish?
This does happen often with halibut, either because the fish has been frozen on the boat, or just because of this particular fish. Next time you cook halibut, I suggest oven-roasting it or broiling it very carefully so as not to overcook it. The grill is another excellent cooking medium for halibut.

Mahi Mahi

Is it true that mahi mahi is a name given to dolphin for marketing purposes? I loved the taste of the fish until I heard that. Is it true?

It is definitely not true. Mahi mahi, or dolphin fish, is not a mammal. Instead, it is a fish that is widely available in Hawaii and off the coast of Florida. It is usually available only in fillets. These should look bright and almost translucent. In Florida markets, I see wonderful-looking mahi mahi, while in New York it is often opaque—a definite indication that the fish is past its prime.

Mahi mahi is at its best when baked with spices, onions, tomatoes, and peppers.

The following is a nice rub for mahi mahi In a bowl, mash 2 large garlic cloves and combine with 1 teaspoon salt, 1 tablespoon coarsely ground black pepper, $\frac{1}{2}$ tablespoon each thyme and oregano, 1 teaspoon sweet paprika or Spanish smoked paprika, and 2 tablespoons soy sauce. Rub the mixture on a 2-pound fillet of mahi mahi and marinate, covered, for 4 to 6 hours. Grill or broil the fish for 6 to 7 minutes on each side.

Salmon

What should I look for when shopping for salmon?

A fresh piece of salmon will boast a layer of glimmering silver skin so shiny you'd swear you could see your face reflected in it. If its skin is dull, don't even consider buying it. Also, with the exception of salmon steaks, try not to buy packaged salmon or skinless salmon.

What is the difference between Atlantic, Pacific, Chilean, and Norwegian salmon? Is one better than the others?

Not really. Some markets and restaurants label Atlantic salmon as Norwegian salmon and try to convince you that one is better than the others, but in fact, they are all farm-raised and pretty similar in flavor. At certain times of year, Atlantic salmon may be a little fattier.

Is there a difference between farm-raised and wild salmon? Is there any way to tell which is which if it isn't labeled?

As you might expect, wild salmon—whether Pacific or Alaskan—is less fatty and more intensely flavored than farm-raised fish. Although wild salmon is not abundant, it can certainly be found in markets in the Pacific Northwest and in specialty fish markets along the Oregon and Washington State coast. Very little wild salmon makes its way to other parts of the country, so it is really a matter of luck or knowing a chef or seafood market that can get it. Is it worth a try? Definitely.

Are there different types of wild salmon? Which is best?

Look for king, sockeye, and coho wild salmon, all of which are extremely flavorful.

What is a salmon trout? Is it some kind of hybrid?

A student once called me with a fish cooking question. She had bought a salmon trout and was following a recipe that called for poaching the fish 15 to 20 minutes. After 20 minutes, the fish still looked pink, so she poached it another 20 minutes. When, after 40 minutes of cooking, it still looked pink, she called me to ask how long it was going to take. My answer? You'd better feed that fish to your cat and start from scratch. What she did not realize is that a salmon trout is not a trout at all, but a small salmon, and the flesh will always be pink. Many markets now call salmon trout Arctic char to make it less confusing.

Do you recommend salmon fillets or salmon steaks?

Each has its place in a cook's repertoire. Thick steaks are moister and better suited for grilling, and they are also very good poached. However, salmon steaks have bones, which may be a problem for some people. The fillets are easier to handle and serve without breaking apart. Try both and see which you like better. It is easier to tell freshness in fillets, since they are generally sold with the skin on, and a salmon's skin is the key to gauging its freshness.

Many Japanese restaurants serve raw salmon. Is it safe to do that at home with store-bought salmon?

Yes, if it is super fresh, which means buying it at a reputable fish store. Remind the fishmonger that you plan to eat it raw and want sushi-quality salmon.

Is it better to pan-sear salmon with or without the skin?

No matter how you are going to cook it—even when preparing a recipe that calls for skinless fillets—always select salmon with the skin on. The skin's color and sheen are the key indicators of freshness, and markets that sell skinless fillets are usually trying to sell you a less than perfect product.

Once you have inspected the skin, you can ask the fish market to remove it. I prefer to cook salmon with the skin on and remove it once it is cooked, because there is a great deal of taste in the skin—actually considered a delicacy—and, just as with a steak, the fat keeps the flesh moist.

No matter what I do, I either undercook or overcook salmon. Is there a reliable way to tell when the fish is perfectly done?

Learning to cook the perfect salmon fillet can be frustrating, because once you've overcooked it, there's no going back. To test for doneness, use the knife method. Cook fillets until nicely browned on one side, then cover the skillet loosely with foil. Once the fillets lose their raw color and all you see is a deep pink dot the size of a dime, turn the fillets over and cook for 50 seconds. Insert the tip of a knife or a metal skewer into the center of the fillet, remove it, and place it on your wrist. If it's warm, the fish is done. If it's cold, the fish is rare, and if it's hot, the fish is well done and maybe overcooked. If all this sounds too complicated, use an instant-read thermometer and remove the fish from the heat when it reads 125° to 130°F. Do keep in mind, though, that the fish will continue to cook. For this reason, remove it from the stove and take it out of the pan when it is still somewhat rare.

TIP Grilled fish will be gently resistant when cooked, never rubbery or tough. The tricky part is testing grilled fish for doneness without cutting into it (which will cause it to fall apart). To do this, insert a metal skewer into the center of the steak or fillet and then carefully push it to one side while it is still inserted, and you should be able to glimpse the center of the fish without pulling it apart.

Some new recipes call for cooking salmon at 500°F. But the standard cookbooks call for 350°F. Which is right?

If you cook any fish steaks at 500°F, you will incinerate them. High-heat roasting can work for a large whole fish, but you have to time it carefully. Low-heat roasting is by far the best way to cook a whole salmon or any fish. See Roasted Sea Bass with a Fricassee of Fennel and Potatoes, page 178.

Skate

Skate is one of my favorite fish. I order it in restaurants all the time but have no idea how to prepare it. Can you help?

Skate has two flat, paired wings, one usually larger than the other. Have the butcher bone the skate, which means removing the central cartilage. You will now have two pieces, one thicker than the other.

To prepare skate in the most classic way, simply dredge the fish lightly in flour, season with coarse salt and freshly ground pepper, and sauté in a mixture of peanut oil and butter or clarified butter for 3 minutes on each side until nicely browned. Break off a little piece to see if the fish is done. To make sure you don't overcook the fillets, sauté the fish over medium rather than high heat. Serve the fish with a browned butter, lemon, and caper sauce.

To make Brown Butter, Lemon, and Caper Sauce
Melt 1 stick butter in a small heavy skillet or saucepan over medium-high heat until the butter turns a golden brown color and has the aroma of toasted hazelnuts. Remove from the heat. Add the juice of 1 lemon, 2 tablespoons well-drained capers, and 2 tablespoons toasted

pine nuts. Swirl the butter and immediately pour it over the sautéed skate wings. Be sure not to let the butter get too dark and to remove the pan from the heat before adding the lemon juice.

Snapper

It seems that every time I go to the fish market, there is a different kind of red snapper available. What kind of snapper should I buy?

First of all, there is snapper and then there is Florida red snapper, which is in a class all its own. Florida red snapper commands a hefty price and is worth every bit of it, since it is a great-tasting fish. There is a quota when it comes to Florida red snapper, so when you see it toward the end of the month, it is not the real thing, since it can be fished for only the first three weeks of the month.

Other snappers, such as white Pacific snapper and New Zealand red snapper, which look very much like the Florida variety, are not in the same league. Never pay top dollar for fillets of snapper even if the skin has the right color, because chances are that you are not getting the Florida snapper variety, unless, of course, you are in Florida at a reputable market that fillets its own fish. In this case always try to buy some snapper bones and heads and make a fish stock. No fish makes a better stock than snapper. Fresh snapper fillets are good simply pan-seared in butter with some fresh herbs; they can also be oven-roasted with some white wine and shallots.

Sole

What is the difference between lemon sole and grey sole?

Grey sole is the mildest tasting of all flounders. It is very popular because it is so unfishy and has become the perfect choice for people who really don't like fish. Traditionally, lemon sole had to come from the Georgia Banks and weigh 3 pounds or more. It was a fish with excellent texture and taste. Now that the fish has become quite scarce, all flounders over 3 pounds are called lemon sole. There is not much difference in flavor between the various types of domestic sole.

Stock

I have trouble getting fish bones for fish stock. Do you have any ideas for substitutes?

In many instances, chicken stock works well in recipes calling for fish stock. For a more pronounced seafood flavor, add two to three handfuls of shrimp shells to the simmering stock, whether it's chicken stock or instant fish broth made from cubes, such as Knorr. Shrimp shells should be easy to get, even from the supermarket, but you may have to ask for them at the fish counter.

When is it important to use real fish stock, and can I use bottled clam juice instead?

I find that a full-bodied fish stock is a must whenever I make a delicate fish soup, seafood risotto, or a sauce for fish. On the other hand, intense flavorings such as saffron, lemongrass, or ginger work with instant fish broth with a fair amount of success. Bottled clam juice is extremely salty and does not provide the right seafood flavor. You can use diluted fish bouillon cubes, but be careful. These are also quite salty; I suggest that you add half again as much water to dilute them.

What are the best bones for making fish stock?

Snapper and bass bones make the best stock. If you live in an area where you have easy access to red or other snapper bones, you are in luck. Don't use sole, flounder, or the bones from other flatfish. They simply do not have enough flavor.

The most flavor is in the fish head. If you can get fish heads, you will be able to make great-tasting stock. I usually use an assortment of fish bones but try to include at least one or two snapper or bass fish heads.

TIP When buying fish heads, check to make sure they still have the gills—a sign of freshness. Then ask the fishmonger to remove the gills for you, since they are not easy to remove at home.

I recently made a fish stock with salmon bones, and the result tasted super fishy. Should I have done done anything differently?

Because salmon is extremely oily, salmon bones are not a good choice for making fish stock. As you discovered, they release a strong, almost unpleasant, fishy flavor.

Whenever I make fish stock, it looks cloudy and opaque. What am I doing wrong?

When fish stock is cloudy, chances are the fish bones and trimmings were not thoroughly rinsed. Place the bones and trimmings in a large bowl in the sink and trickle cold water over them until the water runs completely clear and the bones are snow white.

I have seen several recipes that call for court bouillon for cooking fish. What is this?

A court bouillon is a broth made with vegetables and herbs simmered in water with a touch of vinegar or wine, but without fish trimmings. I generally use court bouillon for poaching fish and braising large salmon fillets. What makes a court bouillon interesting to the seafood cook is that court bouillon can be used several times and frozen in between. After having poached fish in the bouillon a few times, you end up with a delicious full-bodied fish stock.

Swordfish

What are your thoughts on swordfish? I have seen it looking rosy pink and other times it has a grayish cast. Are both good? Is there a particular season for swordfish?

I discussed this with Jeremy Marshall, chef/owner of Aquagrill, one of New York City's most creative seafood restaurants. According to him, the key to the flavor of swordfish is the way it has been caught and at which stage of the game it reaches your fish market. The color varies from region to region, but it is not an indication of freshness. Swordfish can be both line caught and net caught. A line-caught fish is much more flavorful and juicy. Furthermore, the fishing boats go out for days at a time, which means that the last fish caught will come off the boat first and that fish will be fresher than others. If the fish market pays for top-quality swordfish, then you will be paying top dollar as well.

Since swordfish comes from different waters during different seasons, it can be good year-round. Personally, I find myself cooking swordfish more often in the summer, because I like the fish from the North Atlantic and at that time of year I may be lucky enough to find some line-caught fish.

I buy my swordfish at an excellent seafood market. Sometimes it is rich and juicy, while other times it is dry. Is there a way to tell quality by the color of the fish?

Unfortunately, you cannot determine the quality of swordfish by its color. Swordfish must be fatty to be good. The only way to tell is by cutting off a small piece. If the knife comes out clean, the fish is dry. If little bits of fish cling to the knife, it means the fish is fatty. I realize that at this point you have already bought the fish, but based on this little test, you can decide how to prepare it. When swordfish tests dry, I usually do not marinate or grill it. Instead, I pan-sear it in butter or olive oil.

Tilapia

Many seafood restaurants seem to have tilapia on the menu. What kind of fish is it and how should I use it?

Tilapia is a mild farm-raised fish that mostly comes from southern states; it is also imported from Israel or Hawaii. Most markets sell the fish in skinless fillets, but I always look for it with skin on, since the fish is more attractive this way and also cooks better.

Tilapia is excellent roasted whole, either in the oven or on the grill. Be careful not to overpay for tilapia. The fish is often called by other names such as St. Peter's fish, with inflated prices.

Tuna

What is the best tuna to use for tuna tartare?

The most widely available tuna is yellow fin, so chances are that you will be using it for both grilling and tartare. The key is not to use any of the sinew, so be sure to use only the part of the tuna steaks that do not contain it.

What should I look for in tuna? Is color an issue?

The lighter the tuna, the fattier. Most chefs prefer the fattier fish, but dark tuna is extremely flavorful. The most important issue is freshness rather than color. Look for bright trans-lucent flesh and avoid tuna steaks that look opaque.

Whenever I make a tuna steak, it is overcooked by the time it is browned. How can I avoid overcooking tuna?

Always buy a large piece of tuna, enough to serve 4 to 6 people. This way you can buy a 4- to 5-inch piece and then cut it into rectangles or 2-inch cubes. The thicker the pieces, the better your chance of keeping the tuna from being overcooked. If you do not have a hot grill, then pan-sear the tuna quickly in a pan with plenty of very hot oil. The downside of this method is that the fish will release a strong fishy smell because its natural fat will start to burn.

Shellfish

Calamari

What is the difference between calamari and squid?

None. Italians call squid calamari. Spaniards call them calamares, and the British sometimes call them inkfish.

The only place near me that carries fresh squid sells them uncleaned. Can you tell me how to clean them?

Squid are easy to clean. First, pull off the head; most of the innards will follow. Then, work your forefinger deep into the body and pull out the quill (a hard piece of cartilage that feels like plastic) plus any remaining innards. Finally, peel off the skin (if this is difficult, hold the squid under cold running water and the skin will slip right off). Rinse the calamari well under additional cold running water and dry thoroughly with plenty of paper towels.

Is it better to buy small or large calamari?

Actually, large calamari tend to be slightly more tender and less rubbery, but size doesn't matter as much as how they are cooked.

Cook calamari either by sautéing them for no more than 30 seconds or by braising them covered for 1 hour or more to tenderize them. There is no middle way.

My market sells only frozen calamari. Is it okay to use them?

Of course fresh calamari are better, but you can get excellent results with the frozen ones. However, if you plan to freeze some for later use, make sure to ask at the fish market if they have been previously frozen (and hope the answer is truthful), since you should never refreeze seafood.

How much calamari is needed to serve four people?

It depends on whether you are buying them cleaned or uncleaned. Calamari lose about 25 percent of their weight during cleaning, so for a main course that will make use of the tentacles (the most flavorful part of the squid), I would start with 2 pounds to serve four.

Clams

Clams come in so many different varieties. Can you explain which is which?

Sizewise, the smallest clams are Pacific manila clams, followed by littlenecks and cherrystones, all of which are hard-shell varieties and plentiful. Another delicious hard-shell clam is the New Zealand cockle, which is generally only available in top-end fish markets and is pricier than either manila or littleneck. Soft-shell clams are native to the East Coast, from Long Island to Maine, where they are often called steamers. They are the most tender and, because of their scarcity, also the priciest.

Which are better—small or large clams?

Small clams are always more tender. If you like raw clams, the smaller types are best. Large clams have their place, too, though mostly in pasta dishes and soups.

What are the best clams for making clam sauce?

Cherrystone clams are a better buy than littlenecks, and since they are larger and meatier, you can easily dice or chop them. Make sure not to overcook the clams, and remove them from the pot with a slotted spoon as soon as their shells open or they get tough and rubbery.

Is there a season when clams are fresher and less expensive?

Hard-shell clams are plentiful year-round, but I have found them to be less expensive in the summer, when they are easier to dig up.

I saw huge clams at the Pike Market in Seattle. What are they? Can you eat them?

This giant soft-shell clam is called a geoduck (pronounced "gooey-duck"). They generally weigh 3 pounds or more and have 18-inch necks protruding out of their 6-inch shells. The neck is edible when peeled and diced, but the meat is too tough to use in anything other than chowders or fritters. If you're eager to give geoduck a try, the best thing to do is to buy the flesh already cleaned and steamed.

Even after scrubbing my clams with a stiff brush, I still end up with tons of sand in my sauce. What's the best way to rid clams of sand?

A good scrubbing is the only way to remove sand on the outside of the shells, but for internal grit, the best thing to do is to soak the clams briefly in three changes of salted water, using sea salt or kosher salt.

Is there an easy way to open raw clams?

Shucking uncooked clams is tough, but if you put them in the freezer for 30 minutes, they will open slightly, allowing you to insert a clam knife or paring knife easily between the shells to pry them open.

TIP Always soak and rinse shellfish in plenty of salted water. This way the shellfish believes it is still in the ocean and opens its shell and cleanses itself. A saltwater soak also greatly enhances the taste.

Can I use canned or jarred clams in a pasta sauce?

You can, but the taste isn't the same. Since fresh clams are easy to come by, not that hard to clean, and quick to steam open, it's certainly not worth using canned clams. Many markets now carry chopped fresh clams, which are a good choice.

Is clam juice an acceptable substitute for fish stock?

Clam juice is not a good substitute for fish stock, no matter what some cookbooks say. It's too salty, and most bottled brands aren't very flavorful. Use a Knorr fish bouillon cube instead.

Lobsters

Which are sweeter, large or small lobsters?

Both large and small lobsters taste delicious, providing they have been cooked properly. Their size has no bearing on their taste.

When are lobsters in season? They seem to be especially expensive in the summer.

Fresh lobsters are available year-round, but spring lobsters are hard shelled, meaty, and reasonably priced, so late spring is the best time for buying and cooking lobsters. Although summer is considered lobster season, what you will find in summer are new-shell chicken lobsters that are very sweet and tasty and wonderful when steamed, but because of their high water content are unsuitable for grilling, roasting, or baking. So be extremely choosy when buying lobsters in the summer for anything other than classic steamed lobster preparations.

Which is better, a soft-shell or a hard-shell lobster?

The harder the shell, the better. In fact, give the shell a light squeeze and shake the lobster gently. If the shell rattles, it may be soft. Try to compare equal-size lobsters to determine if one feels heavier than the other. Go with the heavier lobster.

Is there a difference in taste between male and female lobsters? Is there any way to tell which is which?

The meat of male and female lobsters tastes pretty much the same. However, only the female has coral or roe. If you appreciate the coral, as I do, look for female lobsters. This is quite easy to do—just check the tiny claws under the tail. A female's claws will appear thin and feathery. In male lobsters these claws are thick and much less delicate looking. If you are still not sure, ask the fishmonger to pick female lobsters for you.

If a lobster is in a tank, does that automatically mean it's fresh, or is there something specific to look for?

In a fish market with large turnover—usually found in coastal areas—you should have no trouble. The further you get from the coast, though, the harder it is to get a truly fresh lobster, even if it is being held in a tank. Chef Jasper White, author of *Lobster at Home* (Scribner, 1998), suggests the following: First, check the antennae. If they are short or caked with an algae-like substance, the lobster has probably been in "the pound" for a long time, which affects the taste. Step back and examine the lobster in a general way. It should be lively. The claws should not droop. If you see a lobster that flaps its tail and swings its claws, buy it.

Why is it necessary to buy live lobsters?

Once a lobster is dead, its meat turns to mush, so it needs to be alive until it goes into the pot for cooking. This is because lobsters have very potent digestive enzymes that start decomposing the flesh the moment they die. The digestive organs are too complex to remove. To check whether a lobster is still alive, pick it up; if the tail curls under, the lobster is alive.

How should lobsters be stored between the market and the cooking pot?

Lobsters should be kept moist but not wet. Wrap them in damp sheets of newspaper. Be sure to keep them separate from each other. They should be stored in the coldest spot in your refrigerator, which is usually located at the rear of the bottom shelf. Store them this way for a few hours at the most. I wouldn't keep a lobster overnight. Absolutely do not store them on ice, as it kills them.

TIP A 1½-pound lobster provides 2½ to 3½ ounces of meat.

It is better to steam a lobster in 2 inches of salt water or to plunge it into lots of boiling water?

Steaming is preferable because it cooks the lobster more slowly, producing more tender meat. Also, steaming is more forgiving than boiling, meaning that it's harder to overcook your lobster that way. Most important, steam does not penetrate the shell the way water does, so lobsters that are steamed do not get watery the way boiled ones do. To steam lobsters, fill a large pot or lobster pot with 2 inches of heavily salted water. Turn the heat to high, cover the pot, and when the water is boiling, place the lobsters in the pot and cover tightly. (The lobsters will be piled on top of each other—since the steam rises and cooks them—which is fine.) Steam for about 10 minutes per pound, or until the shells are bright red. A 1- to 1½-pound lobster will cook in 10 to 12 minutes.

What is the difference between the lobster roe and coral?

The lobster roe and coral are one and the same—the eggs of the female lobster. Green-black when raw, they turn a lovely coral shade when cooked and are absolutely delicious.

What is the tomalley? Is it edible?

Tomalley is the lobster's liver, which turns green when cooked. Lobster connoisseurs consider the tomalley a delicacy and cherish its rich flavor. It is often whipped into the melted butter that accompanies a steamed lobster and is also tasty spread on toast points. However, be extremely careful about tomalley. If a lobster has lived in contaminated water, the impurities will have been absorbed by its liver. If you are not sure about the water where a lobster was caught, you are better off discarding the tomalley.

Mussels

Which are best, large or small mussels?

Personally, I like the medium-sized mussels that are usually labeled "Mediterranean mussels," but small mussels can be extremely tasty as well. Some of the most wonderful small mussels come from Lopez Island in the state of Washington. The freshness of mussels will probably tell you more about their taste than either their size or the variety.

The mussels at my local market come packaged. Is it okay to buy them that way?

Avoid packaged mussels, unless they are in mesh bags. (Most farm-raised mussels are available in 2-pound bags.) It's hard to judge the freshness of packaged mussels, since the plastic holds them shut, and you can't really get close enough to judge them for yourself. If you have no other choice, be sure to rinse the mussels in three changes of salt water. This is called "purging," and it both rids shellfish of impurities and defines their flavor.

Is there a taste difference between farm-raised and wild mussels?

It is practically impossible to find wild mussels commercially. The only difference between one farm-raised mussel and another is the water in which they are raised. If they are in sandy beds, there is a lot of sand in the mussels. If they are raised in beds with current and water that is extremely cold, they will be cleaner and firmer. Looking at the mussel won't offer a clue, but you'll be very aware of it when you clean the mussels. And, yes, there is a great deal more taste in wild mussels than in the farm-raised varieties.

My fish man claims that open shells do not necessarily indicate bad mussels. Is he telling me the truth?

He's telling you a half-truth. If mussel shells are open but close up when you tap them, the mussels are still alive and edible. However, if they are open and don't shut when you tap them, they are no good. Unfortunately, since you will rarely find a fishmonger who will allow you to stick your hands into the fish case and tap away;

I buy only mussels with closed shells. The same goes for mussels you have stored in the refrigerator at home. If they are open, tap them to check for freshness.

What's the best way to store mussels at home? How long will they keep?

Get the mussels home as fast as you can and store them in a pan in the refrigerator covered with a damp (not dripping wet) towel to keep them cool and moist. Stored this way, mussels should last a couple of days. Remove the beards just before cooking. Simply yank them off. A tightly closed fresh mussel will not open when you tear off the beard. If a mussel does open when you tear off its beard, it's dead. Don't use it!

I recently bought mussels from a seafood truck, and they were covered with barnacles that were almost impossible to remove. How do you clean mussels?

The best way to remove barnacles is to rub one mussel against another. If this does not do the job, use a stiff brush. Definitely do not perform this task with a paring knife—you will blunt it permanently.

Is there a surefire way to get rid of the sand in mussels?

This is getting easier all the time, since most of the mussels you buy are farm-raised and therefore virtually sandless. But to be on the safe side, soak them in plenty of very cold water with 1 tablespoon flour added to it for 15 to 30 minutes. This helps disgorge the sand and also plumps them up.

Can you recommend a simple way to serve fresh mussels?

A wonderful and simple way to prepare mussels is to combine 1 cup dry white wine in a large heavy casserole with 2 tablespoons minced shallots, 2 minced garlic cloves, 2 tablespoons fresh thyme leaves or 1 teaspoon dried, 6 peppercorns, and 1 bayleaf. Add 4 to 5 pounds of well-scrubbed mussels. Cover the casserole and cook over medium heat until the mussels open. Serve in individual soup bowls with plenty of French bread.

Scallops

What's the difference between sea scallops and bay scallops? Are they interchangeable in recipes?

Sea scallops are easy to recognize, since they're more than twice the size of bays. They range from ¾ to 1¼ inches across and are about the same thickness. These mighty mollusks are slightly beige to pink in color and have a sweet aroma and a fuller flavor. Sea scallops are found on both the East and West coasts, but the Atlantic scallop is probably the best known and is available year-round. Their size makes them perfect for pan-searing, broiling, and grilling. Smaller bay scallops are also found on the East Coast, but they are seasonally available only from October through early winter. The best bay scallops—sweet and succulent—are from the New England and mid-Atlantic coasts, in the vicinity of Cape Cod and Long Island. Unfortunately, the season for these scallops is short and they are very expensive. Bay scallops are ivory to golden in color and measure about ½ inch across. They cook quickly, in 1 to 3 minutes, which makes them perfect for stir-frying, pan-searing, or marinating raw for seviche.

What are the really tiny scallops in the market year-round?

Those are calicos, which are harvested from the warmer waters of the Carolinas, Florida, and Central America. While they resemble bay scallops, they are vastly inferior. Calicos are shucked by a blast of steam before shipping, which not only destroys their flavor but also makes them prime candidates for overcooking—in which case they have the texture of pencil erasers. Sure, calicos are less expensive and plentiful, but the trade-off in taste isn't worth it.

Sometimes sea scallops are tinged orange. Is it okay to use them?

Don't be alarmed by that orange (sometimes pink) shading. It's from the roe and does not affect flavor or quality.

How can I tell if scallops are really fresh?

Trust your nose. You can identify a spoiled scallop with one whiff. Fresh scallops have a sweet, delicate odor. Any sulfur or iodine smell is a clear signal that these little guys are past their prime. If you're not able to smell them before buying, then by all means sniff before leaving the store and return them immediately if there's a problem. Also, if scallops are swimming in liquid, look opaque, or are even slightly discolored, definitely pass on them. To keep scallops looking fresh, many processors soak them in sodium tripolyphosphates (STP), which reduces water loss and prolongs shelf life. The problem, aside from the added chemicals, is that when they're cooked they release this liquid and end up steaming rather than sautéing. The key is to look for moist scallops that are firm, shiny, and translucent—not milky. If they appear too white, that's a sure sign they've been treated with STP. How to avoid this? Find a reputable fishmonger and insist on "dry," diver, or unsoaked scallops.

What is the best way to store scallops at home, and how long will they last in the refrigerator?

As with all seafood, it's best to cook scallops the day you buy them. But if that's not possible, open the plastic bag or container and rest it in a large bowl of ice. Don't place scallops directly on ice or they will become soggy and won't brown properly. Ideally, store them no more than one day after purchase.

Is it okay to use frozen scallops?

In a word, no. However, there are times when you'll be sold scallops that have been previously frozen without your knowing it. You'll discover this, though, as soon as the scallops hit the hot pan, as they'll exude a lot of juice but won't brown. When that happens, the best way to rescue dinner is to remove the scallops from the skillet as soon as they are cooked, and let the juices cook down to a glaze. Season with salt and pepper, add some minced fresh parsley and the juice of a large lemon, and spoon the sauce over the scallops. They will be delicious.

If bay scallops aren't available, can the larger sea scallops be cut into pieces?

Never halve or quarter sea scallops. Halved or quartered sea scallops will cook up tough, as the cutting process destroys their texture. Scallops can, however, be sliced crosswise.

Shrimp

Is there a difference between shrimp and prawns?

Usually restaurants and cookbooks refer to very large shrimp as prawns. To further confuse the issue, in England all shrimp, regardless of their size, are referred to as prawns. In other words, there's no real difference, other than size.

What should I look for when buying shrimp?

Good fresh shrimp should have no smell at all and not even a whiff of ammonia. The shells should be translucent and unbroken, and the shrimp should fill the shells tightly.

At different times of the year the shrimp in my market are pink, gray, orange, and even black. What's the difference in taste?

The color of shrimp has nothing to do with their flavor. Most of the shrimp we buy are farm raised and have been frozen and defrosted, so the key is not color but freshness.

How many medium shrimp are there in a pound?

There should be 35 to 40 shrimp in a pound of medium-sized shrimp. A smarter way to shop for shrimp is to know fishmongers' lingo. Fishmongers don't refer to medium and large shrimp. Instead they refer to shrimp as U-20 (which means there are about 20 in a pound), U-30 (about 30 in a pound), and U-40 (about 40 in a pound).

Are fresh shrimp worth the extra money?

Freezing has a major effect on both the taste and texture of shrimp, and fresh shrimp are undoubtedly worth seeking out. There are plenty of fresh shrimp in various parts of the country throughout the spring. You can get wonderful shrimp right out of the Gulf of Mexico on Florida's west coast, and the small Maine shrimp with their heads on that appear in markets in early spring are also succulent. In Louisiana, Texas, Georgia, North and South

Carolina, Oregon, and Washington State, fresh shrimp are more widely available. In most other parts of the country, however, the average grocery store rarely offers fresh shrimp. Consult a reputable fishmonger to find out more about what is available in your area.

What's the best method for freezing shrimp at home?

If you are lucky enough to live in a coastal area where you can purchase fresh shrimp (generally in Louisiana, Texas, Georgia, South Carolina, Oregon, Washington, Maine, and Florida), they can be frozen with excellent results. Place the fresh shrimp in water in zippered plastic bags and store them in the freezer. They will keep for about 3 months. Commercial flash-freezing is obviously better than what can be done at home, so don't expect quite the same results. Shrimp must never be frozen twice. The shrimp in almost all grocery stores has already been frozen and then defrosted before hitting the seafood case. If frozen again, they will turn tough and tasteless.

What is the best way to defrost large bags of shrimp?

If you are in a hurry, place the bag in a bowl and run cold water over it. Never use hot water, as it will begin cooking the shrimp. If you have the time, thaw them in the refrigerator.

Can I save time by buying precooked shrimp?

These tend to be dry and tasteless, and I've never understood what the advantage is supposed to be, since it takes no time at all to boil shrimp. In a large saucepan, bring salted water to a boil, add the shrimp, bring the water back to a boil, and simmer for 1 minute. Turn off the heat and let the shrimp cool in the water, about 5 minutes. That's all there is to it.

Is it really necessary to devein shrimp?

This is your lucky day—you now have permission to stop deveining shrimp forever. Yes, that little vein (actually the shrimp's intestinal tract) is not all that attractive, but it disappears when the shrimp are cooked. I never devein shrimp, except the very large blue-gray Thai prawns, which sport particularly unsightly veins.

What's a good marinade for shrimp, and how long should they marinate?

When marinating shrimp, the simpler the marinade the better. Try a mixture of lime juice, olive oil, fresh garlic, and some fresh thyme or oregano. Never marinate for more than 30 to 40 minutes, as the marinade contains an acidic component that "cooks" the shrimp and dries them out.

TIP Always use lime juice rather than lemon juice when marinating shrimp. Lime juice is sweeter and does not overpower the shrimp's delicate taste.

How do you keep rock shrimp from overcooking? They always seem to come out dry.

Cooking tiny, sweet rock shrimp is a challenge. One of the best ways to prepare them is to dip them in a tempura batter (made with 1 cup flour stirred gently into 1 cup of water or beer) and deep-fry them. This dish is very popular in the South, where it is known as popcorn shrimp. Another good way to use rock shrimp is to add them to a tomato-based pasta sauce and just heat them through (for a minute or two) so they don't get tough.

Pan-Seared Arctic Char with Lemon-Chive Essence

Arctic char used to be called salmon trout. It is a mild and delicious fish that takes well to creamy sauces and mild herbs such as dill and tarragon. I like to serve the char with simply boiled new potatoes tossed in a little butter, and some glazed cucumbers.

SERVES 4

LEMON-CHIVE ESSENCE

4 tablespoons unsalted butter

1 cup crème fraîche or heavy cream

½ Knorr fish bouillon cube

3 tablespoons fresh lemon juice

1 to 2 teaspoons finely grated lemon zest

1 tablespoon flour mixed into a paste with
  1 tablespoon softened butter

2 tablespoons minced fresh chives

2 tablespoons minced fresh dill or tarragon

Salt and freshly ground black pepper

FISH

4 fillets of Arctic char (6 to 7 ounces each),
  with skin on

Coarse salt and freshly ground black pepper

2 tablespoons clarified butter (see page 384)

2 large plum tomatoes, peeled, seeded, and
  finely diced

Glazed cucumbers

Minced chives

1. Make the lemon-chive essence: In a large heavy skillet, melt the butter over medium heat. Add the crème fraîche or heavy cream, bouillon cube half, and lemon juice and zest; bring to a simmer, and reduce slightly. Whisk in bits of the blended flour and butter until the sauce lightly coats the spoon. Add the chives, and dill or tarragon; season with salt and pepper, and keep warm.

2. Prepare the fish: Dry the fillets thoroughly with paper towels. Season with salt and pepper.

3. Heat the clarified butter in 2 large, nonstick skillets over high heat. Place 2 fillets in each skillet, skin side down, and cover loosely with foil. Cook for 2 minutes, slightly lower the heat, and cook for an additional 4 to 5 minutes without turning. You may turn the fillets once and cook for about 30 seconds if you want the tops to be browned.

4. Transfer one fillet to each of 4 individual serving plates, skin side up. Spoon some of the sauce around each portion and garnish the sauce with the diced tomatoes and glazed cucumbers. Sprinkle with the chives and serve at once.

Brook Trout en Papillote with Asparagus, Snow Peas, and Dill Butter

Here is a lovely way to prepare brook trout. The mild taste of the fish marries beautifully with asparagus and snow peas. Oven-baked with a fair amount of dill and chive butter, it becomes a delicately flavored dish that needs little in terms of accompaniment. A few boiled new potatoes tossed in parsley and a touch of butter make the perfect side dish.

I usually serve this dish right out of the foil; if you prefer a more elegant presentation, you can fillet the fish in the kitchen and transfer the fillets and vegetables to a warm platter or individual plates.

SERVES 4

2 cups finely sliced asparagus

2 cups fine julienne of snow peas

6 tablespoons butter, at room temperature

2 tablespoons minced fresh dill plus
   2 medium-sized dill sprigs

3 tablespoons minced fresh chives

Coarse salt and freshly ground black pepper

2 brook trout (about 1½ pounds each)

2 slices lemon, each cut in half

1. Preheat the oven to 350°F. In a saucepan, bring lightly salted water to a boil. Add the asparagus and snow peas. Return to a boil and cook for 50 seconds. Drain and immediately run under cold water; drain well.

2. Combine the butter, minced dill, and chives in a bowl and mash with a fork until well blended. Season with a sprinkling of salt and pepper and blend thoroughly.

3. Place each fish on a piece of heavy-duty foil. Place 1 sprig of dill and 2 pieces of lemon in each cavity. Season each fish well with salt and pepper and sprinkle with some of the asparagus and snow pea mixture, as well as placing some under each fish.

4. Divide the dill butter between the 2 fish. Cover with another piece of foil, crimping the foil to firmly enclose the fish. Place on a baking sheet and bake for 20 minutes. Remove from the oven and slide onto a large platter. With sharp scissors, cut open the foil and divide the fish and vegetables among 4 plates. Garnish with sprigs of dill.

Stir-Fry of Calamari, Red Peppers, and Lemon

You can get this zesty calamari dish in numerous tapa bars all over the Catalan coast and in many other parts of Spain. The tentacles are the most flavorful part of the calamari; if you can, be sure to include them. Remember that calamari must be cooked for only 30 to 50 seconds, or else they get tough. You can also make this dish with small whole peeled or unpeeled shrimp. Just cook them for an extra minute and serve with plenty of crusty bread.

SERVES 4

> 1 small lemon
>
> 3 to 4 tablespoons extra virgin olive oil
>
> 1 small dried red chile, broken into pieces
>
> 1 large red bell pepper, seeded and cut into ¾-inch cubes
>
> 1 pound small calamari, cleaned and cut crosswise into ½-inch slices
>
> Coarse salt and freshly ground black pepper
>
> 2 tablespoons tiny fresh cilantro leaves

1. Finely slice the lemon. Cut each slice into quarters.

2. In a large heavy skillet, heat 2 tablespoons of the olive oil over high heat until almost smoking. Add the chile and half the bell pepper and cook for 1 to 2 minutes, or until barely tender.

3. Add half the calamari and stir-fry for 30 seconds, or until just opaque. Immediately add half of the lemon slices and toss for 30 seconds longer, or until the lemon is just heated through. Transfer the calamari mixture to a serving dish.

4. Cook the remaining calamari and lemon in the remaining oil in the same manner. Transfer to the serving dish and season with salt and black pepper. Sprinkle with the cilantro leaves and serve immediately.

Fillets of Lemon Sole in a Lime, Jalapeño, and Caper Butter

SERVES 4

2 large fillets of lemon sole (about 2 pounds)

Coarse salt and freshly ground black pepper

Flour, for dredging

½ cup chicken stock or bouillon

10 tablespoons butter

2 tablespoons lime juice

2 teaspoons grated lime zest

1 tablespoon minced jalapeño pepper

1 tablespoon capers, well drained

2 teaspoons grapeseed or canola oil

Sprigs of flat-leaf parsley or dill

1. Cut the sole fillets into 4 even pieces. Season with salt and pepper. Dredge lightly in flour and set aside.

2. In a small heavy saucepan, heat the stock or bouillon. Cook over medium heat until slightly reduced. Reduce the heat and start adding 8 tablespoons of the butter a little at a time, whisking constantly until all the butter has been added and the mixture is well emulsified. Remove from the heat and add the lime juice, lime zest, jalapeño, and capers. Whisk until the sauce is well blended. Season lightly with salt and pepper and correct the seasoning.

3. In a large nonstick skillet, heat the remaining 2 tablespoons butter and the oil. Add the fillets and sauté over medium-high heat for 3 minutes. Carefully turn the fillets with a fish spatula and sauté for another 2 or 3 minutes. Do not overcook. Carefully transfer the fillets to individual plates or a serving plate and spoon the butter sauce over each fillet.

4. Garnish with the parsley or dill and serve.

Oven-Roasted Mackerel with Caper, Lemon, and Anchovy Butter

Boston mackerel is an East Coast spring delicacy. Because of its oiliness, it must be purchased absolutely fresh. Check the skin and gills. The skin should be silvery and shiny, the gills bright red. If you cannot get Boston mackerel, you can substitute smelts or fresh sardines in this simple but tasty preparation. These, however, will have to be pan-fried rather than baked.

SERVES 2 TO 4

8 tablespoons unsalted butter (1 stick)

2 tablespoons tiny nonpareil capers, drained

2 anchovy fillets, minced

2 tablespoons minced flat-leaf parsley

1 large garlic clove, crushed

Juice of 1 lemon

1 tablespoon grated lemon zest

4 Boston mackerel (1 to 1½ pounds each), cleaned, with heads left on

Coarse salt and freshly ground black pepper

2 tablespoons olive oil

2 lemons, quartered

1. Preheat the oven to 400°F.

2. In a small heavy saucepan, heat the butter over low heat until melted and just starting to brown. Immediately remove from the heat and add the capers, anchovies, parsley, garlic, and lemon juice and lemon zest.

3. Season the mackerel with salt and pepper and brush well with olive oil.

4. Place in a well-oiled roasting pan or baking dish, cover, and bake for 15 minutes. Remove from the oven.

5. Reheat the herb and anchovy butter until it just starts to bubble; do not let it come to a boil. Immediately pour the butter over the mackerel and transfer the fish carefully to individual serving plates. Garnish with the quartered lemons.

Steamed Mussels in Basil-Garlic Cream

Now that mussels are being farmed in several regions of the country, they are becoming more widely available. Unfortunately, farm-raised mussels lack the wonderful briny taste of their wild cousins and need plenty of flavoring. Make sure that the mussels are tightly closed when you buy them, and if possible ask to see the tag that indicates when the mussels were harvested and the sell-by date.

SERVES 4 TO 5

1 cup tightly packed fresh basil leaves

2 large garlic cloves, mashed

3 to 5 tablespoons olive oil

2 tablespoons unsalted butter plus 2 to 4 tablespoons unsalted butter, for enrichment, optional

¼ cup minced shallots

½ cup dry white wine

1 large sprig of fresh thyme

1 sprig of fresh parsley

5 to 6 pounds fresh mussels, well scrubbed

1 cup crème fraîche

1 tablespoon flour mixed into a paste with 1 tablespoon softened butter

Freshly ground black pepper

1. In a blender or food processor, process the basil and garlic with enough olive oil to make a smooth paste.

2. Melt the 2 tablespoons butter in a large heavy saucepan over low heat, add the shallots, and cook for 1 minute without browning. Add the wine, herbs, and mussels and cook, covered, shaking the pan back and forth, until all the mussels open; discard any that do not. Transfer them with a slotted spoon to a bowl.

3. Strain the broth through a fine sieve. Return to the pan together with the crème fraîche and reduce by a third. Whisk in bits of the blended flour and butter until the sauce coats the spoon. Reduce the heat to low and whisk in the basil paste and butter for enrichment. Correct the seasoning by adding a large grinding of black pepper and keep warm.

4. Transfer the mussels to individual serving bowls, spoon some of the sauce over each portion, and serve at once.

Pan-Seared Red Snapper Fillets with Sweet and Spicy Asian Syrup

The first time I tasted this sauce in a San Francisco restaurant, I was intrigued by the interesting flavor combination and could not wait to make it. It has since become one of my favorite ways to serve a variety of fish—in particular, snapper and sea bass. The sauce can be made as much as a week ahead of time. I often double and triple it and keep it on hand for grilled tuna or salmon. Stir-fried snow peas or bok choy are both excellent accompaniments.

SERVES 4

ASIAN SYRUP

1 cup plus 2 tablespoons sake

1 cup plus 2 tablespoons mirin

2 tablespoons finely sliced peeled fresh ginger

2 large garlic cloves, very finely sliced

2 teaspoons finely sliced jalapeño pepper

2 tablespoons light soy sauce

¼ cup very finely diced red bell pepper

¼ cup very finely diced yellow bell pepper

2 tablespoons very finely diced zucchini, skin only

¼ cup corn kernels, optional

FISH

4 red snapper fillets (6 to 7 ounces each), skin on

Coarse salt and freshly ground black pepper

2 tablespoons peanut or canola oil

Sprigs of fresh cilantro

1. Make the Asian Syrup: In a heavy 2-quart saucepan, combine the sake, mirin, ginger, garlic, and jalapeño, bring to a simmer, and reduce until syrupy; this will take about 15 minutes. You should have about ⅔ cup syrup. Strain the syrup into a smaller saucepan. Add the soy sauce and vegetables and simmer for 2 or 3 minutes, or until tender. Keep warm.

2. Season the snapper fillets with salt and pepper. In a large nonstick pan, heat the oil. Add the snapper fillets skin side down and sauté for 3 minutes until nicely brown and crisp. Turn and cook for another minute. Do not overcook.

3. Transfer the fillets to a serving plate and spoon the sauce over them. Garnish with the cilantro and serve immediately.

Pan-Seared Skate with Red Onion, Tomato Jam, and Brown Caper Butter

SERVES 4

2 to 3 tablespoons olive oil

1 large red onion, cut in half and finely sliced

1 tablespoon minced fresh rosemary

Pinch of salt

1 teaspoon sugar

15 grape tomatoes, cut in half

1 large skate wing (about 2 pounds), or
    2 small skate wings, boned and cut into fillets

Freshly ground black pepper

Flour, for dredging

8 tablespoons butter (1 stick)

1 tablespoon grapeseed oil

Juice of ½ lemon or more to taste

2 tablespoons capers, well drained

2 tablespoons minced flat-leaf parsley

1. In a heavy skillet, heat the olive oil and add the onion and rosemary. Season with salt and sugar and sauté over high heat for 1 to 2 minutes. Lower the heat. Cover the skillet and continue to simmer the onion for 15 to 25 minutes, watching carefully so that it does not burn. You may have to add a little more oil.

2. Add the tomatoes and simmer, uncovered, for another 3 minutes. Set aside.

3. Season the fish with salt and pepper. Sprinkle the fillets lightly with flour.

4. Heat 1 tablespoon of the butter and half the grapeseed oil in each of two nonstick skillets. Add the fillets and sauté over fairly high heat for 3 minutes on each side. Transfer the fillets to a warm serving platter and set aside.

5. In a small saucepan, heat the remaining 6 tablespoons butter and cook until the butter turns a deep hazelnut brown. Add the lemon juice and capers and pour the butter over the fillets.

6. Reheat the onion jam and place large spoonfuls on individual plates. Top with a skate fillet, garnish with parsley, and serve immediately.

Roasted Sea Bass with a Fricassee of Fennel and Potatoes

Black sea bass is America's best fish. I am sure some would argue otherwise, but to me, nothing comes close to the sweet taste of this wonderful fish. Roasted whole on a bed of potatoes and fennel, it becomes a splendid one-dish meal. If you cannot get sea bass, try a whole red snapper, which will also be delicious.

SERVES 2 TO 3

6 tablespoons fruity olive oil

4 medium Yukon Gold potatoes, peeled and finely sliced

Coarse salt and freshly ground black pepper

2 medium fennel bulbs, finely sliced, tops removed and reserved

2 medium onions, finely sliced

1 teaspoon fennel seeds

$1\frac{1}{2}$ to 3 pounds sea bass or red snapper

$1\frac{1}{2}$ lemon, cut into wedges

1. Preheat the oven to 350°F.

2. In a large baking dish, heat 3 tablespoons of the olive oil. Add a layer of potatoes, season with salt and pepper, top with a layer of sliced fennel and onions, season with salt and pepper, and sprinkle with fennel seeds. Top with another layer of potatoes, fennel, and onions. Drizzle with a little oil, cover the dish with foil, and bake for 20 to 25 minutes, or until the vegetables are just tender.

3. While the vegetables are in the oven, season the fish with salt and pepper. Fill the cavity with some of the lemon wedges and some of the green fennel tops. Remove the vegetables from the oven, brush the fish with olive oil, and set the fish on top of the vegetables. Roast, uncovered, for 30 to 35 minutes, basting every 10 minutes with the oil that has accumulated in the dish.

4. Test the fish for doneness by inserting the tip of a sharp paring knife into the center. If the knife is warm, the fish is done.

5. Carefully transfer the fish onto a serving platter, garnish with more green fennel tops and lemon wedges, and serve the vegetables right out of the baking dish.

REMARKS A 2½- to 3-pound fish will serve only two to three people, so it is likely that you will have some vegetables left over. These are delicious reheated and served as a side to pan-seared salmon, shrimp, or scallops.

Sauté of Swordfish with Shrimp, Snow Peas, and Three Bell Peppers

Here is a quick stir-fry that only takes minutes to do once you have prepared the snow peas and peppers. I like to serve this dish with a side of steamed jasmine rice flavored with toasted pine nuts or a cumin- and scallion-scented couscous. Be sure not to overcook the fish. Swordfish is at its best when cooked somewhat rare.

SERVES 4

- 2 tablespoons soy sauce
- 2 tablespoons mirin
- 1 garlic clove, mashed
- 3 tablespoons grapeseed or canola oil
- ¾ pound large shrimp, peeled and cut in half
- Salt and coarsely ground black pepper
- 1 pound swordfish, cut into 1-inch cubes, skin removed
- ¾ cup finely diced bell peppers (red, yellow, and green mixed)
- 2 cups snow peas cut into fine julienne
- 2 tablespoons dry sherry
- 2 tablespoons minced cilantro or mint, optional

1. In a small bowl, combine the soy sauce, mirin, and garlic and whisk well.

2. In a large heavy skillet or flat-bottomed wok, heat half the oil. Season the shrimp with salt and pepper and add to the hot oil. Cook for 1 minute or until the shrimp just turn a bright pink. Remove with a slotted spoon to a dish.

3. Add the remaining oil to the wok and when it's very hot, add the swordfish cubes. Season with salt and pepper and sauté over high heat for 2 minutes, turning the fish cubes to brown them evenly.

4. Add the bell peppers and snow peas and sauté for another minute, or until the snow peas are just tender. Return the shrimp to the pan together with the sherry and cook for 30 seconds. Add the soy mixture, bring to a simmer, and immediately transfer the swordfish and shrimp to a serving bowl.

5. Garnish with cilantro or mint and serve immediately.

Sautéed Scallops with Red Bell Pepper and Chili Sauce

Here is a quick flavor-packed sauce that goes well with grilled fish, steaks, scallops, and shrimp. I often make it with leftover roasted red, yellow, or orange bell peppers. The sauce will keep well for a week, so you can double and triple the recipe.

Since the best scallops appear in the market in the fall, I usually serve this dish accompanied by Fricassee of Roasted Eggplants and Two Mushrooms, page 124, or simply boiled and buttered new potatoes.

SERVES 4

3 tablespoons unsalted butter

1 small shallot, minced

2 garlic cloves, minced

1 large roasted red bell pepper, seeded and finely cubed

¾ cup chicken stock or fish bouillon

Salt and freshly ground black pepper

1 teaspoon Thai chili sauce or a few drops of Tabasco

2 tablespoons minced chives

1 pound large sea scallops

½ tablespoon canola oil

Whole chives and sprigs of flat-leaf parsley

1. In a small skillet, heat half the butter. Add the shallot and garlic and cook for 2 or 3 minutes or until soft but not browned. Add the bell pepper and stock. Season with salt and pepper, bring to a simmer, and cook for 5 minutes.

2. Transfer the mixture to a blender and puree until smooth. Add the chili sauce or Tabasco. The sauce should be rather spicy. Transfer the sauce to a bowl. Add the chives.

3. Season the scallops with salt and pepper. In a large nonstick skillet, heat the remaining butter and the oil. Add the scallops and sauté over high heat until they are nicely browned on both sides. Lower the heat and cook for another 2 minutes, or until the scallops are just done. Do not overcook. Transfer the scallops to a dish.

4. Place a dollop of sauce on individual serving plates. Top with 3 to 4 scallops and garnish with the chives and parsley.

Spicy Shrimp and Ginger Fritters with a Ginger-Tamari Dipping Sauce

I am always on the lookout for shellfish recipes, especially those for shrimp, which are so easily available these days. Here is a quick and delicious shrimp fritter that I like to serve as an hors d'oeuvre as well as a topping for the Avocado Salad, page 109.

SERVES 6

DIPPING SAUCE

3 tablespoons tamari or light soy sauce

Juice of 2 limes

1 large garlic clove, mashed

1 teaspoon freshly grated ginger

6 tablespoons extra virgin olive oil

3 tablespoons minced scallions

Freshly ground white pepper

FRITTERS

1 pound medium shrimp, peeled and cubed

¼ cup minced shallots

¼ cup minced scallions

Juice of 1 large lemon

1 tablespoon finely minced jalapeño pepper

2 tablespoons minced peeled fresh ginger

Coarse salt and freshly ground white pepper

Peanut oil, for frying

1. Make the dipping sauce: Combine the tamari or thin soy sauce, lime juice, garlic, and ginger in a small bowl. Whisk in the oil, slowly, until emulsified. Add the scallions, season with pepper, and whisk until well blended. Set aside.

2. Make the fritters: Combine the shrimp, shallots, scallions, lemon juice, jalapeño and ginger in a food processor and puree until smooth. Season highly with salt and pepper.

3. Heat ½ inch peanut oil in a nonstick skillet over medium-high heat. Shape the shrimp mixture with wet hands into 1½-inch disks and fry in batches for about 1 minute, or until nicely browned on both sides. Season with a little salt and serve as a topping for salads or as an hors d'oeuvre with the dipping sauce.

Fillets of Salmon in Teriyaki Marinade with Gingered Carrots

Teriyaki marinade seems to be the marinade of the moment, and it deserves to be popular because it adds such a nice flavor to chicken, beef, and especially salmon. I like to serve this simple dish with carrots or parsnips or butternut squash, which can be prepared the same way as the carrots. A side bowl of jasmine or basmati rice will complement the dish nicely.

SERVES 4

⅓ cup light soy sauce

2 tablespoons mirin

3 tablespoons rice wine vinegar

2 tablespoons brown sugar

1 large garlic clove, crushed

4 salmon fillets (about 7 ounces each)

3 tablespoons unsalted butter

4 large carrots, peeled and cut on the diagonal into thick slices

Salt and freshly ground black pepper

4 fine slices peeled fresh ginger plus 2 teaspoons freshly grated

⅓ cup fish bouillon or water

Sprigs of fresh cilantro

1 avocado, finely sliced, optional

1. In a bowl, combine the soy sauce, mirin, rice vinegar, 1 tablespoon of the brown sugar, and the garlic. Whisk the mixture until well combined. Place the salmon fillets in a zippered plastic bag, add the marinade, and refrigerate for 2 to 4 hours.

2. Forty-five minutes before serving, preheat the oven to 400°F.

3. In a heavy cast-iron skillet, heat the butter. Add the carrots and season with salt and pepper. Sauté the carrots over medium heat until they are lightly browned.

4. Add the remaining 1 tablespoon sugar and the ginger and toss the carrots until they are nicely glazed. Add the bouillon or water. Cover the skillet and place in the oven. Roast the carrots for 10 to 12 minutes, or until tender and nicely glazed.

Remove from the oven and correct the seasoning with salt and pepper.

5. Turn on the broiler. Remove the salmon fillets from the marinade, place in an ovenproof dish, and broil 4 inches from the heat source for 4 to 6 minutes.

6. Place a mound of carrots on individual serving plates, top with a salmon fillet, and garnish with cilantro and avocado. Serve immediately.

Tuna Tartare

Tuna tartare is amazingly easy to make, provided, of course, that you get impeccably fresh tuna. Because I like it so much, I continue to order it in restaurants and have tried many versions. Right now I like this one the best. Don't be daunted by the long ingredient list. All the items except the tuna are pantry basics that you should have on hand at all times. Deep-fried wonton skins make a terrific accompaniment. Place a large spoonful of the tartare between two skins and serve, accompanied by marinated cucumbers or a simple sprig of cilantro.

SERVES 4 TO 5

1 pound very fresh tuna

2 to 3 cornichons, minced

1 tablespoon minced jalapeño pepper

2 tablespoons capers or more to taste

1 small shallot, minced

1 teaspoon finely grated lemon zest

Coarse salt and freshly ground black pepper

2 tablespoons sesame oil

1 teaspoon Thai chili sauce or Chinese Hot oil

2 tablespoons mayonnaise

Finely sliced seedless cucumber, left unpeeled, and small sprigs of dill or cilantro

I. Finely slice the tuna with a very sharp knife. Cut each slice into ¼-inch dice. Add the cornichons, jalapeño, capers, shallot, and lemon zest. Toss gently and season with salt and pepper. Add the sesame oil and chili sauce and toss again. Correct the seasoning. The tartare should be slightly spicy.

2. Fold in the mayonnaise and correct the seasoning. Serve lightly chilled but not cold. Garnish with the cucumber and herbs.

REMARKS Tuna tartare is at its best served within an hour. Although it will change color, it will keep well for several hours.

■ **Broiled Chicken Legs with Herb Butter** ■ **Bouillabaisse of Chicken** ■ **Slow-Braised Chicken Breasts with Peas and Lemon-Dill Sauce** ■ **Provençal Chicken with a Sherry Vinegar–Garlic Essence and Concassé of Tomatoes** ■ **Ragout of Chicken Legs with Fennel Sausage** ■ **Roasted Chicken à la Flamande** ■ **Fried Cornish Hens "al Ajillo"** ■ **Roast Duck with Sautéed Pears** ■ **Fried Marinated Quail** ■ **Grilled Quail with Pineapple Caramel** ■ **Perfectly Roasted Turkey with a Mustard-Herb Rub**

When I was growing up, chicken was a bird that was admired and treated with great respect. The purchasing of a chicken was taken very seriously; its cooking possibilities even more so. Both my mother and grandmother would only buy their chickens from one "chicken lady," Mercedes, at the Barcelona market. At home, we all gathered around to admire the bird's full breast and lovely shape. Settling on a cooking method took time. Would it be better poached or roasted? And how should we flavor it? With herbs, or perhaps just a touch of wine, or the simple way—with some good stock and a generous amount of butter? Some birds begged to be braised with root vegetables and whole cloves of garlic. Others were clearly born to be roasted.

And the discussion didn't end once the chicken was cooked. Was this chicken as good as the one from the week before? Mercedes had seemed slightly less friendly this time around, and maybe that was why her chicken wasn't as good. Should we—heaven forbid—take the unthinkable step of switching poultry sources? That would have meant buying from Mercedes' sister-in-law, who sold equally fine-looking chickens down at the other end of the market. This conversation would last for the length of the meal, yet when we were done, we'd agree that the chicken had been excellent.

My mother and grandmother would remain loyal to Mercedes, and we'd begin, almost immediately, planning our next meal.

If chicken was a religion in my family, then France's Bresse region—home of the famous Poulet de Bresse—was our cathedral. Five times each year, we'd make a pilgrimage from our home in Barcelona to Bresse, where we would always dine at L'Auberge Blanc. I still have vivid memories of the cozy dining room, decorated with large copper casseroles filled with fresh flowers and the flecks of sunlight that filtered through the lace curtains. Reservations for Sunday lunch were a must and had to be made months in advance, and the anticipation made the meal even more wonderful. Everyone there always seemed to be in a celebratory mood, all eager to sample the special bird after miles of travel, and we were never disappointed.

Here, the chicken could be ordered either poached *en garniture*, which included various seasonal vegetables simmered in flavorful broth, or perfectly roasted with homefried potatoes. Occasionally Mme. Blanc would also offer her trademark chicken *en cocotte*, a casserole-braised bird served with plenty of sweet garlic cloves, pearl onions, and cubed bacon.

When I moved to the United States in the seventies, the entire chicken experience changed. I still recall my first American supermarket outing. I stood in awe before a long poultry counter, studying whole chickens, cut-up chickens, family packs of wings, thighs, drumsticks, and even gizzards. Chicken livers by the pound, and skinless, boneless breasts were new to me. The choice was amazing; you could get as much chicken as you wanted, and in any cut or shape or size. I had visions of a succulent roasted bird and richly flavored stock.

I went into a chicken-buying frenzy and soon found myself up to my elbows in bones and wings, not to mention carrots, leeks, celery, and parsley. I cooked all day, with much anticipation, so what went wrong? Why was my stock greasy and flavorless? Why did the birds refuse to brown properly? And why were the livers watery and mushy? More was definitely not better, I learned. American chickens were not the same as their European counterparts. My quest for a flavorful bird was about to begin.

I sought out old-fashioned New York butchers, including several well-known kosher butchers. I trolled through Chinatown on a tip, seeking a fresh chicken from an unnamed storefront there. I tried to improve my luck through cooking methods as well, experimenting with marinades and spice rubs, but the results never rose to the heights of a simple Barcelona market chicken.

I soon learned why. A little research revealed that American chickens were almost all mass produced, raised on a diet that left them fatty and bland. And because of regulations, they were—and still are—soaked in water at length before being brought to market. Also, chickens that arrived "fresh" in grocery stores were actually partially frozen; hence their watery consistency and failure to brown. I almost despaired, but how could I give up on something that had been part of my repertoire for so long and that I knew was open to so many different preparations? And chicken represented something else for me—it represented family, and those leisurely meals and in-depth discussions around the table. So I kept on trying, never giving up on my favorite food.

These days, things are looking up—way up. Poultry farming has changed dramatically, primarily because of the newfound popularity of roasted chicken. As more and more chefs are searching for real flavor in poultry, the public benefits in turn. Organic chicken farming has had spectacular growth, and small producers around the country have found that there is a sizeable market for their free-range birds, despite their higher cost. While most supermarkets continue to sell mass-produced poultry, they are responding to consumer demand for other options. Recently, I walked into a Los Angeles supermarket and found four different organic brands available, two of them free-range as well. What this means is that we as consumers are now in a position to select the optimal bird for a juicy roast, a flavorful sauté, or a wonderful, rich stock. Never have our chicken options been better in this country than they are right now. In the more than twenty-five years since I stood in front of that supermarket counter, chicken has come a very long way.

If you can't locate top-notch chicken in your area, be sure to tell your supermarket manager or local butcher that you, like so many Americans, would be willing to pay a higher price for quality. While our birds do not quite compete with their European counterparts as yet, I firmly believe that before long they will, and eventually Americans will be able to enjoy the kind of bird that has made chicken one of the favorite foods of millions of people around the world.

Is there anything special I should look for when buying a chicken?

I think that you can learn to pick out a really good chicken. A fresh chicken should look plump and rosy. I would avoid buying chicken that is already wrapped, but if you have no other choice, check the package carefully and make sure there is no blood in it and the flesh of the chicken is not bruised or torn. After a while you will be able to tell a good fresh bird every time.

I used to go to a seamstress on the Lower East Side of New York who always seemed to be cooking the best chickens. As soon as I got off the elevator, I would get a whiff of her rich chicken soup or the aroma of a buttery roasting bird. She would treat me to a deliciously tender gizzard or the crunchy tip of a wing, and I begged her to introduce me to her butcher, whom she had been patronizing for fifty years.

At the butcher's, she carefully inspected several chickens until she found one that met with her approval. I roasted the chicken simply, and it was without a doubt the best one I've ever had. Of course, I kept returning to that butcher, and yes, the chickens I got from him were good, but somehow never as good as the one my seamstress had picked out for me that day.

What is a free-range chicken?

In Europe, a free-range chicken is literally a chicken that runs freely and finds its own food. While it's working for its food, the chicken develops some muscle rather than fat. But most free-range chickens here are raised differently. Although they're allowed to go out of their coops, their food is kept in the same place every day and is given to them. So American free-range chickens develop a little more muscle than those that are force-fed around the clock, but I have not found there to be a big difference in taste.

My market carries organic, free-range chicken as well as branded poultry from Perdue and Tyson. Is it worth the difference in price to buy organic or free-range?

It's all a matter of taste and testing. Once when I was in California teaching some classes, I did an experiment with some students. We went to the grocery store and scooped up one of every kind of chicken they carried. There were three brands of organic chicken (remember, this was California), two free-range chickens, and the usual branded chicken as well. We took them back to the school and roasted them all the same way, after which we had a tasting. Most students preferred the organic chickens, while others thought the free-range one was more intensely flavored.

It is important that you try several types of chickens in your area. Organic chickens must be raised in qualifying conditions. They can be vaccinated but not medicated; they must be fed organically and have access to the outdoors.

What is the difference between white- and yellow-skinned chickens?

Skin color is an indicator of feed and not of quality. I find yellow-skinned chickens to be very fatty and try to avoid them.

A lot of food magazines recommend using kosher chickens these days. What makes them better?

Kosher chickens are killed under rabbinical supervision with a special knife. They are then inspected for any defects or scars, any of which cause them to be rejected. After that, they are salted, which makes their texture somewhat firmer. Because of dietary laws, they have to be sold within 3 days of slaughtering, making them fresher than other chickens.

TIP When buying a kosher chicken, you can check the feet. They should be pearly white, an indication of freshness.

What is the difference between a broiler, fryer, and roaster? Is one better than the others?

These names have nothing to do with quality: they refer only to size. Broilers and fryers are pretty much the same size and weigh between 2½ and 3½ pounds, while roasters are larger and weigh between 4½ and 6½ pounds. To confuse matters further, these categories are different on the East and West coasts. On the West Coast, broilers and fryers weight 4½ to 5 pounds, or about a pound more than on the East Coast.

TIP If your chicken comes with a nice-looking liver, don't throw it away! It is a delicacy. Instead, combine it with milk to cover in a small bowl and let it sit for 30 minutes. Pat dry and sauté with a finely sliced onion in a little butter.

Is it better to buy chicken breasts on the bone or boneless?

Buying chicken breasts on the bone makes great sense because it gives you the extra bonus of having bones for stock. These I keep in a tightly sealed bag in my freezer. Once I have about 3 pounds of bones, I combine them with carrots, leeks, some celery, and parsley to make a quick stock.

To make quick chicken stock

MAKES 6 CUPS

2 to 3 pounds breast bones (bones from approximately 4 breasts)

1 chicken bouillon cube

1 carrot

2 celery stalks with tops

1 leek with 2 inches of greens attached, white part only cut in half lengthwise

1 medium onion, unpeeled

3 to 4 sprigs of flat-leaf parsley

Pinch of salt

Combine all ingredients with 8 cups water in a 6-quart pot. Bring to a boil, reduce the heat, and simmer for 30 to 45 minutes. Cool and strain. Store the chicken stock in either the freezer or the refrigerator. Bring the stock back to a boil every 2 days if you store it in the refrigerator.

TIP **It is very important to skim a stock in the very early stages of cooking, because the impurities from the bones rise to the surface as soon as the stock comes to a boil. If the stock is not skimmed, it will remain cloudy and greasy. Also, a stock should not boil, but rather simmer. Bring it to a brisk simmer, reduce the heat, cover it partially, and then simmer gently. This prevents the stock from being too greasy and makes it easier to degrease it once it cools.**

Can the bones from a roasted turkey or chicken be used to make stock?

I have never been happy using cooked bones to make stock. The initial roasting zaps most of the flavor from the bones. For a truly flavorful stock, I much prefer to begin with raw bones.

However, if you are roasting a turkey, it's a shame to throw away that entire carcass. Use it to make turkey stock, but boost the flavor with plenty of leek greens, carrots, and celery. Also, if possible, add some uncooked chicken wings, which are inexpensive and easy to find in every supermarket.

Can I use chicken stock for every kind of soup?

Chicken stock works for every kind of vegetable soup with two exceptions: You should not use it for traditional French onion soup, nor should you use it for classic borscht. Both of these soups are usually made with beef stock. The good news is that I have used chicken stock for seafood soups as well. So for me, it's the most important stock to have on hand.

How do you bone a chicken breast?

The best way to do this is with a boning knife, but you can also use a very sharp 4-inch paring knife. Place the chicken breast in front of you skin side up. Make a sharp slit in the center of the breast and keep your knife very close to the breast bone. Continue cutting the meat away from the bone and keep the knife as parallel to the bone as you possibly can. When most of the meat is detached, make a sharp cut lengthwise, completely detaching the breast meat from the bone. Remove the skin if you like and trim off any bits of fat or tendon.

TIP Once a breast is split, it's much harder to bone, so be sure to buy the whole breast.

If I can't cook a chicken right away, how long can I store it?

Fresh chicken will keep for up to 3 days. Be sure not to leave it in a package or a plastic bag, but rather rinse it lightly and wrap it in a kitchen towel. Do not use paper towels. I have noticed that many organic chickens now have a "cook-by" date, which is a good indication of freshness. Sometimes a "fresh" chicken will have a slight odor when removed from its package. If this does not go away after it is rinsed, be sure to return it to the store.

We hear so much about salmonella these days. What safety measures do I need to take when preparing chicken?

I find that following simple commonsense guidelines is all you need to do. I always rinse the chicken and dry it thoroughly. I also wash my cutting board, knife, and anything else that has come into contact with the raw chicken or its juices in very hot water. However, I do not believe in cooking chicken to death and find that all is well at an inner temperature of 165° to 170°F. Remember to refrigerate all chicken, even when marinating.

What exactly does brining do to a chicken?

Brining is a hot new trend, but it has pluses and minuses. The salt in the brine permeates the chicken so that the meat is evenly seasoned. Brining fans claim that this gives a chicken fuller flavor and firmer texture and keeps the breast meat moist and tender, but it can be difficult to control the level of saltiness. Personally, I like my chickens the old-fashioned way. If you're undecided, try preparing one brined chicken and one non-brined chicken—roasting both—and decide which you prefer. For the brine use ¼ cup kosher salt, ¼ cup sugar, and 2 quarts water. Whisk the mixture to blend thoroughly, then transfer to a zippered plastic bag together with the chicken. Refrigerate for 24 hours. Rinse the brine off and dry the chicken thoroughly with a cotton towel before roasting.

How can I make a roasted chicken that is both crisp and still juicy?

The problem starts with processing of chickens in the United States. American plants use the water-chilling process, in which chicken is dipped in an ice-cold chlorine and water solution to quickly decrease the body temperature and kill bacteria. This is why American chickens get to the market with very wet skins. It is therefore important to dry the chicken thoroughly with a kitchen towel before roasting so you will get a crisp skin.

Also try roasting smaller chickens. Instead of one 5- to 6-pound bird, choose two 2½- to 3½-pound chickens. Yes, it's more work, but the results are worthwhile.

Once the chicken is well seasoned, I roast it at 425°F in a heavy roasting pan without a rack and baste it every 10 to 15 minutes with the pan juices and some broth. You can also use a method that requires less basting: Roast the chicken for 25 minutes on each side, finishing with 10 to 15 minutes breast side up. Roasting a chicken breast side up the entire time will brown it more evenly, but you will lose some juiciness.

TIP The European method of slowly decreasing the body temperature of chicken by using fans and cold air rather than water is slowly gaining popularity among processors of high-quality chickens. It is well worth checking out a good butcher in your area to see if you can find this type of bird.

How can I keep a roasting chicken from sticking to the pan?

There are three steps I usually take. First, I dry the chicken thoroughly. That doesn't mean dabbing it with a paper towel. It means wrapping the chicken in an absorbent tea towel for an hour or even overnight. (Try to do this a day ahead.) Second, be sure to use a heavy-duty roasting pan. The heavier the roasting pan, the less chance that the pan juices will dry out and stick. Third, never let the chicken "fall asleep" in the oven. Instead, keep moving it around a bit and baste every 10 to 15 minutes to keep it from sticking.

TIP When roasting a chicken, it is a good idea to remove the wing tips, especially if the pan is small. The tips will often stick to the side of the pan, so clipping them off gives the chicken less chance to stick.

Do you recommend trussing a chicken for roasting?

I have gone through long periods in my cooking career when I swore by trussing and highly recommended doing it, but now I prefer roasting an untrussed bird. Still, I find that trussing can save the wings from sticking and is still the best way to cook a chicken on a rotisserie.

TIP Using a bulb baster makes basting easy. Be sure to get a glass one that cleans easily, and always use the hot pan juices for basting.

I love the taste and texture of a chicken that has been cooked rotisserie style. Can I duplicate that at home?

A brand-new gadget on the market, which looks like a giant skewer, will do this for you. The one I've seen is the Spanek Vertical Chicken Roaster. Although it makes a big mess in your oven, it produces a crispy, evenly browned bird. However, in addition to the messy cleanup, you also miss out on the delicious pan juices that you get from a traditionally roasted chicken.

Can all the various cuts of chicken parts be used interchangeably in a recipe?

Dark meat and white meat have different flavors. The dark meat (legs, thighs) is juicier and more flavorful, while the white meat (breast) has more subtle flavor, making it more of a blank canvas. In general, white meat goes with milder and lighter sauces such as an herb or cream-based sauce. Dark meat marries well with ethnic flavors, spices, curries, and Middle Eastern and Far Eastern spices and flavors. Then there are dishes that use the whole cut-up chicken and straddle both categories, in which the chicken is braised with tomatoes and herbs. There are also some new "cuts" available now, like drumettes (the fleshy part of the wings), which can be used like mini-drumsticks, and boned and skinned thighs, which I find to be the most flavorful part of the chicken. They can be braised in the oven, broiled, or grilled.

When a recipe calls for grilling chicken, can I use a broiler instead?

The broiler works very well for chicken that has some fat. The advantage of the grill is that you can move the chicken around so that it cooks evenly and thoroughly. The broiler will char the outside quickly while leaving it raw inside. Be sure to watch the chicken carefully and turn the broiler off. Also, grilling lends food a very special "grilled" flavor, which broiling does not.

What is the difference between chicken cutlets and chicken fillets?

In some areas, cutlets are flattened or butterflied chicken breasts. In other areas, the flattened tenderloins are called chicken cutlets.

Recently I have also seen tenderloins sold as both "tenders" and "chicken fillet tenders," which is confusing since the tenderloin and the fillet are one and the same.

Can I prepare chicken cutlets and breasts the same way?

The very best way to prepare a chicken cutlet is to bread it as you would the Viennese schnitzel. Just dredge it lightly in flour, dip it in beaten egg and unseasoned bread crumbs, and then fry it in a mixture of corn oil and butter just as you would a veal cutlet. However, I realize that a lot of people buy cutlets because they like their low-fat aspect, so if you are trying to avoid fat, season the cutlets with salt and pepper and pan-sear over high heat with just a touch of butter or oil. To give a cutlet more flavor, try flavoring it with herbs and some spices, such as a pinch of cumin, ground coriander, and freshly ground black pepper. Marinades such as teriyaki sauce work well, too, because they make the cutlet brown very quickly, so chances are you will not overcook it.

TIP **Pan-seared chicken cutlets are an excellent topping for a mixed green salad.**

Is there a trick to keeping chicken breasts moist?

The most important thing about buying a chicken breast is making sure the tenderloin is still attached. Unfortunately, it's hard to tell if that is the case by looking through the package, because many grocery stores roll the chicken breasts to give you the impression that the breast is plump. When the chicken breast is cooking, the tenderloin forms a layer between the pan and the rest of the meat and keeps it moist.

We eat chicken breasts frequently, so I feel I've made them every possible way. What do you think is the absolute best way to cook boneless, skinless chicken breasts?

Chicken breasts are best when sautéed in some butter and oil, preferably in a cast-iron skillet, then braised, covered, with some good chicken broth for 7 to 8 minutes. At this point you can add a number of interesting herbs and vegetables. I particularly like dill and tarragon with chicken, as well as sautéed wild mushrooms, cucumbers, and peas. Some lemon and heavy cream make interesting additions. Remember that chicken breasts are completely neutral and are open to almost endless possibilities.

I've tried grilling chicken breasts, but they always seem to dry out. What am I doing wrong?

You're probably not doing anything wrong; chicken breasts are low in fat, and they dry out easily when grilled. I'd recommend a gas grill rather than charcoal because a charcoal grill's heat is hard to control. Keep your gas grill on medium-high and cook a chicken breast—with the tenderloin attached—for just 4 minutes on each side, basting it with mixture of lemon juice, olive oil, and fresh herbs. You will be amazed at the delicious and juicy results.

How far in advance can I cook chicken breasts?

It's not really necessary to cook chicken breasts in advance: they cook in less than 10 minutes anyway. But if you brown chicken breasts on top of the stove, cooking them no more than 6 to 8 minutes, or until they are still slightly pink inside, you can prepare them 2 or 3 hours ahead of time. Later, you can reheat them either on top of the stove or by microwaving them for 1 or 2 minutes. Make sure the breasts have the tenderloin attached if you are going to do this; it will help to keep them moist.

I like to tenderize chicken by marinating it. Any suggestions?

Many recipes suggest that a marinade tenderizes chicken. That is not so; what it does is enhance the flavor. You can marinate chicken for as long as 24 hours or as little as 4 hours. For whole chickens and chicken legs, I usually reserve full-flavored marinades that contain strong spices such as hot chiles, ginger, and cumin. For chicken breasts, I use simple marinades that are based on olive oil, lemon juice, and herbs.

I see so many recipes for grilled chicken breasts, but I prefer the legs. Any suggestions for quick ways to prepare them?

Although I'm not a big fan of broiling, I think this method does an excellent job on chicken legs. Simply season them with salt, pepper, and a touch of cayenne, then run them under the broiler until well browned. Finish cooking the legs in a 400°F oven for 15 minutes. For chicken legs with a delicious sauce, see Broiled Chicken Legs with Herb Butter, page 201.

I see family packages of chicken wings in my market. Are there any interesting ways to use them?

There isn't a lot of meat on chicken wings, but they do make a very tasty appetizer when broiled, grilled, or deep-fried. I usually count about 3 wings per person, although many of my friends can consume a lot more than that.

TIP **Think dipping sauces when grilling chicken wings; a zesty vinaigrette, a spicy jalapeño-flavored mayonnaise, and a mustard-garlic dressing are some flavorful ideas.**

I like to stir-fry chicken. Which cut should I use?

One of the best quick-cooking cuts for chicken stir-fries is the chicken tenderloin, sometimes sold as "chicken tenders." The tenderloin is juicy, cooks quickly, and doesn't dry out as much as chicken breasts. When you want to cook chicken together with root vegetables, which takes a little more time, use boneless and skinless thighs, cut in half.

What's the best way to prepare chicken for chicken salad?

Contrary to what most recipes suggest, I don't believe that chicken breasts make great chicken salad. My first choice is a roasted chicken. If you prefer the breast, poach bone-in chicken breasts in a light bouillon with some aromatic vegetables such as leeks, carrots, celery, onions, and a couple of unpeeled garlic cloves. Do not overcook. Let the chicken cool completely in the broth before making the salad.

TIP **For a terrific chicken salad, I often buy a ready-cooked rotisserie chicken and cut it up. Then, rather than binding it with mayonnaise, I like to toss the chicken in a mustard vinaigrette, adding some diced red bell pepper, a diced dill gherkin, and a little minced red onion, and let the salad marinate for an hour or two before serving.**

Any tips for roasting a juicy turkey at Thanksgiving? I usually make a 24-pounder, and it is always somewhat dry.

I can easily say that I am a fanatic about not using large turkeys. I'd rather use two 10- to 12-pound birds than one that large. Remember that your turkey needs attention. You simply cannot leave it in the oven, go for a long walk, and then come home expecting a perfectly roasted bird. It can, however, be amazingly good if it is treated carefully. Choose smaller birds and don't stuff them. Season them well and baste every 15 minutes. Keep in mind, too, that you can't have it both ways. If you want juicy dark meat, you will have to sacrifice the breast somewhat. Smaller birds, 10 to 12 pounds, roast more quickly, which gives the white meat less of a chance to dry out.

Does stuffing keep a turkey moist?

That depends on the kind of stuffing you use. Since bread absorbs moisture, bread stuffing will draw out much of a bird's natural juices. Sausage stuffings are a good choice because they're somewhat fatty and will help baste the bird from the inside.

I find turkey very bland. Will a marinade make it tastier?

A turkey will absorb the flavors of a marinade and take on a somewhat different character. However, since turkey has such a mild flavor, I prefer a full-flavored dry rub (see Perfectly Roasted Turkey with a Mustard-Herb Rub, page 216). Keep in mind that at holiday times, even those who like to try new flavors usually prefer the simply roasted turkey that tradition dictates.

I've read that brining a turkey is a good idea. What is the advantage of brining and how do I do it?

Brining a turkey has become the favored method of many cooks, who feel that it renders a juicier bird and firms up the meat. Personally, I only brine smaller turkeys, because brining requires placing the bird in a large zippered plastic bag full of water, and that takes up a great deal of refrigerator space. To brine, coat the turkey with 1 cup coarse salt and transfer to a large zippered plastic bag. Fill the bag with water, place it in the fridge, and let sit for 24 hours. Rinse thoroughly, dry with an absorbent towel, and use it for any recipe of your choice.

I've heard you shouldn't leave a stuffed turkey at room temperature. Is that true?

Yes, I definitely suggest refrigerating a turkey once it has been stuffed, particularly if you use a sausage mixture. However, I do not believe you should concern yourself too much regarding the whole issue of not stuffing a bird until just before putting it in the oven. If it is refrigerated, it will be fine for several hours before roasting.

Is it better to roast a turkey breast side down or breast side up?

I have tried it both ways, and here's the difference: When you roast it breast side down, you may end up with a somewhat moister breast, but you're also running the risk of having the skin stick if you let the pan juices run dry. If you roast it breast side up, you absolutely must tend to it by basting every 15 minutes to keep it moist.

I often see a good buy at the supermarket on turkey breasts. Does it make sense to roast the breast alone?

When well seasoned and simply roasted, a turkey breast is delicious, and it also makes for a good-natured and inexpensive main course. It's more efficient, too, since it cooks more quickly than a whole bird. If you really like turkey, the breast is the perfect size for six or eight people. It benefits greatly from a rub or a marinade, after which I roast or grill it simply, basting often with chicken bouillon.

Is there an easy way to grill a turkey?

Absolutely. Follow the directions for indirect grilling on page 350. Place it off the heat and roast to 160°F, and then let it sit for 10 to 15 minutes before carving. I usually stick with small turkeys (12 to 13 pounds), which take about 1 hour 30 minutes to 1 hour 45 minutes and do not require basting.

TIP **For a lovely smoky flavor, add some wood chips to the fire when roasting a turkey. Best woods are apple, lilac, and hickory. Be sure to soak the chips in water for 20 minutes before adding to the coals. Depending on the size of the turkey, you may have to add wood more than once.**

I'm always looking for low-fat meats, so turkey burgers appeal to me. How should I prepare them?

Ground turkey is low in fat, but it is also low in flavor. It needs all the help it can get, so seasoning assertively is very important. Try this: Sauté a minced onion until just soft and incorporate it into the ground turkey together with some minced parsley, 1 mashed garlic clove, lots of freshly ground pepper, salt, a touch of cayenne, and a sprinkling of thyme. Pan-sear the burgers in some butter and oil or grill until just cooked, being careful not to overcook. Keep in mind, though, that unless the ground-turkey package promises that it is 5 percent fat or less, your fat savings are not that great.

TIP **Ground turkey is especially good in meatloaf when it is cooked to well done with a lot of seasoning and possibly served with a tomato sauce. Substitute ground turkey for some or all of the ground beef in your favorite meatloaf recipe.**

Is it better to buy an organic or a free-range turkey? How do you feel about frozen turkey?

I usually go with organic and have not found that the "free-range" tag warrants the difference in price. Also, there is no longer any reason to buy a frozen turkey. As long as you give your market a day's notice, it should be able to come up with a fresh one.

What are Cornish game hens? Can I prepare them the same way I would prepare a chicken?

In fact, you can do a lot with them, more than people think. Cornish game hens are not wild fowl; they are a small variety of chicken. On the practical side, they're a lovely dinner party entree, because they cook quickly. They have no distinctive flavor, and every preparation for whole chickens works with Cornish hens, as long as you adjust the cooking time. They do well on the grill, where they cook in 25 to 30 minutes, and when cut in half or quartered, they make very good finger foods. Cornish hens are also great roasted or braised.

I love the taste of squab and always look for it on restaurant menus. It does not seem to be as popular as it deserves to be and I would like to prepare it myself. How can I get it?

I agree with you. Squab is one of my favorite foods as well and I always order it when it is on the menu. Most good grocery stores will order squab for you if you give them one or two days' advance notice. Otherwise, you can order it from D'Artagnan (see Sources, page 398). The squabs they carry have plump breasts and are extremely flavorful.

Why is squab so much more expensive than chicken? Is it because it is wild?

Squabs are farm raised but take much longer to raise than chickens. A squab cannot be artificially inseminated, the birds are wed for life, and the courtship takes its time. It is followed by at the most nine baby chicks, which means that raising squabs is both time consuming and expensive. They come to market when they are twenty-eight days old and they must never have flown. If they have, they will be tough. This is a wonderful-tasting bird that is worth the splurge.

Can I substitute Cornish hens in recipes that call for quail or squab?

No. Quail and squab are more gamy, leaner birds that need a very short cooking period.

Is it okay to use frozen ducks? That's all my grocery store carries.

Yes. Frozen ducks are fine, so long as they don't show any signs of freezer burn. With most food, defrosting has to take place in the refrigerator.

Do remember to remove the bird from its plastic package as soon as it is defrosted and wrap it in an absorbent kitchen towel to get it nice and dry before popping it in the oven.

What exactly is a Long Island duck?

At one time, the eastern part of Long Island was home to many duck farms. Now that the building boom in that area has chased out farmers, ducks continue to be referred to as "Long Island ducks" when they are really Peking ducks raised in several other states, including Maryland, Delaware, and Pennsylvania.

Are duck breasts available individually like turkey breasts? Where can I get them?

The best duck breasts are those of Muscovy ducks, but sadly these are not yet available commercially. Moulard duck breasts are an equally fine substitute, which you can find in many supermarkets as well as by mail order. Many good grocery stores do carry vacuum-packed duck breasts, though. If you can't find a store near you, contact D'Artagnan, a company that provides many restaurants with specialty meats and poultry (see Sources, page 398).

I order duck in restaurants, but I've never tried to cook it at home. Is it complicated?

You're not alone. Many people seem intimidated by cooking duck, but in fact, it's one of the most good-natured foods you can prepare. It's literally foolproof. Whether you buy your duck frozen or fresh, medium or large, you almost can't go wrong if you follow this simple technique: roast it in a low oven for a long period of time (approximately 3 hours at 350°F). Besides all its other advantages, duck can be roasted well ahead of time and kept warm without a change in taste or texture. For me it's the number-one poultry in terms of flavor and ease of cooking. Try the Roasted Duck with Sautéed Pears, page 212, and you'll see what I mean.

TIP **If you prick the duck all over before roasting, roast it slowly at 350°F in a heavy-duty pan, baste it often with hot broth, and remove the fat from the pan with a bulb baster about every 15 minutes, you will end up with a duck that is very crisp with absolutely no fat underneath the skin.**

I'd like to buy a duck breast, but I don't know how to prepare it.

The secret to cooking a duck breast is to score the skin side first in a diamond pattern, then pan-sear it over low heat, skin side down, on top of the stove in a heavy cast-iron skillet until the skin is crisp and has released all or most of its fat. Then finish cooking in a 400°F oven for 10 to 12 minutes. Always serve duck breast rare or medium-rare. Since duck breast is a restaurant favorite, several cookbooks by top chefs contain wonderful recipes for it.

I love to grill chicken but have never attempted duck. Can it be done?

Because of its high fat content, duck does not lend itself to grilling; the fat melts and drips onto the coals, and then the flames flare up and burn the duck. I have, however, worked around this by poaching the duck first, then wrapping it in a towel and leaving it in the refrigerator overnight. The next day I slow-smoked it, and the results were delicious. Still, it's much easier and quicker to roast a duck in the oven, and the flavor is just as good. If you really crave that grilled taste, you can place a roasted duck on a gas grill for a few minutes after it is cooked through.

What is foie gras?

The ancient Egyptians noticed that ducks and geese stored extra calories in their livers just before they migrated, and that those livers were super tasty. Ever since, these birds have been cultivated for their livers, now known as foie gras, which can be incorporated into terrines or mousses, or sliced and cooked.

Can you use the liver that comes with a duck as a substitute for foie gras?

If only that were possible! Alas, the livers from store-bought ducks have very little flavor, and it's not really worth bothering with them. Do spring for some foie gras once or twice a year—it's a treat.

How do you cook foie gras?

Nothing can be simpler. The liver must be very cold. Dip your knife in hot water and make ½-inch slices. Heat a dry skillet to almost smoking, add the foie gras slices, and cook for 1 minute on each side. Drain on a double layer of paper towels before serving.

I finally made a Christmas goose and it was so tough. What could I have done wrong?

Usually it means that your goose was too old. For a goose to be delicious and tender, it needs to be young, so look for a smaller goose in the market. Be sure to roast the goose at 325°F and spoon off the fat every 15 to 20 minutes. Save the goose fat for sautéing anything from a steak to fish fillets. I usually freeze the fat in one-cup containers and use it all year as I need it.

Is it okay to buy a frozen goose? I cannot get a fresh one where I live.

Frozen geese are fine. Be sure to let them defrost in the refrigerator. This may take up to 2 days. Choose a goose that has a nice plump breast and plenty of fat that looks clean and unblemished.

Last Christmas a friend sent me two guinea hens and they are still in my freezer. How shall I prepare them?

Guinea hens are best simply roasted. Start by seasoning the hens with coarse salt, freshly ground pepper, and a sprinkling of thyme. Trussing the birds will keep the breast meat from drying out. Brown on top of the stove in a mixture of butter and oil and roast the birds on their sides at 400°F for 45 to 55 minutes, basting with good chicken stock every 10 minutes. The hens are done when the inner temperature is 145°F. Serve with a ragout of mushrooms, or a creamy risotto.

Broiled Chicken Legs with Herb Butter

Although I am not a great fan of the broiler, I find that I often turn to this recipe for a quick main course. Serve the chicken legs with a simple couscous and sautéed seasonal vegetables.

SERVES 4

8 chicken drumsticks

8 chicken thighs

Juice of 2 lemons

$^1/_4$ cup olive oil

2 tablespoons fresh thyme or 2 teaspoons dried thyme

$^1/_2$ teaspoon cayenne

Coarse salt and freshly ground black pepper

5 tablespoons unsalted butter, at room temperature

2 tablespoons minced fresh parsley, plus small whole leaves

1 tablespoon minced shallot

1 tablespoon minced fresh tarragon

$^3/_4$ cup chicken stock or bouillon

Lemon wedges

1. Place the chicken pieces in a large baking dish. Sprinkle with lemon juice, olive oil, thyme, and cayenne. Season with salt and pepper and chill for 4 to 6 hours.

2. In a bowl, combine the butter, minced parsley, shallot, and tarragon. Season with a pinch of salt and pepper and blend thoroughly.

3. Preheat the broiler. Transfer the chicken to a broiler or roasting pan and set 6 inches from the source of heat. Broil for 10 minutes on each side, making sure the chicken does not burn. Remove the pan from the oven, discard all the fat that has accumulated in the pan, and add the bouillon. Place a dollop of the herb butter on each piece of chicken.

4. Reduce the oven temperature to 400°F. Return the pan to the oven and continue to cook for another 5 minutes, or until the herb butter has just melted.

5. Transfer the chicken pieces to a serving plate. Spoon herb butter over them. Garnish with parsley leaves and lemon wedges.

Bouillabaisse of Chicken

What does a chicken bouillabaisse have in common with the great classic seafood stew? Not much. Still, the wonderful aroma and taste of saffron and a creamy garlicky aioli lend authenticity to this delicious chicken stew. Don't be put off by the length of the recipe; it is extremely easy to make and is even more flavorful reheated the next day.

SERVES 4

3 tablespoons olive oil

2 medium onions, quartered and finely sliced

1 small fennel bulb, quartered and finely sliced

3 large tomatoes, seeded and cubed

1 teaspoon dried thyme

1 teaspoon fennel seeds

Salt and freshly ground black pepper

8 chicken drumsticks

8 chicken thighs

10 cups chicken stock or bouillon

$\frac{1}{4}$ teaspoon loosely packed saffron threads

3 small Yukon Gold potatoes, peeled and cubed

2 small zucchini, cubed

1 large red bell pepper, seeded and cubed

2 cups cubed butternut squash

Minced flat-leaf parsley

Bowl of Puree of Celery Root, Potatoes, and Sweet Garlic (page 117), as accompaniment

1. In a large heavy casserole, heat the olive oil. Add the onions and fennel. Cook over medium heat, stirring occasionally, until slightly browned.

2. Add the tomatoes, thyme, and fennel seeds. Season with salt and pepper and continue to cook for 5 to 8 minutes, or until most of the tomato water has evaporated.

3. Season the chicken with salt and pepper and add to the casserole together with the chicken stock. Add the saffron. Bring to a boil, reduce the heat, and simmer for 35 to 40 minutes, or until the chicken is tender but not falling apart.

4. Skim off the fat and add the potatoes. Simmer until the potatoes are almost tender, about 10 minutes. Add the zucchini, bell pepper, and squash. Continue to simmer until the vegetables are soft, about 10 minutes longer. Taste and correct the seasoning. Serve hot in deep soup bowls, garnished with parsley and topped with a dollop of the puree.

Slow-Braised Chicken Breasts with Peas and Lemon-Dill Sauce

Grilled, sautéed, baked, or roasted chicken breasts are popular fare in every one of these preparations. And chefs and home cooks are always looking for interesting ways to prepare them. The mild taste of the chicken breasts takes well to many herbs and vegetables, and even fruit and lemon are perfect partners. When fresh peas are not available, you can use asparagus tips or cubed mushrooms instead. You can also substitute a mixture of tarragon and chives for the dill depending on your mood. Serve the dish with a simple Parmesan-flavored risotto.

SERVES 6

$\frac{1}{2}$ cup heavy cream

Juice of 1 lemon

3 whole boneless, skinless chicken breasts, cut in half

Salt and freshly ground white pepper

All-purpose flour, for dredging

3 tablespoons unsalted butter

2 teaspoons peanut oil

$\frac{1}{2}$ to $\frac{3}{4}$ cup chicken stock or bouillon

1 tablespoon flour mixed into a paste with 1 tablespoon softened butter

$\frac{1}{2}$ cup cooked fresh peas, optional

2 to 3 tablespoons minced fresh dill

1. In a small bowl, combine the cream and lemon juice, mix well, and set aside to develop flavor.

2. Dry the chicken breasts thoroughly with paper towels. Season with salt and pepper and dredge lightly in flour, shaking off the excess.

3. Melt the butter together with the oil in a large heavy skillet over high heat. Add the chicken breasts without crowding the skillet and sauté until nicely browned on both sides. Add a little stock or bouillon, reduce the heat, and simmer, covered, for 7 minutes, or until the juices run pale yellow when the chicken is pricked near the bone. Add a little more stock or bouillon to the skillet if the pan juices run dry before the chicken is done. Transfer the chicken to a dish.

4. Add the remaining stock or bouillon to the skillet, bring to a boil, and reduce to ¼ cup. Add the lemon-cream mixture, bring to a boil, and reduce slightly. Whisk in bits of the flour-and-butter paste until the sauce lightly coats the spoon. Correct the seasoning.

5. Reduce the heat to low. Return the chicken to the skillet together with the peas and just heat through. Transfer the chicken to a serving platter, spoon the sauce over, and garnish with dill, chives, or tarragon. Serve hot with buttered orzo or couscous.

Provençal Chicken with a Sherry Vinegar–Garlic Essence and Concassé of Tomatoes

We tend to think of roasted chicken as "comfort food," something best suited for cool weather, to be enjoyed with a side dish of buttery mashed potatoes. This is a summer version, which feels cool and inviting because of the creamy tomato sauce added to the pan juices just before serving. Serve with butter-braised yellow zucchini and crusty French bread.

SERVES 6

> 2 large ripe tomatoes, seeded and cut into
> $\frac{1}{2}$-inch dice
> 2 tablespoons extra virgin olive oil
> $\frac{1}{3}$ cup plus 2 teaspoons sherry vinegar
> 3 tablespoons fresh thyme leaves
> 2 tablespoons minced fresh chives
> Coarse salt and freshly ground black pepper
> 2 small whole chickens (about $2\frac{1}{2}$ pounds
>   each)
> 1 cup crème fraîche
> 2 teaspoons tomato paste
> 2 teaspoons Dijon mustard
> 2 garlic cloves, mashed
> 2 tablespoons unsalted butter
> 1 teaspoon canola or grapeseed oil
> 1 cup chicken stock or bouillon
> 2 tablespoons minced fresh flat-leaf parsley

1. Prepare the tomato concassé: In a small bowl, combine the tomatoes, olive oil, the 2 teaspoons vinegar, 1 tablespoon of the thyme, and the chives. Season with salt and pepper and mix well. Set aside to marinate.

2. Preheat the oven to 375°F.

3. Dry the chicken thoroughly with a kitchen towel. Sprinkle with the remaining 2 tablespoons thyme, the salt, and pepper; truss and set aside.

4. Combine the crème fraîche, tomato paste, mustard, and mashed garlic in a small bowl.

5. In a large heavy flameproof baking dish, melt the butter together with the canola oil over medium-high heat. Add the chicken and brown lightly on both sides. Add the remaining ⅓ cup sherry vinegar, bring to a boil, and cook until reduced to a glaze.

6. Add ½ cup of the stock to the baking dish, place in the center of the oven, and roast the chickens for 1 hour to 1 hour 15 minutes, or until the juices run pale yellow when the meat is pricked near the bone. Baste the chickens with hot stock every 10 to 15 minutes. Be careful not to let the pan juices run dry. When the chickens are done, remove them to a cutting board.

7. Thoroughly degrease the pan juices and return them to the baking dish together with any remaining stock. Place over medium heat. Whisk in the crème fraîche mixture and reduce slightly.

8. Add the tomato concassé and just heat through; do not let boil. Taste the sauce, correct the seasoning, and keep warm.

9. Carve the chickens and place on a serving platter. Spoon the sauce over the chickens and sprinkle with the parsley. Serve at once.

Ragout of Chicken Legs with Fennel Sausage

Here is a wonderfully gutsy, cool-weather chicken dish that is open to seasonal variations, such as roasted bell peppers cut into fine julienne or some shiitake mushrooms sautéed in a touch of olive oil. Serve the ragout with a side dish of soft polenta or buttery mashed potatoes.

SERVES 6

8 chicken drumsticks

4 tablespoons extra virgin olive oil

1 pound fresh sweet Italian (fennel) sausage

Coarse salt and freshly ground black pepper

$\frac{1}{4}$ cup minced shallots

3 garlic cloves, minced

$\frac{1}{2}$ cup dry white wine

3 large ripe tomatoes, peeled, seeded, and
    minced, or one 16-ounce can Italian plum
    tomatoes, drained and finely chopped

2 teaspoons tomato paste

2 tablespoons minced fresh thyme

1 teaspoon dried oregano

$\frac{1}{2}$ cup chicken stock or bouillon

2 teaspoons finely grated lemon zest

3 tablespoons minced fresh parsley

1 tablespoon capers, well drained

1. Ask the butcher to cut each drumstick in half crosswise and to cut off the tips. Dry the drumsticks well with paper towels and set aside.

2. In a large heavy skillet, heat 2 tablespoons of the olive oil over medium-high heat, add the sausage, and sauté until nicely browned all over. Remove from the pan and reserve.

3. Add a little more oil to the skillet, add the chicken pieces, partially cover the skillet, and sauté, turning, until nicely browned all over. Season with salt and pepper. Remove the chicken to a plate.

4. Add more oil to the pan if needed. Add the shallots and 2 of the minced garlic cloves and cook just until soft. Add the wine, bring to a boil, and reduce to a glaze. Add the tomatoes, tomato paste, thyme, and oregano. Bring to a simmer and cook, uncovered, until some of the tomato liquid has evaporated.

5. Return the chicken to the pan along with any juices that have accumulated on the plate and just 2 to 3 tablespoons stock. Cover the skillet tightly and simmer over low heat for 20 minutes.

6. Cut the sausage crosswise into ½-inch rounds and add to the skillet. Continue to simmer for another 10 minutes, or until the chicken is done and the juices run pale yellow when it is pricked near the home.

7. While the chicken is cooking, prepare the garnish. In a small bowl, combine the lemon zest, parsley, capers, and remaining garlic and mix well.

8. When the chicken is done, transfer it together with the sausage to a deep serving platter. Place the skillet over high heat, add the remaining stock, and reduce the pan juices until they heavily coat the spoon. Add the garnish and simmer the sauce for 2 or 3 minutes. Taste and correct the seasoning.

9. Spoon the sauce over the chicken and sausage, and blend carefully with 2 spoons.

REMARKS If you want more sauce, add a small amount of arrowroot or cornstarch mixed with a little stock to the pan to thicken the sauce. The sauce will be more flavorful, however, if allowed to reduce and thicken to the desired consistency without any thickening agent.

You can add some pitted black niçoise olives to the sauce or more capers to taste. If you are using fresh tomatoes, you may need a little more chicken stock, since spring tomatoes are not very ripe or juicy.

Roasted Chicken à la Flamande

The concept of cooking a vegetable alongside a roasting chicken has great appeal, because you get the benefits of the vegetable absorbing the flavors of the pan juices. Endives work perfectly like this, and the result is delicious. If you don't mind a touch of cream, add about $\frac{1}{3}$ cup to the pan juices just before serving. Sliced roast potatoes or hash browns and roasted parsnips make excellent accompaniments.

SERVES 3 TO 4

$3\frac{1}{2}$-pound whole chicken

Coarse salt and freshly ground white pepper

$1\frac{1}{2}$ teaspoons dried thyme

1 large garlic clove, mashed

3 tablespoons butter

1 tablespoon corn or peanut oil

4 large Belgian endives, trimmed and cut in half lengthwise

1 to $1\frac{1}{4}$ cups chicken stock or bouillon

1 teaspoon flour dissolved in 3 tablespoons cold chicken bouillon

1. Preheat the oven to 400°F.

2. Season the chicken with salt, white pepper, and thyme. Rub with the mashed garlic. In a large cast-iron skillet, heat the butter and oil. Add the chicken and cook over high heat, turning, until brown all over, about 7 minutes.

3. Add the endives cut side down and pour in $\frac{1}{3}$ cup of the stock. Place the skillet in the oven and roast the chicken for 45 minutes, basting every 10 minutes with a little more of the hot broth. Turn the endives over halfway through the cooking to be sure they do not burn. Season with salt and pepper.

4. When the chicken is done, quarter it and transfer to a serving platter. Garnish with the roasted endives.

5. Place the skillet over direct heat, add any remaining stock, and whisk in a little of the dissolved flour. Bring to a boil, whisking, to thicken the pan juices. Spoon over the chicken.

Fried Cornish Hens "al Ajillo"

Chicken fried *al ajillo* is one of southern Spain's most popular everyday dishes. Small chicken nuggets are rubbed with fresh garlic and quickly deep-fried in olive oil. Served hot with nothing more than quartered lemons and some fried garlic cloves, they make a delicious simple main course. Here is a variation that uses Cornish hens instead. The garlic-parsley oil makes a nice dipping sauce, which can also be used with grilled flank steak or pan-seared burgers.

SERVES 3 TO 4

1 cup extra virgin olive oil

2 to 3 garlic cloves, finely minced, plus 3 large
    garlic cloves crushed through a press

3 tablespoons finely minced parsley

2 teaspoons minced jalapeño or more to taste

Coarse salt and freshly ground black pepper

3 Cornish hens, cut into eighths, wing tips removed

Pinch of cayenne

Flour, for dredging

2 quarts corn or peanut oil, for frying

Sprigs of parsley

2 lemons, quartered

1. Prepare the garlic-parsley oil: In a small bowl, combine the olive oil, minced garlic, parsley, and jalapeño. Season with salt and pepper. Stir until well blended and set aside until serving.

2. Thoroughly dry the Cornish hen pieces with paper towels. Rub each piece with some of the crushed garlic. Season generously with salt and pepper and sprinkle very lightly with cayenne. Dip the pieces very lightly in flour, shaking off any excess.

3. In a large saucepan or heavy casserole, heat the corn or peanut oil. Add the Cornish hen pieces a few at a time without crowding the pan. Deep-fry at 350°F for 6 to 8 minutes, or until nicely browned.

4. Remove to a double layer of paper towels and continue to deep-fry the rest of the Cornish hens, keeping a close eye on the oil, which must not burn. Transfer to a serving platter. Garnish with parsley and lemon quarters and serve accompanied by the garlic-parsley oil.

Roasted Duck with Sautéed Pears

Whenever I teach a roast duck recipe in one of my cooking classes, students are amazed at how easy and undemanding it is to prepare. All the ducks need is to be slow-roasted for as long as $2\frac{1}{2}$ to 3 hours to release all the fat under the skin. The ducks can be roasted hours ahead of time and reheated under the broiler.

SERVES 6 TO 8

2 ducks (about $4\frac{1}{2}$ pounds each)

Coarse salt and freshly ground black pepper

$1\frac{1}{2}$ teaspoons dried thyme

5 tablespoons unsalted butter

1 tablespoon peanut oil

$1\frac{1}{4}$ cups chicken stock or bouillon

2 Bartlett pears, peeled and quartered

1 tablespoon sugar

2 tablespoons lingonberries in syrup

A few drops of lemon juice

2 teaspoons arrowroot mixed with a little broth, optional

Large pinch of fresh nutmeg

1. Rinse the ducks and dry thoroughly with paper towels. Season with salt, pepper, and thyme.

2. Melt 2 tablespoons of the butter and the oil in a large rectangular roasting pan, add the ducks, and brown on all sides on top of the stove. Discard all but 3 tablespoons fat and add $\frac{1}{2}$ cup of the stock.

3. Place the ducks in the center part of the oven and roast for 2 hours 30 minutes, turning them once during the roasting time. Remove the fat every 15 to 20 minutes and baste with 3 to 4 tablespoons more stock.

4. While the ducks are roasting, prepare the pears. In a large heavy skillet, heat the remaining 3 tablespoons butter. Add the pears, season lightly with salt, pepper, and sugar, and sauté over fairly high heat until they are nicely glazed and brown. Set aside.

5. When the ducks are done, transfer them to a baking sheet. Set aside.

6. Thoroughly degrease the pan juices and add to the pears together with the lingonberries and drops of lemon juice. Taste and correct the seasoning.

7. If the pan juices seem too thin, add a little of the arrowroot mixture, just enough to thicken the sauce lightly.

8. Quarter the ducks and place on a serving platter. Spoon the pears and pan juices around the ducks, sprinkle the pears with nutmeg, and serve accompanied by soft polenta or the Puree of Rutabaga and Potato with Crispy Shallots, page 144.

Fried Marinated Quail

Quail makes wonderful eating. It is usually served grilled, but I like it just as much fried. Here is a dish to be enjoyed with friends when manners do not count, since it makes a great finger food. I usually serve quails as an appetizer, but they make a wonderful main course, as well, accompanied by mascarpone-flavored risotto, page 281.

SERVES 6 TO 8

⅓ cup tamari or soy sauce
1 tablespoon grated tangerine zest
⅓ cup fresh tangerine juice
1 tablespoon peeled and grated fresh ginger
1 tablespoon minced garlic
1 jalapeño, minced, or ⅛ teaspoon cayenne
1 teaspoon sugar
5 to 6 quails, quartered
3 to 4 cups corn oil, for frying

1. Combine all the ingredients except the quails and corn oil in a large bowl with 6 tablespoons water. Add the quails, turn, and marinate in the refrigerator overnight.

2. Drain the quails and place on a triple layer of paper towels and dry as well as possible.

3. In a deep cast-iron skillet, heat 2 inches of oil until very hot. Add half or one-third of the quail pieces and cook until nicely browned all over. Do not crowd the skillet and do not overcook. You will have to do this in 2 or 3 batches. Drain the fried quails on a double layer of paper towels and serve with a tiny bowl of coarse salt and the coarsely ground peppercorn mixture that follows.

Peppercorn mixture

MAKES ABOUT 2 TABLESPOONS
1 teaspoon Tellicherry peppercorns
1 teaspoon freeze-dried green peppercorns
1 teaspoon Sichuan peppercorns
1 teaspoon pink peppercorns or mixed colored peppercorns
1 teaspoon toasted cumin seeds, optional

Grind all the ingredients together in a spice grinder.

Grilled Quail with Pineapple Caramel

The slightly gamy but rich taste of quail benefits enormously from this sweet spicy marinade. Grill the quails and serve with a well-seasoned couscous or the Creamy Risotto with Vine-Ripe Tomatoes, Fresh Rosemary, and Mascarpone, page 281.

SERVES 4 TO 6

2 cups unsweetened pineapple juice

1 small serrano pepper, sliced

¼ cup brown sugar

6 black peppercorns, coarsely cracked

2-inch-long piece ginger, peeled and minced

2 garlic cloves, finely sliced

oil

Coarse salt and freshly ground black pepper

4 to 6 quails, cut in half lengthwise

Sprigs of fresh cilantro

1. In a bowl, combine the pineapple juice, serrano pepper, brown sugar, cracked peppercorns, ginger, and garlic. Whisk in the oil and season with salt and pepper.

2. Place the quails in a large zippered plastic bag and add the pineapple juice mixture. Transfer the bag to a baking dish and refrigerate for 12 to 24 hours.

3. Preheat the grill. While the fire is getting hot, remove the quails from the marinade and pat dry thoroughly with plenty of paper towels.

4. As soon as the fire is ready, place the quails skin side down and grill for 3 minutes. Turn and grill for another 3 minutes. Remove the quails to a dish and serve hot, garnished with the cilantro.

Perfectly Roasted Turkey with a Mustard-Herb Rub

Whenever I make a roasted turkey, friends ask me for the recipe. All it takes is getting a good fresh turkey, and it does not have to be either organic or free-range. Just season it assertively, baste it every 15 minutes with good stock, and do not forget it. I promise your friends will ask you for the recipe.

SERVES 8

10- to 12-pound fresh whole turkey
2 tablespoons Dijon mustard
2 teaspoons dried thyme
2 teaspoons dried marjoram
2 teaspoons imported sweet paprika
2 large garlic cloves, peeled and mashed
Coarse salt and freshly ground black pepper
2 tablespoons unsalted butter
1 teaspoon peanut oil
4 small onions, cut in half crosswise but
   not peeled
3½ cups chicken stock or bouillon
1 tablespoon flour mixed into a paste with
   1 tablespoon softened butter
Bouquet of fresh herbs

1. Preheat the oven to 425°F.

2. Dry the turkey thoroughly with kitchen towels. Combine the mustard, thyme, marjoram, paprika, and garlic in a small bowl and mix well. Rub the mixture all over the turkey (but not on the bottom), season with salt and pepper, and truss the turkey.

3. In a large heavy flameproof baking dish, melt the butter together with the oil over medium heat. Add the turkey, breast side up, and place the onions cut side down in the baking dish together with ¼ cup of the stock. Set in the center of the oven and roast for 1 hour 30 minutes to 1 hour 45 minutes, or until the internal temperature on a meat thermometer registers 165°F in the thigh and the juices run pale yellow when the meat is pricked near the bone. Add a little stock to the pan every 10 to 15 minutes and baste with the pan juices. If the turkey becomes too dark before it is done, tent loosely with foil and continue roasting.

4. When the turkey is done, remove it from the oven and transfer to a carving board. Remove and discard the trussing string and let the turkey sit for at least 5 to 10 minutes before carving. Remove the onions from the roasting pan, peel, and set aside.

5. Degrease the pan juices and return them to the baking dish together with the remaining stock. Bring to a simmer. Whisk in bits of the flour-and-butter paste until the sauce lightly coats the spoon. Taste and correct the seasoning. Keep warm.

6. Carve the turkey, place on a large serving platter, and surround with the roasted onions. Garnish with herbs and serve hot with the sauce on the side.

REMARKS You may puree the roasted onions in a food processor and add to the reduced sauce instead of thickening it with the flour-and-butter paste. The sauce will have a velvety texture and a delicious roasted onion flavor.

The onions can also be served as a side dish at room temperature, drizzled with a touch of sherry vinegar and extra virgin olive oil, and sprinkled with coarse salt and freshly ground black pepper.

■ **Beef Tenderloin and Portobello Mushroom Kebabs** ■ **Roast Beef with Caramelized Onion Sauce** ■ **Marinated Grilled Flank Steak with Wilted Watercress** ■ **Pan-Seared Rib-Eye Steak in Herb and Shallot Butter** ■ **Viennese Goulash Soup** ■ **Boulettes Basquaise** ■ **Spring Ragout of Veal Shanks with Mushrooms and Peas** ■ **Braised Lamb Shanks with Vegetables Niçoise** ■ **Pork Tenderloin with Prunes and Port Sauce**

Meat is back on American tables. If you have any doubts, just pick up a magazine or the food section of your local paper. Food magazines run recipes that call for short ribs, lamb shanks, and veal osso buco. Steak restaurants are opening everywhere, and even seafood menus offer diners several meat choices, such as rib-eye steaks and double pork chops. Unfortunately, because of years of consumer pressure to lower the fat in the American diet, producers have been breeding and raising animals to be leaner and, therefore, less flavorful. Pork was never meant to be lean, and you can't have chops that are both juicy and fat free.

I often opt to teach a beef stew at a cooking class, using the robustly flavored chuck. When my students see me degrease the sauce, the inevitable question comes up, "Can I use a less fatty cut? How about the tenderloin?"

I always find myself explaining that the tenderloin is not meant for stews. When, in another class, I brine and oven-roast a pork shoulder butt to be served with lentils and sautéed winter vegetables, occasionally a student will want to make the dish more elegant by using a boneless loin of pork. Yes, it will look good, but with today's lean pigs, chances are the meat will lack the rich, hearty flavor we are counting on to accentuate the other ingredients.

An important principle in cooking all meat is that tender cuts will remain tender only by being cooked quickly with dry heat. Overcook them, and they toughen. The tougher, more flavorful cuts require a marinade or rub to tenderize them and bring out the hearty flavors. These are best cooked slowly with moisture—stewed or braised.

So, how do you learn which cuts are tender and which are tougher? In earlier times, most grocery stores had butchers who could be relied on to give you this kind of information. You could count on their expertise and knowledge. Now most meat comes to the supermarket already cut, and few butchers have in-depth information about the product they sell. Today's shopper has to be much more knowledgeable and cautious to avoid disappointment.

My first recommendation to anyone interested in cooking meat of any kind is to learn the anatomy of the animals we eat. It is important to keep in mind that flavor and tenderness depend on where the meat comes from on an animal. The tenderness of a piece of meat depends on the amount of work a particular muscle does. Thus, it is not surprising that the same cuts that are tender in beef are also so in veal, pork, and lamb.

Unfortunately, the average grocery store is more than happy to provide the shopper with the most popular cuts, such as rib roast, tenderloin, strip steaks, chuck, and sirloin. But when it comes to wonderful flavorful and inexpensive cuts, such as oxtails, shoulder of veal, the tri-tip, or even short ribs or skirt steak, chances are that you will have to shop around or ask the butcher to get it for you.

Fortunately, distinguishing tender cuts from tough ones is not difficult, because the key barn animals we eat all use their muscles in pretty much the same way. The rib and loin sections are the most tender, because they run along the sides and back and do not get exercised as much. The rib-eye, the tenderloin, the rack of lamb, and the pork tenderloin come from this part of the animal as well and are perfect for roasting, pan frying, and grilling. The parts of the animal that get more exercise, the shoulder and legs, need to be cooked in moist heat for a longer period of time to become tender and juicy. The brisket, flank, and shoulder are tougher, but to me, they have more of that rich meaty taste. They should be reserved for braising, pot roasting, or stewing. As soon as you become familiar with these various cuts, you will be the best judge of what you should use for which type of recipe. When it comes to beef, choosing the right cut can be confusing because different cuts are sold by different names, depending on where you live.

When preparing pork, the challenge facing all cooks is to keep it moist, which can only be achieved by undercooking it slightly or by brining, or both. Here, too, it is the lesser cuts, such as the shoulder butt or the picnic roast, that will give you the most tender and flavorful results if you cook them slowly. If you are not squeamish about fat, also consider the robust flavor of spare ribs. Grill or slow-roast them, and they will be juicy and delicious.

On those days when you decide to go with lamb, you will be in luck, since good lamb is now widely available. American lamb from California, Colorado, Vermont, and Washington State is excellent. You may run into trouble when you decide to make a lamb stew, because butchers like to sell you the leg for everything. When used for kebabs or a stew, the leg meat becomes tough; it does not benefit from slow moist cooking.

Once you get your meat home from the market, don't just toss it into the fridge or the freezer. Take the extra few minutes to store it properly. Remove all meat from the package and, if you are not going to be using it the same day, wrap it loosely in freezer paper, waxed paper, or, best of all, brown butcher's paper, which you can easily get from the meat counter. Large cuts will keep well this way for 3 or 4 days, and small cuts such as veal and lamb chops or flank steaks will keep for 2 days. I have actually "aged" both rib-eye and strip steak in the cold part of the fridge for as long as a week with excellent results. Never wrap meat in foil or a zippered plastic bag, because the key to keeping it fresh is to allow air to circulate around the meat. Remember good meat is expensive, and you deserve to get your money's worth, but also remember the endless diversity of meat and the wonderful cooking opportunities it presents.

In the following Q & A's, I try to answer some of the many questions students have asked me over the years, and my advice continues to be the same: Try to break away from the common and the familiar and be willing to experiment. You will find it extremely rewarding.

Beef

■■

Many cookbooks and television cooks suggest asking the butcher for meaty beef bones for stock, but I have to rely on the supermarket for stock bones. What should I do?

It is important and actually rather easy to establish a relationship with the butchers at the supermarket. You will be surprised how helpful they usually are. Ring the service bell and ask for meaty bones for stock. Or look for inexpensive packages of extra bones called "soup bones." For these my first choices are beef shank bones and rib bones.

It's a good idea to build up a supply of veal and beef bones as well as chicken backs and wings, which you can keep in a sturdy plastic bag in the freezer. You can use these straight from the freezer whenever you want to make stock.

TIP **Invest in a heavy cleaver so that you can chop the beef, veal, or poultry bones into 3- or 4-inch pieces. These produce the most flavor in a stock.**

What exactly does the labeling of beef mean, and what should I look for?

The labeling of beef is becoming more and more confusing. Because there is very little real aged prime beef available anymore, you must make sure to choose Choice or Top Choice. Avoid any fancy names such as Butchers' Prime or Market Choice. This labeling is done by individual markets and has nothing to do with U.S.D.A. labeling. To be on the sure side when it comes to beef, try to buy certified Black Angus, which has a high degree of marbling and excellent beef flavor.

I always bought beef that was bright red but now hear that darker beef is a better choice because it means it has been aged.

In certain cuts such as a New York strip steak, a darker color can mean that the steak has been aged. Generally I look for a light cherry red color with marbled interior fat and white external fat, and a smooth tight grain in the meat.

Color is not a reliable indicator of quality, since many butcher cases use special lighting to give beef a misleading bright red hue.

Many of my friends buy their beef at wholesale club stores in vacuum-sealed bags, but the meat looks very dark to me. Is it really okay?

You can do very well buying beef this way, especially when it comes to the large cuts. The lack of oxygen in vacuum-packaged meat gives it a dark purplish color, but once the bag is opened, the meat will go back to its reddish color. Also, don't be alarmed if the meat gives off a strong odor. It will disappear after a few minutes of exposure to the air.

I find all the various beef cuts confusing. Can you tell me in simple terms what cut to use for what?

You do not need to be an expert to understand the important cuts of beef. The rib, short loin, sirloin, and tenderloin all come from the back area of the steer. They are all fine grained and tender and all can be used in oven-roasting, grilling, sautéing, and pan-searing. These cuts are best cooked rare to medium-rare.

For braising, the best cuts are the chuck roast and the brisket, which come from the shoulder and sides of the steer. These cuts are tougher and need long, slow cooking but deliver great taste in pot roasts and stews.

Other cuts, such as flank and skirt steak, take well to marinades and are best quickly grilled. Chances are your market will also carry the rump roast and the eye round. These less tender cuts need long, slow oven-braising, but I find them too chewy and too dry no matter what you do with them. Much of the round is

sold ground, and I even avoid that because I feel that the meat lacks the more fatty and interesting taste and texture of the chuck.

My market does not label its ground beef by fat content but rather by the cut. How can I tell the amount of fat the ground beef contains?

Ground chuck, which is my first choice, contains 20 to 25 percent fat while ground sirloin has 15 to 20 percent, and ground round 15 percent or less.

Unfortunately, labeling is inconsistent around the country and changes from area to area. In fact, the name of a cut is no guarantee that the meat is actually ground from a specific cut. Your best bet is to check the package and see if it is full of white specks, which is an indication of fat. Be sure to question your butcher about the fat content of the ground meat the market sells.

What is the secret of successful broiling? Why can't I get the same results as a restaurant does?

Meat broiled at home frequently ends up dry because a home range simply does not put out enough heat. Since the surface of the steak is not sufficiently seared, the flavorful juices escape. A home broiler reaches about 500°F while a restaurant range can get up to 700°F, and that makes a difference in taste and texture.

What should I look for in a great steak?

I think that you will find a lot of different opinions among steak lovers. Many beef eaters swear by the tenderloin and the almost fatless filet mignon. Others like myself much prefer the more assertive taste and texture of either the T-bone steak, which is the New York steak with a bit of the tenderloin attached, or the New York strip steak, which has the bone attached but not the tenderloin. This can be most confusing, since the New York strip steak is called by various names depending on what part of the country you are from. It can be called Kansas City steak, club steak, shell steak, or Delmonico. Another cut that makes a great steak is the rib-eye steak, either bone-in or boneless. This cut has more fat and is somewhat more chewy but very flavorful.

What is the difference between a tournedo, filet mignon, and chateaubriand?

A filet mignon comes from the small end of the tenderloin and is usually 1 to 2 inches thick. The tournedo is essentially the same piece of meat wrapped in bacon to add juiciness to this very lean cut. The chateaubriand is a French cut of the finest part of the filet mignon, usually reserved for restaurants.

What exactly is a porterhouse steak?

The porterhouse is the T-bone steak with a large portion of the tenderloin attached. (The T-bone is the strip steak with a small portion of the tenderloin attached.) The porterhouse is a favorite for the grill, which is the way I recommend using it, since it is too large for top-of-the-stove cooking.

What exactly is the London broil, and what is the best way to use it?

London broil is the name given to the top round. It is a rather tough cut that should be marinated and then quickly grilled. It looks somewhat similar to the sirloin steak, but the sirloin—although more pricey—is a much more interesting and flavorful cut.

Do you recommend tenderizing a steak?

I do not recommend using any meat tenderizer, because it changes the texture and flavor of beef.

What is the ideal thickness of a steak for pan-searing?

For pan-searing, a steak must be at least ¾ inch thick and up to 1¼ inches thick. If you cook on a gas range that puts out plenty of heat and have a well-seasoned black cast-iron skillet, you can go to as much as 1½ inches in thickness.

I always have trouble cooking a steak on top of the stove. Should I cook a thick steak on high or medium-high heat?

It all depends on the thickness and your pan. If it is a thick steak, it is important to pan-sear it in clarified butter on high heat in a heavy cast-iron skillet. However, if you are cooking on a gas range such as a Viking or a Garland, then medium-high heat is ideal.

TIP Always remove meat from the fridge an hour before cooking and never use a lightweight nonstick pan for pan-searing or cooking steaks or chops.

Many recipes suggest pan-broiling a steak or a burger; others call for sautéing. What is the difference?

Pan-broiling is done in a heavy skillet without oil or butter, while for sautéing you need to start with some fat. I start with a little butter and oil, and once the steak or burger has released some fat, I pour it off to make sure the meat continues to sauté and does not end up frying.

My market offers three or four choices of ground beef at a time. Which ground beef do you recommend?

Your first choice in ground beef should be the chuck. Because this cut has more fat in it than the sirloin or the top round, the burgers remain juicy and flavorful. Do not buy lean or extra-lean ground beef. You are not actually getting much less fat, but you are giving up a great deal of flavor.

TIP **If you have a food processor with a very sharp blade, I highly recommend grinding your own beef. Be sure to chill the blade and the bowl in the freezer for 30 minutes. Cut the meat and its fat into ³/₄-inch pieces and grind in small batches. The taste of freshly ground beef is far superior to anything you can buy at the market.**

Is it best to season steaks and burgers before cooking or after?

I believe in seasoning a steak with coarse salt and freshly ground black pepper prior to cooking. When it comes to burgers, mixing the salt and pepper into the raw meat makes a world of difference in taste.

What cut do you suggest using for a roast beef and how much should I get per person?

For great beefy taste, nothing beats a standing rib roast, also called prime rib. The entire roast is made up of ribs from the upper section of the back of the steer, which weighs over 16 pounds, but rib roasts are also sold in smaller pieces of 2 to 6 ribs. My favorite is a 3-rib roast from the back of the rib section, which is the small end. The meat from this section is lean, tender, and very flavorful. However, if you plan to serve

roast beef to a large group of people, you may prefer the large end of the rib. This cut has much more fat on it and is harder to carve.

Another terrific cut that I often use is the boneless rib-eye. This can run into quite a bit of money, but there is no waste, it is packed with flavor, and it is very easy to carve. Because it is boneless and very manageable, I like to serve it for a dinner party of six to eight people. If you prefer a roast with the bone in, you may want to go with a bone-in rib-eye.

You should always buy at least a 3-rib roast that serves four people with some leftovers for sandwiches. This cut will weigh 6 to 7 pounds. If you want to serve 12 people, you will have to go for a 5-rib roast, which weighs between 10 and 12 pounds.

TIP **Always buy a rib roast from the small end of the ribs rather than the large end. This cut is more tender, leaner, and more flavorful.**

Is there a surefire method for cooking a roast beef? I have tried three or four methods and have either undercooked or overcooked the roast each time.

Nothing can be simpler than making a roast beef, but I admit I overcooked several roasts before I got it right. Preheat the oven to 500°F. Season the roast with plenty of salt and pepper. Place it fat side down in a heavy roasting pan and sear it on top of the stove until nicely browned on all sides. Place the roast fat side up in the oven and roast for 15 minutes. Reduce the oven temperature to 350°F and continue to roast, counting eighteen minutes per pound or to an inner temperature of 115°F for rare and 120° to 125°F for medium-rare. Remove the roast from the oven and let it rest for

15 minutes. By this time the inner temperature should read 130° to 135°F, which will give you a perfectly cooked medium-rare roast.

Why do so many recipes these days suggest using an instant-read thermometer rather than tell you how many minutes per pound it takes to cook a roast?

The instant-read thermometer has been an absolute savior for many cooks, and I recommend using it with all roasts. Recipes should give you an approximate time, but so much depends on whether the meat has been cold or at room temperature, whether your oven is properly calibrated, and whether you are roasting in a gas or electric oven. However, I do not use the instant-read thermometer for steaks and chops of about 1½ inch thick. I prefer the knife method, in which you insert the tip of a very sharp paring knife into the center of the chop or steak while it is being pan-seared. If the tip of the knife comes out cold, the meat is underdone; if it is warm, it is medium-rare; and if the knife tip is hot, the meat is well done and overcooked.

What cut of beef do you suggest using for kebabs?

There are several cuts I like for this preparation. The chuck steak from the rib section is delicious and inexpensive. It takes well to various marinades and to quick grilling. I also like to use the tenderloin, which may sound extravagant, but when using it for kebabs, a little goes a long way and you can either marinate it or not. A less tender choice but equally flavorful is the sirloin. However, this cut is only good when served rare.

Do not buy pre-cut shish kebabs. Chances are these nice-looking lean cubes have been cut from the top round, which cooks up dry no matter what you do to it.

What cut of beef do you use for making fajitas?

My choice and probably the only choice is the skirt steak. Be sure to marinate it for 4 to 6 hours or overnight (see the marinade, page 234), then grill directly over the coals on a hot grill for 2 to 3 minutes per side. Do not overcook.

My family loves a good beef stew. Sometimes the meat is tender after less than 2 hours, and other times it remains tough no matter how long it is in the oven. Why does this happen?

You are probably making the mistake of buying pre-cut stew meat. You have no idea what cut you are getting, since most meat markets try to get rid of lesser cuts. Instead, buy a piece of chuck and cut it up yourself into 1½- to 2-inch pieces, or have the butcher cut it up for you. It will be less expensive, and your stew will cook evenly every time.

What is the best way to cook short ribs?

Short ribs make the most delicious stew, and they take well to braising since they benefit from slow, long cooking. Have the butcher cut them into 3-inch chunks, brown them in a little oil, and then braise them, covered, with plenty of chopped onions, minced garlic, some carrots, a little celery, and some stock for 3 to 6 hours. Because short ribs tend to be fatty, they must be cooked a day ahead of time so that you can properly degrease the sauce. But nothing beats short ribs for fabulous beef flavor.

How do you cook oxtails and beef shank bones?

Both are delicious cuts that are used in soups and stews. You can cook oxtails or beef shank bones as you would chicken soup, with some carrots, leeks, and a couple of celery stalks for 2 to 3 hours. Chill overnight, degrease the broth, and return it a boil. Add ½ cup tiny pasta and cook until tender. Serve this soup as a simple one-dish meal.

Calf's Liver

Whenever I broil calf's liver, it becomes tough. What am I doing wrong?

Calf's liver is best seared in butter in a very hot cast-iron skillet no more than one to 2 minutes on each side, depending how thick the slice, and then seasoned with salt and pepper. Another good way to serve calf's liver is to cut it into 1-inch strips, quickly sauté them, and combine the liver with a soft onion jam.

TIP Avoid buying pre-cut liver and, if you can, check the color and make sure it is pale and rosy, and not blotchy. If the liver seems dark and has some bloody spots, place it in a rectangular dish and cover with milk. Soak for 1 to 2 hours, then dry well with paper towels.

Lamb

I like to make lamb kebabs. Sometimes I am very successful, other times the kebabs are tough. What is the reason for this?

Lamb kebabs are actually very forgiving, especially if they have been marinated, but you will get the most tender results from shoulder meat or the inexpensive sirloin. Most pre-cut kebabs are from the leg, which becomes tough if not cooked rare.

What is the best marinade to use for lamb kebabs?

Yogurt-based marinades work well for lamb. My favorite is a take-off on the Indian tandoori marinade: Combine 1½ cups plain yogurt with ½ cup olive oil, ¼ cup lemon juice, and 1 tablespoon each minced ginger, garlic, and serrano pepper. Add 1 tablespoon each ground cumin,

coriander, and cardamom and 1 teaspoon each salt and freshly ground black pepper. Place all the ingredients in a food processor with 2 large whole bunches of cilantro, stems and all, and blend well. Place the lamb cubes in a zippered plastic bag, add the marinade, and refrigerate overnight. About 2½ pounds of lamb cubes will make 4 to 6 servings.

I followed a recipe for lamb stew, and although I cooked it for twice as long as the recipe called for, the meat was still tough. What did I do wrong?

It was probably the cut you used. Next time, insist on lamb shoulder and have the meat cut into 2-inch cubes. This is an unpopular cut with supermarket meat departments, who are not too happy to have to bone the whole shoulder for stew and prefer selling it as bone-in shoulder chops.

I see a lot of recipes that call for lamb shanks, but my market does not carry them. Can I use the leg of lamb instead?

The leg of lamb is not a substitute, since the two cuts require totally different cooking methods.

The leg requires short roasting and is best served rare to medium-rare, while the shank needs to be braised in a low oven for as long as 3 to 4 hours until it is so tender that the meat almost falls off the bone.

Lamb shanks have recently become extremely popular. Your market should be able to get them for you if you order them in advance.

Pork

What is the difference between the pork loin and the pork tenderloin?

Although both cuts come from the part of the hog that runs on either side of the backbone, the two are very different. The pork loin is the most common and popular pork roast. It is sold either bone-in or boneless and usually weighs between 3 and 4 pounds. The tenderloin, or fillet of pork, is a thin cylindrical roast that weighs between ½ and ¾ pound. It is juicy and tender and is usually sold vacuum packed one or two fillets at a time. It is to the hog what the beef tenderloin or filet mignon is to the steer.

What is the best cut to choose when making a pork roast for a dinner party?

I am surprised by the consistent popularity of the pork loin roast, since this cut dries out no matter what you do to it. But you have two other excellent choices. First on my list is the pork tenderloin, which you can get from the oven to the table in 15 minutes. Another more humble cut of pork, but one that is loaded with taste, is the Boston butt or the shoulder butt. This cut is much fattier than the tenderloin and lacks the showy presentation of

the pork loin roast, but it makes up for it in flavor.

My market carries various kinds of ribs. Which ones do you recommend?

For meatiness and delicious pork flavor, spareribs are the best. Make sure you buy heavier slabs, weighing more than 3 pounds. This will guarantee you the right meatiness. But make sure that they are not too fatty. For a leaner meal, try baby back ribs; these are relatively more expensive since they have almost no meat on them. Look for ribs that are the leanest and have the most meat on them. Plan on serving one slab for one to two people.

Country-style ribs are an inexpensive choice. They can be fatty but are delicious when marinated and grilled slowly over indirect heat (see page 350 for indirect heat information).

Do baby back ribs come from a baby pig?

Not at all. Baby back ribs are the bones of the loin ribs with the boneless pork chops removed. The name is one of the great pork marketing gimmicks, but since the ribs are tasty, we are willing to pay a high price for a bony cut with very little meat.

What is a good method for cooking pork chops so they don't dry out?

For years we shied away from pork because it was too fatty and "not good for you," with the result that farmers are growing larger, leaner pigs. The result is dry, tasteless pork. There is little you can do to pork chops these days to keep them juicy other than to flavor brine them and undercook them slightly so as to keep them somewhat more juicy.

Every cookbook I read seems to suggest a different inner temperature for cooking pork. What should it be?

The business of overcooking pork for health reasons goes back a long time and was drummed into a whole generation of cooks. In reality, trichinae, the parasites that cause trichinosis, are killed at 137°F or medium-rare. Lean cuts, such as loin chops, should be taken off the heat at that stage and left to rest for another 10 to 20 minutes, at which point the inner temperature will increase by 5 to 10 degrees. Don't be alarmed if the meat is still a faint pink in the center and the juices run pink as well. These colors are perfectly safe and it means the pork will be juicy.

Pork roasts, on the other hand, need to be cooked a little longer—to anywhere between 150°F inner temperature for the tenderloin to 160°F for a pork shoulder roast. Ignore all cookbooks that suggest that you cook pork to 180°F. At 160°F it is more than done, and at 180° it is inedible.

My butcher suggests very thin pork chops rather than thick ones, because they cook quickly and stay juicier. Is that true?

I prefer chops that are 1 to 1½ inches thick, but the key is that they must be uniformly cut. Many butchers have the tendency to cut chops thick at the bone and thin at the periphery. Pass these by and request evenly cut ones; otherwise the outside part of the chop will be done while the meat near the bone will still be raw. This is also the problem with a thin bone-in chop. It is almost impossible to get the meat near the bone cooked properly without the rest of the chop tasting like cardboard.

Which is juicier—the rib or loin pork chop?

Rib chops have a little more fat and, therefore, stand a better chance of not drying out. Either way, buy the chops at least 1 to ½ inches thick.

TIP When choosing the pork loin roast, always buy it "bone in" rather than boneless, and have the butcher crack the bones for easier serving.

I recently got 1½-inch-thick pork chops from my meat market and tried to pan-sear them on top of the stove, but while they were practically charred on the outside, they were still raw inside. Is there a good method for getting them cooked through?

Whenever you have a thick chop or steak, you should cook it in clarified butter (see page 384) or rendered duck fat, which you can now buy at the meat counter of many supermarkets. (It is packed by D'Artagnan and comes in small plastic containers; see Sources, page 398.) Sear the chops in a heavy cast-iron skillet. Once they are nicely browned on both sides, and I mean deeply browned, turn down the heat only slightly, so that the chops continue to sizzle. Do not lower the heat to the point that the sizzling stops, because if the heat is too low, the chops will sweat, and the juices will exude, leaving the meat dry.

Cover the pan and continue to cook for 3 to 4 minutes. Use an instant-read thermometer after 2 minutes: If it registers 140°F, the chops are done. Let them rest for 5 minutes, which will bring the inner temperature up to 145 degrees. The chops may still be slightly rosy inside but, believe me, they are done.

TIP Whenever you sear any kind of chop or steak in a black iron skillet, be sure to remove the meat to a warm platter to let it rest. If left in the skillet, which retains heat, the meat will keep cooking.

How long should I marinate pork, and does a marinade tenderize it?

A marinade does not tenderize all types of meat, but it does add a great deal of flavor. For the marinade to be effective, however, you must marinate the meat overnight in a zippered plastic bag. For pork, I especially like the following:

Citrus Spice Marinade

MAKES ¾ CUP

¼ cup lemon juice

¼ cup orange juice

1 large onion, finely chopped

2 teaspoons ground cumin

2 teaspoons chili powder

1 tablespoon minced serrano pepper

1 tablespoon minced garlic

½ cup olive or grapeseed oil

1 teaspoon coarsely ground black pepper

1 teaspoon coarse salt.

Combine all the ingredients in a bowl and whisk until well mixed. Put 4 chops or a 2- to 3-pound shoulder butt roast in a zippered plastic bag, add the marinade, and refrigerate overnight.

Veal

■■

What cut of veal is osso buco? What dishes is it used for?

Osso buco is not a cut but a classic northern Italian dish in which the cut-up veal shank is braised with white wine, onion, and tomatoes until very tender. Traditionally, it is served with a saffron-flavored risotto. While I like this dish, I find more interesting uses for the veal shank, such as a veal ragout—a traditional French dish in which the shank is cooked with a variety of mushrooms with spectacular flavor results (Spring Ragout of Veal Shanks with Mushrooms and Peas, page 240).

The shank is also delicious braised whole in the oven and served with sautéed shitake mushrooms or roasted parsnips. Because the meat is cooked on the bone, it is done in a relatively short time and the collagen in the bone produces intensely flavored pan juices.

What is the right cut to use for a veal stew? When I buy pre-cut veal, the results are uneven. Some pieces are tender while others remain chewy and tough.

Stewing veal is expensive and you do not know what you are getting. Try to have your butcher cut up a veal shoulder roast, or buy boned veal shoulder and cut it up yourself into 2-inch cubes. It is not difficult at all. If you have a knowledgeable butcher, you could ask him for the meat from the neck area. This slightly gristly cut is full of collagen, so the meat is tender and flavorful, resulting in a delicious sauce.

TIP **If you happen to find a good batch of veal scaloppine, remember that it freezes well for several weeks. Place a small sheet of waxed paper between each scaloppine, then wrap the whole package in foil and slip into a zippered plastic bag. Be sure to defrost in the refrigerator rather than at room temperature to avoid losing precious juices.**

My market carries inexpensive ground veal. How is it used?

Veal meatballs are easy to prepare and, when combined with the Quick Tomato Sauce, page 274, are great tossed into freshly cooked tubular pasta, such as ziti, fusilli, or penne. They are also good served over creamy polenta. You can combine ground veal with an equal amount of ground pork and season with grated onion, salt, pepper, and a touch of oregano. Use it this mixture to stuff vegetables, such as green or red bell peppers or hollowed-out small zucchini. Drizzle with olive oil and roast the vegetables for 45 minutes at 350°F. Serve hot or at room temperature as a light main course.

Is it a good idea to marinate veal?

Try marinating veal chops for 2 to 3 hours in a mixture of olive oil and fresh lemon or lime juice with some minced fresh thyme, rosemary, or oregano. Veal has a delicate flavor, and a long, intensely seasoned marinade would compete with its lovely flavor.

Beef Tenderloin and Portobello Mushroom Kebabs

Few dishes look prettier than skewers of marinated beef or lamb tenderloin alternating with peppers, onions, and cherry tomatoes. Here is a slight variation on the classic, in which I use only peppers and portobello mushrooms. You may add onions if you like and a mix of red and yellow peppers. Be sure to use a long sturdy spatula to turn the skewers to prevent the food from rolling around. Another hint is to thread the kebabs on two skewers instead of one. Remember to soak the bamboo skewers in water for 20 minutes before threading them, so they won't burn. You will need 8 to 10 skewers.

SERVES 4 TO 5

2 pounds beef tenderloin

1/3 cup sake

1/2 cup mirin

1/2 cup soy sauce

1/3 cup canola oil

1 tablespoon minced peeled fresh ginger

3 large garlic cloves, crushed

1 dried hot chile pepper, crumbled

1 1/2 teaspoons ground cumin

3 large portobello mushrooms, stems
    removed, caps cut into large cubes

2 tablespoons olive oil

Coarse salt and freshly ground black pepper

1 large red bell pepper, cut into 1-inch cubes

1 teaspoon coarsely cracked black pepper

1. Cut the beef into 1-inch cubes. In a bowl, combine the sake, mirin, soy sauce, and canola oil. Add the ginger, garlic, chile, and cumin. Whisk until well blended. Add the beef to the marinade and transfer to a zippered plastic bag. Marinate for 4 hours, or overnight.

2. The next day, light a hot fire in a barbecue grill. Toss the mushrooms with the olive oil and season with salt and pepper.

3. Thread the kebabs onto the bamboo skewers, alternating the beef cubes with mushrooms and bell pepper. Season with cracked pepper and grill for 4 minutes on each side. Serve with corn on the cob or Corn and Chive Fritters, page 120.

Roast Beef with Caramelized Onion Sauce

Most people believe that when it comes to a well-roasted piece of meat, less is more, and I tend to agree. Excellent meat needs little or no adornment. However, when you are looking for a simple change, caramelized onions slightly flavored with mustard and balsamic vinegar are an excellent choice. Serve the roast with a gratin of buttery potatoes or a puree of potatoes flavored with either celery root or rutabaga, and a well-dressed salad.

SERVES 4 TO 6

6-pound rib roast

Coarse salt and freshly ground black pepper

4 tablespoons butter (½ stick)

1 tablespoon peanut oil

2 large Spanish onions, quartered and finely sliced

1 teaspoon sugar

1 tablespoon Dijon mustard

2 tablespoons balsamic vinegar

¾ cup beef stock or bouillon

2 teaspoons arrowroot mixed into a paste with a little stock

1. Preheat the oven to 500°F.

2. Rub the roast well with salt and pepper.

3. In a heavy roasting pan or large cast-iron skillet, heat 2 tablespoons of the butter. Add the roast and brown over medium-high heat on both sides. Place the roast top side down and continue cooking until the fat is well browned and crisp.

4. Spoon off all but 2 tablespoons fat from the pan. Place the roast in the oven and cook for 15 minutes.

5. Reduce the heat to 325°F and continue cooking for 45 minutes, or up to 18 minutes per pound.

6. While the roast is in the oven, heat the remaining 2 tablespoons butter and the oil in a large cast-iron skillet. Add the onions. Season with salt, pepper, and sugar and cook for 5 to 7 minutes, or until the onions start to brown. Lower the heat and continue to cook the onions for 45 minutes, stirring every few minutes and keeping an eye on them to be sure they do not burn, until they are very soft and lightly caramelized. Add the mustard and balsamic vinegar and continue to cook for another 3 to 4 minutes. Taste the onions and correct the seasoning.

7. When the meat is done, transfer it to a serving plate.

8. Discard all the fat from the pan. Place the pan over direct heat, add the stock, and whisk in the arrowroot mixture. Cook the pan juices until they heavily coat the spoon. Add the onions and stir into the sauce. Transfer the onion sauce to a serving bowl.

9. Carve the roast and serve on individual plates with a dollop of the onion sauce either on the side or over the roast.

REMARKS The onion sauce can be varied by adding minced fresh thyme or rosemary. If you really prefer your roast beef simple and unadorned, just follow the recipe, omitting the onion sauce altogether.

Marinated Grilled Flank Steak with Wilted Watercress

Here is a very interesting marinade that is actually a paste made out of shallots, garlic, and lemongrass. If you cannot find fresh lemongrass, you can use it dried and add the juice of a lime to the paste. You can also use this marinade with skirt steaks, beef kebabs, and a sirloin steak. Wilted watercress has a slightly bitter, assertive flavor similar to broccoli rabe, which you can use as well if you cannot get watercress in large bunches.

SERVES 4

MARINADE

3 large shallots

6-inch-long piece lemongrass, outer leaves removed

5 large garlic cloves

⅓ cup canola or grapeseed oil

3 tablespoons sesame oil

2 tablespoons nam pla (Thai fish sauce)

1 tablespoon soy sauce

2 tablespoons sugar

1 chile in adobo sauce, or 1 teaspoon pure chile flakes

STEAK

1½ to 1¾ pounds flank steak

3 tablespoons olive oil

2 garlic cloves, finely sliced

2 large bunches watercress, 2 inches of stems removed

Coarse salt and freshly ground black pepper

2 grilled red peppers, cut into julienne

1. Place all the marinade ingredients in a food processor or a small chopper and blend until finely chopped. Transfer together with the flank steak to a large zippered plastic bag and make sure the meat is well covered with the paste on all sides. Refrigerate overnight.

2. The next day, heat a gas grill and cook the steak over high heat for 3 minutes on each side. Remove to a platter and let the steak rest for 5 minutes before carving.

3. While the steak rests, heat 1½ tablespoons of the olive oil in a large nonstick skillet, add a few of the garlic slices, and, as soon as they start to brown, add half the watercress. Stir-fry for 2 minutes, or until just wilted. Transfer to a bowl and cook the second batch the same way. Divide among 6 serving dishes and set aside.

4. Slice the meat on the diagonal into thin slices and divide among the 6 plates. Garnish with grilled peppers and serve immediately.

Pan-Seared Rib-Eye Steak in Herb and Shallot Butter

Food trends come and go, much like fashion. Beef in green peppercorn sauce was the "in" dish in the seventies; now it seems somewhat outdated. Personally, I think this combination of flavors deserves its place among the classics. Here, the addition of fresh tarragon and double-poached garlic cloves gives it a new dimension. When buying green peppercorns, avoid those that are pickled in vinegar and instead use the ones packed in brine.

SERVES 3 TO 4

3 tablespoons clarified butter (see page 384)

1½-pound rib-eye steak, 2 to 2¼ inches thick

Coarse salt and freshly ground black pepper

2 tablespoons minced shallots

½ cup Scotch whiskey

1 cup brown stock or beef bouillon

1 teaspoon brined green peppercorns, drained

2 teaspoons arrowroot dissolved in a little stock or bouillon

2 tablespoons minced fresh tarragon

12 cloves Double-Poached Garlic Cloves (page 388), optional

1. Heat the butter in a cast-iron skillet over high heat, add the steak, and sauté for 3 minutes. Turn and sauté for another 3 minutes or until nicely browned. Season with salt and pepper, reduce the heat, and continue to cook for 10 minutes. Turn the steak once more and cook for an additional 8 to 10 minutes for medium-rare. Transfer to a cutting board and let the meat rest for 5 minutes.

2. Discard all the fat from skillet, add the shallots, and cook for 1 minute. Add the Scotch and reduce to a glaze. Add the stock and green peppercorns and whisk in a little of the arrowroot mixture until the sauce lightly coats a spoon. Add the tarragon and double-poached garlic, and taste and correct the seasoning.

3. Slice the steak thinly on the bias, place on a serving platter, and spoon the sauce over the steak. Serve at once with roasted portobello mushrooms, page 132.

Viennese Goulash Soup

Here is a hearty one-dish meal that is easy to make with ingredients that you can get in every grocery store. It is one of those dishes I fall back on when I crave something undemanding yet full of flavor. Be sure to make enough, because this soup gets better every day and also freezes well.

SERVES 4 TO 6

3 tablespoons vegetable oil

1 dried hot chile pepper

3 cups finely diced onions

3 garlic cloves, finely minced

1 tablespoon imported sweet paprika

2 tablespoons tomato paste

2 pounds beef chuck, cut into 1-inch pieces

Coarse salt and freshly ground black pepper

2 tablespoons caraway seeds

1 teaspoon dried marjoram

8 cups beef stock or bouillon

2 parsnips, peeled and cubed

2 medium red potatoes, peeled and cubed

Sour cream

Minced flat-leaf parsley

1. In a 6-quart heavy casserole, heat the oil. Add the chiles and cook until they turn dark. Add the onions and garlic and cook over medium heat until the onions are soft and lightly browned, about 7 minutes.

2. Stir in the paprika and tomato paste. Add the beef and season with salt and pepper. Mix well into the onion mixture and season with the caraway seeds and marjoram. Add the stock. Bring to a boil, reduce the heat, and simmer for 1 to 1½ hours.

3. Add the parsnips and continue to cook until they are tender, about 10 minutes. Add the potatoes and continue to simmer until the potatoes and beef are tender, about 10 minutes longer. Correct the seasoning. You may need quite a bit more salt, since the parsnips tend to sweeten the soup. Serve hot in deep soup bowls, garnished with a dollop of sour cream and some parsley.

Boulettes Basquaise

Boulettes is the French a word for meatballs. I grew up with this recipe and still enjoy making it to this day. I sometimes make the meatballs with ground lamb instead of beef and vary the dish by adding a roasted pepper and a diced zucchini. The very best accompaniment to this homey preparation is mashed buttery potatoes or a well-flavored couscous. The meatballs can be made a day or two ahead of time and will reheat perfectly in the microwave.

SERVES 4 TO 6

2 pounds ground beef, preferably chuck

1 small onion, grated, plus 1 large onion, quartered and sliced

2 garlic cloves, mashed

2 tablespoons minced flat-leaf parsley

1 teaspoon dried thyme

Salt and freshly ground black pepper

2 eggs, beaten

¼ cup unflavored bread crumbs

¼ cup club soda

2 tablespoons butter

1½ tablespoons olive oil

1 green bell pepper, diced

1 teaspoon hot paprika

One can (32 ounces) Italian plum tomatoes, well drained and chopped

1 teaspoon dried oregano

Minced flat-leaf parsley, for garnish

1. In a bowl, combine the ground meat, grated onion, 1 mashed garlic clove, 2 tablespoons parsley, and thyme. Season with salt and pepper.

2. Add the eggs and bread crumbs and work the mixture with your hands until smooth and well blended. Add the club soda and work the mixture again with your hands until well blended. If the mixture seems heavy, add a little more soda.

3. Form the mixture into round but somewhat flat meatballs about 1½ inches in diameter.

4. In a large heavy skillet, heat the butter and olive oil. Add the meatballs and sauté over medium-high heat until nicely browned all over. Carefully remove with a spatula to a dish.

5. Add a little more oil to the skillet and when hot, add the sliced onion, remaining garlic clove, and bell pepper. Sauté the mixture for 2 to 3 minutes, or until soft.

6. Add the paprika, tomatoes, and oregano. Season with salt and pepper and bring to a simmer. Return the meatballs to the skillet. Cover tightly and cook for 25 minutes. Correct the seasoning. The sauce should be highly seasoned. Transfer the meatballs to a deep serving bowl, garnish with parsley, and serve hot.

Spring Ragout of Veal Shanks with Mushrooms and Peas

The veal shank is suitable for many wonderful preparations. Most Americans are only familiar with the classic Italian osso buco, in which the veal is braised with tomatoes and wine and served with a saffron risotto. Here the shanks are braised with plenty of mushrooms, garlic, and herbs, and the dish is given a spring touch with the addition of fresh peas. The traditional accompaniment of saffron risotto works perfectly here, too. You can make this dish up to 2 days ahead of time and reheat it slowly in a low oven.

SERVES 6

3 tablespoons unsalted butter

1 tablespoon peanut oil

2 medium onions, finely chopped

3 large garlic cloves, crushed

Salt and freshly ground black pepper

3 small sprigs of fresh thyme

1 small sprig of fresh rosemary

$\frac{1}{2}$ cup dry white wine

$4\frac{1}{2}$ pounds veal shanks, cut crosswise into 2-inch-thick pieces

$1\frac{1}{2}$ to 2 cups Brown Chicken Stock (page 389) or beef stock or bouillon

$\frac{3}{4}$ pound cremini mushrooms, stemmed, caps cubed

1 cup cooked peas

$\frac{1}{3}$ cup heavy cream

1 tablespoon flour mixed into a paste with 1 tablespoon softened butter

3 tablespoons minced flat-leaf parsley

1. Preheat the oven to 350°F.

2. In a large heavy casserole, heat the butter and oil. Add the onions and garlic and season with salt and pepper. Sauté the mixture over medium-high heat until nicely browned. Add the herbs and wine. Bring to a boil and cook until all the wine has evaporated.

3. Season the veal with salt and pepper. Add to the casserole together with $1\frac{1}{2}$ cups of the stock and the mushrooms. Bring the mixture to a simmer. Cover the casserole tightly, first with foil and then the lid, and place in the oven. Braise the veal for 1 hour 45 minutes, or until fork tender. Check every 30 minutes to make sure that there is enough broth in the pot, adding the remaining ½ cup stock if necessary.

4. When the veal is done, place the casserole on top of the stove and add the peas. Heat through and transfer the veal to a deep serving platter together with the mushrooms and peas. Add the cream to the pan juices and whisk in bits of the blended flour and butter, just enough for the sauce to thicken slightly. Taste the sauce and correct the seasoning. Spoon the sauce over the veal and garnish with parsley. Serve hot.

REMARKS Brown cremini mushrooms are far tastier, with a better texture, than all-purpose white mushrooms. Cremini are now available in many supermarkets, where they are often labeled brown mushrooms. If you cannot find them, substitute all-purpose white mushrooms in this dish.

Braised Lamb Shanks with Vegetables Niçoise

Traditionally, lamb stews are synonymous with spring, but since the quality of American lamb is consistent year round, I find that a good lamb stew is equally delicious and welcome in the fall. This ragout, typical of the Nice region of France, makes use of the season's last ripe tomatoes and garden-fresh basil. The intense flavors blend and improve when allowed to develop for a day or two. Roasted bell peppers and sautéed cubed eggplant can be added to the ragout for additional texture and interest.

SERVES 6

6 whole lamb shanks

5 tablespoons unsalted butter

2 tablespoons olive oil

Salt and freshly ground black pepper

3 medium onions

3 large garlic cloves, minced

$\frac{1}{3}$ cup dry white wine

4 large ripe tomatoes, peeled, seeded, and chopped, or 1 can (28-ounce) Italian plum tomatoes, drained and chopped

2 tablespoons fresh thyme leaves

1 sprig of fresh rosemary

2 tablespoons fresh oregano leaves or 1½ teaspoons dried

2 cups Brown Chicken Stock (see page 389) or beef stock or bouillon

1 large leek, all but 1 inch of greens removed, leek cut into ½-inch cubes and washed

1 large zucchini, trimmed and diced, seedy center discarded

1 large red bell pepper, cut into ½-inch cubes

1 large yellow bell pepper, cut into ½-inch cubes

Finely grated lemon zest and juice of 1 lemon

4 tablespoons minced fresh basil

4 anchovy fillets, drained and minced, optional

2 teaspoons cornstarch, mixed with a little cold stock or water

3 tablespoons minced flat-leaf parsley mixed with 2 minced garlic cloves

I. Preheat the oven to 350°F. Dry the lamb shanks thoroughly with paper towels.

2. Melt 2 tablespoons of the butter with 1 tablespoon of the olive oil in a large cast-iron skillet over medium-high heat. Add the shanks and brown nicely all over. Transfer to an oval casserole or large, deep cast-iron skillet. Season with salt and pepper.

3. Reduce the heat to medium and add the remaining 1 tablespoon oil to the skillet. Add the onions and garlic and sauté for 5 to 7 minutes, or until nicely browned. Add the wine, bring to a boil, and reduce to a glaze. Add the tomatoes, thyme, rosemary, and oregano. Bring to a boil and transfer to the casserole containing the lamb. Add the stock, cover tightly, and place in the center of the oven. Braise the lamb for 1½ to 1¾ hours, or until tender when pierced with a fork.

4. While the lamb is braising, prepare the vegetables. In a large skillet, melt the remaining 3 tablespoons butter over medium-low heat. Add the leek, zucchini, and bell peppers, season with salt and pepper, and add 2 tablespoons water. Reduce the heat, cover, and simmer for 8 to 10 minutes, or until tender. Stir in the lemon zest, lemon juice, basil, and anchovies.

5. When the shanks are done, transfer them with a slotted spoon to a dish. Degrease the pan juices and strain them through a fine sieve back into the casserole. Place over high heat and cook until reduced by half. Whisk in enough of the cornstarch mixture to thicken the sauce so that it lightly coats a spoon. Correct the seasoning.

6. Return the lamb shanks and vegetables to the casserole and just heat through. Garnish with the parsley and garlic mixture and serve hot directly from the casserole with plenty of crusty French bread.

Pork Tenderloin with Prunes and Port Sauce

SERVES 6

2 dozen unpitted or pitted prunes

1 cup tawny port

$\frac{1}{4}$ cup sherry vinegar

$\frac{1}{4}$ cup sugar

$1\frac{1}{2}$ to 2 cups beef stock or bouillon

4 pork tenderloins ($2\frac{3}{4}$ to 3 pounds each)

Coarse salt and freshly ground black
   pepper

2 teaspoons dried thyme

2 tablespoons butter

1 tablespoon canola oil

About 1 tablespoon flour mixed into
   a paste with 1 tablespoon softened
   butter

1. In a nonreactive medium saucepan, combine the prunes with the port. Bring to a simmer and cook for 5 to 7 minutes.

2. In a small, heavy, nonreactive saucepan, heat the vinegar and sugar. Cook the syrup until it becomes a thick caramel and is reduced to 2 tablespoons. Immediately add $\frac{1}{2}$ cup of the beef stock and boil for another 2 minutes.

3. Preheat the oven to 400°F.

4. Season the pork tenderloins with salt, pepper, and thyme. In a heavy roasting pan, heat the butter and oil. Add the tenderloins and sauté over medium-high heat, turning, until nicely browned all over, about 5 minutes. Add a little more stock to the pan and transfer to the oven.

5. Roast the tenderloins for 12 to 14 minutes, or until an instant-read thermometer registers 135°F. Remove from the oven and let rest.

6. Strain the prunes, reserving the port. Add the port to the roasting pan together with the sugar-vinegar broth and the remaining stock. Bring to a boil. Gradually whisk in the blended flour and butter. Cook the sauce until is slightly thickened, 2 to 3 minutes.

7. Add the prunes, taste, and correct the seasoning, adding a large grinding of black pepper. Slice the pork tenderloins into ½-inch slices. Place them overlapping on a serving platter and spoon the prune sauce over and around them. Serve hot.

■ Fettuccine with Jalapeño-Lime Cream and Shrimp ■ Fettuccine with Zucchini and Goat Cheese in a Ginger-Tomato Fondue ■ Bow Ties with Creamy Tomato Sauce, Bacon, and Radicchio ■ Linguine with Mussels in a Creamy Tomato-Saffron Fondue ■ Penne with Broccoli, Peppers, Tomatoes, and Smoked Mozzarella ■ Spaghettini with Tuna, Capers, and Black Olives ■ Quick Tomato Sauce ■ Catalan Chicken Paella ■ Oven-Baked Rice Pudding with Lemon and Cranberries ■ Risotto with Clams and Tomato-Saffron Fondue ■ Leek and Stilton Cheese Risotto with Mascarpone ■ Creamy Risotto with Vine Ripe Tomatoes, Fresh Rosemary, and Mascarpone ■ Braised Bulgur with Two Peppers and Lemon ■ Couscous with Spinach, Red Peppers, and Carrots ■ Corn-Studded Polenta with Parmesan ■ Cumin-Scented Quinoa with Yogurt and Mint ■ Chickpea, Tomato, and Cilantro Salad ■ Lentil Salad with Goat Cheese and Roasted Peppers ■ Stew of Pinto Beans and Shrimp with Fragrant Indian Spices ■ Ragout of White Beans with Bacon and Radicchio ■ White Bean and Chorizo Soup

One of my favorite memories is of the summer I spent with the Manfreddi family while I attended the University of Parma in Italy. La Nonna, the grandmother, made the best homemade pappardelle and gnocchi I have ever tasted, and I was lucky enough to learn firsthand about pasta from her. I watched how she made the dough by hand, with very basic ingredients—water, olive oil, flour, and salt—kneaded and rolled it to perfection, then cut and laid it out to dry on clean dish towels sprinkled with cornmeal. We ate pasta every day at the Manfreddis', and the varieties of shapes and sauces always amazed me.

When Sr. Manfreddi came home for lunch, he would shout from the bottom of the staircase, *"Mama, butta la pasta"* ("throw in the pasta"). His booming voice could easily be heard up to the fourth floor, and Nonna would immediately put a large pot of water on the burner. By the time Sr. Manfreddi walked through the door, the water would be at a rolling boil, and all of us would be seated at the big wooden table waiting for the pasta to be done. The rule is that pasta is never made to wait.

During my stay with the Manfreddis, I picked up some wonderful pasta-making techniques and recipes for homemade sauces. There's a whole art to preparing pasta, and Italians are very serious about cooking it properly and matching different shapes with the right sauce. The wonderful thing about pasta is its versatility. It is one of those foods that can fit anywhere on a menu. You can dress it up or dress it down. It can be an appetizer or an entree, and it can be served any time of year.

Pasta has become an American classic whose popularity continues to soar. There are lots of questions about pasta, especially since there are so many varieties and so many different ways of preparing it. Here are a few of the questions most frequently asked by my students all over the country.

What is the difference between dried and fresh pasta?

Dried pasta is simply fresh pasta that has been dried for a period of time in large commercial ovens. Usually dried pasta does not contain eggs and, in the case of imported Italian brands, is made with durum semolina flour. Fresh pasta generally does contain eggs; it is more pliable and requires a much shorter cooking time. I find that commercial fresh pasta, even from very good markets, is not very good. Which is why I suggest learning to make your own. Also, it is very important not to overcook fresh pasta, because it quickly turns mushy. Instead, look for dried egg pasta. There are several excellent domestic brands on the market these days as well as a number of artisinal imported ones. Test several brands, and when you find one you like, stock up on it.

I keep reading that dried pasta can be used for just about any pasta dish. Are there any preparations for which fresh pasta is much better?

The taste and texture of good fresh pasta is quite different from that of dried pasta. Fresh pasta is best for cream- or butter-based sauces, such as the classic Roman Alfredo sauce.

TIP To keep fresh pasta from cooking too quickly, dry it for a couple of hours by loosening the strands and spreading them on a large linen towel sprinkled with cornmeal. Drying the pasta overnight is even better. You can store it in your pantry in a large plastic bag.

What brand of dried pasta do you recommend?

DeCecco is a good all-around imported brand that is now available everywhere. Avoid domestic brands, because they tend to cook too quickly, and the result can be a rather mushy consistency.

What about the expensive, flavored varieties of pasta? Are they worth the extra money?

Some specialty pastas are simply trendy or gimmicky and aren't really worth the extra cost. The only purpose of vegetable-flavored pastas, especially those flavored with tomatoes, beets, or spinach, is to add color, not taste, to a dish. Some spices, in particular black pepper and saffron, will flavor it and, depending on the brand, can be quite good.

When you want color in a pasta dish, try a combination called *paglia y fieno*, "grass and hay." This is a classic mixture of white and green pasta usually served in a creamy Parmesan and butter sauce.

Many cookbooks and magazines call for pasta artisanale. What exactly is that?

Pasta artisanale, literally translated as "craft made," is available in many specialty stores and upscale grocery stores. Two excellent brands worth trying if you can find them are Rustichella d'Abruzzo and Benedetto Cavalieri. What is the difference? The large commercial pasta companies dry their pastas in enormous ovens for about an hour, producing noodles that are practically pre-cooked. *Pasta artisanale*, on the other hand, is generally produced by small companies who use better-quality flour and mineral water (versus tap water) and who dry the pasta for up to 12 hours at a much lower temperature. This produces pasta with a far superior texture. Good *pasta artisanale* can cost almost double the price of commercial brands, but it is definitely worth it.

TIP If you decide to serve a "designer pasta" colored with beets or squid ink, think about how it will actually look once it's cooked and sauced.

What is pasta asciutta? It appears in recipes and on restaurant menus, but I'm not sure what it means.

Pasta asciutta simply means dried pasta. It is a mixture of durum semolina flour and water that does not contain any eggs and, once formed into various shapes of pasta, is fully dried. This differs from fresh pasta, which may be dried later, but always contains eggs.

How much pasta should I cook per person? Is there an easy way to estimate how much is enough?

It depends on whether you are serving the pasta as an appetizer or a main course. If you plan on serving it as an appetizer, figure on 3 ounces of dried pasta per serving, or 5 ounces as a main course. Italians believe that when you eat pasta as a main course, you will be hungry within 2 hours, and they usually serve it as a starter.

Many recipes call for salting the pasta water; others do not. What's best?

Salt the water, adding about 1 tablespoon coarse salt to 14 cups water. If you forget to salt the water, don't worry. The seasoning in the sauce and the accompanying ingredients usually provide the necessary flavor. Some Italian cooks believe that seasoning the water gives you the option of using some of the pasta water for thinning out the sauce of a finished dish, but I find that unsalted water does just as well. Adding salt to make water boil faster is a myth.

What is the proper amount of water to use for cooking pasta?

Fourteen to 16 cups, or 4 quarts, water is about what you need to cook a pound of pasta. Why so much? You need to keep the noodles from sticking to each other and to the bottom of the pot. When pasta boils, it releases a fair amount of starch, and if there is not enough water, the pasta will cook unevenly. The key is to give the noodles as much room as possible to swirl around during cooking, and this means lots of water.

If you add a splash of olive oil to the water when cooking tubular pasta, such as ziti, fusilli, rigatoni, and penne, it will keep the pasta from sticking. However, many Italians and pasta purists frown on adding oil. They believe that oil makes the sauce slide off the pasta.

TIP If you do not add oil when cooking any of the tubular shapes, just make sure that you stir the pasta gently with a wooden spoon several times during cooking.

Recipes frequently call for cooking pasta "al dente." What exactly does that mean?

Literally it means "to the tooth," and when applied to pasta, it means the pasta should offer slight resistance when bitten. This does not mean it is half cooked, but that it keeps an interesting texture; overcooked pasta could be called "al mushy." Also remember that pasta continues to cook after draining and saucing. Is there a formula? Not really. The only way to master the timing is to practice, make a lot of pasta, and learn as you cook and eat.

I have heard that one of the best ways to tell whether pasta is done is to fling a couple of strands against the wall and see if they stick. Is there an easier way to tell when it is done? And is there a foolproof guideline?

Fortunately, you don't need to fling pasta around the kitchen to see if it's done. The best way to tell if pasta is ready is to taste the noodles several times during cooking. Keep in mind that pasta continues to cook even after it has been drained. A good rule of thumb is 7 to 9 minutes for flat, imported strands of pasta, and 10 to 12 minutes for tubular pasta.

TIP The best tool to use for testing pasta is a wooden or stainless steel pronged pasta fork. The noodles are easily caught in the fork and the wooden handle stays cool.

Can I substitute one shape of pasta for another? And do certain sauces call for particular shapes?

Within a general category, you can usually use any shape you want. Penne, ziti, and fusilli are shapes that can be used interchangeably in pasta recipes. So are strands of pasta like spaghetti, spaghettini, and linguine. Most sauces can be used on any shape of pasta except for the creamy Alfredo sauce, which is traditionally served over fettuccini.

I sometimes find myself with several boxes of pasta, each about a quarter full. Can I mix the various shapes?

If you have leftover penne, ziti, fusilli, or pennete, all of the same brand, it is possible to mix them. I wouldn't mix different brands, though, even if the shapes were the same, because cooking times vary from one brand to another. You can also use these small amounts in soups. Keep in mind that the older the pasta is, the longer it takes to cook.

TIP Italians use much less sauce on their pasta than we do in America. That's because they want to taste the pasta, and pasta tastes best if it's not swimming in sauce. Be frugal with the sauce and generous with the pasta. You can always add more sauce, but you can't remove it once it's been tossed with the noodles.

I would like to go beyond the standard tomato sauce over spaghetti. Do you have any suggestions?

First, stock your pantry with some basics: several shapes of dried pasta, canned plum tomatoes (preferably the brand imported from the San Marzano region of Italy), a chunk of good Parmesan cheese (Parmigiano-Reggiano), extra virgin olive oil, fresh garlic, onions, shallots, flat anchovy fillets, capers, oil-cured black olives, fresh lemons, crushed hot red pepper or dried chile peppers, canned tuna packed in olive oil, fresh flat-leaf parsley, and maybe some fresh or smoked mozzarella. Once you have these basic ingredients, you can make lots and lots of different sauces and match them with a variety of pasta shapes.

My homemade pasta cooks in less than 2 minutes, and it turns out mushy, even if I use special pasta flour. What am I doing wrong?

By its nature, homemade pasta is soft, particularly if it contains eggs. You can firm it up by drying the cut pasta on a rack for several hours. Be sure to use durum semolina flour to give the pasta the necessary firmness. You may want to try buying imported egg pasta. It cooks in 2 or 3 minutes but retains a more toothy texture.

When should grated cheese be served with pasta?

In this country, we assume that grated Parmesan should be served with nearly every pasta. In fact, many dishes do not call for cheese. Never add cheese to pasta with a seafood sauce. Many sauces that contain meat, butter, vegetables, and cream, however, are greatly enhanced by the addition of Parmesan. You can also use Asiago and pecorino, but to me nothing really compares with true Parmigiano-Reggiano imported from Italy. If it is not available, I prefer serving the dish without any cheese. Whatever you do, avoid domestic Parmesan or the one imported from Argentina, which comes with a black rind marked "imported."

TIP It's best to buy Parmesan in chunks and grate only enough for use in your meal. Once grated, Parmesan loses its unique aroma and texture within a day or two.

Is pasta fattening?

If you eat lots of pasta, it is right up there on the fat scale, especially if you lead a sedentary life. Pasta is a complete carbohydrate, which means it is great fuel if you exercise regularly and can burn it off. The other thing to remember is that when we are talking pasta, we are talking sauce, olive oil, butter, cream, and other flavorful toppings that add to the calorie count.

TIP Take a close look at the way Italians eat pasta. Their portions are small and so is the amount of sauce. If you can handle that, you can enjoy your pasta and eat it too.

Can I freeze leftover pasta?

There is not much point in freezing leftover pasta unless it is a baked dish like lasagna that can be reheated in the oven. You can freeze sauces, such as those made with tomatoes and meat, but it's best to cook the pasta at the last moment.

Grains

■■

Bulgur

I read a recipe that called for bulgur, and the instructions called for 5 minutes of cooking. Even after 45 minutes the grain was still tough. Why?

Sometimes bulgur and cracked wheat are mislabeled, and you probably bought cracked wheat.

True, they are the same grain, but bulgur has been processed so that it cooks much quicker. Cracked wheat can take as long as an hour or more to cook; bulgur, depending on the size of the grain, may only need to be soaked in water or cooked for 5 minutes. Bulgur comes in three sizes: fine, medium, and coarse. Only the fine bulgur can be left to soak up the water; medium and coarse bulgur should be steamed just like rice.

What grain is used for tabbouleh?

Bulgur is fine or medium-grain cracked wheat that has been par-boiled and dried, so it is essentially instant. For the salad, the soaked grain is mixed with parsley and flavored with lemon juice and olive oil. Bulgur is available in all health food stores and Middle Eastern markets.

Couscous

What is the difference between bulgur and couscous? Can they be used interchangeably?

If you are looking for a quick side dish flavored with spices or herbs, both couscous and bulgur can be prepared the same way. Just soak them in broth or water: they'll plump up to a fluffy consistency in very little time. Good quick couscous, especially the superior French varieties, is ready in about 10 minutes. Add a little butter and some melted scallions to your couscous, and you've got a lovely and effortless side dish. Add some diced tomatoes and sliced cucumbers to a bowl of bulgur, sprinkle it with fresh cilantro, lemon juice, and olive oil, and you're ready to serve a tangy salad that's refreshingly different.

I had a delicious fluffy couscous in a Moroccan restaurant, but the one

I make is nothing like it. What am I doing wrong?

Making real couscous is very time consuming. If you want to know more about it, read Paula Wolfert's chapter on couscous in her cookbook *Mediterranean Grains and Greens*.

The instant couscous you are probably making can never have that wonderful fluffy texture, but it is quick and can be quite delicious when combined with herbs and spices.

What is the difference between couscous the dish and couscous the grain?

Couscous is not a grain but a tiny pasta made from semolina wheat. Couscous, the dish, is composed of fluffy-textured couscous served with a meat broth, cooked lamb, or poultry as well as vegetables. It is a popular dish in Morocco and Tunisia.

What is Israeli couscous?

Israeli couscous is not couscous at all. It is a novelty pasta in the shape of very tiny, pearly balls. It can be cooked in water just like pasta and flavored with butter, herbs, and spices. However, I prefer to sauté it first in a little oil until nicely browned and then cook it in some broth, like a risotto. It makes for a lovely side dish, which can be made seasonal with bits of asparagus, tomatoes, zucchini, red peppers, and fresh herbs.

Polenta

What exactly is polenta?

The word *polenta* refers to a cornmeal product imported from Italy, and to the northern Italian dish of the same name. When cooked, it resembles cornmeal mush or cooked grits. Somewhat like cooked pasta or rice, it is rather bland but takes well to many toppings and sauces.

The three classic preparations usually associated with polenta are sautéed chicken livers, grilled quail, and sautéed peppers and sausages. From here, you can be as creative as you want and use polenta as a bed for tomato- and meat-based sauces in place of pasta.

I understand that polenta is time consuming and difficult to cook. Is there an easy way to make it?

Actually polenta is quite easy to prepare, and although the traditional method does take 25 minutes, you can now get quick-cooking polenta that is just about foolproof and can be cooked in as little as 10 to 12 minutes. Here's how to do it.

To make quick polenta Bring 3¼ cup skim milk or water to a simmer. Season with a pinch of salt. Add ¾ cup quick-cooking polenta in a slow steady stream and cook over moderate heat, stirring constantly, for 10 to 12 minutes, or until thick and smooth. Correct the seasoning, then stir in 2 to 3 tablespoons of unsalted butter for enrichment.

I see various kinds of polenta in the markets. What should I buy? Does it matter if it's fine or coarse?

The texture of polenta varies, depending on how and where the corn has been milled; some varieties will absorb more liquid than others. I personally like a medium-coarse polenta that retains a nice texture when cooked, but I suggest you try various brands and types of polenta to discover what you like best. The finer the polenta, the more baby-food texture it has.

Coarser-textured polenta is more interesting to me.

I recently bought a bag of polenta that smells stale. Does this mean it's gone bad?

Fresh polenta should smell sweet. If you have had the box for a while or it's languished on the store shelf, there is a good chance that the polenta has become stale and may even have an unpleasant cardboard smell. Do not use it because the staleness is difficult to disguise.

If I cannot get imported Italian polenta, can I use cornmeal instead?

Yes, but I would use only stone-ground cornmeal. It has wonderful taste, and when I am willing to give it the time it needs, I actually prefer it to imported Italian polenta. To maximize the taste of cornmeal, you must stir it constantly for anywhere from 25 to 35 minutes and then enrich it with butter and freshly grated Parmesan.

I love pan-fried polenta, but whenever I attempt to make it, the slices fall apart. What am I doing wrong?

If you plan to pan-fry polenta, you have to start with a firm mixture, one that has not been enriched with either butter or cheese. In this case, I use a ratio of 1 cup imported polenta or cornmeal to 3½ cups skim milk. If you use water, use only 3 cups. Spread the cooked polenta about ¾ inch thick in a buttered pan and chill for several hours before slicing and frying.

I don't recommend grilling polenta. It is not easy, and I usually opt for frying. Even at my favorite restaurant in Florence, famous for their grilled squab with polenta, they use the grill only to give the polenta squares decorative grill marks before transferring it to a flat pan to finish cooking.

TIP **To fry polenta shapes, dip them first in beaten egg and then in fine cornmeal; sauté in olive oil or a mixture of olive oil and butter.**

I have tried to make polenta several times, and it was always lumpy. Any suggestions?
There are two simple, very important steps to take when making polenta. First, the liquid cannot be too hot. Second, add the polenta in a fine stream, never all at once.

TIP **I often suggest to my students that they use a large-hole shaker for adding the polenta to the pot.**

How long can I store cooked polenta?
Polenta cooked in water or broth will keep for as long as 4 to 5 days, but when made with milk, it will keep only for 2 or 3 days. Be sure to wrap it well to keep it from picking up refrigerator smells.

The specialty market in my neighborhood carries prepared polenta logs. What do you think of them?
Now that you can get quick-cooking polenta that cooks in about 10 minutes, there is no reason to bother with these. First, they are expensive for what they are, and second, they have a rubbery texture that cannot be changed.

Quinoa

In recent years, I've read a lot about quinoa but am still not sure what it is or what it goes with. Can you give me some ideas how to use it?
Quinoa is a protein-packed grain that is now becoming increasingly available. The cooked grain is similar in texture to tapioca; its taste is unique. You can find it either imported from South America or in a domestic variety. On the East Coast, it is usually available only in health food stores and specialty food markets, but west of the Rockies it is quite popular and widely available in supermarkets.

What is the best way to cook quinoa?
First, you must rinse the grain well under cold running water, just as you would rice. Bring 2 cups vegetable broth or chicken bouillon to a boil. Add 1 cup of quinoa, cover, and simmer for 12 to 15 minutes, or until all the liquid is absorbed and the quinoa is tender. 1 cup dry quinoa will serve four to five people.

I recently cooked some quinoa, and it had a bitter aftertaste. What did I do wrong?
You didn't do anything wrong. That off-taste probably came from saponin, a natural chemical that often occurs on the outside of the quinoa. Usually this harmless coating is removed during processing, but sometimes you will still find quinoa that has some saponin clinging to it. Simply rinse quinoa in a fine-mesh strainer until the water runs clear.

Rice

I still remember one of my mother's favorite weekday dishes from when I was growing up in Barcelona, Spain. It was a simple rice preparation, what she called a "poor man's paella," made with bits of vegetables and some sausage or chicken. We would sit down to lunch, and invariably my mother would exclaim, "I like potatoes but I love rice," and so did I. This recipe was forever changing depending on the season or what was fresh at the market or in our garden. It was good at room temperature and just as flavorful as a cold snack. It made a good side dish as well as a fine picnic dish. It taught me to appreciate rice years before I ever knew what a risotto or a biryani was.

Many years later, after having tasted many varieties of rice and learning a variety of rice cooking techniques, I would always encourage my students to give rice a chance. Now that we can easily find good-quality Arborio rice in most grocery stores, making a risotto at home should not be daunting. And a bowl of simply steamed jasmine or basmati rice is an easy and delicious side dish to just about any entree.

Having grown up in Barcelona, I know nothing can top the taste of saffron-tinged paella rice that's slow-cooked on the grill. But there is much more to rice than even the best of paellas, from a spicy shrimp pilaf to a Thai braised rice in lime-coconut milk. Rice is quick to prepare, goes with everything, and is so very satisfying.

Even risottos, which have always demanded a great deal of time and attention from the cook, are possible to create with a short-cut method that doesn't short cut the rich, intense taste. I think my simplified version on page 281 is perfect for the everyday cook. I'm no longer rigid about how I make risotto or how I serve it. I often make it the main course, preceded by a soup or a salad or a quick skillet sauté of shellfish. When I choose a grilled or pan-seared fish as my main course, I balance it with a hearty risotto as an appetizer.

Whenever I teach a class I try to include a quick rice dish, and I am amazed by the response. Many of my students have only cooked converted or flavored rice, or they feel that rice is hard to make. For some reason, they are intimidated by it and do not realize how good-natured the grain really is. Rice is more forgiving than pasta. As long as it is not mushy, it is fine. In many cases it can be prepared in advance, as it reheats well.

In other cultures, cooks are familiar with their typical rice dishes because they make them almost daily. Venetian or Milanese cooks can eye their risottos and get the perfect result without measuring the broth. An Indian can make a perfect biryani, and a Japanese cook knows exactly how to make sushi rice. Of course, they've been practicing for years. Each of these cooks is looking for a familiar texture and taste. One of the difficulties facing American cooks is that they embrace so many cuisines and need to change gears every time they are cooking a different type of rice with a different technique. The cook who makes a fluffy pilaf of rice one day, a risotto the next week, and a rice pudding as well needs to understand the difference that each type of rice brings to a dish.

Sometimes the selection is not really critical. Basmati and Texmati are very similar, although Texmati does not have quite the aroma of the real thing. But if you are in Texas, then Texmati will do just fine. If you cannot get La Bomba paella rice, you can make good paella with Arborio, and if your store does not carry Superfino Italian rice, then go with a lesser brand.

Experimenting with many international cuisines makes rice-cooking a challenge; it also makes it fun. With three types of rice—a long-grain such as basmati or jasmine, a short-grain such as Arborio, and a medium-grain such as La Bomba—you can make endless wonderful rice dishes.

Remember that rice needs to be stored properly. Although cookbooks tell you rice keeps indefinitely, some types draw bugs and develop an "off taste" after a while. To be sure, store rice in an airtight container, and in the case of Arborio, keep it refrigerated.

The important thing is to give rice a chance and enjoy the fabulous flavors it can deliver.

Buying rice can be very confusing. Can you recommend one or two types of rice that can be served with everything?

When you consider that there are over 7,000 varieties of rice produced around the world, you would think that choosing two would be practically impossible to do. However, since most grocery stores offer only a limited choice, the task is not difficult.

Start with one type of flavorful long-grain rice, such as long-grain Carolina rice or jasmine rice, both of which can be simply steamed. I also recommend a short-grain rice such as the Italian imported Arborio. Arborio superfino is excellent; Carnaroli and Vialone Nano are even better.

There are three preparations that require short-grain rice: classic risotto, Spanish paella, and rice pudding.

I have recently seen medium-grain rice in my grocery store. It comes in 10-pound bags and is very inexpensive. What do you use it for?

Years ago, you could get medium-grain rice only in western states, especially California, where it is grown. But now it is becoming widely available, especially in areas with large Hispanic communities. Medium-grain rice is a compromise kernel, since it is shorter than long-grain, but not as dense or glutinous as traditional short-grain. It is amazingly flavorful and works well in all sorts of dishes, especially in paella and rice pudding. In fact, I have met chefs in Cali-

fornia who use medium-grain rice for risotto and swear by it.

How important is it to stick to the exact variety of rice called for in a recipe?

It is always a good idea to stick to the type of rice called for in a recipe. If the recipe calls for long-grain rice, you have many choices, such a long-grain basmati or jasmine. When a recipe calls for short-grain rice, you can use either a medium-grain California rice, Spanish-style Valencia, or Arborio, which is creamier and has a more interesting taste.

What is instant rice? Is there a particular brand that you recommend?

I am not a fan of instant rice; it lacks taste and texture. And there is really no reason to use it, since rice cooks in 15 minutes on top of the stove, or in less than 10 minutes in the microwave.

What does enriched rice mean? Does it mean it has more calories?

Enriched rice means that the rice has been spiked with iron, calcium and assorted vitamins. It should not be rinsed, since you would be rinsing some of the vitamins and minerals down the drain. It has the same amount of starch and calories as other types of rice.

What exactly is converted rice?

Converted rice is parboiled rice that has been steamed and pressure-cooked before milling. This process supposedly conserves vitamins, making it higher in vitamin content than regular rice. In spite of its obvious popularity, I am not fond of converted rice, because it lacks character and is not as aromatic as other types of rice. Also, it takes longer to cook and has a tendency to lose its nice texture when left on the stove for a period of time.

What is the difference between basmati and Texmati rice? Are they from different regions?

Basmati is a fine-textured long grain rice. It has been grown for thousands of years in the Punjab region of northern India, in Pakistan, and in the foothills of the Himalayas. It has a distinct aroma and a nutlike flavor. When cooked, it is soft, with the grains remaining separate. Texmati is a hybrid grown in Texas, and Calmati comes from California. They have neither the assertive flavor of true basmati nor the fluffiness of other domestic long-grain rices.

What is paella rice?

Paella rice is a short-grain rice similar to Arborio, but much less expensive. You can substitute Arborio in any recipe that calls for paella rice or use a medium-grain California rice.

What kinds of flavored rice do you recommend?

I really do not recommend using flavored rice. It is so easy to season rice that there is no reason to pay the extra money for something you can do better yourself. Using flavored rice sounds easy, but it is often harder to adjust the seasoning than to start from scratch.

What is risotto rice and how do you make risotto?

Risotto is not a type of rice but a preparation that is usually made with Arborio rice, a grain unique to the Po Valley in northern Italy. It is shorter and rounder than other short-grain rice and contains the right degree of starch needed to create the creamy texture that binds a risotto. In this classic northern Italian dish, the kernels should be tender on the outside but still retain a touch of chewiness on the inside.

My market does not carry Italian Arborio rice but does carry Italian-style rice. Is it okay to use for risotto?

In a pinch it is fine, but it is worthwhile to stock up on Arborio rice, which you can easily get through a good mail-order resource. Be sure to buy Arborio superfino, which is more expensive than the regular rice but has larger, plumper kernels.

Recipes for risotto sound long and quite difficult. Can you recommend any shortcuts?

A properly cooked risotto takes 25 minutes of almost nonstop stirring to make and should be served as soon as it is done. However, I have developed a method that requires only 10 minutes of stirring and works beautifully (see Creamy Risotto with Vine-Ripe Tomatoes, Fresh Rosemary, and Mascarpone, page 281.) Do not be tempted by recipes that suggest making a perfect risotto in the microwave. If you have ever tasted a really good risotto, you will agree that it is well worth spending 10 to 12 minutes to make this exquisite dish.

What is a rice pilaf and what kind of rice do you use to make it?

Pilaf is a classic Turkish peasant dish. The rice is first sautéed in some butter until the grains turn translucent, then baked in either vegetable or chicken broth. Toward the end, currants or raisins are gently folded into the rice. It is served as an accompaniment to grilled meats and seafood.

In classic French cooking, pilaf is simply braised rice that is either baked in the oven or cooked on top of the stove over very low heat.

Herbs such as parsley, dill, and basil can be added toward the end of cooking, as can cooked peas, bits of asparagus, and other parboiled vegetables.

Many pilafs are started with a small amount of minced shallots or finely minced onions that are first sautéed in a little butter, which adds more taste to the rice. I usually use long-grain rice to make a pilaf but have also used converted rice, which takes a little longer to cook.

I like to cook simple Chinese food and never know what kind of rice to make with it.

Look for short-grain Asian rice, such as White Rose, which is starchy and has a sticky consistency when cooked. In Japan and China, this rice is known as glutinous rice and is considered best when it is young, because that is when it cooks into a soft mass ideal for picking up with chopsticks. Look for California-grown short-grain rice rather the Japanese brands, which are much more expensive.

I love Thai food and find the rice in Thai restaurants especially tasty. Is there a special rice or does the cooking method make a difference?

The rice of choice in Thai cooking is jasmine rice. It is exceptionally aromatic, and now that it is grown in the United States, it is widely available.

What is the best rice to use for rice pudding?

Many recipes suggest using long-grain rice, which results in a lighter-textured pudding. Spanish and French rice puddings are usually made with a short- or medium-grain rice, such as Arborio, then oven baked. These puddings are denser and creamier.

Many recipes suggest rinsing rice well, others say not to. What do you suggest?

When it comes to rinsing rice, every cook has an opinion. As a rule, I never rinse rice for a risotto or paella because it is the starch in the rice that binds the ingredients and gives these preparations their special character. I do rinse all long-grain rice because it makes for a fluffier consistency.

Some recipes recommend soaking rice for up to 8 hours. Is this a good idea?

In many Asian countries, rice is soaked anywhere from 30 minutes to 8 hours. Soaking does produce fluffier rice, and I often do it when I remember, but it is not a must.

Is there a foolproof recipe for cooking rice?

Here is the basic recipe using long-grain rice: In a heavy 2-quart saucepan, bring 2 cups lightly salted water to a boil. Add 1 cup rice. Cover the pan tightly, lower the heat, and simmer for 15 minutes, or until the rice is fork tender. Remove from the heat and season to taste with salt and pepper. I often use chicken bouillon instead of water, for additional flavor. I also like to flavor the cooked rice with a tablespoon or two of butter, but this is not a must.

What should the consistency of rice be like when it is done?

If you go around the world asking what sort of texture perfectly cooked rice should have, you will get different answers everywhere you go. Basmati or jasmine rice should be light and quite dry, with separate fluffy grains. Sushi rice must be soft and sticky. Generally I like the mouthfeel of separate grains—tender but not mushy, with just a little bite left in them. Uncover the rice two or three times during its cooking and taste to see if it is done. Slightly overcooked rice is not a disaster, but undercooked rice is unpleasant to eat.

What is the best way to reheat rice?

It depends on the rice. Both long-grain and converted rice can easily be reheated in a low oven or in the microwave. You can also reheat Arborio rice, but it is not advised; there is a definite change in texture and it gets somewhat gummy.

What exactly is brown rice?

Brown rice is the whole, unpolished grain with the outer husk intact. It is much chewier than white rice and takes twice as long to cook, because each kernel is enclosed in a delicate layer of high-fiber bran. The bran adds a nutty flavor to the rice, plus, of course, a slew of vitamins and minerals. But it is the fiber that is the main reason to include brown rice in your diet.

I know that brown rice is healthier than white rice, but I am always put off by the long cooking time. Is there any way around it?

Not really. I soak brown rice overnight. This makes for more tender rice, but does not shorten the cooking time, which, I admit, is long. Try cooking the rice in the oven. Although the cooking time is the same, somehow it does not feel as long as when the rice is cooked on top of the stove.

TIP **If you do not have a saucepan with a tight-fitting lid, wrap the lid with a tea towel, which keeps steam condensation inside the lid while the rice cooks. This is also a good way to put a risotto on hold and keep it from drying out.**

I have been saving a bag of Arborio rice for over a year, and when I opened it, it was full of bugs. How should I store rice?

All varieties of rice can be stored for a long time. But it is always best to transfer the rice to airtight jars. Keep the rice in a cool place, or refrigerate it, and it will last indefinitely.

Wild Rice

How is wild rice related to other types of rice?

Wild rice is not actually rice at all but the seeds of an annual aquatic marsh grass that grows naturally in the northern Great Lakes area in both the United States and Canada. There is also commercial production in California and the Midwest. It is the only cereal native to North America, and the only wild grass plant that produces a grain large enough for use as a food.

Because of the way wild rice is harvested, you'll need to clean it before cooking. Put it in a bowl of water, swish it around, and strain off any plant material that floats to the top.

What is the best way to cook wild rice? I find the kernels stay too hard or become mushy.

There is no real formula for cooking wild rice because the amount of liquid needed and the cooking time can vary enormously from one variety of rice to another. I usually use 3 cups water to 1 cup wild rice and allow at least 45 to 50 minutes of cooking. If the rice is tender but has not absorbed all the liquid, you can strain it off. Don't worry about letting the rice sit. It is better to give yourself plenty of time, and if the rice is done before you are ready to serve it, you can keep it hot in a warm oven or reheat it in the microwave.

I love the taste of wild rice but find buying it confusing, since there are such enormous price variations. What is the difference between the expensive kind and the inexpensive rice?

Unfortunately, there are no bargains when it comes to wild rice. The real stuff is very expensive and very delicious. Organic hand-picked wild rice from the Great Lakes region is a superb-tasting grain that is difficult and time consuming to harvest and, therefore, commands the mighty price ticket.

To be on the sure side, buy only organic wild rice and look for kernels that are long with black-brown hues. I find it best to buy wild rice from a reputable mail-order source, since supermarket brands are usually inferior and never seem to cook evenly.

What wild rice mixes do you recommend?

I do not recommend any wild rice mixes, although I realize that they are quite popular. Good wild rice has a unique flavor and texture that is best served on its own.

Beans

With the continuing interest in peasant cooking of every type, beans are gaining in popularity, and I am delighted. I grew up with wonderful bean soups, lentil ragouts, and chickpea salads. The bean stand in the Boqueria Market in Barcelona was one of my favorite stops for many years, and strolling through the aisles with my small cone-shaped bag of warm white beans drizzled with olive oil continues to be one of my favorite things to do when I am there.

That beans are extremely versatile and packed with nutrition is widely known by now, so why is it that beans are have been so slow to gain the popularity they deserve? For starters, legumes in general, and especially chickpeas and beans, require advance preparation and do not fit easily into the lifestyle of the spur-of-the-moment cook. They need to be soaked in water overnight, and while some cookbooks recommend a cooking method in which the beans are brought to a boil for a minute and then left

to soak briefly before cooking, this method does not work as well as overnight soaking.

Also, even though they are dried, legumes need to be fresh. In spite of the fact that we are led to believe that beans have an indefinite shelf life, this is far from the truth. The older the bean, the tougher the shell, and the longer it takes to cook, resulting in mushy, unevenly cooked beans, which can be less than digestible. In Europe, packages of beans are dated and are meant to be consumed within a year of purchase.

Some types of beans are easier to buy fresh than others. Pinto or cranberry beans as well as black beans are usually delicious if you can buy them in a Hispanic neighborhood, because the turnover is such that the beans are fresh. If you have access to a Middle Eastern store, the same holds true for chickpeas. Other beans, especially great northern and cannellini beans, can be more of a problem. Try a good mail-order resource, but always check first to find out if the resource dates their beans. If not, you are much better off buying your beans at a health food store that has a large turnover.

Avoid buying beans in fancy cook shops or specialty stores, because, again, chances are that they are not fresh. There is a good chance that a lot of effort will have gone into the packaging and not into the product.

Since beans are often called the caviar of Tuscany, I am always on the lookout for them when I go to Italy. To me beans are worth that kind of search, because when they are good they are as good as caviar and equally memorable.

The choice of beans can be very confusing. Which of them do you recommend having in the pantry?

I usually stock up only on the beans I use regularly. There is no point in hoarding beans, which is something I used to do, because they do not keep long. Here is a list of my basic pantry beans:

- Black beans
- Pinto beans
- Great Northern beans or cannellini beans
- Red kidney beans
- French Puy lentils

When a recipe calls for a specific type of bean, can you substitute one type for another?

It depends entirely on your recipe. If you are making something as simple and gutsy as chili, you can use red, pinto, or pink beans, but if you are making a French cassoulet or the French garbure (a traditional soup made with cabbage, root vegetables, and beans), you will need a good-quality white kidney bean, such as Sois-

son or Great Northern. The famous Italian soup pasta e fagioli is traditionally made with cannellini beans, but it works with Great Northern beans. Black beans, also called turtle beans, are more problematic because of their distinct color and taste, and cannot be substituted in recipes.

Are organically grown beans a better choice? Organically grown beans are usually fresher but also pricier. If a bag of beans is clearly marked with an expiration date and appears fresh, it doesn't matter if they are organically grown. For mail-order sources of organically grown beans, see Sources, page 397.

Can dry fava beans be substituted in recipes that call for fresh?

Fresh fava beans, one of the oldest members of the bean family, are just starting to show up in supermarkets around the country, but the going is slow. Your best bet for fresh is in Italian neighborhoods, specialty markets, and greengrocers during the spring and early summer. The dried bean, which is very popular in the Middle and Far East, is practically another vegetable.

Cook fava beans only when you see them fresh at your market in the spring. Choose those that have bright green, velvety-textured skin with no black spots.

TIP Unlike peas, which are ready to eat out of the pod, fava beans have both an outside pod and a tough skin that needs to be removed to expose the delicate bean inside. Blanch the shelled beans in a pot of boiling water for 30 seconds, and this protective skin will slip right off.

Can I use canned beans, such as kidney beans and chickpeas, in bean soup?

I use canned beans as an accent when they are needed mainly for texture, not flavor, as in minestrone or winter cabbage soup. But for real bean soups, such as the White Bean and Chorizo Soup, page 292, you must begin with dried beans that have been soaked overnight.

What is the difference between a garbanzo bean and a chickpea?

Just the name. Garbanzo bean is the Spanish name for chickpea; the Italians call it *ceci*, and the French *pois chiche*.

Why do I have more trouble cooking chickpeas than other legumes?

As with most legumes, chickpeas should be less than a year old if they are to cook quickly. It is best to buy them from a Middle Eastern or Latin market or health food store. Chickpeas older than a year will practically never soften, no matter how long you cook them. Be sure to soak them in water to cover for 24 hours with about ¼ teaspoon baking soda added to the water. Drain and then cook them in plenty of unsalted water.

Can canned chickpeas be used in recipes that call for the dried legume?

Sometimes that works, especially when the chickpeas are only used for additional texture. Use the Mexican or Goya brands, which are firmer than the American varieties.

TIP Spring water is a good choice for cooking beans because it is softer. Many Spanish cooks believe that it makes a more tender legume.

What is the difference between the basic brown lentil and green, yellow, pink, and red lentils? Are they interchangeable in recipes?

The brown lentil you see in your grocery store is the common lentil most often consumed in the West. It is a good-natured legume, extremely high in protein; it needs no presoaking, and it cooks quickly. It deserves to be high up there in everyone's cooking repertoire because it is healthful, inexpensive, and extremely versatile. Pink, yellow, red, and green lentils, except for the French Puy lentils, can be classified as Indian lentils, since it is in India that they are consumed the most. All Indian dals are made from split lentils and many of India's vegetarian dishes are based on this legume.

French green lentils, so often mentioned in cookbooks and food magazines, are not available in my grocery store. Can I substitute brown lentils for the French ones?

The taste and texture of brown lentils is quite different from the French ones. You can easily get Puy lentils through a good mail-order source (see page 397). Since they have a long shelf life, they are good to have on hand.

TIP When shopping for any type of bean, look them over carefully. If you find many that are broken and split, it means that they are old and will stay tough no matter how long you cook them.

Black beans are hard to find dried in my area. Are canned acceptable?

Personally, I do not recommend canned black beans because they are usually mushy and often too salty. Good-quality dried black beans will look dark and glossy. They are available through mail-order sources (see page 397).

Do all beans need soaking? Is there a shortcut that you can recommend?

All presoaked beans have a better texture and better overall flavor than those that have not been soaked. If you find yourself pressed for time, here is a shortcut: Cover the beans with water, bring them to a simmer, then let them stand off the heat for 1 to 2 hours. Drain, cover with fresh water by an inch, and cook over low heat either on top of the stove or in the oven.

At what point in cooking should beans be seasoned?

Never salt beans until they are almost tender, or they will be tough. You can flavor the bean cooking water with a whole unpeeled onion and a whole unpeeled head of garlic. You can also use fresh herbs, such thyme, rosemary, and bay leaf.

Beans also must be tender before being combined with a tomato mixture, because the acidity in the tomato will keep the cell walls of the bean from softening.

I find beans very hard to digest. Is there any way to get around it?

There is no question that beans are hard to digest. Be sure to soak your beans 12 to 14 hours or overnight, changing the water at least once and using fresh, cold water to promote the softening of the starches. Do not use hot or boiling water to start cooking soaked beans because they will not cook evenly. Always cover the beans with at least 2 inches of water. This helps extract the oligosaccharides, a string of sugar molecules that our normal digestive enzymes can't deal with. Beans have high levels of these compounds because they are seeds, and plants store high levels of certain sugars in their seeds to ensure their survival.

I always add 3 to 5 drops of Beano, a natural enzyme available in all health food stores, for each portion of beans.

Fettuccine with Jalapeño-Lime Cream and Shrimp

Pasta has moved beyond the classic preparations and can now be found prepared with a variety of interesting ingredients. I first sampled this dish in a Santa Fe restaurant, and it has been one of my favorites ever since. For a variation, use grilled diced chicken instead of the shrimp.

SERVES 2 TO 3

3 tablespoons olive oil

$\frac{1}{2}$ pound peeled medium shrimp

Coarse salt and freshly ground black pepper

1 cup green bell pepper, cored and cubed

1 cup yellow bell pepper, cored and cubed

1 cup red bell pepper, cored and cubed

1 medium red onion, cubed

1 tablespoon minced jalapeño pepper, seeds removed

Juice of $\frac{1}{2}$ lime or more to taste

$\frac{1}{2}$ cup heavy cream

$\frac{1}{2}$ pound egg fettuccine

Minced fresh cilantro or basil

8 grape tomatoes, cut crosswise in half, optional

I. In a large heavy cast-iron skillet, heat 2 tablespoons of the olive oil. Add the shrimp and sauté over high heat until nicely browned and slightly charred. Season with salt and pepper. Remove to a cutting board and, when they are cool enough to handle, cube the shrimp.

2. Add the remaining 1 tablespoon oil to the pan. Add the bell peppers and red onion. Season with salt and pepper and cook over medium-high heat until soft and slightly charred, 3 to 5 minutes. Be sure not to burn the peppers.

3. Lower the heat and add the jalapeño, lime juice, and cream. Bring to a simmer and correct the seasoning. Set the sauce aside.

4. In a large pot, bring plenty of salted water to a boil. Add the fettuccine and cook for 3 to 4 minutes, or until just tender. Drain and return to the pot.

5. Pour the pepper-and-shrimp sauce over the pasta; toss with two spoons. Add a large grinding of black pepper and the minced cilantro, and serve in individual soup bowls sprinkled with the sliced tomatoes, if using.

Fettuccine with Zucchini and Goat Cheese in a Ginger-Tomato Fondue

Here is a lovely pasta dish packed with flavor and texture. Be sure to use good-quality dried egg fettuccine here. DeCecco is acceptable, but Rustichella D'Abruzzo is a sturdier and much more flavorful pasta that is ideal for this recipe. You can vary the dish by using red, yellow, and green peppers and yellow zucchini instead of green. I also like to add some gaeta olives to the dish for additional piquant flavor.

SERVES 4 TO 5

4 tablespoons extra virgin olive oil

3 small zucchini, quartered lengthwise and cubed

1 red bell pepper, cored and cubed

1 small dried hot red pepper, broken into pieces

2 large garlic cloves, minced

1 tablespoon minced fresh ginger

1 large shallot, minced

1½ cups Creamy Tomato Sauce (page 268)

1 tablespoon minced fresh oregano, optional

Salt and freshly ground black pepper

½ pound egg fettuccine

4 tablespoons minced fresh basil

1 cup crumbled mild goat cheese

Freshly grated Parmesan cheese

1. Heat 2 tablespoons of the olive oil in a large heavy skillet over medium-high heat. Add the zucchini and bell pepper, and sauté quickly until lightly browned, about 3 minutes, Transfer to a dish with a slotted spoon.

2. Add the remaining 2 tablespoons oil to the skillet and when hot, add the hot pepper and cook until dark. Remove and discard the pepper. Add the garlic, ginger, and shallot and cook for 1 minute without browning. Add the tomato sauce and oregano, if using, and season with salt and pepper; simmer, covered, for 15 minutes.

3. Bring plenty of salted water to a boil in a large saucepan, add the fettuccine, and cook for 3 to 5 minutes, or until just tender. Drain well and return the pasta to the pan.

4. Mix the tomato sauce and zucchini-and-pepper mixture together with the basil and goat cheese and toss lightly; the goat cheese should just be warm, not melted. Taste and correct the seasoning. Transfer to a serving bowl. Serve at once with a bowl of the Parmesan.

Bow Ties with Creamy Tomato Sauce, Bacon, and Radicchio

A quick basic tomato sauce is probably the most important sauce to have on hand when making pasta. I usually make a large batch of it and freeze it in 1- and 2-cup containers. Here the sauce is enriched with a touch of cream, and when tossed into pasta with some sautéed bacon and radicchio, it makes for a delicious main course.

SERVES 4

2 tablespoons butter
½ cup diced pancetta or blanched bacon
1 tablespoon olive oil
1 large garlic clove, finely sliced
1 large head of radicchio, cored and cut into eighths
Salt and freshly ground black pepper
1 cup Quick Tomato Sauce, page 274
¼ cup heavy cream, optional
½ pound bow ties (fusilli)
2 to 3 tablespoons freshly grated Parmesan cheese

1. In a large heavy skillet, melt the butter over medium heat. Add the pancetta or bacon and sauté for 2 minutes, or until crisp. Remove with a slotted spoon to a dish and reserve.

2. Add the olive oil to the skillet and when hot, add the garlic and radicchio. Season with salt and pepper and sauté for 2 minutes, or until just wilted. Transfer to a side dish.

3. Heat the tomato sauce, and add the cream; taste and correct the seasoning. Keep warm.

4. In a large pot, bring salted water to a boil. Add the pasta and cook over high heat for 8 minutes, or until just tender. Drain, reserving ½ cup of the pasta water.

5. Return the pasta to the pot together with the tomato sauce, pancetta, and radicchio. Toss with two spoons. Add a large grinding of pepper and 2 tablespoons of the Parmesan. If the sauce seems too thick, add a little of the reserved pasta water. Taste and correct the seasoning. Serve hot in deep soup bowls.

REMARKS When choosing radicchio, be sure to buy light, large, fluffy heads. Separate the leaves, folding them in half lengthwise and cutting out the white triangle with a sharp knife.

Linguine with Mussels in a Creamy Tomato-Saffron Fondue

Here is a terrific gutsy pasta preparation. It can be made more elegant by shelling the mussels, leaving 6 to 8 in their shells as a garnish. Other pasta shapes, such as spaghetti or dried egg fettuccine, can be used as well. Serve this as a main course preceded by a well-seasoned salad or a soup.

SERVES 4 TO 5

1 large shallot, thinly sliced, plus 2 large shallots, minced

¾ cup dry white wine

2 sprigs each of thyme and flat-leaf parsley

6 whole black peppercorns

2 to 3 pounds fresh small mussels, well scrubbed

2 tablespoons unsalted butter

1 teaspoon extra-virgin olive oil

1 small dried hot red peppers, crumbled

2 large garlic cloves, minced

4 ripe medium tomatoes, peeled, seeded, and chopped

1 tablespoon minced fresh thyme

Salt and freshly ground black pepper

¼ teaspoon saffron threads

½ cup crème fraîche

3 to 4 tablespoons fine julienne of fresh basil

1 pound fresh linguine

Tiny leaves of fresh basil, for garnish

1. In a large flameproof casserole, combine the sliced shallot, wine, thyme and parsley sprigs, and peppercorns. Bring to a simmer over medium heat. Add the mussels and simmer, covered, shaking the pan, until the mussels open, 5 to 7 minutes; discard any that do not. With a slotted spoon, transfer the mussels to a large bowl and reserve. Strain the mussel broth through a double layer of cheesecloth and set aside.

2. Melt the butter together with the olive oil in a heavy skillet over medium heat. Add the hot peppers, minced shallots, and garlic and cook for 1 minute, stirring constantly. Add the tomatoes and minced thyme and season with salt and pepper. Reduce the heat and simmer, partially covered, until all the tomato liquid has evaporated.

3. Add the reserved mussel broth and saffron; simmer until slightly reduced. Transfer the mixture to a food processor and puree until smooth. Return the sauce to the skillet. Add the crème fraîche and julienne of basil. Heat just through. Keep warm.

4. Bring plenty of salted water to a boil in a large pot. Add the fresh pasta and cook for 3 to 4 minutes, or until just tender. Immediately add 2 cups cold water to the pot to stop further cooking. Drain well and return the pasta to the pot. Add the warm sauce and reserved mussels and toss gently. Taste and correct the seasoning.

5. Transfer the pasta to individual serving bowls and garnish each portion with a few of the reserved mussels in their shells and tiny basil leaves. Serve at once.

Penne with Broccoli, Peppers, Tomatoes, and Smoked Mozzarella

I always have some homemade tomato sauce on hand either in the re-frigerator or the freezer, which makes it much easier to come up with a pasta dish like this almost on the spur of the moment. Smoked moz-zarella is also best kept in the freezer; let it thaw just enough so you can grate it into the finished pasta dish. Leftover pasta is delicious at room temperature the next day. Just sprinkle with additional minced fresh basil, a few drops of good olive oil, and freshly ground pepper.

SERVES 4 TO 5

5 tablespoons extra virgin olive oil

1 large shallot, minced

4 large garlic cloves, thinly sliced

10 ripe Italian plum tomatoes or one 32-ounce can Italian plum tomatoes, drained

1 tablespoon fresh oregano or 2 teaspoons dried

4 tablespoons fine julienne of fresh basil

Coarse salt and freshly ground black pepper

1 bunch of fresh broccoli

½ to ¾ cup chicken stock or bouillon

1 red bell pepper, cored, quartered, and thinly sliced

1 yellow bell pepper, cored, quartered, and thinly sliced

½ pound imported penne

1 cup finely diced smoked mozzarella

Freshly grated Parmesan cheese

1. In a heavy 2-quart saucepan, heat 3 tablespoons of the olive oil over medium heat. Add the shallot and 2 of the garlic cloves and cook until just soft. Add the tomatoes, oregano, and basil, season with salt and pepper, and simmer, covered, for 25 minutes, or until all the tomato water has evaporated and the mixture is quite thick. Transfer the mixture to a food processor and process until smooth.

2. Trim the broccoli into florets. Peel the stalks with a veg-etable peeler. Remove any leaves and slice the stalks crosswise into ½-inch slices.

3. In a large cast-iron skillet, heat the remaining 2 tablespoons olive oil over medium heat. Add the remaining 2 garlic cloves and the broccoli florets and stems and season with salt and pepper. Add ½ cup of the stock, cover, and simmer for 5 to 7 minutes, or until the broccoli is tender. Be careful not to overcook. Set aside off the heat.

4. Bring water to a boil in a steamer. Add the bell peppers and steam, covered, for 2 to 3 minutes, or until just tender.

5. In a large pot, bring salted water to boil. Add the penne and cook until just tender. Immediately add 2 cups cold water to the pot to stop the penne from further cooking and drain well.

6. Return the pasta to the pot. Add the broccoli, peppers, and tomato mixture and season with salt and pepper. Add the smoked mozzarella, toss gently, and serve immediately in shallow soup bowls accompanied by a bowl of the Parmesan.

Spaghettini with Tuna, Capers, and Black Olives

Here is a wonderfully simple pasta dish I make almost weekly and vary according to what I see fresh in the market and seasonally. Some interesting additions could include cubed and sautéed eggplant, a couple of fire-roasted red peppers, or a medium zucchini cubed and sautéed in a little oil. Now that pitted black olives are widely available, this dish can be put together in a matter of minutes. A well-seasoned salad is the perfect accompaniment.

SERVES 2 TO 3

$\frac{1}{2}$ cup extra virgin olive oil

4 tablespoons minced flat-leaf parsley

3 large garlic cloves, minced

$\frac{1}{2}$ cup minced fresh basil, optional

1 teaspoon dried oregano

4 medium tomatoes, diced, or 14 grape
    tomatoes, cut in half

One 7$\frac{1}{2}$-ounce can tuna packed in olive oil

4 flat anchovy fillets, drained and minced

$\frac{1}{2}$ cup oil-cured black olives, preferably
    kalamata, diced

Salt and freshly ground black pepper

$\frac{1}{2}$ pound spaghettini

1 cup cubed smoked mozzarella, optional

1. Heat the olive oil in a large heavy skillet. Add 2 tablespoons of the parsley, and the garlic, basil, and oregano. Cook just until the garlic is soft, about 2 minutes.

2. Add the tomatoes and cook for another 3 to 4 minutes, or until the tomatoes are soft. Add the tuna, anchovies, and olives and heat through. Season with salt and pepper and set aside.

3. In a large pot, bring salted water to a boil. Add the pasta and cook for 7 to 8 minutes, or until it is just tender. Drain and return to the pot. Add the sauce and toss with two forks. Add the remaining 2 tablespoons parsley and the mozzarella and serve immediately.

Quick Tomato Sauce

A quick basic tomato sauce is a wonderful sauce to have on hand if you are a pasta fan. I usually make a large batch of it and freeze it in 1- and 2-cup containers. The sauce can be enriched with a touch of cream, which gives it a more mellow, delicate flavor that works especially well with homemade or egg-based pasta.

MAKES 2 CUPS

2 tablespoons olive oil

1 tablespoon butter

⅓ cup minced shallots

2 large garlic cloves, minced

1 dried hot red pepper, optional

One 32-ounce can Italian plum tomatoes, drained and chopped

1 teaspoon dried oregano

1 teaspoon sugar

Salt and freshly ground black pepper

¼ cup heavy cream and 2 tablespoons butter, optional

1. In a 2-quart heavy saucepan, heat the olive oil and butter. Add the shallots, garlic, and hot pepper. Sauté the mixture until soft but not browned. Add the tomatoes, oregano, and sugar. Season with salt and pepper. Bring to a boil, reduce the heat, and simmer for 30 minutes, stirring from time to time.

2. Transfer the tomato sauce to a food processor or a blender, add the cream and butter, and puree until smooth. Taste and correct the seasoning. Transfer the sauce to a covered jar and refrigerate for up to 5 days, or freeze for longer storage.

Catalan Chicken Paella

Although a traditional paella calls for a combination of seafood and poultry, this classic Spanish dish changes according to the region. In the Pyrennees it is often made with rabbit, chicken, and chorizo sausage. Here I use only chicken, but if you can get fresh rabbit do try it, because it gives the dish another flavor dimension that is quite interesting. Serve with a crusty loof of bread.

SERVES 6

3½ cups chicken stock or bouillon

¼ teaspoon loosely packed saffron threads

4 small whole chicken legs, cut in half at joint to make 4 thighs and 4 drumsticks

4 tablespoons extra virgin olive oil

Salt and freshly ground black pepper

1 or 2 small dried hot red peppers, broken into pieces

1 large onion, quartered and thinly sliced

3 large garlic cloves, minced

2 cups peeled, seeded, and chopped Italian plum tomatoes or one 16-ounce can Italian plum tomatoes, drained and chopped

1 red bell pepper, cubed

1 green bell pepper, cubed

1¼ cups Arborio rice or medium-grain Spanish

½ pound smoked chicken, cut into ½-inch cubes

½ cup cooked peas

Lemon wedges

Tiny leaves of flat-leaf parsley

Thinly sliced pimientos

1. In a small saucepan, combine the stock and saffron threads. Bring to a boil, reduce the heat, cover, and simmer for 20 minutes. You should have 3 cups saffron stock; if not, boil to reduce the stock to 3 cups.

2. Preheat the oven to 350°F. Dry the chicken pieces thoroughly with paper towels. In a large, deep cast-iron skillet, heat 2 tablespoons of the olive oil over medium-high heat. Add the chicken pieces and brown nicely on all sides. Remove the chicken from the skillet and drain on paper towels. Season with salt and pepper.

3. Discard all but 1 tablespoon of fat from the skillet. Add the hot peppers; cook until dark and discard. Heat the remaining 2 tablespoons oil in the skillet. Add the onion and garlic and cook, stirring often, for 10 minutes, or until the onion is soft and nicely browned.

4. Add the tomatoes and bell peppers. Season with salt and pepper and continue to cook until the tomato water has evaporated.

5. Add the rice, stirring it thoroughly into the onion and tomato mixture. Add the reserved saffron broth and browned chicken pieces. Bring to a boil, cover tightly, and place in the center of the oven. Braise for 20 minutes. Add the smoked chicken and peas and continue to cook for 5 to 10 minutes longer, or until the rice is tender.

6. Remove from the oven, correct the seasoning, and garnish with the lemons, parsley, and pimientos. Serve at once.

Oven-Baked Rice Pudding with Lemon and Cranberries

For an easy and satisfying weekend dessert, few recipes are as delicious and homey as a rice pudding. Once placed in the oven, it needs no attention, and the result is a no-nonsense dessert that will be devoured in a matter of a day. I often vary the pudding by adding dried cherries or raisins. The strawberry sauce, page 395, adds a refreshing finishing touch.

SERVES 6

$3\frac{1}{2}$ cups whole milk

1 cup sugar

$\frac{1}{2}$ cup long-grain rice

Zest of 1 lemon, cut into fine julienne

$\frac{1}{4}$ cup dried cranberries

2 extra large eggs, separated

1 teaspoon vanilla extract

Ground cinnamon or freshly grated nutmeg

1. Preheat the oven to 325°F.

2. Heat the milk in a large ovenproof saucepan together with all but 2 tablespoons of the sugar, and stir until dissolved. Add the rice, lemon zest, and cranberries; cover loosely with foil and bake for 2 to $2\frac{1}{2}$ hours, stirring once or twice. The rice should be quite tender and all the milk absorbed. Remove from the oven and whisk in the egg yolks and the vanilla.

3. Beat the egg whites with the remaining 2 tablespoons sugar until stiff but not dry; fold into the rice. Transfer to a serving dish, sprinkle with cinnamon or nutmeg, and serve at room temperature or slightly chilled.

Risotto with Clams and Tomato-Saffron Fondue

If you like spaghettini with clams you will love this risotto. The rice can be infused with the delicious briny flavor of clams and ripe tomatoes. Serve the risotto as a light main course preceded by a seasonal salad or a quick sauté of seasonal vegetables, or as an appetizer. Leftovers reheat beautifully in the microwave, but I doubt that you will have any.

SERVES 4

2 dozen littleneck clams
4 tablespoons extra virgin olive oil
1 dried hot red pepper, crumbled
½ cup white wine
2 cups fish stock or bouillon
2 tablespoons minced shallots
2 garlic cloves, minced
3 ripe tomatoes, peeled, seeded, and chopped
¼ teaspoon powdered saffron
Coarse salt and freshly ground black pepper
1 cup Carnaroli or Arborio rice
2 tablespoons minced flat-leaf parsley

1. Wash the clams thoroughly, scrubbing well with a hard brush.

2. In a large saucepan, combine 2 tablespoons of the olive oil, the hot pepper, and wine. Add the clams. Cover the saucepan and simmer the clams until they open. Discard any unopened clams. Remove the clams from the broth, discard the shells, and dice the clams. Reserve the broth and the clams separately.

3. Measure the clam broth, adding enough fish bouillon to make 5 cups.

4. In a 3½-quart heavy saucepan, heat the remaining 2 tablespoons olive oil. Add the shallots, 1 clove of the garlic, the tomatoes, and saffron. Season with salt and pepper and cook the mixture over medium heat until all the tomato juice has evaporated.

5. Add the rice and cook for 1 minute or until it turns opaque. Add 2 cups of the clam broth. Cover the pan and simmer over low heat for 12 minutes, or until the rice is barely tender.

6. Start adding more broth, ¼ cup at a time, stirring constantly and switching to fish bouillon as needed. When the rice is done, it should be soft but still slightly chewy. Add the clams and taste and correct the seasoning.

7. Add the parsley and the remaining garlic clove and simmer for another minute or two. Serve immediately in deep bowls accompanied by a bottle of extra virgin olive oil.

Leek and Stilton Cheese Risotto with Mascarpone

Leeks and rice make a wonderful combination, especially when teamed in this buttery risotto, which gets a kick from Stilton cheese. If you can't find good Stilton, try another blue, such as Danish or Maytag. Serve the rice as a starter or a side dish to a veal roast or pan-seared veal chops. Pass a bowl of grated Parmesan cheese on the side.

SERVES 6

½ cup mascarpone

2 ounces Stilton cheese, diced, or more to taste

2 tablespoons unsalted butter

2 cups minced leeks, rinsed and drained

5 cups chicken stock or bouillon

1½ cups Arborio rice

Salt and freshly ground black pepper

3 tablespoons freshly grated Parmesan cheese

Minced flat-leaf parsley

1. Combine the mascarpone and Stilton in a food processor and puree until smooth.

2. In a heavy 3-quart saucepan, melt the butter over low heat. Add the leeks and 3 tablespoons of the stock and braise, covered, until tender, about 5 minutes. Add the rice, season with salt and pepper, and stir well with the leek mixture. Add 2 cups of the stock, cover tightly, and simmer over very low heat for 10 minutes.

3. Raise the heat to medium and uncover the saucepan. Gradually add the remaining stock, ¼ cup at a time, stirring constantly, until each addition has been absorbed, for the next 10 minutes; you may not need all of the remaining stock. The rice should be tender on the outside but somewhat chewy on the inside.

4. Add the Stilton mixture and the Parmesan and fold gently. Taste and correct the seasoning. Garnish with parsley and serve at once.

Creamy Risotto with Vine-Ripe Tomatoes, Fresh Rosemary, and Mascarpone

Here is a wonderful "tomato season" risotto, which I make as soon as I get really good tomatoes at my farm stand or when my own are finally ready for picking. Other herbs, especially basil and chives, are good additions. Be sure not to cook the risotto any longer once the tomatoes are added. Serve the rice either as an appetizer or as a side dish to grilled pork tenderloins, quail, or flank steak.

SERVES 4

2 tablespoons extra virgin olive oil

1 medium onion, finely diced

¼ cup dry white wine

1½ cups Arborio rice

4 cups hot chicken broth or bouillon

Salt and freshly ground black pepper

2 large ripe tomatoes, seeded and diced

⅓ cup mascarpone

2 tablespoons julienne of fresh basil, plus sprigs for garnish

1 tablespoon minced fresh rosemary

2 to 3 tablespoons coarsely grated Parmesan cheese, plus some for sprinkling

1. Heat the oil in a heavy 3-quart saucepan over low heat, add the onion, and cook until soft. Add the wine and reduce to a glaze. Add the rice and cook for 1 minute, stirring constantly.

2. Add 2 cups of the broth or bouillon, set over the lowest possible heat, and simmer, covered, for 10 minutes. Raise the heat to medium, uncover the saucepan, and add the remaining broth or bouillon ¼ cup at a time, stirring constantly, for the next 10 minutes, until each addition has been absorbed; you may not need all of the remaining broth. The rice should be tender on the outside but still slightly chewy on the inside. Season with salt and pepper.

3. Fold in the tomatoes, mascarpone, herbs, and Parmesan, correct the seasoning, and serve immediately in shallow soup bowls, garnished with sprigs of basil and accompanied by grated Parmesan.

REMARKS If you cannot get mascarpone, you can still make this risotto successfully by adding 2 tablespoons of heavy cream or crème fraîche to the rice. If getting good Parmesan is a problem, it is better not to use it at all, since this is a rather delicate risotto that could easily be overpowered by a stronger or salty cheese.

Braised Bulgur with Two Peppers and Lemon

Bulgur is a favorite grain in the Middle East, where it is used much like rice but also as stuffing for various vegetables. It is also the main ingredient for the famous tabbouleh. Bulgur comes two ways: fine or medium grained. I use medium-grained bulgur for everything, since I find its texture to be more interesting. Serve this flavorful dish as a side to shish kebabs or grilled fish steaks, veal chops, or chicken. Make enough to have leftovers, since this dish can easily be reheated.

SERVES 4 TO 6

2 tablespoons virgin olive oil

$\frac{1}{2}$ cup minced red onion

1 teaspoon minced jalapeño pepper, seeds included

1 medium red bell pepper, finely diced

1 cup medium-grained bulgur

$2\frac{1}{2}$ cups chicken stock or bouillon

Juice of $\frac{1}{2}$ lemon or more to taste

2 tablespoons minced flat-leaf parsley or cilantro

Salt and coarsely ground black pepper

1. In a saucepan, combine the olive oil, onion, jalapeño and bell pepper. Stir in the bulgur. Add the stock. Cover tightly and simmer over low heat for 20 minutes, or until tender.

2. Add the lemon juice and parsley; season with salt and pepper and more lemon juice if it needs it. Serve hot or at room temperature.

Couscous with Spinach, Red Peppers, and Carrots

Couscous makes a wonderful side dish to many preparations. I like to serve it with all types of grilled or pan-seared fish steaks, lamb chops, or a butterflied leg of lamb. You may add several spices to the couscous, depending on your mood. Cumin, saffron, and curry powder all work well. Leftover couscous can be turned into a delicious salad by adding the juice of a large lemon, some fruity olive oil, and a mincing of flat-leaf parsley.

SERVES 5 TO 6

3½ cups chicken stock or bouillon

¼ teaspoon saffron

2 tablespoons unsalted butter

½ cup finely diced red bell pepper

½ cup finely diced carrots

2 large scallions, minced

1½ cups couscous

Salt and freshly ground black pepper

2 cups fresh spinach leaves, washed, dried and
　　cut into fine julienne

1. In a small saucepan, combine the stock and saffron. Bring to a boil, reduce the heat, and simmer, covered, for 20 minutes, or until the stock is infused with the saffron and is reduced to 2 cups.

2. Melt the butter in a 2-quart saucepan over low heat. Add the bell pepper and carrots. Cook, covered, until just tender, 5 to 6 minutes. Remove the cover and add the scallions and a little broth. Simmer for 2 to 3 minutes until the scallions are just wilted.

3. Add the couscous to the pan together with the broth and season with salt and pepper. Bring to a boil, cover tightly, and let stand off the heat for 10 minutes, or until all the stock has been absorbed. Return to the stove over very low heat, add the spinach, and fold gently until the spinach has just wilted. Correct the seasoning. Serve at once as an accompaniment to grilled lamb or swordfish steaks.

Corn-Studded Polenta with Parmesan

Fresh corn adds a crunchy texture to this lovely creamy polenta. You can be quite creative with this recipe by substituting grated Cheddar or smoked mozzarella for the Parmesan; or add some heat to it with 1 tablespoon minced red or green chile pepper. When fresh corn is not in season, I use canned corn with excellent results. If you make the polenta ahead of time, keep it warm in the top part of a double boiler and whisk in 2 tablespoons of butter just before serving.

SERVES 4 TO 6

3¼ cups skim milk, or use half whole milk
   and half water

Salt

¾ cup semolina or yellow cornmeal

5 tablespoons unsalted butter

2 cups cooked corn kernels

⅓ cup freshly grated Parmesan cheese

Freshly ground black pepper

1. In a heavy 3½-quart saucepan, combine the skim milk or whole milk and water and 1 teaspoon salt and bring to a slow boil. Sprinkle in the semolina or cornmeal very slowly to avoid lumping, whisking constantly, until all has been added. Reduce the heat to very low and simmer, covered, for 20 minutes, stirring often. A skin will form on the bottom of the pot; do not be alarmed.

2. Remove from the heat, add the butter, corn, and Parmesan, and stir until well blended. Taste and correct the seasoning, adding a large grinding of black pepper, and serve at once.

REMARKS A trick for making polenta without lumps is to place the cornmeal in a grated cheese shaker and shake the cornmeal slowly into the hot liquid.

VARIATION Add 4 ounces crumbled goat cheese in addition to the Parmesan and 2 tablespoons fresh thyme leaves to the finished polenta and just heat through.

Cumin-Scented Quinoa with Yogurt and Mint

When I first tasted quinoa I was not particularly keen on it, but after a trip to Ecuador, where quinoa is used extensively in soups, fritters, and desserts, I started to appreciate this interesting and healthy grain. Now I often add it together with root vegetables to a home-made chicken stock or serve it as a side dish with grilled chicken or pan-seared lamb chops.

SERVES 4 TO 5

1 cup quinoa
2½ to 3 cups chicken stock or bouillon
Salt
2 tablespoons olive oil
½ cup finely diced red onion
2 teaspoons minced serrano pepper
1 teaspoon ground cumin
⅛ teaspoon ground coriander
Freshly ground black pepper
½ cup plain yogurt
2 to 3 tablespoons minced mint

1. In a saucepan, combine the quinoa with 2½ cups of the stock. Season lightly with salt and cook, covered, for 10 to 12 minutes, or until the quinoa is tender and all the broth has been absorbed.

2. In another heavy saucepan, heat the olive oil. Add the onion and serrano pepper and sauté for 2 or 3 minutes, or until the onion is soft but not browned. Add the cumin and corian-der and cook for another minute. Add the quinoa, season with salt and pepper, and simmer for 2 to 3 minutes.

3. Add the yogurt and mint and blend well into the quinoa. Taste and correct the seasoning. Serve hot.

REMARKS When made ahead of time, the quinoa may get quite thick. Thin it out with a little broth or add more yogurt. It should have the texture of thick oatmeal. If possible, use the imported Greek yogurt, which has a wonderful thick texture and delicious flavor.

Chickpea, Tomato, and Cilantro Salad

Chickpeas are amazingly versatile legumes that are delicious both hot and cold. I like to serve this salad as a starter, often topped with cubed feta or goat cheese, but it also makes an excellent accompaniment to grilled flank steak, salmon steaks, or grilled shrimp. If you plan to use canned chickpeas, be sure to use a Spanish brand such as Goya.

SERVES 4 TO 5

4 to 5 cups cooked chickpeas

2 ripe tomatoes, seeded and finely cubed

1 cup diced red bell pepper

½ cup diced red onion

1 to 2 tablespoons diced jalapeño pepper

1½ tablespoons sherry vinegar

Juice of 1 lemon

8 tablespoons extra virgin olive oil

Coarse salt and freshly ground black pepper

3 tablespoons tiny cilantro leaves

1. In a bowl, combine the chickpeas, tomatoes, bell pepper, onion, and jalapeño pepper.

2. In another bowl, combine the sherry vinegar, lemon juice, and olive oil. Season with salt and pepper and whisk the mixture until smooth. Combine with the chickpea and tomato mixture and toss gently. Add the cilantro, taste, and correct the seasoning. Cover and chill for 2 to 4 hours before serving.

Lentil Salad with Goat Cheese and Roasted Peppers

Early on I knew that there was a trick to making a good lentil salad. My grandmother taught me this little trick and I never forgot it. The key to the success of all legume salads is that the dressing is poured over the warm legumes and that the beans or lentils should then remain over low heat for as much as 30 minutes before serving. Any dried bean or lentil dressed the day before will taste even better, so always plan on making a little more for tasty leftovers. Since excellent goat cheese is hard to get outside large metropolitan areas, I suggest you use something as easily available as Montrachet, but freeze it lightly so slices it neatly. Drizzle this cheese with olive oil and some fresh thyme to give it the flavor it needs. If you are pressed for time, you can use jarred roasted red bell peppers.

SERVES 4

1 cup green Puy lentils
Salt
1 medium shallot, minced
1 large garlic clove, mashed
2 tablespoons balsamic vinegar
6 tablespoons extra virgin olive oil
Freshly ground black pepper
4 slices of goat cheese, cut about $\frac{1}{2}$ inch thick
Minced fresh thyme, for garnish
2 roasted red bell peppers, peeled, cored, and
   finely sliced

1. In a saucepan, combine the lentils with water to cover, season lightly with salt, and cook over medium heat for 15 minutes, or until the lentils are tender but not falling apart.

2. While the lentils are cooking, prepare the vinaigrette. In a bowl, combine the shallot, garlic, balsamic vinegar, and olive oil. Whisk the dressing until thoroughly emulsified. Add the lentils and toss. Season with salt and pepper. Let stand for 30 minutes Taste and correct the seasoning.

3. Divide the lentil salad among 4 salad plates, top each portion with a slice of goat cheese, sprinkle with thyme, and drizzle with olive oil. Add a mound of roasted peppers and serve accompanied by crusty bread.

Stew of Pinto Beans and Shrimp with Fragrant Indian Spices

All legumes take well to spices, but pinto beans are especially deli-cious when teamed with curry and other Indian spices. Here is a gutsy one-dish meal that is best made a day or two ahead of time. Serve it accompanied by chilled yogurt, a bowl of fragrant jasmine rice, or a refreshing cucumber salad. Try to find Greek yogurt, which has a more interesting texture and taste than domestic varieties and is now quite widely available.

SERVES 6

4 tablespoons olive oil

1 cup finely diced slab bacon, blanched

2 small dried hot red peppers, broken into pieces

$\frac{1}{2}$ pound medium shrimp, peeled

Salt and freshly ground black pepper

2 large onions, quartered and thinly sliced

3 large cloves garlic, minced

2 teaspoons minced fresh ginger

1 teaspoon tomato paste

3 to 4 large ripe tomatoes, peeled, seeded, and chopped

1 tablespoon curry powder, preferably Madras

$\frac{1}{2}$ teaspoon ground cumin

4 to 5 cups Cooked Pinto Beans (page 392)

2 medium red bell peppers, roasted, peeled, and thinly sliced

2 tablespoons minced flat-leaf parsley

I. In a large heavy skillet, heat 2 tablespoons of the olive oil over medium heat, add the bacon, and cook until almost crisp. Remove to a dish with a slotted spoon.

2. Add the hot peppers; cook until dark and discard. Add the shrimp and cook until just lightly browned. Season with salt and pepper; set aside.

3. Add the remaining 2 tablespoons olive oil to the skillet and, when hot, add the onions and cook, stirring constantly, until they begin to brown, about 5 minutes. Reduce the heat and continue to cook, partially covered, stirring occasionally, for 30 to 40 min-utes, or until soft and nicely browned.

4. Add the garlic, ginger, tomato paste, tomatoes, curry powder, and cumin; season with salt and pepper and simmer, uncovered, for 20 minutes, or until all the tomato juices have evaporated.

5. Add the pinto beans and roasted bell peppers and continue to simmer for another 10 minutes. Add the shrimp and bacon and just heat through. Taste and correct the seasoning, garnish with parsley, and serve hot or at room temperature with crusty French bread.

Ragout of White Beans with Bacon and Radicchio

Here is a wonderfully tasty bean dish that is a delicious accompaniment to lamb, pork, and grilled fish steaks. You can cook the beans 2 or 3 days ahead of time and store them in their cooking broth. You can also serve this as a one-dish meal by adding some smoked diced kielbasa or chorizo sausage to it.

SERVES 6

2 tablespoons virgin olive oil

1 head of radicchio, cored and cut into eighths

Salt and freshly ground black pepper

2 tablespoons butter

1 cup finely cubed blanched bacon, or 1 cup cubed pancetta

3 tablespoons minced shallots

2 large garlic cloves, minced

2 tablespoons tomato paste

4 cups cooked or canned cannellini or other white beans, cooking broth or liquid reserved

2 cups bean cooking broth or chicken bouillon

2 tablespoons minced flat-leaf parsley

I. In a large nonstick skillet, heat the olive oil. Add the radicchio, season with salt and pepper, and sauté until limp and lightly browned.

2. In a large cast-iron skillet, heat the butter. Add the bacon and sauté for 2 or 3 minutes, or until almost crisp. Remove with a slotted spoon to a dish.

3. Add the shallots and garlic to the skillet and sauté for 1 minute or until soft and lightly browned. Add the tomato paste and beans together with the reserved bacon. Add 1 cup of bean broth and season with salt and pepper. Cover the pan and simmer over low heat for 15 to 20 minutes, adding a little more broth if the beans seem dry.

4. Add the radicchio and toss gently into the beans. Taste and correct the seasoning.

5. Transfer the beans to an oval serving dish, garnish with parsley, and serve as an accompaniment to grilled lamb chops, a roast leg of lamb, or pan-seared or grilled sausages.

White Bean and Chorizo Soup

This soup is really a one-dish meal. You can start or follow it with a well-seasoned salad and finish with a bowl of fruit and a nice piece of cheese. Perfect for Sunday nights and simple suppers.

SERVES 4 TO 6

½ cup extra virgin olive oil

1 large onion, minced

6 garlic cloves, minced

½ cup minced fresh parsley

3 ripe tomatoes, peeled, seeded, and chopped

1 tablespoon tomato paste

1 teaspoon dried oregano

4 to 5 cups Cooked White Beans (page 394)

6 to 7 cups chicken stock or bouillon

Salt and freshly ground black pepper

⅓ cup uncooked thin spaghetti, broken up

2 cups tightly packed fresh basil leaves

½ cup freshly grated Parmesan cheese, plus
  some for sprinkling

1 cup thinly sliced chorizo sausage

1. Heat 3 tablespoons of the olive oil in a large, heavy flame-proof casserole. Add the onion, 2 of the garlic cloves, and the parsley and cook for 2 to 3 minutes, or until the onion is soft but not browned. Add the tomatoes, tomato paste, and oregano, and continue cooking until all the tomato juices have evaporated. Add 2 cups of the beans and 1 cup of the stock, season with salt and pepper, cover, and simmer for 10 minutes.

2. Remove the casserole from the heat and let the bean and tomato mixture cool. Place it in a blender and puree until smooth. Pour the puree into the casserole, add the remaining stock and beans, and season with salt and pepper. Add the spaghetti and simmer for 10 to 12 minutes, or until the spaghetti is done. If the soup seems too thick, add more stock.

3. In a blender, combine the remaining 4 garlic cloves, the basil, the remaining olive oil, and the Parmesan. Blend the mixture until smooth.

4. When the soup is done, whisk in the basil mixture. Taste and correct the seasoning. Add the sliced sausage and heat through, but do not let the soup come to a boil.

5. Serve the soup hot, with a bowl of freshly grated Parmesan cheese and crusty bread.

■ Spiced Applesauce ■ Three-Berry Coulis with Nectarines ■ Caramelized Banana Tatin ■ Blueberries in Lemon Sabayon ■ Classic Cherry Clafoutis ■ Chocolate and Pear Tart ■ Terrine of Citrus Fruit with Strawberry Sauce ■ Cranberry, Ginger, and Orange Chutney ■ Crab and Mango Salad ■ Poached Pears in Sherry Sabayon ■ Sliced Oranges in Red Wine–Cinnamon Coulis ■ Stewed Peaches in Muscat, Cinnamon, and Vanilla Syrup ■ Pear Crisp with Brown Sugar and Ginger ■ Persimmon Mousse ■ Pineapple Caramel Compote with Oranges ■ Italian Plum and Almond Tart ■ Vanilla-Scented Pots de Crème with Raspberries ■ Rhubarb and Strawberry Pecan Crisp

On a trip to the South of France in early June two years ago, I soon realized that it was the beginning of the melon season. Along the roads, stand after stand displayed rows of the beautiful small Cavallon melons—always showing one cut in half to assure you that the melons were ripe.

The Cavallon melon is named after a small town in Provence where it is grown and prized for its superb taste and texture. Since I was working in the kitchen of a local restaurant that week, I was looking forward to sampling the region's prized melons.

On my second day, I joined the chef on his weekly trip to the Antibes market. The intoxicating aroma of ripe melons was in the air. As we walked through the market, I was hoping that Lucien would choose some for the restaurant, but he didn't. We stopped at several stands, but without even a sniff, he decided the melons were not yet ripe enough. However, as we were about to leave, he spotted a small heap of rather unattractive melons that looked as if they were about to burst open. "These," he said, "are perfect!" We bought all the melons they had, and I will never forget the taste of the melon sorbet we had that evening or of the fresh slices that appeared on the breakfast table the next morning.

It was a lesson in restraint. After decades of purchasing fruit, always following the calendar, trusting and believing that when fruit is in season, it must be good, I realized how much more there is to fruit than eye appeal. Americans are especially vulnerable. We live in a country that produces masses of fruit of every kind. Not only do we expect to find almost every fruit year-round, we want our fruit to look perfect with taste to match. Unfortunately, we rarely get what we are hoping for, at least not when it comes to summer fruit—or more precisely to store-bought summer fruit.

The most frustrating aspect of fruit shopping is having to wait for ripe fruit to arrive in the market. I have spent many a summer unable to make a good peach cobbler and many spring seasons without sampling a single juicy strawberry. Because today's fruit is less about cooking than about eye appeal and instant pleasure, many people are only vaguely aware of the seasonal importance of fruit. And yet, is there anything more rewarding than a lovely ripe peach for dessert or a baked apple bursting with buttery juices, or a ripe piece of cool melon?

Today's fruit has been bred primarily to withstand shipping and handling. Flavor is secondary, and people who do not live in areas where a specific fruit is grown may never get to taste a truly sweet, tree-ripened example. Many of our favorite fruits are packed green, are gassed along the way to ripen them visually, and arrive at market looking quite lovely but tasteless. We are led to believe that 2 or 3 days on the countertop will ripen them. Of course, all stone fruit—peaches, nectarines, and plums—will ripen eventually, but that does not mean that they will be flavorful or juicy. Unfortunately, even the most intense sugar syrup cannot add true flavor to any fruit.

I still remember one spring when I was conducting a workshop in Fresno, California, and had my fill of the ripest, juiciest apricots I had had in years. Come spring, I still look longingly at apricots, which are my very favorite fruit, but after a sniff, I move on. Even though that experience was more than ten years ago, I have rarely had a ripe apricot since.

Unless you live in Florida, Arizona, or parts of California, you may not even be aware that oranges or lemons have a season; or that limes are better in the summer, while lemons are juicier in the winter months. I have had students searching for tangerines in July, and others looking for an interesting recipe for raspberries in January.

The good news is that with the growing proliferation of farmers' greenmarkets, we can now get wonderful local berries in the spring and juicy, flavor-packed apples and pears well into late fall. Also, because of consumer interest, more large supermarket chains are beginning to offer local varieties of fruit, making it easier for the cook to make a fruit tart or cobbler on the spur of the moment.

With education, product availability, and greater sophistication about food, we are going back to buying fruit on the basis of taste rather than eye appeal. We are learning to trust our instincts and to ask questions. And the more we ask, the more we learn about fruit, saving ourselves both money and disappointment. I may not be able to answer all your questions, but the dialogue that follows should lead you to a much better understanding of how to buy, cook, and enjoy fruit.

Apples

■■

Which is your favorite cooking apple?

Different preparations require different cooking apples. It all depends upon whether you want the apples to retain some shape or to become a smooth puree, and whether you are looking for a flavor that is sweet or tart. For sautéed apples and tarts, my favorite is the Golden Delicious, but when I'm cooking a chunky applesauce or baking a pie, I look for Jonathans, Cortlands, or Empires. For making applesauce without sugar, try Braeburns and Golden Delicious. I try not to get stuck on one type or another but look for those that are tastiest and in the best condition.

Apples are available all year long and are grown nearly everywhere, but this does not mean they are always top quality. For example, if the Golden Delicious look bruised and mealy, I'll go with Granny Smiths or switch to McIntoshes for applesauce. For a more complex flavor, try a combination of varieties. A mixture of all those flavor and aroma molecules can be something quite splendid.

I love the soft, tender texture of a good baked apple, but mine explode in the oven. Am I using the wrong apple?

To prevent the apples from bursting open, peel about a third of the skin from the top of the apple and fill the cavity loosely. When it comes to baked apples, you can't beat Rome Beauties for texture and flavor, although they require about 10 minutes longer in the oven than other apples, so adjust recipes accordingly. These are perfect candidates because they can take a lot of heat without collapsing or cracking.

What apples make the best applesauce?

Macs are considered a good sauce apple because they're widely available, but they tend to dissolve during the long, slow stewing required for applesauce, rather than retaining a little texture. I get much better results with Cortlands, which stay chunkier, but your best bet is to do a little research and try some of the regional varieties in your area.

What is the best way to keep apples from discoloring?

Discoloration is caused by exposure to oxygen and a naturally occurring enzyme, polyphenol oxidase, also known as tyrosinase, that is released when the apple is cut. To keep browning to a minimum, rub the exposed area with the cut side of a lemon. This works for several hours. If you are going to use sliced or chunked apples for fruit salad, be sure to add some kind of acidity to the apples, such as orange juice or a sprinkling of lemon juice. If you plan to sauté the apples, don't bother. Sautéing itself browns the apples and camouflages any discoloration, and cooking, of course, immediately stops any chemical reaction.

What is the best way to store apples, and how long do they keep?

Although it is lovely to have a big bowl of apples on a table or counter, if your goal is eating rather than decorating, keep your apples in the refrigerator. Apples purchased in season—that is, late summer through the first hard frost—will keep for quite a while. Years ago, people used to store them for months in an

APPLES AT A GLANCE

VARIETY	DESCRIPTION	USES	SEASON
Braeburn	Crisp, moderately tart, spicy, juicy, tender skin	Fresh, sauce, pie	November–January
Cortland	Fine-textured, mild, tart-sweet, juicy, thin skin	Fresh, sauce, pie, baking	October–December
Empire	Mildly tart, crisp, juicy, thick skin, mealy if overripe	Fresh, good in sauce, pie, cooks quickly	September–November
Fuji	Tangy-sweet complex flavor, snappy crisp texture	Best fresh, takes longer than average to cook	January–April
Gala	Sweet with tart accent, crisp, juicy, tender skin	Best fresh, creamy in sauce, needs little sugar	January–April
Golden Delicious	Rich, sweet aromatic flavor	Fresh, sauce, pie, needs little sugar	September–October
Granny Smith	Balanced tart and sweet, firm, crisp, juicy	Fresh, sauce, pie, falls apart when baked	Sweetest after mid-October
Gravenstein	Aromatic, tart-sweet, crisp, juicy	Good fresh, juicy, sauce, bakes quickly	July–September
Jonathan	Rich, tart, distinctive flavor, thin skin	Good fresh, smooth juicy sauce, retains shape when baked	August–November
McIntosh	Mildly tart, aromatic, juicy, tough skin separates from flesh	Best fresh, dissolves in sauce, falls apart in pie	September–October
Red Delicious	Sweet and aromatic with hint of tartness	Best fresh, flavor weakens when cooked	September–March
Rome Beauty	Mild flavor with little acid, somewhat mealy, sugar enhances flavor	Only fair fresh, best for baking, pies	September–November

unheated garage. Today, wholesalers keep apples to be used in the fall and early winter in cold storage. Those scheduled to go to market after the first of the year are held in a controlled atmosphere of reduced oxygen. This keeps them in good shape. However, once taken out of storage, the apples deteriorate quickly, losing crispness and flavor ten times faster at room temperature than they do at 32°F. When purchasing apples during the winter, refrigerate them right away and consume them as soon as possible.

Do you have a recipe for a quick apple dessert?

Apples sautéed in butter and sugar make a great quick dessert served with either vanilla ice cream or sugared crème fraîche. Use Golden Delicious or Granny Smith. Here is how to to sauté them: Peel 4 apples; core them and cut into eighths. In a large skillet, melt 3 tablespoons butter over medium-high heat. Add the apples to the pan and sprinkle with 2 tablespoons sugar. Sauté until nicely browned on all sides, 5 to 7 minutes. Add a sprinkling of grated fresh nutmeg and serve warm or at room temperature.

Bananas and Plantains

■■

Often the bananas in my market are hard and green. Why is it so difficult to buy a ripe banana?

Bananas often arrive in markets hard and green because ripe bananas are very fragile and can easily be damaged during packing and transport. On arrival, they are gassed with ethylene, which begins the ripening process. This triggers the synthesis of naturally occurring enzymes. Fortunately, bananas ripen perfectly off the tree. Be sure that they are at least greenish-yellow when you buy them. At that point they will take as long as 3 days to ripen at room temperature. During the ripening process, bananas go from 25 percent starch and 1 percent sugar, to 20 percent sugar and 1 percent starch, making them sweet and succulent. Don't be concerned about a few brown spots: this just means that the banana is perfectly ripe.

What is the best season for bananas?

Bananas are in the markets all year, but their selection can be spotty in the winter. This is when you find more jade green bunches than nice yellow ones. A deep green color is an indication that the bananas have been chilled and will never ripen properly.

Is it necessary to wait until bananas turn black to make banana bread?

Overripe bananas, with their soft, super-sweet pulp, make terrific banana bread. But there is no need to wait until they turn black on their own. You can help them along by simmering the whole, unpeeled fruit for 3 to 4 minutes in water to cover until the skin turns black before continuing with your recipe.

What are plantains? They look like large bananas, but I am not sure how to use them.

Plantains look like overgrown, green bananas, but unlike their sweet cousins, plantains are eaten as a vegetable, rather like a tropical potato. The two fruits have very different textures, too. Bananas are soft and buttery and are good both raw and cooked; the starchier plantains must be served cooked. Plantains hold their shape well and are best sautéed or fried. Here's how: Peel and slice the plantains into 1-inch-thick slices. Lightly dust them with flour, shaking off the excess, and sauté for 2 or 3 minutes in equal parts butter and peanut oil. Sprinkle with salt and pepper and serve as a side dish for grilled chicken, pork, or lamb.

When a recipe calls for plantains, can I use bananas instead?

No. You won't get acceptable results because the two, while related, have very different textures and react differently when cooked. Bananas are delicious raw, lightly sautéed, or baked. Plantains, on the other hand, have a firmer texture and can never be eaten raw. They are best fried or baked.

Will plantains ripen at room temperature, like bananas?

Yes. To ripen plantains, leave them in a bowl at room temperature for several days. Their degree of ripeness determines how best to cook them. Fully ripe, black-skinned plantains are best for mashing or frying. Starchier, less ripe fruit, with yellow-green skin—with or without brown spots—are best served fried.

If I refrigerate bananas and plantains, will they last longer?

Refrigerating ripe bananas affects the color of their skin but not their flavor, and they will keep for a couple of days longer. If you want to store bananas for any length of time, freeze them, peeled and wrapped in plastic. Once defrosted, they are great for making banana breads and muffins.

Refrigeration stops the ripening of plantains and will allow you to keep them for about a week. Since they will be cooked anyway, their texture in the raw state is not that important. Wrapped tightly in plastic, peeled plantains freeze well.

TIP Bananas ripen faster when stored in a brown paper bag. Adding an apple to the bag ripens the bananas even faster, because the ethylene gas given off by the apple signals the bananas to ripen.

How do I use those red bananas and baby yellow bananas available in some markets?

They are wonderful for eating raw and also for cooking. Red bananas, which signal their ripeness by taking on a purplish tinge, are deliciously sweet and creamy. The little apple, or finger, bananas turn dark yellow when ripe and remain quite firm. They are excellent sautéed and caramelized in butter and sugar and served with ice cream. Unlike other bananas, these have slightly crunchy seeds, which give them an unusual, interesting texture. Here's a tasty way to prepare both red and finger bananas: Preheat the broiler. Peel the banana and slice it in half lengthwise. Put it on a well-buttered baking dish, dot with bits of butter, and top with a sprinkling of sugar. Broil for a few minutes, until lightly browned. Sprinkle with grated orange zest and serve warm.

Blueberries, Raspberries, and Strawberries
■■■

Is there a difference between wild blueberries and the ones in the supermarket? Do the wild ones taste better?

Visually, wild blueberries, often called huckleberries, are quite different. Dark blue and very small, they have an intense flavor that the cultivated berries lack, and some purists prefer them. Unfortunately, they are rarely available outside the Northwest, except in Maine during the summer season. If you do come across wild blueberries at a farmers' market, be sure only to rinse them lightly and never to soak them.

TIP All berries should be rinsed quickly; they become waterlogged if soaked.

Is it all right to wash blueberries, or does that bruise them?

Blueberries are not particularly delicate; the new cultivated varieties are actually quite thick skinned. A quick rinse will not bruise them.

I usually find a fair number of pale, unripe blueberries in a box. Will these late bloomers ripen if I leave them at room temperature?

Once picked, unripe blueberries, or any other berries for that matter, will not ripen or get any sweeter. Unripe berries have their uses. They are higher in pectin than ripe berries, so if you plan to make jam, preserves, compotes, pies, or cobblers, they will help thicken them. Pectin is a naturally occurring carbohydrate that "sets" or jells cooked fruit.

How can you tell a really fresh blueberry?

Color is the number-one clue. The best blueberries have a velvety, true blue color and look as if they were dusted with very fine powder. This lighter surface color, known as a berry's "bloom," is natural and not due to spraying, as many people think. Above all, it is an indicator of freshness. It will not rinse off, but it does fade as berries get older. Dark, shiny blueberries are not as fresh, firm, or flavorful.

Raspberries are my favorite fruit, but they're so expensive! Is there any way I can use frozen ones instead?

Frozen raspberries make a terrific dessert sauce. Once the berries are pureed, pass the sauce through a fine-mesh sieve to remove the seeds.

At what time of year are raspberries least expensive?

Depending on where you live, June, July, and August are peak months in the United States. If you happen to live in or travel through the Northwest or Michigan during the summer, you can pick up whole flats of sweet, juicy raspberries for a fraction of the price they cost elsewhere.

I like the idea of serving raspberries for dessert. Do you have any suggestions for serving them other than with a sprinkling of sugar?

While fresh unadorned berries are good, raspberries become even more appealing when teamed up with something creamy. I like mine served as a topping for Vanilla-Scented Pots de Crème (page 342).

Why is it getting harder than ever to get really juicy strawberries?

Growing strawberries has become big business, with California producing more berries than anywhere else in the world. Growers focus more on size than taste; large strawberries are easier to pick, pack, and ship. Unfortunately, bigger doesn't mean better. These giant "gourmet" berries are frequently hollow and tasteless. You can still find good strawberries, but it takes effort. Be sure to shop seasonally and locally and look for berries in the spring and early summer, when they are at their best.

Do you have any tips for buying strawberries?
First of all, try to buy them loose. If that is not possible, always check the bottom of the carton and pass on those in which there are only a few ripe strawberries. Once you get them home, be sure to transfer strawberries to a bowl as soon as you can, since one moldy berry can easily ruin the rest in a very short time. Also, check the fragrance of strawberries. If you smell more container than berry, chances are they will taste like the container as well.

Do you know a quick method for making chocolate-covered strawberries?
Chocolate-covered strawberries are easy and fun to make.

To make chocolate-covered strawberries Line a baking sheet or sheet pan with waxed paper. Select 16 well-formed strawberries with stems attached. Rinse and dry them, but leave the leafy stem in place. Melt 6 ounces bittersweet or semisweet chocolate and 2 tablespoons butter in the top of a double boiler set over medium-low heat. Holding a berry by its stem, dip it in the chocolate so that the bottom half is coated. Transfer the berry to the prepared baking sheet. Repeat with the remaining berries. When all are dipped, refrigerate for at least 10 minutes to set the chocolate.

Are there any desserts in which frozen strawberries can be used instead of fresh ones?

Frozen berries are fine for a strawberry sauce. Use the unsweetened fruit and add just enough sugar to taste with a few drops of fresh lemon juice. Serve this delicious sauce with sliced oranges or cantaloupe or drizzled over ice cream (see Strawberry Sauce, page 395).

TIP If you plan to sweeten the berries with a little sugar, do so at least 30 minutes before serving. This gives the sugar time to draw some of the moisture from the berries so they will be nice and juicy.

What is strawberry coulis?
Coulis is a French term for sauce, and it most often refers to a fruit puree. But the term has become so popular that it is sometimes used for tomato sauce as well.

TIP Instead of heavy cream, try topping strawberries with a spoonful of sour cream, like the northern Europeans do. Or toss them in fresh orange juice or a high-quality balsamic vinegar, like the Italians.

Recipes sometimes call for "macerating" berries. What does this mean?
To macerate means to soften by marinating and refers exclusively to fruit preparations. Strawberries are macerated by sprinkling them with sugar and letting them sit for 30 minutes or so to release their juices. Other fruits may be tossed with liqueur or juice and left to macerate. Macerated strawberries and raspberries are often used as an accompaniment to cakes and ice creams, but they are also delicious on their own topped with a little sugared crème fraîche. To macerate strawberries, rinse them

quickly; hull and slice them. Sliced berries absorb sugar more readily. If they are very small, you can leave them whole. Place in a bowl and sprinkle heavily with sugar. Let them sit at room temperature for 30 to 60 minutes before serving.

TIP Refrigerate berries for storage, but never serve them chilled. They taste best at room temperature.

I have bought strawberries in June at a pick-it-yourself stand, hoping for juicier berries, but with no luck. The berries can't get any fresher than that, so why don't they taste better?

Just because berries are in season does not mean they are good. So much depends on soil and weather. After a wet spring, they will be watery and less tasty. If you live in Florida,

chances are that the berries will not be as sweet as those grown in California. Keep in mind that less-than-perfect strawberries still make excellent jams and sauces and if you have had fun at the berry patch, you've had a good day.

Are the large, fancy strawberries sold with their stems more flavorful than those sold in the cartons?

Absolutely not. These fancy berries are usually hollow and less juicy than their small, unassuming cousins. But they are lovely as a garnish, dipped in chocolate or powdered sugar.

Should strawberries be hulled before or after being rinsed?

Always rinse strawberries before removing the stems or else they become waterlogged. With a small paring knife, cut down and around the stem end. This way, you can leave them whole and hollowed out, or you can slice and sugar them.

Cherries

When is the best time to buy cherries?

Cherry season is short. It begins in June and ends in late July. Even when cherries are plentiful in the markets, they are pricey—unless, that is, you live in Michigan or the Northwest, the two premier cherry growing areas in the country. I have bought flats of cherries for next to nothing at a pick-your-own farm in Oregon. As the cherry season tapers off, cherries of various shades of red show up in the bins. This is because produce markets tend to mix up varieties to extend the season. You might find some late-harvest Bings mixed with Lamberts and Lari-

ans. The latter, however, lack the flavor and firmness of Bings.

I know there are different varieties of cherries, but I have never seen them named. How can I tell the difference?

The season opens with Tartarian and Burlatt cherries, which are not especially sweet. But as soon as the Bings, Lamberts, and Raniers arrive in the markets, you are in for a treat. Bings are dark colored, crisp textured, and juicy—characteristics that put them in a class by themselves. Lamberts, which ripen a little later, are similar to Bings, but they are smaller. Raniers, which are cream colored with rosy cheeks, are juicy and meaty. They bruise easily and are not as readily available. No matter; even Raniers do not compare in taste to a good Bing cherry.

I used to love Queen Anne cherries, but I rarely see them in the market anymore.

Queen Annes are now used mainly for maraschino cherries and have been replaced in the market by the Raniers, which are bigger, firmer, and sweeter.

I have a recipe that calls for tart cherries and another one that calls for pie cherries. What is the difference and where can I get them?

The major variety of tart cherry grown in the United States is the Montmorency. Tart cherries, which are sometimes called pie cherries or sour cherries, are seldom sold fresh. They are usually canned or frozen, so your best chance to get them fresh is at local farmers' markets in Michigan, Utah, New York, Wisconsin, Washington, Oregon, and Pennsylvania. They are mostly available in July.

If I buy cherries that are not sweet, will they develop more flavor if they are kept for several days at room temperature?

Cherries do not ripen once they are picked and will not get darker or sweeter. So taste a couple of cherries at the store and buy only those that are crisp and sweet. Also be sure to pick those with green rather than black stems

Does the size of cherries have anything to do with their taste?

Bigger is better. Large, firm cherries may be more expensive, but they taste great. For cooking, however, smaller cherries are fine.

Do I need to pit cherries for a pie or cobbler? How do you go about doing that?

A cherry pitter is a handy gadget sold in kitchenware shops and through kitchenware catalogs. It is inexpensive and small enough to be stored easily. It is really indispensable when pitting cherries for pies or cobblers, but I often use unpitted cherries in a compote and for the Classic Cherry Clafoutis (page 327). Just be sure to warn family and guests.

Cranberries

■■■

I love making cranberry bread, muffins, and coffeecake, but I can find fresh cranberries in the markets only around Thanksgiving. Why is this?

That's because fresh cranberries are a seasonal crop, harvested between October and December. They start appearing in markets in late September and last only until the end of the year. But the good news is they're great keep-

ers. Fresh cranberries last up to a month in the refrigerator, and frozen berries will keep for as long as a year.

Is there a difference in flavor between fresh and frozen cranberries?

Once cranberries are cooked, it's almost impossible to tell the difference between fresh and frozen, whether cooked into a sauce or baked into a muffin. Around Thanksgiving, I always make it a point to buy an extra bag or two to pop into the freezer. This way, I have some on hand when I get a craving for a cranberry tart in the middle of July. And they are so easy to use. You don't even have to thaw them first; just give them a quick rinse under cold running water, and they're ready to go.

Since all cranberries come bagged, how do I pick fresh berries?

Just follow the bouncing berry. Cranberries are called "bouncing berries" because in the old days, barrels of cranberries were overturned down a flight of stairs. Fresh berries bounced like mad down the steps. Overripe or underripe berries never made it past the top steps and were discarded.

Of course, today the berries are locked in plastic bags, but you can inspect them before you buy. Look for berries that are dry, plump, firm, and a bright, dark red. Apply gentle pressure on a few through the bag—if they squish easily, their bouncing days are over. Pass on any bag that contains mostly pink berries; these are underripe. The closer to Thanksgiving you can buy them, the better. This is peak cranberry marketing time, and so you are apt to get the cream of the crop.

Can I use cranberries raw, or do they have to be cooked?

Cranberries are exceptionally tart, so plan to pucker if you pop a raw one in your mouth. Raw berries are harmless, but taste much better cooked. Their delightful tartness is what I love in breads, sauces, pies, and even in turkey stuffing. A lot of people like a quick relish made with chopped raw cranberries mixed with sugar and orange peel, but I prefer cooked cranberry sauce, which softens the skins. These little bright berries are showcased in the Cranberry, Ginger, and Orange Chutney (page 332). It is the best possible accompaniment to a roasted turkey or duck, and it sure beats the canned stuff that accompanies many holiday dinners.

Is there a taste and quality difference between large and small cranberries?

The New England cranberries called early blacks are rather small but more flavorful than the larger ones grown in the Midwest and the Northwest. They are also more perishable. If you open a bag and find that the berries are small, use them right away. Larger berries, on the other hand, keep well in the refrigerator for 4 to 6 weeks.

Why are dried cranberries so much sweeter than fresh cranberries?

Practically all dried cranberries have some sweetener added. In most cases this is sucrose, common table sugar, but if you search you might find some that are sweetened with apple juice.

What is the best way to use dried cranberries?

In many recipes, you can use dried cranberries just like raisins. For instance, sprinkle some into rice or couscous or stir them into your favorite muffin or scone batter. Dried cranberries look like bright red raisins. Once they are plumped, they make a wonderful garnish for roasted duck, turkey, or pork. Another idea is to add dried cranberries to chutney and relish recipes along with the fresh ones. The tartness of dried cranberries can also enhance salads, especially when the salad includes some blue cheese and toasted nuts such as walnuts or pecans.

Dried cranberries are great for snacking because they're high in vitamin A and fiber and low in sodium and calories.

Grapefruit

■■■

What is the difference between pink, red, and white grapefruit?

Quality, not color, is what counts. Chose fresh, firm fruit that feel heavy for their size. Pink and red grapefruit are generally sweeter than white varieties, but they are also about 20 percent more expensive.

Which are better grapefruit, the ones from Texas or the Florida varieties?

Both are excellent. It comes down to the quality of the particular variety. Florida's Indian River grapefruit are superb, and so are Texas Ruby Reds and Star Rubys. The price and availability of these depends on where you live and the time of year. The season starts with Florida grapefruit; the ones from Texas appear a little later. Also, you will find more Florida grapefruit in the Northeast, and Texas, Arizona, and California fruit in the Midwest and along the West Coast.

TIP To enjoy their full flavor, let refrigerated grapefruit return to room temperature before serving.

Should grapefruit be thin- or thick-skinned? Does shape matter?

Both the thickness of the skin and the shape of the fruit indicate the quality of the grape-fruit. Thin skin is better, and a flatter, disk-shaped grapefruit is better than a round one with a pointy stem end. However, if you live in a grapefruit-producing state, you may find wonderful-tasting fruit that is thick skinned and very juicy.

I love the refreshing taste of grapefruit, but I know only one way to serve them: halved and eaten for breakfast. Do you have any other suggestions?

There's no reason not to eat a good, juicy grapefruit as you would an orange: peel it and enjoy the segments. I also like grapefruit salad, where the sections are served with soft, buttery greens and a slightly sweet dressing. For a simple dessert, try broiled grapefruit: Preheat the broiler. Halve a grapefruit and set the halves in a shallow broiling pan. Sprinkle with brown sugar and broil just until the sugar starts to melt and caramelize and the fruit juices bubble.

TIP Use grapefruit zest as you would orange zest—to flavor muffins, pound cakes, a fruit salad, or a sabayon. Be sure not to include any of the white membrane, or pith, which is very bitter. It is always best to blanch grapefruit zest for 2 minutes before using it in any recipe.

Lemons and Limes

I have trouble finding really juicy lemons in the summer. Why?

Lemons and almost all citrus fruit except limes are at their best in the winter, so I always use limes instead of lemons at that time of year. Also, you will find that during the summer, limes have twice as much juice as lemons. If you like the combination of lemon and berries as much as I do (see Blueberries in Lemon Sabayon, page 326), use a little more lemon juice than the recipe calls for and add some lemon zest for extra kick.

TIP For maximum juice, let lemons sit at room temperature for at least 30 minutes. Before cutting and squeezing, firmly roll the lemon under the palm of your hand on the countertop to break up some of the juice-filled membranes. Or pop the lemon in the microwave for a few seconds to warm it up and release its juices.

Is it better to buy large lemons or small ones?

When it comes to lemons—or more accurately, when it comes to juicy lemons—bigger is not better. Smallish thin-skinned lemons are much juicier, but you get more zest out of the large thick lemons; so choose lemons with an eye to the dish you are preparing.

There often seems to be a bitter flavor when I add lemon peel to a dish. What am I doing wrong?

Chances are that you are including some of the white pith, which is extremely bitter. Be sure to use only the outer yellow zest. Also, be sure to get a good zester, and if in doubt, before using the zest, parboil it in a little water for 2 to 3 minutes to remove any traces of bitterness.

I hear a lot about Meyer lemons. What makes them so special?

Meyer lemons are very large and very juicy; they are much less tart than other lemons, but still not exactly a fruit you'd eat out of hand like an apple. They are too smooth skinned to provide good zest. More and more Meyer lemons now appear in specialty fruit stores, but most of the time the only way to get your hands on Meyer lemons is to befriend someone with a tree in his or her yard.

TIP Only need half a lemon? Immerse the other half in a glass of water and store it in the refrigerator. Change the water every other day, and it will keep for a week to 10 days.

Can I substitute lemons for limes in marinades and vice versa?

As a general rule, yes, but I prefer limes to lemons in seafood marinades because limes are less tart and more fragrant. I also prefer the milder taste of limes in vinaigrettes to be drizzled over shellfish and avocados.

In Mexico I have tasted wonderful, pebbly little limes that are quite different from the limes I buy at the grocery store. How can I duplicate their taste?

Unfortunately, their taste cannot be duplicated, but Mexican limes (called *limones*) are becoming more available, particularly on the West Coast and in the Midwest. You can usually find these little green gems in Latin grocery stores everywhere. Their unique flavor enhances seafood and poultry, and they can be used in any recipe that calls for Key limes.

How much juice can you expect to get out of the average lime or lemon?

In summer, a single lime will yield at least ¼ cup juice while a lemon will yield at the most 2 tablespoons; but in the winter it is the reverse, and a juicy lemon will yield at least ¼ cup juice.

Mango

■ ■

Do you have any tips for picking a good mango?

Be sure to buy mangoes only during their peak season from early spring through late summer. Especially avoid buying mangoes in the winter. At the market, use your nose. Ripe mangoes have a tropical, fruity aroma, and they give slightly to the touch. Although mangoes come in all sizes, you'll find that the larger the mango, the more fruit you'll get in relation to the big pit.

Books and magazine articles on mangoes recommend specific varieties, but my supermarket doesn't label them. How can I tell the good ones by sight?

Picking a mango by variety is really a problem, since there are more mango varieties in the world than there are apples.

Avoid the beautiful but stringy Tommy Atkins variety. You can easily spot this mango by its attractive red skin and lovely oval shape. Instead go for the Haden. This is a fairly small mango with yellow skin and red cheeks. While it is less showy than the Tom Atkins, it rates a "10" as far as flavor and texture are concerned. Other good mango varieties that you can occasionally find in June and July are the Keitt and the Kent. Both are fairly large with green skin and reddish cheeks. If you want to learn more about mangoes, take a look at *The Great Mango Book*, by Allen Susser (Ten Speed Press, 2001).

I understand that Mexican and other Central American mangoes are heavily sprayed with chemicals and that they are unsafe to eat. Is that true?

There is no question that you must rinse a mango thoroughly before serving, but once you do so and peel it, the mango is perfectly safe to eat. However, there are more and more organic mangoes in the markets these days, so if you have the choice, do buy those.

Can a mango be ripened at room temperature? Does it get sweet?

As with most fruit, your best bet is to buy a mango that is at least semiripe. Mangoes do ripen within 2 or 3 days at room temperature, but I never feel that they become as sweet as the ones that are picked ripe off the tree.

TIP Make sure that when you buy a ripe mango its skin is taut and never flabby, and pass on any mangoes with soft spots.

Once a mango is sliced, how long will it keep?

A ripe mango will keep for as long as a week. Once it is cut, it will keep for 2 or 3 days in the refrigerator.

When I cut into a mango, I always seem to hit the pit. Is there a right way to cut into a mango?

There is no neat way to slice a mango. One way is to first peel it, either with a vegetable peeler or, if the mango is very ripe, by scoring the skin into quarters and pulling it off. Then cut the mango on either side of the long flat seed that runs lengthwise. The other way is to cut the unpeeled mango in half, doing your best to avoid the pit. Score the flesh into small squares, turn the half inside out, and the cubes will pop up and can be cut easily from the skin.

I live in Florida, and we get heaps of ripe mangoes at the farmers' market. Do you have any interesting mango recipes?

Mangoes can be used in various interesting ways. You can use them in a mango "soup," in which the fruit is pureed and combined with diced strawberries and finely sliced mint. I often serve sliced mango with finely sliced prosciutto, much the same way you would serve melon.

TIP One of the fun ways to enjoy a really ripe mango is to roll it back and forth on the counter as you would a lemon, then make a small incision at the stem end and suck out the nectar-like pulp.

Melons

My market carries cantaloupes practically year-round, but I still have a hard time picking a good one. Is there a trick to picking a good cantaloupe?

This reminds me of one of my favorite melon stories. Several years ago I was standing at a farmers' market in Connecticut. It was early spring, and there was still a light frost on the ground. A woman picked up a melon and asked whether it was locally grown. Without missing a beat, the salesperson said, "Yes, it is grown locally in California."

We tend to forget that all melons, including cantaloupes, are seasonal and are one of the most disappointing fruits during the winter months. A good cantaloupe is fabulous at its peak from June through September. If you live on the West Coast, you can probably get a jump on the season and find a good ripe melon as early as April, but not much before that.

What is the difference between a cantaloupe and a muskmelon?

The terms cantaloupe and muskmelon are used interchangeably in the United States. True cantaloupes (cantalupensis) are mainly found in southern Europe, especially Provence. They are smallish and have a hard scaly rind and orange or green flesh. Muskmelons have a netted rind.

MELONS AT A GLANCE

VARIETY	CHARACTERISTICS	SEASON
Cantaloupe	Ripe when fragrant and skin is yellow under netting. Flesh ranges from golden to orange. Best comes from California and Arizona.	June–November
Casaba	Ripe when skin is pale yellow. Freckles indicate high sugar content. Flesh is white, juicy, but not very flavorful.	July–December
Charentais	Rind gray green and slightly ribbed. Ripe when it has a sweet aroma. Flowery taste, bright orange flesh. Imported from Europe.	June–September
Crenshaw	Very large melon. Ripe when skin is golden and velvety and flesh is golden yellow. Sweet and juicy.	August–December
Galia	Looks like a pale, smooth cantaloupe. Light green flesh. Sweet and juicy with smooth texture. Best imported from Israel.	November–February
Honeydew	Ripe when very fragrant and skin is the color of butter, velvety and slightly tacky.	August–October
Juan Canary	Ripe when skin is bright yellow with no green and feels slightly waxy. White flesh. Sweet, but perfectly ripe ones are rare.	June–October
Persian	Large round melon. When vine ripened, skin shows orange through heavy netting. Flesh is deep orange, sweet and musky.	August–September

I live in the Northeast, and my farmers' market carries local muskmelons in late August. They smell heavenly but have no taste. Why is this?

It is simply a matter of soil and sun. No matter how we look at it, California probably grows the world's best cantaloupe melons. I am often tempted to buy local muskmelons at my farmers' market in Connecticut, but unfortunately they do not deliver tastewise. If you find yourself tempted by the wonderful aroma but the melon seems to lack sweetness, a sprinkling of fresh lemon juice and sugar will do the trick.

What kind of melons are good in winter?

The only good winter melon is the Israeli Galia. It looks somewhat like a cantaloupe but has green flesh. You can now find Galia melons imported from Latin America. I don't think they are as sweet as those grown in Israel.

Is there a trick to picking a good honeydew? Frequently they are hard and tasteless.

A good honeydew is a great fruit, but it is not easy to come by. I have seen heaps of honeydews at supermarkets without a single ripe one. The reason is that honeydews, much like ripe tomatoes, are too delicate to withstand rough handling.

So what to do? If possible, buy your melon

at a good greengrocer, one that handles ripe fruit and knows how to pick a good melon. But if that is not possible, look for three things: skin color, skin texture, and a slight softness at the blossom end. A truly ripe honeydew is not green or white outside; it is the color of creamy butter. The skin must be velvety. If it is too smooth and shiny, it is not ripe. And finally, the blossom end must give to very gentle pressure, the kind of pressure you would apply to a ripe avocado.

Last, if you do not want to be disappointed, buy honeydews only during their peak season, which is August and September, when there is a good chance you will find a perfectly ripe one.

TIP When you shake a honeydew and the seeds go "slurp," don't buy it. It is overripe, and overripe melons can actually cause an upset stomach.

I am totally confused by all the different varieties of melons I see in the market in the summer. Which do you recommend?

Picking a good melon even in peak season can be a challenge, especially in California and Arizona, where the choices can be overwhelming. Here are some of my favorites:

■ **Crenshaw** This is a huge gold-colored melon that is sweet and juicy with an almost buttery texture. Many markets offer a half Crenshaw, which is a good way to buy it, since you can easily see if it is ripe. If the skin is not golden yellow, pass on it. Best in August.

■ **Persian melon** This, too, is a fabulous melon if you can get a ripe one. Be sure to check the skin carefully. The color peeking through the webbing must be orange, not green.

■ **Orange-fleshed honeydews** This is a rather new hybrid that combines cantaloupe flavor with the more flowery taste of the honeydew. Here again, it is not easy to tell ripeness. The skin must have a velvety texture. If it is slick and hard, pass on it.

■ **Charentais** This is a French import that you can now find in high-end grocery stores. Not as delicious as the famous French Cavallon melon, it is still well worth looking for. The skin of these firm-fleshed, flowery-tasting melons is slightly ribbed, with a gray green rind. Check the blossom end for ripeness and make sure it has a sweet floral aroma.

Oranges

I love freshly squeezed orange juice, but some of the oranges I buy are full of seeds while others aren't. Is there a way to tell which ones are seedless?

Many of the better markets will display a cut orange so you can see what you're getting.

Other than that, there's no way of telling. But the fact is, if you want delicious juice you will have to accept seeds. One of the best juicing oranges is the Florida Pineapple variety. It's packed with seeds, but it's also the sweetest and juiciest.

CITRUS AT A GLANCE

FRUIT	CHARACTERISTICS	SEASON
GRAPEFRUIT		
Marsh	White flesh, good flavor, very juicy. Few seeds.	April–November
Red Blush	Red flesh, good flavor, very juicy. Few seeds.	mid-January–November
Star or Texas Ruby	Deep red flesh, with some red on peel. Very sweet.	mid-January–May
Pomelo	Very large fruit, good sweet-sour flavor. To serve, peel and segment.	December–May
KUMQUATS		
Nagami	Small, oblong, orange fruit. Entire fruit is edible with mildly sweet rind. Good for preserving, marmalades.	December–mid-March
LEMONS		
Lisbon and Eirela	Highly acid and juicy, thick peel. Good for zesting or grating.	Year-round, best in winter and spring
Meyer	Slightly sweeter than other lemons. Very juicy, thin skinned.	Year-round
LIMES		
Key or Mexican	Small green to yellow fruit, Highly acid and aromatic, very juicy. Few to many seeds.	July–December
Bears or Persian	True lime flavor, very acid, few seeds. Picked and used green. Ripe fruits are yellow.	Year-round, peak June–August
MANDARINS		
Clementines	Sweet and juicy, easy to peel. Many seeds.	November–mid-April
Satsuma	Mild, sweet, and juicy, easy to peel. No seeds.	November–mid-April

FRUIT	CHARACTERISTICS	SEASON
MANDARINS (continued)		
Dancy tangerines	Sprightly rich flavor, moderately juicy and easy to peel. Many seeds.	November–mid-April
Honey tangerines	Small but very rich and juicy.	January–March
ORANGES		
Blood	Red flesh, rich, sweet, distinctive flavor. Few seeds.	December–May
Skaggs Bonanza navel	Medium-large fruit, rich and sweet. Easy to peel, no seeds.	November–May, peak January–March
Washington navel	Large fruit, rich flavor, moderately juicy. Easy to peel, no seeds.	November–May, peak January–March
Pineapple or Arizona Sweet	Small fruit, rich, aromatic, juicy, Used in commercial juices.	November–March, peak January–February
Seville	Juicy and sour, easy to peel. Many seeds. Best for marmalade.	November–March
Shamouti or Jaffa	Fragrant, sweet, juicy. Few or no seeds.	mid-December–May
Valencia	Sweet and juicy. Hard to peel, few seeds. Best for juice.	February–October
HYBRID CITRUS FRUIT		
Calamondin	Cross between mandarin and kumquat. Small round fruit, juicy with acidic flavor. Good for preserves.	December–September
Tangelo–Minneola	Cross between mandarin and grapefruit. Easy to peel, few to many seeds.	January–mid-May
Temple (also called Tangor)	Cross between mandarin and orange. Rich, spicy flavor, juicy. Easy to peel. Many seeds.	Late December–March

Which are better oranges, those from Florida or California?

It depends on where you live, the time of year, and whether you want an orange for eating or juicing. Oranges are at their sweetest and juiciest from November until April, when both the Florida and California seasons are in full swing. The California oranges look better because their skins are cleaner and brighter. They're also easier to peel and are great for eating. But don't be fooled. If it's juice you're after, the Floridas make the best juice, even though their skin is thinner and they're harder to peel. A good rule of thumb is to choose Californias for eating and stick to Floridas for juice.

What is the easiest way to make orange zest?

The perfumed, pigmented outermost layer of all citrus fruits is the zest, and that's where the fruits' essential oils are. Cooks value the zest for its intense flavor; it adds a lot of depth to many dishes. The best way I know to remove the zest is to use a zesting tool, but a swivel-bladed vegetable peeler works well, too. First wash and dry the fruit well. Then remove the colored peel in long strips, but don't dig in too deep or you'll get some of the fruit's bitter, white membrane, or pith. Lay the strips on a cutting board and use a very sharp paring knife to cut the zest into fine slivers. Be sure to put the slivered zest immediately into a bowl of water to prevent it from drying out.

What is the best orange for zesting?

I prefer using the Florida Temples or tangelos, which appear in markets around February or March. All three are great for zesting, but if they're not available, I find that a thick-skinned California navel works just fine.

Can orange zest be stored?

Orange zest keeps well for a day or two immersed in cold water and refrigerated, but if poached and simmered in sugar syrup, it will keep almost indefinitely.

To preserve orange zest Combine the zest of 2 large oranges with 1 cup water and simmer for 2 minutes. Drain and reserve. In a small saucepan, combine 1 cup water and ¾ cup sugar. Bring to a simmer and stir until the sugar dissolves. Add the blanched zest and simmer for 2 to 3 minutes. Transfer the zest and its syrup to a jar, let cool, then cover and refrigerate.

TIP Add a tablespoon or two of grenadine to the sugar syrup. It will turn the zest a pretty crimson color. Use this lovely bright red zest as a garnish for pork roast, poached pears, sliced oranges, or sugared strawberries.

Many Latin recipes call for sour orange juice. Does that require a certain kind of orange?

What you want are Seville oranges, a nubby, rough-skinned variety that has bitter juice. These are the oranges used for marmalade. Seville oranges are available for only a short time in just a few specialty markets.

To make 1 cup of sour juice Combine 6 tablespoons each of orange and grapefruit juice with 4 tablespoons lemon juice and 2 teaspoons freshly grated grapefruit zest. This will give you about the same amount of bitterness as a Seville.

What's so special about blood oranges?

From the outside, blood oranges look like regular oranges with a slight reddish blush. But slice one open, and you'll see they range from a beautiful deep pink to speckled red to burgundy. Sections of tart-sweet oranges are a lovely addition to an endive and arugula salad, simply drizzled with a light sherry vinegar dressing.

Should I avoid oranges that have a green tinge?

Bright color doesn't mean better flavor when it comes to oranges. The green coloration has nothing to do with ripeness; it only shows that the fruit has been through some cold nights before picking.

Papayas

■ ■

How can I tell when a papaya is ripe?

A ripe papaya will have bright gold skin and give slightly when you press it with your thumb. You can quicken the ripening process by placing it in a brown paper bag at room temperature for a few days.

Papaya seeds are so beautiful that I hate to throw them away. Can I use them for something?

No matter how many times I cut open a papaya, I am surprised and delighted to see the beautiful, black, pearl-like seeds nestled together at its core. Papaya seeds are, indeed, edible and contribute a peppery flavor, but their greatest talent is visual. Try adding papaya seeds to a vinaigrette or tossing them into a fruit salad to punch up the flavor.

What is a green papaya, and how do you use it?

A green papaya, common in both Vietnamese and Thai cuisine, is simply the unripe fruit. It has a pleasant bite and a cucumber-like texture and is usually cubed or grated into salads.

Peaches and Nectarines

■ ■

What exactly are nectarines? Can I use them in recipes that call for peaches?

There seems to be a difference of opinion over whether a nectarine is a fuzzless peach or a cross between a peach and a plum, but, yes, you can substitute nectarines in many recipes that call for peaches, especially in a cobbler and a compote.

I now see nectarines in my market practically year-round. Is there a real nectarine season?

Ripe nectarines are difficult to come by even at the height of their season, which is from June through August. The nectarines you see during the winter months are Chilean imports; because of long shipping and handling, they are never as sweet as the California- or Georgia-grown summer varieties. Also, depending on where you live, you may find fabulous tree-ripened Washington State–grown nectarines in September. These have superb flavor and juice.

Can unripe nectarines and peaches ever become really sweet?

It is getting harder and harder to get ripe stone fruit. Nectarines, like peaches, are extremely fragile, and with the large demand for this summer fruit and the mishandling by self-serve consumers, few markets can afford to bring in tree-ripened produce.

Unripe nectarines will ripen at room temperature in 2 or 3 days, but they are rarely as sweet as naturally ripe fruit. One clue to quality, however, is size. Don't buy small fruit, which has probably been picked before it has had a chance to fully mature; instead, go with medium to large nectarines. Also, avoid oversized fruit, which has probably been bred for appearance.

If you have access to a gourmet produce market, you actually may have a chance of getting tree-ripened nectarines. Just make sure they are not bruised, and do not refrigerate them until they are fragrant and slightly softened.

What is the easiest way to peel a peach without sacrificing some of the fruit?

The best way to peel peaches is to blanch them briefly in simmering water. First, cut a small cross at the blossom end with the tip of a sharp paring knife. Then immerse them in a large pot of simmering water for about 30 seconds. Remove them promptly and drop the fruit immediately into a bowl of ice water to stop further cooking. The peel should slip off easily.

Which peaches are more flavorful—the white or the yellow variety? Is there a flavor difference between cling and freestone peaches?

In the past few years, white peaches have been making a comeback, and they are my first choice for pickling and compotes. Generally, yellow peaches have a more intense peach flavor, but on the whole, the flavor depends more on ripeness than color. Both cling and freestone peaches can be absolutely delicious or flavorless, depending on their stage of ripeness.

Pears

I understand that some pears are better for eating and others for cooking, but I am confused as to which is which. Can you help?

The Bartlett pear is good for both eating and cooking. For strictly eating, a ripe Comice is excellent. Bosc pears, with their rather crunchy texture, are good for eating and poaching, but not for baking; Bosc pears marry particularly well with cheese. The most common winter pear, the Anjou, is unfortunately often shipped so unripe that it is green and hard. If you do come upon some good Anjou pears—still firm, but yellowish green in color and quite fragrant—use them for cooking rather than for eating.

Is there one really terrific pear I can always count on?

The Bartlett is by far the best all-round pear. However, Bartletts are pretty much out of season by Christmas, so look for them as early as late summer and throughout the fall when they're at their best.

PEARS AT A GLANCE

VARIETY	DESCRIPTION	USES	SEASON
Bartlett (red or yellow)	Sweet and juicy	Eating, poaching, baking, roasting	August–December
Anjou	Juicy and slightly peppery	Sautéing and poaching	October–April
Comice	Very juicy; crunchy, buttery texture	Dessert	October–March
Bosc	Crunchy and buttery texture	Eating, poaching, roasting	October–March, best in October
Forelle	Crunchy and sweet; somewhat one-dimensional	Eating, roasting	October–April

Are yellow Bartlett pears better than red ones?

I much prefer yellow Bartletts, but when I say yellow I don't mean greenish-yellow, which indicates that they are underripe, or deep golden yellow, which means they are overripe and therefore mealy. It is a challenge to find a Bartlett that is just the right color and consistency, but when you bite into it and the juice runs into your mouth, you know it's worth it.

What is the best way to poach pears?

There are three ways to poach pears: in a water-based syrup, in a red wine syrup, or in a white wine syrup. The sugar to liquid ratio is the same for all three types.

To poach pears As a guideline, for 4 to 6 pears, you should use 1½ to 2 cups sugar for 4 cups water, white wine, or red wine; use less if the pears are quite ripe and sweet. I add a cinnamon stick, a 2-inch piece of vanilla bean, and a long strip of lemon zest to the poaching liquid.

Poach for 8 to 10 minutes, testing pears with a fork every few minutes. Some may be done before others. Chill pears in the poaching liquid.

TIP To keep pears from discoloring, place a circle of parchment inside the casserole, using it to cover the pears in the bowl as well.

I live in an area with lots of pear orchards and fruit stands. What are some interesting ways of using pears?

When it comes to pears, don't underestimate the power of sugar to enhance flavor. Combine them with cranberries in a luscious tart. Use them instead of apples in your favorite crisp recipe. Make a spiced pear butter out of very ripe ones to serve as a topping for pancakes, crepes, or waffles. Simply slice and serve your favorite ripe pear with some blue cheese or a ripe Brie for dessert.

For a refreshing salad, roast peeled pear halves in red wine, sugar, butter, salt, and pepper with a pinch of nutmeg until tender, then fan out the cooled slices on a bed of fresh greens and top with a dollop of sugared crème fraîche. Or use the unpeeled hollowed-out roasted halves as edible containers for all kinds of sweet and savory fillings, such as a sweetened ricotta cheese or a sauté of leeks, walnut, and goat cheese mixture.

What are Asian pears and how do I serve them?

Asian, or Japanese, pears are actually a variety all to themselves. While they have the same granular texture and taste of a soft, ripe pear, they look and even taste more like a crisp, juicy golden apple. They're best served raw on salads and are used frequently in Asian cooking, especially in spicy noodle dishes where their sweet, cool taste helps temper the fire. They're also delicious sautéed with sliced toasted almonds or preserved ginger and served as a side dish.

I now see charming-looking small greenish pears in the market. What exactly are they?

They are the tiny, spicy Seckels, which are pricey but worth it. They have a dull olive-green color with a bit of a blush and are perfect for eating when you just want that spicy pear taste. But don't confuse the succulent Seckel with the Forelle, another miniature variety that is usually half yellowish green fading into a deep red. While cute as can be, the Forelle is virtually tasteless unless it's roasted unpeeled in butter and plenty of sugar, but then just about everything is good prepared this way.

I like Bosc pears, but because of their brown skin I can never tell when they are ripe.

The color of Bosc pears does change slightly. The unripe pears will be quite green under the brown skin. When they are ripe, they become a yellowish brown with a distinct pear aroma.

TIP A pear is ripe when a light squeeze at the base of the neck yields lightly to pressure. To ripen hard pears, put the unripe fruit in a paper bag for 2 to 3 days.

Persimmons

■■

I have heard that freezing an unripe persimmon ripens it overnight. Is that true?

Unfortunately, that is not the case. When the unripe persimmon is defrosted, it will have a mushy consistency but it will still be unripe.

I can never find a ripe persimmon in my market and have tried to ripen them at room temperature for as long as 3 or 4 days. Is there a way to ripen a persimmon quickly?

Not really. In fact, 3 days is a short time for an unripe persimmon. It may take as long as 6 days, and you can never rush it, either, because in order to be really sweet and flavorful, the persimmon has to be almost mushy. When choosing persimmons, pick those that are already slightly soft; otherwise they simply take forever to ripen and sometimes never do.

There seems to be more than one kind of persimmon around. Is one variety better than the other? Which one is sweeter?

Hachiya is the most common variety, but the round Fuyu is becoming increasingly available. They have very distinct flavors, and the Fuyu does not lend itself to puddings. The major advantage of the Fuyu is that you can eat it even when it is hard, and I always choose it when I see it in the market. Besides that, it is also almost tannin free and does not have the astringency that is common in a less than perfectly ripe Hachiya persimmon.

Should a persimmon be served peeled or unpeeled?

The ripe persimmon is very hard to peel. To serve, slice it lengthwise, then free the flesh from the peel with a sharp paring knife, much as you would prepare a grapefruit. Score the flesh into small cubes and drizzle with a squeeze of lime juice. You can eat the skin of a very ripe Hachiya persimmon, but the skin of the Fuya is rather hard and somewhat bitter.

Pineapple

I always try to select a good pineapple, but the ones I end up with are still hit or miss. Any tips?

For a pineapple to be sweet, it must be picked when ripe, since, unlike bananas, the fruit has no starch reserve that can be converted into sugar. This means that a pineapple will not ripen once it is off the plant. The fruit should be slightly soft to the touch, and the skin color should be full and rich looking (color will vary somewhat depending on the variety and time of year). The base of the pineapple should give off a distinctively fruity aroma. Finally, disregard the old wives' tale about pulling a leaf from a pineapple's crown—it doesn't work. You should, however, look for fresh, crisp leaves.

Del Monte has a brand called Hawaiian Gold that is consistently sweet, with a deeper tropical flavor. You may pay a bit more, but you will be able to count on great flavor.

Is a Hawaiian pineapple a specific variety, or does that just refer to the place where it's grown?

The latter. Almost all of the pineapples sold in the United States are grown in Hawaii, although Costa Rica and Honduras also have large pineapple crops. By far the most common variety of pineapple sold here is the Smooth Cayenne variety, although occasionally you can find the Red Spanish pineapple, which is delicious.

Pineapples seem to be available all year. Is there a season when they are better?

Because sun and heat are the prime promoters of sweetness in pineapples, it follows that the sweetest fruit will come to market in the warmest months. Hawaii has somewhat cooler weather between December and April, so pineapples harvested then generally have a lower sugar to acid ratio, which leads to fruit that is less sweet.

I recently bought a small "baby" pineapple that was the sweetest one I have ever had. Does size have anything to do with flavor?

You most probably tasted a pineapple from Africa's Ivory Coast. These are usually much smaller than Hawaiian varieties and are deliciously sweet.

Sometimes I get a pineapple with little brown seeds in it. What are these?

They're just what you think they are, pineapple seeds. While most varieties of pineapple grown for sale are seedless, there are a few seeded varieties; sometimes different varieties are grown close together, and they cross pollinate, unbeknownst to the growers. Pineapple seeds are small and brown and resemble apple seeds. They are perfectly harmless, but you wouldn't want to eat them.

TIP Whenever you buy a pineapple, check the green tops and do not buy one with a double crown, which usually is an indication of a double core as well.

What's the best way to store a pineapple for a few days? Should I refrigerate it or leave it out on the counter?

If you are not going to use a pineapple right away, the best thing to do is to cut out the flesh, place it in an airtight container, and refrigerate it. (Although you may find, as I do, that you can't stop yourself from snacking on pineapple chunks.) Since a pineapple won't ripen further once it's picked, leaving it at room temperature may allow the skin to become more golden, but it will not become any sweeter.

What is the best way to cut up a pineapple?

The traditional way is to quarter the whole unpeeled fruit right through the green crown. Lay the quartered pieces on their sides and slice off the hard core. Next, place the pieces flesh side up, cut the flesh away from the skin with a sharp paring knife, and then cut crosswise into $1/2$-inch pieces.

I have a recipe for a gelatin dessert that uses canned pineapple. Since I don't like to use canned fruits when I can find fresh, I tried it with fresh pineapple instead. It was a disastrous blob. What went wrong?

Pineapple contains an enzyme called bromelain, which breaks down the protein in gelatin so it never sets. (Some people also think bromelain helps digestion, but this has never been proven.) Canned pineapple is processed at a high temperature, which destroys bromelain. Boiling breaks down bromelain, so either cook your fresh pineapple before adding it to gelatin or reach for a can.

Plums

What is the best eating plum?

My favorites are the bright red or dark red-skinned, large Japanese varieties. The dark reds are quite round, have very small pits, and, when perfectly ripe, are loaded with juice and a refreshing tart-sweet flavor. Look for Laroda, considered the quintessential plum and a real winner because this one does it all—it's great for eating, cooking, and jam. Also El Dorado, Queen Anne, and Friar are outstanding. Excellent bright red varieties are usually more oval in shape and can be identified by the "Rosa" in their names. They are the Santa Rosa, which is packed with flavor, Queen Rosa, and Simka Rosa. Unfortunately, many markets don't label their plums, which makes it difficult to identify them.

What is an Italian Plum?

For marketing purposes, European plums are often called Italian plums, or prune plums. This does cause some confusion, possibly because the Latin word for plums is *prunus* and in the English language the words *prunes* and *plums* are used interchangeably. They're oval-shaped, purple in color, and can be as small as 1 inch in diameter or up to 3 inches in diameter. Sometimes they can be very sweet but not juicy and are best reserved for cooking and baking.

There are so many varieties of plums throughout the summer. Which are good for eating and which are better for baking?

Plums seem to come in every size, shape, and color imaginable, and that does make the choice confusing. There are two clear distinctions of plums: European and Japanese. The more common eating plums are the Japanese varieties that come in red, yellow, and green. These are essentially eating plums, since they practically dissolve when cooked. The small, ovoid purple European varieties that have a green flesh are best for baking and poaching; they make excellent tarts. These are the plums that are dried to make prunes.

TIP To minimize the confusion when you're shopping for plums, remember that the Japanese varieties are simply called plums, and the European, English, or Italian varieties are called prune plums.

Are green plums as juicy as the red ones?

If you buy a green plum, make sure it's a Kelsey or Greengage, or you'll be sorely disappointed. Other green varieties are bitter and tough. Otherwise, chances are that red plums will be juicier and more flavorful. Greengage plums, are originally from England and are best eaten when fully ripe. They have a juicy, yellow flesh. Slice and toss with fresh greens for a wonderful salad.

What's the best season for plums?

The Japanese varieties come from California and start arriving in markets in May, but the peak season is July through September. Don't buy the first plums that come on the scene. By July, they'll be so much more juicy and flavorful. Prune plums don't show up until mid-August and are best in early to late fall.

Spiced Applesauce

I love a simple buttery applesauce and usually serve it warm with a side dish of sugared crème fraîche. I also flavor it with prepared hot horseradish and a touch of sour cream and serve it as a side dish to boiled beef. If you feel ambitious, you can use some applesauce as a filling for a butter crust, top it with additional finely sliced Golden Delicious apples, and bake it until the apples are nicely browned.

SERVES 6

4 pounds McIntosh apples or a mixture of
  Macs and Jonathans

½ cup granulated sugar

2-inch piece lemon zest

1-inch-long cinnamon stick

2 to 3 tablespoons brown sugar

2 tablespoons unsalted butter, optional

Freshly grated nutmeg

Crème fraîche, as accompaniment

1. Core and quarter the apples, but do not peel.

2. Combine the apples, ½ cup water, and the sugar in a large saucepan. Add the lemon zest and cinnamon stick and cook for 15 to 20 minutes, or until the mixture is very soft.

3. Discard the cinnamon stick. Pass the apple puree through a food mill. Add the brown sugar, the butter, and freshly grated nutmeg. Taste for sweetness and serve warm accompanied by a bowl of sweetened crème fraîche.

Three-Berry Coulis with Nectarines

I start making this compote in June when good blueberries, black-berries, raspberries, and strawberries become more readily available. Although I call it a coulis, the French word for a fruit sauce, this is more of a compote, especially with the addition of nectarines or peaches. Serve the coulis as a sauce with vanilla ice cream or by itself as a fruit soup topped with sugared crème fraîche. You do not have to wait for good nectarines; just the berries are delicious by themselves.

SERVES 6 TO 8

2 ripe nectarines or freestone peaches
2 pints blueberries
1 pint blackberries
¾ to 1 cup sugar
1 pint strawberries
Small scoops of peach sorbet
Small sprigs of mint

1. In a pot of boiling water, blanch the nectarines or peaches for 30 to 50 seconds. Drain and remove the skins. Cut each nectarine or peach into eighths and set aside.

2. Thoroughly rinse the blueberries and remove all stems. In a large heavy saucepan, combine the blueberries, blackberries, sugar, and ½ cup water. Bring to a simmer and cook for 15 minutes.

3. Add the strawberries and simmer for 5 minutes. Add the nectarines or peaches and cook for another 5 minutes, or until the nectarines are just soft.

4. Transfer the mixture to a bowl and chill for several hours before serving. Serve in individual bowls, topped with scoops of peach sorbet and sprigs of mint.

Caramelized Banana Tatin

A tatin is essentially an upside-down fruit tart. Apple Tatin is one of France's most famous desserts, but the same technique can be used for pears or, as here, bananas. Choose bananas that are just ripe or else they will become mushy as they bake. To save time, you can use store-bought pastry. It will likely be less flaky but still delicious.

SERVES 6 TO 8

½ cup sugar
4 large semiripe bananas
3 tablespoons unsalted butter
½ recipe Basic Tart Dough (page 385)

1. Preheat the oven to 375°F.

2. In a small saucepan, combine the sugar and 3 tablespoons water. Bring to a boil and stir once to dissolve the sugar. Continue to boil without stirring until the syrup turns hazelnut brown.

3. Immediately remove the saucepan from the heat and pour just enough of the caramel into the bottom of a 9-inch round, nonstick cake pan to cover it completely. As you are pouring, turn the cake pan at the same time to create an even layer of caramel. Set aside to cool completely.

4. Peel the bananas and slice them on the diagonal into ¼-inch slices. Dot the caramel with the butter and arrange the banana slices in a single layer, tightly overlapping them to create a circular pattern.

5. Roll out the dough on a lightly floured surface to about 9½ inches in diameter and about ⅛ inch thick. Place the dough over the bananas to cover completely, tucking the edges into the pan. Prick with a fork and place in the center of the oven.

6. Bake for 30 to 35 minutes or until the dough is crisp and nicely browned. Removed the pan from the oven. If there are any excess pan juices, remove them from the cake pan with a bubble baster and reserve.

7. Invert the tatin carefully onto a platter and let cool.

8. Place the banana juices in a small saucepan, bring to a boil, and reduce until syrupy. Serve the tart cut into wedges, with a drizzle of the reduced juices and a small scoop of vanilla ice cream on top.

Blueberries in Lemon Sabayon

This recipe was first published in 1973 in my cookbook *The Seasonal Kitchen*, and made the cover of *House & Garden* magazine that year. It is still one of my favorite desserts. I have since adjusted the lemon sabayon, which in the original recipe was quite fragile and could not be made ahead of time. The revised version will keep well for 3 to 4 days. It can also be frozen and served as an iced lemon mousse.

SERVES 6

1 quart blueberries, washed and stemmed

1 cup sugar

5 extra large eggs, separated

Juice of 2 large lemons

2 teaspoons finely grated lemon zest

1 cup heavy cream, whipped

Tiny leaves of fresh mint

1. Place the blueberries in a glass serving bowl. Sprinkle with ¼ cup of the sugar and set aside.

2. In a double boiler, combine the egg yolks and remaining ¾ cup sugar. Whisk until fluffy and pale yellow. Add the lemon juice and zest and whisk until well blended. Set over simmering water and whisk constantly until the mixture is thick and heavily coats a spoon, about 5 minutes. Be careful not to overcook, or the eggs will curdle. Immediately transfer the sabayon to a stainless steel bowl and let cool completely.

3. Beat the egg whites in a large bowl until they form firm peaks. Add them to the cooled sabayon and fold in gently but thoroughly. Add the whipped cream and again, fold in gently but thoroughly. Cover and chill until very cold.

4. Spoon the sabayon over the berries, garnish with mint leaves, and serve at once.

Classic Cherry Clafoutis

Cherry clafoutis is a classic French dessert that appears in pastry shops all over France when fresh cherries are in season. Unfortunately, it is rarely very good, but I don't give up and continue to sample it whenever I am in France during cherry season. Last year, I discovered a delicious cherry clafoutis at a market café in St. Remy and begged the owner for the recipe. Here it is.

SERVES 6 TO 8

½ pound Bing or sour cherries

1¾ cups sugar plus 2 tablespoons

1 cinnamon stick

4 eggs

3 tablespoons flour

½ cup heavy cream

½ cup milk

2 teaspoons vanilla extract

One 9-inch partially baked pastry crust

1. Preheat the oven to 350°F.

2. Remove the stems from the cherries. Combine 2½ cups water, 1¼ cups of the sugar, and the cinnamon stick in a large saucepan. Bring to a boil, reduce the heat, and add the cherries. Simmer for 25 to 30 minutes, or until the cherries are very tender. Let the cherries cool completely in the syrup; then drain thoroughly, reserving the syrup. Pit the cherries and set aside.

3. In a bowl, combine the eggs, ½ cup of the sugar, and the flour. Whisk until thoroughly blended. Add the cream, milk, and vanilla extract. Taste. If you like it sweeter, add the remaining 2 tablespoons sugar. Strain the custard into a bowl to make sure it is completely smooth.

4. Add the cherries to the custard and pour into the prebaked crust. Be sure to distribute the cherries evenly.

5. Bake the clafoutis for 30 minutes, or until the custard is set and a knife inserted in the middle comes out clean.

6. Serve slightly warm or at room temperature.

REMARKS The clafoutis can be reheated in a low oven the next day. For a nice addition to this homey dessert, I usually cook the cherry syrup until it is well reduced, fold in a little crème fraîche, and serve it as a sauce. Other fruits, especially sautéed summer peaches and roasted Bartlett pears, can be used instead of the cherries.

> **TIP** Since I pit the cherries after they are poached, no pitter is needed; gently squeeze the fruit and the pit will pop right out.

Chocolate and Pear Tart

Many people like the taste of raspberries or strawberries with chocolate, but to me the marriage of pears and chocolate in unbeatable, whether the pear is simply poached and drizzled with hot chocolate sauce or baked in this delicate yet easy-to-make tart. Although all tarts are best baked and served the same day, this one can be made a day ahead of time and still be quite delicious. Make sure the pears are at least semiripe before making the tart.

SERVES 6

2 tablespoons unsalted butter

3 large, slightly underripe pears, preferably Bartlett, peeled, cored, and cut into ½-inch wedges

5 tablespoons sugar

½ cup heavy cream

1 large egg

1 partially baked 10-inch Basic Tart Shell (page 386) in a pan with a removable bottom

5 ounces bittersweet chocolate, preferably Lindt or Tobler, coarsely chopped

½ cup sliced blanched almonds

Lightly sweetened crème fraîche, as accompaniment

I. Preheat the oven to 375°F.

2. In a large skillet, melt the butter over medium-high heat. Add the pears, sprinkle with 2 tablespoons of the sugar, and sauté quickly until nicely browned. Reduce the heat and cook until tender, about 15 minutes. Drain the pears in a colander and set aside.

3. Combine the heavy cream, egg, and 1 tablespoon of the sugar in a bowl and whisk until smooth.

4. Sprinkle the bottom of the partially baked tart shell with the chopped chocolate. Arrange the pears in a decorative pattern over the chocolate and drizzle with the cream-egg mixture. Sprinkle the top with the sliced almonds and remaining 2 tablespoons sugar. Place in the center of the oven and bake for 30 to 35 minutes, or until the custard is set and the almonds are nicely browned. Remove from the oven and let cool.

5. Cut the tart into wedges. Serve with a bowl of lightly sweetened crème fraîche.

Terrine of Citrus Fruit with Strawberry Sauce

Here is an impressive yet simple dessert that is really nothing more than "upscale" Jell-O. Although I like the terrine look of this refreshing dessert, you can also spoon the mixture into martini glasses and serve topped with a dollop of sugared crème fraîche and a light grating of lime or orange zest.

SERVES 6 TO 8

Flavorless oil (preferably almond oil) for the terrine

1½ tablespoons unflavored gelatin

2 cups fresh orange juice, strained

2 pink grapefruit

4 navel oranges

Strawberry Sauce (page 395)

Sprigs of fresh mint

1. Lightly oil the inside of a 1½-quart terrine, preferably porcelain.

2. Combine the gelatin and orange juice in a small saucepan and let stand 5 minutes, or until the gelatin has softened.

3. Peel the grapefruit and oranges with a sharp knife, removing all traces of the rind and white pith. Cut each segment away from the membrane on either side, then cut each segment in half crosswise.

4. Heat the orange juice and gelatin mixture over medium-low heat, stirring constantly until the gelatin has completely dissolved. Remove from the heat and transfer the mixture to a large stainless steel or glass bowl. Chill until the mixture begins to thicken but is not set. (The thickened juice will keep the fruit suspended throughout the gelatin mixture instead of letting it sink to the bottom of the terrine.)

5. Fold the fruit into the gelatin mixture and pour into the oiled terrine. Cover and chill overnight.

6. The next day, remove the terrine from the refrigerator and run a hot knife around the inside of the terrine to loosen the molded fruit. Invert onto a sheet of plastic wrap and shake to free the molded fruit from the terrine. Wrap completely in the plastic wrap and place in the freezer for 3 to 4 hours or until just frozen.

7. To serve, cut the molded fruit into ½-inch slices and place 1 slice on each individual dessert plate. Let sit for a few minutes, then wipe excess liquid from the plate with a paper towel. Surround with strawberry sauce and garnish with sprigs of fresh mint.

Cranberry, Ginger, and Orange Chutney

I love the puckery sour taste of cranberries. Cooked with fresh orange juice, fresh ginger, and cinnamon, cranberries take on a chutney-like texture, which I find works well as a condiment with roasted turkey, duck, and pork. It also goes well with French toast, pancakes, and as a filling for crepes. It is a good idea to double the recipe, since the chutney will keep for at least 6 months.

MAKES 8 CUPS

3 packages (12 ounces each) fresh cranberries

3 semiripe Golden Delicious apples, peeled, cored, and cubed

1½ cups golden raisins

1½ cups sugar

1¼ cups freshly squeezed orange juice

2 tablespoons finely grated orange zest

3-inch-long cinnamon stick, or 2 teaspoon ground cinnamon

2 tablespoons minced fresh ginger

¼ teaspoon freshly grated nutmeg

⅓ cup Cointreau, optional

1. Place all ingredients except the liqueur in a large non-reactive saucepan. Bring to a boil; reduce the heat to low and simmer, uncovered, stirring often, until the mixture thickens, about 25 minutes.

2. Remove the saucepan from the heat, stir in the liqueur, and let the chutney cool to room temperature. Cover and refrigerate overnight. Serve lightly chilled.

REMARKS The chutney will keep in the refrigerator, in tightly covered jars, for months. You may also "pack" the chutney in pint jars, leaving ½ head space, and process them for 20 minutes.

Crab and Mango Salad

Aqua Grill is one of New York's best restaurants, and this salad is just one of their delicious seafood salads. It is best to dress the crab right before serving, but you can prepare the fruit and make the vinaigrette hours ahead of time. A few baby greens tossed in the dressing would make a lovely accompaniment.

SERVES 4

THE VINAIGRETTE

2 tablespoons finely minced shallots

Juice of ½ orange plus 1 tablespoon orange zest

1 tablespoon lemon juice plus 1 tablespoon lemon zest

1 tablespoon sherry vinegar

1 tablespoon soy sauce

1 tablespoon honey

½ cup grapeseed oil

½ to 1 teaspoon Thai chili sauce

Salt and freshly ground black pepper

THE SALAD

1 pound lump crabmeat

1½ cups finely diced jicama

1 large ripe mango, peeled and diced

2 tablespoons minced fresh cilantro

Tiny leaves of cilantro and mint, for garnish

1. In a bowl, combine the shallots, orange juice and zest, lemon juice and zest, vinegar, soy sauce, and honey. Whisk until well combined. Slowly add the oil and whisk until the vinaigrette is lightly emulsified. Stir in Thai chili sauce to taste. Season with salt and pepper.

2. In another bowl, combine the crab with just enough vinaigrette to bind it. Season with salt and pepper to taste.

3. In a third bowl, combine the jicama with the mango and cilantro. Season with salt and pepper.

4. To serve, place 2 tablespoons of the mango-jicama mixture in the center of individual serving plates. Top with 2 spoonfuls of the crab and garnish with small cilantro and mint leaves. Drizzle a little of the leftover vinaigrette around each serving and serve the salad slightly chilled.

Poached Pears in Sherry Sabayon

SERVES 6 TO 8

1½ cups sugar

3-inch-long cinnamon stick

1 vanilla bean, split

6 large pears, preferably Anjou or Bosc, peeled

3-inch piece lemon zest

Sherry Sabayon (recipe follows)

Tiny leaves of fresh mint, for garnish

I. Start by poaching the pears: In a large flameproof casserole, combine 5 cups water, the sugar, cinnamon stick, and vanilla bean. Bring to a boil over high heat and cook for 5 minutes.

2. Add the pears and lemon zest, reduce the heat, and simmer, partially covered, until the pears are tender when pierced with the tip of a sharp knife, 15 to 20 minutes. Remove the cinnamon stick and vanilla bean and set the pears aside to cool completely in their poaching liquid.

3. Drain the pears well and pat dry on paper towels. Cut in half lengthwise, core, and place cut side down on round shallow plates in a decorative pattern. Top each portion with a large dollop of sabayon. Garnish with tiny leaves of mint and serve at once.

Sherry Sabayon

MAKES ABOUT 2½ CUPS

4 extra large egg yolks

¼ cup sugar

⅔ cup cream sherry

1 cup heavy cream, whipped

I. In the top part of a double boiler, combine the egg yolks, sugar, and sherry; place over simmering water and whisk constantly until the mixture is thick and heavily coats a spoon.

2. Immediately place the top of the double boiler in a large bowl of ice and stir constantly until the sabayon is thick and cool. Chill for 2 hours.

3. Fold in the whipped cream gently but thoroughly, cover, and chill the sabayon until serving time.

Sliced Oranges in Red Wine–Cinnamon Coulis

Whenever I have some leftover red wine, I turn it into syrup, which keeps indefinitely. Besides pairing with oranges, it is equally delicious with grapefruit segments, baked apples, or stewed prunes. Make sure to remove the cinnamon stick after a few days, or it will give the wine a bitter flavor.

SERVES 4 TO 5

3 cups red wine, preferably Bordeaux

1½ cups sugar

1 cinnamon stick

3-inch piece vanilla bean

6 black peppercorns

two 1-inch pieces of lemon zest

4 large navel oranges, peeled and sliced
  crosswise into ¼-inch slices

2 tablespoons Grand Marnier

Zest of 1 large navel orange, cut into fine
  julienne strips, and small whole
  strawberries, for garnish

1. In a heavy nonreactive saucepan, combine the wine, sugar, cinnamon, vanilla bean, and peppercorns. Add the lemon zest and bring to a boil, reduce the heat, and simmer until the wine is reduced by half and the mixture is syrupy. Discard the lemon zest, transfer the wine syrup to a bowl, and chill for 4 hours or overnight.

2. Divide the orange slices among 4 or 5 glass serving dishes. Sprinkle with Grand Marnier. Spoon the wine coulis over the oranges and garnish with the orange zest and whole strawberries. Serve chilled.

Stewed Peaches in Muscat, Cinnamon, and Vanilla Syrup

I love peaches and cannot wait until July, when I can pick them at our local orchard. Unfortunately, many people are less fortunate and often spend entire summers without tasting a single juicy ripe peach. Here is a good way to use fruit that is less than perfectly ripe. However, don't fool yourself into thinking that you can use hard unripe fruit even when stewed with sugar, because while the compote will be sweet, it will lack that real peach flavor. Enjoy a glass of the leftover Muscat wine over crushed ice and a few drops of peach liqueur.

SERVES 6

5 large semiripe or ripe peaches or nectarines
2½ cups Muscat wine
½ cup sugar
3-inch-long cinnamon stick
3-inch piece vanilla bean
two 1-inch pieces lemon zest
2 tablespoons peach liqueur, optional
Honey-sweetened ricotta, optional
Tiny mint leaves

1. In a large saucepan, bring plenty of water to a boil. Add the peaches or nectarines and cook for 1 minute. Drain and peel; the skin should slip off easily. If it does not, cook for another minute. Slice the peaches into ½-inch pieces and reserve.

2. In a nonreactive medium saucepan, combine the Muscat wine with the sugar, cinnamon, vanilla, and lemon zest. Add the peaches and poach for 5 to 8 minutes, or until the fruit is just tender and the syrup is lightly reduced. Chill the peaches in the syrup until serving.

3. Serve in individual glass bowls, topped with a drizzle of peach liqueur and a dollop of sweetened ricotta and a few tiny mint leaves.

REMARKS The compote will keep for at least a week. Remove the cinnamon stick and vanilla bean after a day.

Pear Crisp with Brown Sugar and Ginger

Everyone loves a good apple crisp, but I find the taste of pears to be more interesting and am always on the lookout for good pears to make this crisp. Bartletts are my first choice, but ripe Boscs or Anjous work well too. Serve with sugared crème fraîche or vanilla ice cream.

SERVES 6

6 ripe medium pears, preferably Bartlett
$^{1}/_{4}$ to $^{1}/_{3}$ cup granulated sugar
1 teaspoon ground ginger
1 tablespoon candied ginger, minced, optional
$^{2}/_{3}$ cup tightly packed dark brown sugar
$^{3}/_{4}$ cup all-purpose flour
8 tablespoon (1 stick) unsalted butter

1. Preheat the oven to 375°F.

2. Peel the pears with a vegetable peeler, core, and quarter. If the pears are large, cut them into eighths. Place the pears in a bowl and sprinkle with one-fourth cup of the granulated sugar (or more, depending upon the sweetness of the pears), the ground ginger, and optional candied ginger.

3. In a small bowl, combine the brown sugar, flour, and 6 tablespoons of the butter. Work the mixture with your hands until it resembles cornmeal.

4. In a large oval flameproof gratin dish, heat the remaining 2 tablespoons butter over low heat, add the pears in one layer, and sprinkle with the brown sugar topping. Place the dish in the center of the oven and bake for 30 minutes, or until the topping is golden and crisp.

5. When the crisp is done, remove from the oven and let cool for 30 minutes before serving. Serve with vanilla ice cream.

REMARKS You may substitute Golden Delicious apples, peeled and cored, for the pears.

Persimmon Mousse

A ripe persimmon needs little enhancement, but it is not an easy fruit to serve with style. Whenever I can, I simply dice the fruit and combine it with some sugared crème fraîche and freshly grated nutmeg. Remember that persimmons are sold quite firm, and it can take as long as 10 days to ripen them.

SERVES 4

4 ripe persimmons, peeled

1 cup crème fraîche

3 to 4 tablespoons sugar

1 tablespoon minced candied ginger,
  optional

Freshly grated nutmeg and mint leaves,
  for garnish

1. In a food processor or a blender, combine the persimmons, crème fraîche, and sugar. Blend gently; do not over-process. Add the minced ginger. Transfer to individual glass bowls and top with a generous grating of fresh nutmeg and mint leaves.

2. Cover and chill for 2 to 4 hours. Serve in martini glasses.

Pineapple Caramel Compote with Oranges

A sweet ripe pineapple needs little enhancement, but occasionally it is fun to use it creatively. Here the cubed fruit is tossed with an orange-flavored caramel and combined with fresh orange segments for a light dessert.

SERVES 4 TO 5

½ cup sugar

1 pound finely cubed pineapple

2 tablespoons Grand Marnier

2 navel oranges, peeled and cut into segments
   or cubed

Fresh sprigs of mint, for garnish

1. In a small heavy saucepan, combine the sugar with ¼ cup cold water. Bring to a boil and cook without stirring until the syrup turns hazelnut brown. Do not let it get too dark. Immediately remove the caramel from the heat and pour in ¼ cup hot water. Whisk the caramel until it becomes a smooth syrup. Pour over the pineapple, toss gently, and chill for several hours.

2. An hour or 2 before serving, add the Grand Marnier and the oranges and toss gently.

3. To serve, transfer the compote to individual glass serving bowls. Garnish with sprigs of fresh mint and serve chilled.

Italian Plum and Almond Tart

This was one of my mother's favorite recipes and I still make it as soon as fresh prune plums appear in the market in early fall. Unfortunately, the season for these small fleshy sweet plums is rather short, so take advantage of it either by making this luscious tart or by poaching them in a wine, sugar, and cinnamon syrup and serving them with sweetened crème fraîche.

SERVES 8

1 cup finely ground slivered almonds,
   lightly toasted

½ cup plus 2 to 3 tablespoons sugar

1 teaspoon lemon zest

½ teaspoon ground cinnamon

¼ teaspoon almond extract

1 extra-large egg

One 9-inch unbaked dessert tart shell
   (see Remarks, page 387), in a removable-
   bottom tart pan, frozen

2 dozen small Italian prune plums, halved and
   pitted (quartered if large)

2 tablespoons unsalted butter

Lightly sweetened crème fraîche or
   mascarpone mixed with a little whipped
   cream and honey

1. Preheat the oven to 400°F.

2. To make the almond paste: Combine the almonds, the ½ cup sugar, and the lemon zest in a food processor and process until the almonds are finely ground. Add the cinnamon, almond extract, and egg and process until a smooth paste is formed. Spread the almond paste in an even layer in the bottom of the prepared tart shell.

3. Arrange the plum halves very close together in a decorative pattern over the almond paste. Sprinkle with 2 to 3 tablespoons sugar, according to the sweetness of the fruit, and dot with the butter. Set the tart shell on a baking sheet and place in the center of the oven. Immediately reduce the heat to 375°F and bake for 1 hour to 1 hour 30 minutes, or until the crust is evenly browned and the juice from the plums has evaporated.

4. Remove the tart from the oven and let cool completely on a wire cake rack. Remove the tart shell carefully from the tart pan, transfer to a serving platter, and let cool to room temperature. Serve cut into wedges, with a dollop of sweetened crème fraîche or mascarpone.

Vanilla-Scented Pots de Crème with Raspberries

When I was growing up, pots de crème was a familiar weekday dessert at our house. The little custards, flavored with coffee, chocolate, or vanilla, were served in decorative covered porcelain ramekins especially designed just for this dessert. Today, I still love making these custards, but I simply bake them in 6-ounce porcelain ramekins. The toppings vary according to the season, but my favorite is always some kind of seasonal berry. Strawberries, raspberries, and blackberries work best, but if you flavor the custard with some lemon zest, then blueberries are a good choice as well.

SERVES 6

¾ cup whole milk

½ cup heavy cream

2 extra large whole eggs

2 extra large egg yolks

⅓ cup sugar

1 teaspoon vanilla extract

Toppings: Fresh raspberries or other spring berries, such as blueberries, raspberries, or sliced strawberries

1. Preheat the oven to 350°F. Heat the milk and cream together in a saucepan and keep warm.

2. Combine the whole eggs, egg yolks, sugar, and vanilla in a bowl and whisk until fluffy and pale yellow. Add the warm milk-cream mixture and whisk until well blended. Pour the custard into six 4-ounce porcelain ramekins.

3. Place the ramekins in a heavy baking dish, fill the dish with enough boiling water to reach halfway up the sides of the ramekins, and bake for 15 minutes or until the tip of a knife comes out clean. Do not overcook; the centers should remain slightly soft. Remove from the oven and from the water bath and let cool. Refrigerate for 2 to 4 hours before serving.

4. Top with fresh raspberries or other spring berries, and serve lightly chilled.

Rhubarb and Strawberry Pecan Crisp

The marriage of rhubarb and strawberries seems to be unbeatable, whether in a compote or in this delicious crisp. Serve the dessert with lightly sugared crème fraîche or good vanilla ice cream.

SERVES 8 TO 10

2¼ pounds rhubarb, trimmed and washed

1 cup plus 2 tablespoons granulated sugar

2 pints strawberries, rinsed and hulled

1 cup plus 3 tablespoons all-purpose flour

1 cup packed light brown sugar

2 teaspoons grated fresh ginger

½ teaspoon ground ginger

½ cup coarsely chopped pecans

9 tablespoons unsalted butter, cut into small pieces, at room temperature

1. Preheat the oven to 375°F. If the rhubarb stalks are more than 1 inch thick, split them in half lengthwise. Using a sharp knife, cut the rhubarb stalks into 1-inch pieces.

2. Place the cut rhubarb in a bowl, add the 1 cup granulated sugar, and toss well. Let sit for 20 minutes, or until the rhubarb starts to release some liquid and the sugar is moist.

3. Depending on the size of the strawberries, cut them in half or quarters. Toss with the remaining 2 tablespoons granulated sugar and add to the rhubarb. Add the 3 tablespoons flour and toss gently. Spoon the fruit mixture into a 1½-quart casserole.

4. Combine the remaining 1 cup flour, the brown sugar, fresh and ground ginger, pecans, and butter in a medium bowl. Mix well with your fingertips, crumbling any lumps. Work the mixture gently until it resembles coarse crumbs. Sprinkle the crumb topping evenly over the fruit mixture.

5. Set the dish in the center of the oven. Bake for 50 minutes to 1 hour, or until the topping is golden and the filling is bubbling. Serve warm or at room temperature.

REMARKS The crisp can be prepared up to 8 hours in advance and refrigerated. Bring to room temperature before serving.

■ **Lemon-Herb Grilled Chicken "Under a Brick"** ■ **Lime-Marinated Chicken Kebabs** ■ **Smoked Chicken Wings with Spicy Peanut Sauce** ■ **Lemon- and Thyme-Scented, Apple-Smoked Cornish Hens** ■ **Fresh Fennel with Grilled Fennel Sausage** ■ **Butterflied Leg of Lamb with Shallot, Garlic, and Lemongrass Rub** ■ **Grilled Lamb Chops in Shallot and Herb Butter** ■ **Citrus-Marinated Grilled Pork with Sweet-and-Sour Red Onion Confit** ■ **Grilled Quail with Pineapple Caramel** ■ **Brochettes of Swordfish Grilled in Sesame Marinade** ■ **Grilled Salmon Kebabs in Dill and Mustard Marinade** ■ **Grilled Scallops with Mango and Jicama Salad** ■ **Grilled Shrimp with Mushrooms and Bell Peppers** ■ **Middle-Eastern Char-Grilled Skirt Steaks in a Cumin and Cilantro Marinade** ■ **Grilled Marinated Cremini Mushrooms** ■ **Grilled Eggplant** ■ **Grilled Green Tomatoes in Basil Vinaigrette** ■ **Roasted Red Bell Peppers** ■ **Grilled Tomato Salsa**

I am not quite sure what it is about grilling that makes people embrace the fire with a confidence they would never have with other cooking methods. More than 80 percent of American households own at least one type of grill, but unfortunately too many of them sit unused after a few unsuccessful experiences. No matter how reassuring grill cookbooks try to be, the fact remains that grilling is an inexact science, prompting more questions from my students than any other cooking technique. To begin with, you are dealing with a live fire and its constantly changing dynamics, which means that while it is exciting and fun to grill, it is also very challenging. Temperature varies with the type of grill you own, fuel source, even the weather.

For many cooks outside the developed world, grilling is the only way to produce hot food. Often it is a way to make a living. In China, Morocco, Thailand, Greece, and New York City, street vendors cook on a grill with the most rudimentary resources, producing delicious, succulent morsels of meat, sausage, and poultry. In many countries, including some regions of the United States, grilling lies at the very core of a culture's culinary identity. What would a Malaysian street festival be without skewers of chicken satay or a Mexican fiesta without roasted corn on the cob, or a Texas barbecue without sizzling ribs?

Having grown up in Europe, I came to grilling by participating in the all-American experience, the backyard cookout. When I first met my husband, we would spend many summer weekends with his family in Pennsylvania. On Saturdays we would make our way through the Amish farmers' market, ending up with wonderful fresh corn, juicy vine-ripened tomatoes, plump sausages, and jars of homemade pepper slaw. Our last stop was always at Michael's Meat Locker, where the sides of aged beef hanging made us all think of wonderfully succulent, perfectly grilled steak.

By late afternoon, our friends would arrive, bringing side dishes and dessert, and over a glass of cider or wine, my husband would start the grill. Things rarely went smoothly. Often the fire was too hot, which resulted in charred steaks and overly browned sausages. Other times the fire was not hot enough, and we would stand around wondering what to do. "Let's add more starter fluid," or "It needs more charcoal," or "Take the steak off for a while" were some of the suggestions. But somehow it all worked out, and everyone had a good time. I can still remember the lively conversations, satisfying aroma of searing meat, and sense of well-being that only an outdoor cookout can provide.

That said, most people would love to have their grilled steak or pork chops be juicy and tender rather than something akin to shoe leather; so if you want to grill, it's a good idea to learn some techniques. Successful grilling is determined by some very basic rules that when properly applied will lead to a delicious outcome almost every time.

When buying a grill your first decision is whether to go with charcoal or gas. Nothing beats a charcoal grill for infusing food with the characteristic flavor that comes from the interplay of wood and smoke. Be sure to invest in a big one, since the larger the surface, the more room you have to move foods around and keep them from burning. It also allows you to cook all kinds of additional vegetables to serve alongside the meat or have on hand for another meal.

When using charcoal, be patient and wait until the coals are covered with a fine gray ash before adding the food. Over the years I have been to many cookouts where "let's throw something on the grill" was a recipe for disaster, because the fire was not ready. I have since concluded that waiting for the right moment to put the steak, chicken, or chops on the grill is the key to success.

The next challenge is to choose the right cuts and the grilling technique you plan to use. Uncovered direct grilling is similar to broiling, except that the source of heat is on the bottom. This method is perfect for small cuts of meat, fish steaks, or chops. If you love thick pork chops or double veal chops, be ready to use the grill cover or to create a small oven by tenting the chops with a pie plate or by finishing them in the oven. The indirect method is more like roasting in that the heat from the fire—gas or charcoal—radiates from the sides of the grill but not directly beneath the food. This is the best method for small roasts, whole chickens, or turkeys. Also, once you have achieved a smoky taste, it is safer to finish cooking food indoors or over indirect heat rather than taking the risk of burning your steak or chops by keeping them directly over the fire. Whenever I make a small fire for a quick grill I choose foods that do not require much time on the grill. Best choices are single rib lamb chops, medium-sized shrimp, small fish steaks, or chicken breasts.

Always season assertively when grilling, using plenty of coarse salt and freshly ground pepper. When you've chosen an exceptional piece of meat, these seasonings will allow the true taste to come through. If you're looking for more exotic flavors, spices, rubs, or marinades can turn even chicken parts into a delicious feast.

Now with the great choice of fruit woods, you can vary the flavors by adding aromatic chips or twigs to the fire. To me there is nothing more wonderful than going out into the garden and snipping off some lilac or fresh apple wood twigs to sprinkle over the coals to add dimension to a roast pork or Cornish hens. For those who do not live near an orchard, there is now a wealth of excellent mail order resources available.

Learning when food is done is key to grilling, since the time between when a piece of meat or fish is perfect and when it is overcooked is very short. In the following pages you'll learn several ways to do that. It's very important to have your side dishes ready and made ahead of time, so that you can give all your attention to the grill. Even the pros concede that grilling is an unpredictable art. But when all the theories have been debated and the techniques experimented with, the real purpose of grilling is to have a good time in your backyard, porch, or at the beach. There is something about being outside and smelling the rich aromas of food as it cooks that makes this form of cooking so much fun and enjoyable.

What is the difference between grilling and barbecuing?

We frequently use these terms interchangeably, but in fact they refer to two different techniques.

Grilling is done rather quickly at high heat, either directly over coals or indirectly off to the side. If the grill has a lid, it is kept off. Choose only tender cuts to grill because the cooking is done quickly and does not have time to break down the fibers. When grilling meat, watch it closely so it does not burn.

Barbecuing involves cooking meat very slowly in a covered grill or smoker, surrounding the food in hot smoke until it becomes tender.

I am about to buy my first outdoor grill. Do you recommend charcoal or gas grills?

Grilling on gas and charcoal are very different experiences. Gas is cleaner, simpler, and more predictable, while charcoal grilling is more challenging as well as more work. When it comes to the flavor of the food, I don't think there is any comparison: food cooked properly over hardwood charcoal is far more flavorful. It has that real grill taste that you just cannot get from a gas grill.

What type of charcoal grill do you recommend?

To me, there is only one great charcoal grill, and that is the Weber kettle. It has everything a good charcoal grill needs. You can control the cooking temperature by opening the vents on the bottom of the grill and in the lid. As long as you buy the medium- or large-sized grill, you can easily use either direct or indirect grilling methods.

When you shop for a grill, keep this checklist with you:

- Are the legs sturdy?
- Is the grill made of heavy-gauge metal?

- Does it have a tight-fitting lid with vents in it?
- Does the grill have vents in its base?
- Is the grate hinged or easy to lift so that you can add more coals to the firebox easily?

Some grills have wire side baskets that hold coals for indirect grilling and a shallow ash-catching plate for easy cleaning.

The Weber kettle grill pretty much fits the bill, although older versions have no side baskets. But I don't find that much of a deterrent.

There is room for only a very small charcoal grill on my balcony. Can I grill successfully on one of these small models?

Street food around the world is cooked on small grills with great success. If you watch food vendors on the sidewalk in Vietnam or Thailand, you will see them fan the fire to increase the heat. These small grills, which often are hibachi-style, are very good for grilling small cuts of meat, poultry pieces, and seafood. Because they do not come equipped with lids and because they are just too small, they cannot be used for indirect grilling or for grilling large cuts or whole birds.

What should I be looking for when shopping for a good gas grill?

Heat and more heat. The more BTUs the better—35,000 is good, 40,000 is better, and 60,000 is the best. High BTU means a hotter grill. These grills get sufficiently hot that they can be used uncovered. This means you can sear thick cuts of beef on the grill as well as foods that don't have any fat at all, such as vegetables or fish fillets.

Remember that you are looking for a grill, not an oven. Make sure that it comes with adjustable controls so that you can set it on high,

medium, or low. Three adjustable heating zones are important, too. Many grills come with only two, which I do not consider to be enough. You should be able to move the food around and keep some things hot over a lower heat while others are cooking over high.

A warming rack is another nice feature. This, too, allows you to keep some foods warm while others are grilling. If you want to keep the main course warm while you are serving an appetizer or drinks, this is extremely useful.

Will I get the same results using my built-in stovetop grill as I do grilling outdoors?

Indoor grills are wonderful for preparing low-fat foods, but you will never get that assertive grilled taste that you get from a very hot gas grill or a charcoal grill. When grilling indoors, stick to thin chops, fish fillets, sliced vegetables, and boned chicken breasts.

Recently I've heard that charcoal briquettes are not safe and produce an off taste. Do you agree?

Briquettes are a reliable product, which is good to know since they are so much easier to find than lump charcoal. Briquettes are made of charcoal, coal, and starch and so do not burn as cleanly as lump charcoal, which is nothing more than carbon.

The food will taste fine if cooked over charcoal briquettes, but it will never have the distinctive, pure grilled flavor of food cooked over natural lump charcoal. The irregular pieces are sold under various names, including charwood, lump charcoal, and natural charcoal.

This burns hotter than briquettes and while you may have to wait a little longer before the fire is ready, the natural charcoal gives food fabulous flavor. It does not impart any unpleasant odor, so when the fire dies down, you can add more charcoal without worrying about fumes. This is one of the best things about lump charcoal as far as I am concerned.

If you use briquettes, shop carefully. Some of them are impregnated with chemicals to make them self-lighting. Avoid these at all costs. Stick to known brand names. Inexpensive briquettes can burn "dirty" and smell unpleasant.

Mesquite seems to be the trendy wood for grilling. What is it and where do I find it?

More natural lump charcoal is made from mesquite than from any other wood. This might be because the mesquite tree, considered a "weed tree," grows with little help from human cultivation in arid regions of both North and South America and is easy to gather. Mesquite, which has a light distinctive aroma, is also popular for charcoal because it burns hot and stays hotter longer than other charcoals.

How much charcoal do I need to grill a butterflied leg of lamb or steak to feed four to six people?

For most grilling needs, start with about 5 pounds of charcoal. If you also plan to grill some shrimp and vegetables for appetizers, and will be grilling for longer than 45 minutes, you will need more.

To determine how many coals to light for direct-heat grilling, lay the charcoal in a single layer under the area where the food will be. Toss in a few extras chunks for good measure, and you have your fuel. If you will be grilling the food over indirect heat (more on this later in the chapter), you will probably need more charcoal. Mentally divide your grill into three sections. In one outside section, pile the coals 4 to 5 inches deep. Create a middle section with one layer of coals. Leave a third of the grill without coals. This allows you to cook food at different temperatures as required.

What is the best way to light a charcoal fire?

If your grill is near an electrical outlet, electric starters work well. They are inexpensive and easy to find at hardware stores. Unfortunately, these devices have a short life span—they break easily, particularly if you leave them in the grill for more than 20 minutes. It's good to have more than one on hand, since they tend to break at the most inconvenient times. (For this same reason, I recommend you have an extra tank of propane gas on hand if you use a gas grill!)

You might also try the chimney, which is reliable and very popular. If you like to grill as much as I do, you should have one. These are cylindrical metal containers with room on the bottom for crumpled newspapers and on the top for charcoal. The newspaper easily ignites, which in turn ignites the charcoal. When the coals at the top of the chimney are covered with light gray ash, tip them out of the chimney into the firebox of the grill.

What about using starter fluid to light charcoal?

I stay away from it when I'm at home, but when I am camping—one of my favorite things to do—or when we picnic down by the river near my house, I use it. If you let it burn off, it's okay. Follow the directions on the can carefully. Give the fluid time to seep into the coals before you light them and never squeeze any fluid onto hot coals. Once the coals are lit, they will have to burn for at least 30 minutes to reach the correct temperature. By then, any noxious fumes in the fluid will be long gone.

I hear about "direct" and "indirect" grilling. This sounds confusing. What do they mean?

Direct grilling is exactly what it implies. You put the food directly over the hot coals, which, for this kind of cooking, can range from hot to medium-hot. Direct grilling is best for steaks, chops, chicken breasts, fish steaks, and vegetables—in other words, foods that cook quickly and need little time on the grill.

Indirect grilling is really a form of roasting. It does, however, add a nice grilled flavor. I usually start by searing the food directly over hot coals (direct grilling) and then move it to a cooler part of the grill to finish cooking. Once the food is moved off the coals, I cover the grill and keep the vents open. Indirect grilling works best for foods such as loin of pork, bone-in leg of lamb, or a whole turkey or chicken.

How can I tell when the coals are ready?

Unfortunately, there's no foolproof method— like any other cooking technique, the more you do it, the better you become. Practice is important, but so is patience. Most fires made from charcoal can take as long as 40 minutes until they are ready. A good rule of thumb is to count on 35 to 40 minutes for a hot fire, 45 minutes for a medium fire, and about 50 minutes if you want a low fire.

The recipe should tell you how intense the fire should be. Watch the coals and when they are covered with a fine gray ash, check their temperature by using the "hand test": Hold your hand 5 inches above the coals and if you can hold it for 6 seconds before yanking it away, the fire is low; if you can hold it over the coals for only 5 seconds, the fire is medium-hot; and 1 or 2 seconds means a very hot fire.

TIP Patience is a virtue, but by being too careful, you may find that the fire has literally burned away before you have even begun cooking! If this happens, add a few more coals and give the fire another 10 to 15 minutes to regain its proper temperature.

How do I prepare the grill for indirect grilling?

Most cookbooks suggest that you make two piles of coals on opposite sides of the grill and leave a space in between them for a drip pan. Each pile of coals is ignited, and the food is positioned over the drip pan.

I usually don't do this. Instead, I arrange the coals on one side of the grill, put the food on the other side, and rarely bother with a drip pan. Although you may lose pan juices—which are minimal at best—my technique is simpler and much more straightforward. Remember that you can always divide the smoldering coals and set a drip pan between them, which is a useful technique when grilling a turkey or large roast.

Once you try indirect grilling, it will begin to make sense and you won't find it difficult. In fact, it will expand your grilling repertoire.

Can I use a gas grill for indirect grilling?

Absolutely, as long as you can turn off part of the grill. The best gas grills come with three zones, or burners, which allows plenty of choices. Even if your gas grill has only two burners, you can grill indirectly by turning off one element and putting the food on that side.

The food on my gas grill seems to cook slowly and does not develop a true "grill flavor." How do I get the food going? Can I sprinkle it with oil or is that dangerous?

For years I had the same problem. I realized it was because my gas grill just did not get hot enough. Even when I used marinades with large quantities of oil, the food didn't taste grilled. After a bit of research I discovered that in order to be effective, the gas grill must heat up to 600° or 700°F, which means the grill should have at least 35,000 BTU. If your grill does not generate enough heat to begin with, it may not maintain the heat when the lid is opened, resulting in food that is baked, rather than grilled.

As far as using oil while grilling to "get the food going," all you will accomplish is flare-ups—which are not only dangerous, but result in burned, bitter-tasting food.

I like the taste of smoked food and have experimented with some wood chips, but I am still not exactly sure how to use them.

Start by soaking the wood chips for 20 to 30 minutes in a bucket or similar container. This will allow them to smoke before they burn. Then make packages from heavy-duty foil with about two handfuls of wet chips. Perforate the packages in two or three places and set them on top of the coals. The size of the food dictates how many foil packages you will need. For example, if you are grilling a small turkey, you will need at least two packages of chips, while if you are grilling a butterflied leg of lamb, one may be enough. When you grill something like chicken breasts, quail, or fish steaks, which cook quickly, simply scatter the wet wood chips directly over the hot coals—this will impart the smoky flavor you're after.

When should I add wood chips to the grill?

This depends on two factors. The first is the choice of chips; some impart a more intense fla-

vor than others—particularly hickory. The second factor is the size of the piece of meat, poultry, or fish you are grilling. For large cuts of meat, I add the wood chips (wrapped in foil packages) 20 to 30 minutes into the grilling process so the smoke does not overwhelm the food. I usually add more packages once or twice before the food is done.

For small cuts, such as chicken breasts, quail, or fish steaks, I sprinkle wet chips directly on the coals right at the beginning, because the grilling time is so short.

The taste of hickory can be overwhelming. What other wood chips do you recommend?

If you don't care for hickory, you have other wonderful choices and can change them seasonally. For instance, in the cold winters of New England, I use heavier woods such as oak, apple, and maple for more robust foods. Toward spring, I switch to lighter woods such as lilac, alder, and cherry. Alder and mesquite are great for summer grilling because of their pleasingly mild flavor. Dried herb twigs, such as rosemary and fennel stalks, are good choices as well.

Do wood chips impart enough smoke to actually smoke food?

Using wood chips and hot coals to grill food is not the same as smoking food, which is a cool cooking method. The food will taste smoky, but it will be grilled, not smoked.

To smoke food, you need to set aside a lot of time—usually 5 or 6 hours—and cook the food over very low coals. Be prepared to tend the fire closely. It's important to keep the coals at 140° to 150°F and add soaked chunks of hardwood and wood chips every 20 to 25 minutes. Add only enough to produce smoke, but not so many that you risk extinguishing the fire.

Additionally, you will have to add live (already lit) coals to the fire every 45 minutes or so. That means you need a separate grill or chimney filled with smoldering coals because the key to proper cold smoking is to maintain an even temperature at all times.

If you like to smoke foods, consider investing in a commercially made smoker, which I find to be a great tool.

When a recipe calls for grilling, can I use a broiler instead?

The broiler works best for foods with some fat, such as pieces of chicken on the bone or chops. It does not work as well for delicate foods such as vegetables, scallops, and skinless fish fillets. Basically grilling and broiling are two different cooking techniques. One cooks the food from below, the other from above, so there will be a difference in taste and texture. Also grilling lends food a very special "grilled" flavor, which broiling does not.

What is the purpose of marinating meats and seafood before grilling?

Marinades are popular because they are fun to concoct and add a certain flavor dimension to the food. But, unless they are packed with intensely flavored herbs and spices (hot peppers, cumin, cardamom, cinnamon, cloves, coriander, and so on), their flavor tends to dissipate during cooking.

Which foods should be marinated? Does marinating improve the flavor?

Traditionally, marinades have been used in countries where the quality of the raw ingredients (fish, poultry, meat) was not always of utmost freshness. The marinades were used to mask or perk up dull flavors. This is not the case today, although we still tend to marinate lesser cuts of meat, especially flank and skirt steak and a butterflied leg of lamb.

A good rule of thumb is that the higher the quality of the raw ingredient, the less marinating it needs. There is nothing more wonderful than tender baby lamb chops simply enhanced with a touch of rosemary and some garlic, or a great steak properly seasoned with coarse salt and freshly ground pepper before it's grilled over hot coals. Of course, with truly fresh fish, less is more—a grinding of sea salt and black pepper and a squeeze of fresh lemon is all it needs. This is not a hard-and-fast-rule. If you prepare chicken or lamb often, marinades are good ways to add a spectrum of tastes.

Ironically, marinades can have an adverse effect on seafood and fish. If these are marinated for too long, they become dry and rubbery. While meat and poultry can withstand hours in a marinade, seafood and fish should be removed after 30 minutes.

Fish steaks, such as swordfish and tuna, are good when marinated for short periods of time, but I prefer salmon simply grilled and lightly smoked with wood chips, served with an interesting sauce on the side.

TIP Don't be tempted to use the marinade as a sauce unless you cook the marinade, too. This means bringing it to a boil and then letting it simmer briskly for at least 5 minutes to destroy any harmful bacteria that the raw food might have imparted. For this same reason, don't baste food with the marinade in which it has soaked except during the very early stages of cooking.

If I am in a hurry and have no time to plan ahead, can I marinate something for 1 or 2 hours even if a recipe calls for 12 to 14 hours?

Depending on the food, even short periods of marinating will give you excellent results; in fact fish and shellfish only need 30 minutes. In recipes that call for long marinating times in the refrigerator, you can get pretty good results by marinating at room temperature for 1 to 3 hours, as long the temperature of the kitchen does not exceed 65°F.

TIP If you want to marinate for a short period of time, it is best to use yogurt-based marinades in terms of taste and texture. Be sure to use yogurt with a live, active bacterial culture.

Recipes usually say to marinate in nonreactive pans. What is does nonreactive mean?

A nonreactive pan is one that will not react with acidic ingredients, which include vinegar, tomatoes, citrus juice, and wine, all commonly used in marinades. The most common reactive containers are non-anodized aluminum, un-lined copper, and cast iron, all of which should be avoided. They can impart a metallic taste to the food and cause it to darken. A pan with an aluminum core is fine for marinating if it is coated with stainless steel. Glass, ceramic, and plastic are good materials for containers used to hold marinades.

Over the years, I have marinated in many different types of containers and have become a fan of zippered plastic bags. Once the food and the marinade are enclosed in the bag, they mingle in close quarters. It's easy to turn the food, allowing you to distribute the marinade evenly. Also the pliable bag fits more easily in a crowded refrigerator.

If I put a steak or chicken on the grill and there is a flare-up, should I move it to a cooler part of the grill or remove it entirely?

I suggest taking it off the fire right away and giving the fire time to cool down a little. Even if you move it to a cooler part of the grill, it will still cook and possibly burn. It will also throw off your timing. This is why I feel so strongly about exercising patience and waiting for the coals to reach the correct temperature. They should be covered with gray-white ash before starting to grill. If you are using a gas grill and there is a flare-up, it is best to remove the food and turn down the heat.

Can every vegetable be grilled?

Most vegetables are delicious grilled while a few fare less well. My favorites are peppers, zucchini, onions, eggplant, and mushrooms. I am not a fan of potatoes, leeks, and winter squash, such as butternut, but they too will soon join the ranks of the all-popular classics. As with everything, I suppose, it's a matter of personal taste.

I have tried to cook spareribs on the grill, but always end up with a charred mess. What is the secret?

There are two methods that will allow you to grill spareribs so that the meat is tender but the ribs are not charred. The first is to roast the ribs in a 350°F oven for about 45 minutes to cook them, then place the racks directly over medium-high coals for about 15 minutes, until brown and crisp. The other method is to grill them over low indirect heat in a covered grill for about 45 minutes before finishing them over direct heat for the same 15 minutes.

TIP Never brush barbecue sauce on the ribs until the last 2 minutes of cooking. The sugar and tomatoes in the sauce will quickly caramelize and burn the surface of the meat. Even when you apply the sauce during the final minutes of grilling, watch the ribs very carefully to avoid charring.

What is the best way to cook chicken on the grill—whole, halved, or in pieces?

My two favorite ways are whole or cut in half and grilled "under a brick" (see page 356). When I grill a whole chicken, I cook it first over indirect heat for about 35 minutes and then set it directly over medium-high coals to continue cooking until the internal temperature of the dark meat is 165°F. Then I remove it from the grill, cover it loosely with foil to keep warm, and let it rest for 10 to 15 minutes before serving. During this time, the internal temperature of the dark meat will rise to the correct 180°F.

If you have your heart set on grilling cut-up, bone-in chicken pieces, start them over medium-high direct heat, turning them once or twice until the skin is browned. Move them to the cooler side of the grill for 15 to 20 minutes, or until cooked through. Quickly sear them again over direct heat, if necessary, for a crispy finish.

I keep reading that cutting into meat causes it to lose its juices. Is this true?

Certain cuts of meat such as skirt and flank steaks as well as a butterflied leg of lamb can be tested by cutting into them. You may lose some juice, but there should be no loss of flavor. Cutting into poultry is also not a problem, but I never cut into smaller cuts of meat, such as steaks and chops. Instead I use a meat thermometer, which has become the "tool of the grill" or the tip of the knife method, which will give you an accurate reading every time.

TIP Insert the tip of a sharp paring knife into the thickest part of a piece of meat, chicken, or fish. Test it against the inside of your wrist (the same place you test the heat of the milk in a baby's bottle). If it feels cold, the food is still raw; if it's just warm, it is medium-rare; and if the tip of the knife feels hot, the food is cooked through and may actually be overdone.

I am always nervous when I grill fish because I can never tell when it's done.

It takes experience and a lot of overcooked and undercooked fish before you learn how to tell when fish is perfectly cooked. Never trust the exact times given in a recipe, because so much depends on the heat of the grill. When grilling fish steaks, remove them from the grill at about the time you think they may be done. Once off the fire, use the "tip of the knife" method employed by all professional chefs to determine doneness. For salmon, tuna, and swordfish you want the fish to be medium-rare.

This is not the optimum method for a whole fish, which should be opaque all the way through. Always test a whole fish in a couple of places and especially near the bone where a little translucency is okay.

What is the best way to grill a whole fish?

Unless you have incredible expertise, a whole fish is challenging to cook on the grill, especially if it weighs more than 2 to 2½ pounds. You can roast a fish that is wrapped in foil fairly easily, because you can easily remove it from the grill and test the flesh for doneness. Also, the fish will not stick.

My salmon steaks or fillets tend to fall apart on the grill. What's the secret to keeping them whole?

If you want your grilled salmon to look pretty as well as taste delicious, make sure that your fillets or steaks (either cut is okay in this case) still have their skin attached. Also, cook them through almost all the way before turning them. If you turn them more than once, they are sure to fall apart.

I have heard you can cook food buried in the ashes. Is this safe when you use charcoal briquettes?

When the charcoal has burned down to the point of ashes, it is quite safe to cook foods nestled in them. Whatever chemicals may have been in the charcoal have burned off long ago. Unless the food has a protective skin (like a potato or corn on the cob), wrap it in heavy-duty aluminum foil before burying it in the ashes.

Is it necessary to clean the grill after each use?

It depends on what grill you use. A charcoal grill should not be emptied of ashes since they allow for better conduction of heat. However, if the ashes are wet, you are better off starting from scratch. As for the grill itself, a quick scrubbing with a grill brush will do. When using a gas grill, be sure to scrape food particles off the rack every time you use the grill.

Lemon-Herb Grilled Chicken "Under a Brick"

The method of cooking chicken under a brick is popular in many countries around the Mediterranean. The Italians call it Chicken Fra Diabolo, in Spain it is Pollo Planchado, and in Russia it is called Truck Chicken, "because the chicken looks like it has been run over by a truck." No matter, the result is delicious and a great addition to one's summer cooking repertory. You can use Cornish hens with equally good results.

SERVES 2 TO 4

2 to 4 small poussins (about 1¼ pounds each)

MARINADE

1 tablespoon soy sauce

Juice of 1 large lemon or lime

1 tablespoon minced fresh thyme

1 tablespoon minced fresh rosemary

3 large garlic cloves, smashed

⅓ cup fruity olive oil

1 teaspoon coarsely ground black pepper

2 teaspoons diced serrano chile, optional

2 to 4 sprigs fresh thyme

2 to 4 tiny sprigs fresh rosemary

Salt and freshly ground black pepper

Large pinch of cayenne pepper

Lemon wedges, a sprinkling of *fleur de sel*, rosemary sprigs, for garnish

1. Split the chickens in half and cut off the backbone. Place the chicken between 2 sheets of waxed paper and pound until flattened evenly. Set aside.

2. Combine all the marinade ingredients. Transfer to one or two large zippered plastic bags. Add the chickens, turn to coat, and marinate for at least 4 hours or overnight.

3. The next day, remove the chickens from the marinade and dry thoroughly with paper towels. Carefully lift the skin, separating it from the breast meat without tearing, and insert some fresh minced thyme and rosemary under the skin. Set aside.

4. Heat a gas grill to medium-high. Place the chickens skin side down on the grill rack and top each half with a brick wrapped in foil. Grill for 10 to 12 minutes, or until the skin is nicely browned but not burned.

5. Remove the bricks, turn the chickens over and again top with the bricks. Grill for another 12 minutes, or until cooked through but still juicy. Transfer the chickens to a serving platter, season with salt and pepper, and a sprinkling of cayenne. Garnish with a sprinkle of *fleur de sel*, quartered lemons, and rosemary sprigs, and serve hot.

REMARKS Be sure to check the chicken after the first 5 minutes. If the skin seems to be cooking too quickly, turn off one side of the grill and move the chicken to the cooler side; return the chicken to the hot part of the grill once it has been turned over.

Lime-Marinated Chicken Kebabs

I don't know of any grilled food that is more popular than chicken, and deservedly so. Chicken cooked on the grill is both versatile and satisfying. Here I use just the thighs, but you can also add some drumsticks and drumettes, the fleshy section of the wing. A teaspoon of turmeric or a pinch of real saffron will add a brilliant yellow color to the chicken, which makes for an interesting change.

SERVES 6 TO 8

3 medium onions, coarsely chopped

1 cup fresh lime juice

1 cup extra virgin olive oil

2 cups cilantro leaves and stems

Coarse salt and freshly ground black pepper

½ teaspoon turmeric

Large pinch of powdered saffron, optional

16 to 18 boneless chicken thighs

1. In a food processor combine the onions, lime juice, olive oil, and cilantro. Puree until blended but still coarse. Season with coarse salt, turmeric, saffron, and lots of black pepper. Transfer the mixture to a large zippered plastic bag. Add the chicken and refrigerate for 4 to 6 hours or overnight. Let the chicken return to room temperature 30 minutes before grilling. Drain and scrape off the marinade.

2. Make a charcoal fire on one side of the grill and when the coals are white, place the well-drained chicken pieces directly over the coals. Grill for 5 minutes on each side, or until the thighs are nicely browned but not charred. Transfer to the cooler side of the grill, cover, and continue to cook for another 10 to 12 minutes. Serve hot, accompanied by a platter of grilled peppers of assorted colors and Charcoal-Grilled Eggplants with Lemon-Scallion Mayonnaise (page 126).

Smoked Chicken Wings with Spicy Peanut Sauce

Whenever I grill, I think of various ways to use the hot coals. Vegetables or chicken wings are delicious served as part of a cookout or as finger food with drinks for dinner the next day. If you cannot get hickory chips, use any other fruitwood or omit it altogether.

SERVES 4

1 medium onion, quartered

4 large garlic cloves

2 tablespoons peeled fresh ginger

1 small jalapeño pepper

2 cups plain yogurt

½ to 1 tablespoon tandoori seasoning,
   (see Sources, page 397)

2 teaspoons ground cumin

Coarse salt and freshly ground black pepper

2 cups hickory chips, soaked in water for
   1 hour

20 chicken wings, cut in half at joint and
   tips removed

Spicy Peanut Sauce (recipe follows)

1. Combine the onion, garlic, ginger, and jalapeño in a food processor and grind to a fine paste. Add the yogurt, tandoori seasoning, and cumin and process until well blended. Transfer to a large zippered plastic bag, add the chicken wings, and seal the bag. Refrigerate for 6 hours or overnight, turning the bag often.

2. Prepare the grill with the charcoal placed to one side only. Open all the vents.

3. When the coals are white, remove the wings from the marinade and scrape off any bits. Sprinkle the wings with salt and pepper and place on the grill directly over the cool side of the grill. Drain the hickory chips and add to the coals. Cover and continue to grill for 15 to 20 minutes, or until the juices run pale yellow.

4. Transfer the wings to a serving platter and serve hot with individual bowls of warm peanut sauce on side.

Spicy Peanut Sauce

1 tablespoon peanut oil

2 teaspoons minced garlic

2 teaspoons minced peeled fresh ginger

2 tablespoons tomato paste

⅔ cup chicken broth

1½ teaspoons Chinese chili paste

2 tablespoons hoisin sauce

2 tablespoons creamy peanut butter

2 tablespoons toasted sesame oil

Heat the peanut oil over low heat in a skillet. Add the garlic, ginger, and tomato paste and cook for 1 minute. Add the broth, 1 teaspoon of the chili paste, the hoisin sauce, and peanut butter, whisk until well blended, and simmer for 3 minutes. Add the sesame oil and the remaining chili paste and keep warm.

Cornish hens each serve one person nicely and are perfect dinner party food. They make a beautiful presentation and are easier to grill than regular-sized chickens because they take less time to cook. Fresh lilac or apple wood added to the coals infuses the birds with a lovely flavor. Serve with a side dish of grilled vegetables. For this recipe, you will need both charcoal briquettes and some fresh apple wood.

SERVES 4

4 small whole Cornish hens (about 1 to 1¼ pounds each)

Juice of 1 large lemon

2 large garlic cloves, mashed

2 tablespoons minced fresh thyme leaves, plus sprigs for garnish

2 tablespoons minced fresh flat-leaf parsley

1 teaspoon coarsely ground black pepper

6 tablespoons extra virgin olive oil

Coarse salt

1. Marinate the hens: Place the hens in a large zippered plastic bag. In a small bowl, combine the lemon juice, garlic, thyme, parsley, and pepper. Whisk in the oil and pour the marinade over the hens. Seal the bag, place in a shallow dish, and refrigerate overnight, turning the hens in the marinade several times.

2. Prepare the fire: Use a medium-sized charcoal grill. Open all vents. Place 30 briquettes to one side of the lower grill and, using an electric or cylindrical starter, ignite the charcoal. Set a rectangular, disposable drip pan beside the coals and position the cooking grill in the kettle with one handle directly over the pile of coals. This will allow you to add briquettes through the opening by the grill handle during smoking.

3. Remove the hens from the marinade, truss them, and season with coarse salt. Place the hens on the grill, breast side up, directly over the drip pan. Add a few twigs of apple wood to the pile of coals, cover the kettle, and "roast" the hens for 1 hour, or until the juices run clear and a meat thermometer registers an internal temperature of 165°F. The hens will need no basting or turning, but every 15 minutes add 6 to 8 briquettes and a few twigs of apple wood to the pile of burning coals, through the opening on the cooking grill.

4. When the hens are done, transfer them to a cutting board and let rest for 5 minutes. Cut the hens in half and place 2 halves on each of 4 serving plates. Garnish with fresh thyme and serve either warm or at room temperature.

Fresh Fennel with Grilled Fennel Sausage

Fennel-flavored sausage has a natural affinity to the sweet and slightly licorice taste of fresh fennel bulbs. Together they make a lovely and easy supper course when served with crusty peasant bread or buttery mashed potatoes. I like to poach the sausage prior to grilling; this removes much of the fat and also eliminates flare-up. However, if the sausage is very lean, you can put it directly on the grill.

SERVES 4

1½ pounds sweet Italian fennel sausage

2 small fennel bulbs, tops removed, bulbs quartered

2 to 3 tablespoons extra virgin olive oil

Coarse salt and freshly ground black pepper

2 tablespoons coarsely chopped flat-leaf parsley

1. In a deep skillet, combine the fennel sausage with water to cover. Bring to a boil, reduce the heat, and poach the sausage for 3 minutes. Drain and reserve.

2. In a large saucepan, bring salted water to a boil. Add the fennel pieces, return the water to a boil, reduce the heat, and simmer for 3 minutes. Drain and set aside.

3. Preheat a gas grill. Place the fennel on a rack and sprinkle very lightly with olive oil, salt, and pepper. Transfer to the grill together with the sausage. Cover and grill over medium-hot heat for 5 minutes on each side, or until nicely browned.

4. Transfer the sausage and fennel to a serving dish. Drizzle with the remaining olive oil and parsley and serve accompanied by crusty bread or garlic mashed potatoes.

REMARKS Two grilled red bell peppers cut into ½-inch slices are a delicious and colorful addition to this simple dish, and excellent olive oil is a must!

Butterflied Leg of Lamb with Shallot, Garlic, and Lemongrass Rub

Lamb is a wonderful meat for grilling, and it takes well to many marinades. Make sure that the meat is actually butterflied and not just boned, and that the pieces are as evenly thick as possible. You are looking for a thickness of 1 to 2 inches. You can then cut the lamb into three to four sections, which allows you to remove the thinner pieces off the grill as they are done.

SERVES 5 TO 6

1 lemongrass stalk (bottom 6 to 7 inches)

3 large shallots, coarsely chopped

5 large garlic cloves, coarsely chopped

1 jalapeño pepper, coarsely chopped

2 tablespoons chopped fresh oregano, or 1 teaspoon dried

½ cup peanut or grapeseed oil

3 tablespoons Asian sesame oil

3 tablespoons Thai fish sauce

1 tablespoon sugar

1 tablespoon coarsely ground black pepper

4- to 5-pound butterflied leg of lamb

1. Combine the lemongrass, shallots, garlic, jalapeño, oregano, peanut oil, sesame oil, and fish sauce in a food processor and blend until finely minced. Add the sugar and pepper and blend well.

2. Rub the lamb thoroughly with the paste and place in a zippered plastic bag. Marinate for 6 hours, or overnight.

3. Build a fire on one side of a grill that can be covered. Remove the lamb from the marinade and pat it dry with paper towels. Place the lamb directly over the hot coals and sear until well browned, 3 to 4 minutes.

4. Move the lamb to the cool part of the grill. Cover, leaving the vents open, and cook for 15 to 20 minutes. After 10 minutes check the thinner pieces by cutting into one and if done, remove from the grill.

5. Remove the rest of the lamb from the grill when it is done to your liking. Let the meat rest for 5 minutes before serving. Serve accompanied by the Chick Pea, Tomato, and Cilantro Salad (page 287).

REMARK If you are using an instant-read thermometer, it should read 135°F for medium-rare.

Grilled Lamb Chops in Shallot and Herb Butter

A juicy grilled lamb chop needs little in the way of a sauce. However, the flavor is highly enhanced by this compound butter that melts nicely into the chop. You may vary the herb, keeping in mind that lamb has a particular affinity to character herbs such as rosemary, sage, oregano, and of course, garlic and shallots. Serve the chops with Mascarpone and Chive Mashed Potatoes (page 139) or Braised Leeks with Shiitake Mushrooms (page 131).

SERVES 2

6 tablespoons unsalted butter, softened
2 tablespoons minced shallots
2 tablespoon minced flat-leaf parsley
2 teaspoons minced rosemary
1 large garlic clove, minced
Coarse salt and freshly ground black pepper
4 double loin lamb chops, cut 1¼ to 1½ inches thick
sprigs of fresh rosemary

1. Combine the softened butter, shallots, parsley, rosemary, and garlic in a small bowl. Mash with a fork to blend thoroughly. Season with salt and pepper. Refrigerate for 30 minutes.

2. Bring water to a simmer in a 2-quart saucepan, set a heavy 10-inch dinner plate on top of the pan, and put half of the herb butter in it. Keep warm over low heat.

3. Preheat a gas barbeque grill to 500° or 600°F. Place the chops on the grill and cook for 2 to 3 minutes on each side. Be careful not to char them. Check for doneness with an instant-read thermometer: the chops should have an internal temperature of 120°F. If they are well browned and not cooked to medium-rare, turn off one side of the grill and place the chops on the cool side for another 2 to 3 minutes, or until done. Remove from the heat and season with salt and pepper.

4. Transfer the chops to the plate with the melted herb butter, cover tightly with foil, and let the chops absorb the butter, about 2 minutes. Serve at once, topped with the remaining herb butter and garnished with sprigs of rosemary.

Citrus-Marinated Grilled Pork with Sweet-and-Sour Red Onion Confit

Pork takes beautifully to citrus and spices. I particularly like the shoulder butt, which is an inexpensive cut usually available in Asian markets and German grocery stores. Grilled over fruitwood and served with melted onions, it is a wonderful early fall dish. The onions can be prepared several days ahead and reheated. The pork roast can be grilled 2 or 3 hours ahead of time and served at room temperature. Depending on the season, a side dish of Puree of Sweet Potato and Carrots (page 143), Roasted Vidalia Onions (page 136), or a plateful of grilled shiitake mushrooms would complete this dish beautifully.

SERVES 4 TO 5

⅓ cup olive oil

Juice of 1 orange

Juice of ½ lemon

1½ teaspoons dried oregano

1 teaspoon ground cinnamon

½ teaspoon ground coriander

½ teaspoon ground cardamom

Coarse salt and freshly ground black pepper

2 medium onions, thinly sliced

3 large garlic cloves, minced

1 tablespoon minced peeled fresh ginger

2½- to 2¾-pound pork shoulder butt, rolled and tied or 2¾-pound boned loin of pork, rolled and tied

Sprigs of fresh thyme

Red Onion Confit (recipe follows)

1. In a small bowl, combine the olive oil, orange juice, lemon juice, oregano, cinnamon, coriander, cardamom, and salt and pepper. Whisk until well blended. Add the onions, garlic, and ginger and stir to mix. Place the pork butt in a large zippered plastic bag, pour the marinade over the pork, and seal the bag. Set the bag in a shallow dish and refrigerate for 24 hours, turning the pork several times in the marinade.

2. The next day, remove the pork from the marinade and dry thoroughly on paper towels. Strain the marinade and reserve.

3. Prepare the charcoal grill: Place charcoal briquettes or charwood on one side of the grill. When the coals are very hot and white, divide in half and carefully push an equal amount to each side of the grill. Set a disposable rectangular pan, slightly larger than the pork butt, in the center of the lower grill between the piles of coals. Position the cooking grill in the kettle with the handles directly over each pile of coals. This will allow you to add briquettes through the openings by the grill handles during "roasting."

4. Sprinkle the pork butt with salt and place it on the center of the cooking grill directly over the roasting pan. Add a few green twigs of lilac or apple wood to each pile of coals, cover the kettle, and cook the pork for about 1 hour 10 minutes, or to an internal temperature of 155°F on a meat thermometer. Every 15 to 20 minutes, add a little more charcoal and a few twigs of wood to each pile of burning coals. Baste often with the reserved marinade; stop basting at least 5 minutes before the meat is done, so no "raw" marinade is left on the meat.

5. When the pork is done, transfer to a carving board and let rest for 5 minutes before carving. Reheat the red onion confit.

6. Cut the pork butt crosswise into ½-inch slices and place in an overlapping pattern on a serving platter. Garnish with the thyme and serve warm or at room temperature with the red onion confit on the side.

REMARKS You can use other fruit woods, such as alder or cherry. These come in chips and are easy to obtain through mail order.

Red Onion Confit

SERVES 4 TO 5

3 tablespoons rendered duck fat or
  2 tablespoons butter and 2 tablespoons
  corn oil

6 large red onions, quartered and thinly sliced

2 teaspoons sugar

2 tablespoons fresh thyme leaves

Salt and freshly ground black pepper

1 to 2 tablespoons sherry vinegar

1. In a nonreactive, large heavy skillet, heat the duck fat or a mixture of butter and oil over high heat. Add the red onions, sprinkle with the sugar, and cook for 3 to 4 minutes, stirring constantly, until the onions begin to brown.

2. Reduce the heat to low, add the thyme, and season with salt and pepper. Continue to cook, partially covered, until the onions are soft and caramelized, 40 to 45 minutes.

3. Add the sherry vinegar to the onions and cook, stirring often, until it has evaporated, 1 to 2 minutes. Set aside at room temperature for up to 3 hours or refrigerate in a covered container for up to 1 week.

REMARK Duck fat packed by D'Artagnan is now widely available in many supermarkets and most specialty shops.

Brochettes of Swordfish Grilled in Sesame Marinade

To me, swordfish tastes best grilled. Here it is marinated in a teriyaki-like marinade and quickly grilled. A quick sauté of baby bok choy with red peppers or the Avocado Salad on page 109 and couscous tossed with cilantro make perfect accompaniments.

SERVES 6

¼ cup soy sauce

¼ cup rice vinegar

1 tablespoon minced peeled fresh ginger

2 large garlic cloves, minced

1 tablespoon sugar

1 tablespoon minced jalapeño pepper

2 tablespoons minced lemongrass, optional

⅓ cup fruity olive oil

2 tablespoons toasted sesame oil

3 to 6 drops Tabasco sauce

2½ to 3 pounds swordfish steaks cut into 1-inch cubes

2 bell peppers (a mix of red, yellow, orange, or green)

1 large white onion, cut into 1¼-inch cubes

Coarse salt and freshly ground black pepper

Small leaves of fresh cilantro

1. Combine the soy sauce, vinegar, ginger, garlic, sugar, jalapeño, and lemongrass in a medium mixing bowl. Whisk in the olive and sesame oils in a slow stream. Add the Tabasco and swordfish cubes and marinate for 2 to 4 hours. While the swordfish is marinating, soak 6 wooden skewers in water.

2. Prepare a hot fire in a charcoal grill. Remove the swordfish from the marinade and thread 4 cubes, alternating with the bell peppers and onion, onto each wooden skewer. Sprinkle with a little salt and pepper. Grill the swordfish brochettes over very hot coals 3 to 4 minutes per side, or until browned outside and almost opaque in the center. (Test by removing one piece of swordfish and checking it for doneness.)

3. Transfer the brochettes to serving plates and garnish with cilantro.

Grilled Salmon Kebabs in Dill and Mustard Marinade

Now that good fresh salmon is available everywhere, I find that I am always looking for new and interesting ways to prepare this fish. Here the salmon is marinated and grilled on skewers. Depending on the season, I like to serve the kebabs with sautéed cucumbers, a few simply boiled potatoes, and some roasted beets. In the summer, a cool cucumber and radish salad would make a lovely side dish as well.

SERVES 4 TO 5

1 large bunch of dill, large stems removed, dill
    coarsely chopped

¾ cup peanut oil

Juice of 1 large lemon

1 cup sliced scallions

1½ tablespoons sugar

1 heaping tablespoon Dijon mustard

1 teaspoon coarsely cracked black pepper

1 teaspoon ground coriander

2 pounds boneless, skinless center-cut salmon
    fillets, cut into 1-inch cubes

1 large red onion, cut into 1¼-inch cubes

Coarse salt and freshly ground black pepper

Spigs of dill

1. In a food processor combine all the marinade ingredients and puree the mixture until smooth. Transfer to a zippered plastic bag. Add the salmon cubes and coat well in the marinade. Chill for 3 to 4 hours.

2. When ready to grill, remove the salmon cubes from the marinade and wipe dry with paper towels. Skewer the fish cubes onto metal or bamboo skewers, alternating with pieces of red onion.

3. Grill the fish for a total of 6 to 8 minutes, turning the skewers after 3 minutes. The kebabs should be nicely browned but not charred. Test for doneness with the tip of a sharp paring knife: it should come out warm, not hot. Season with salt and pepper.

4. Remove the kebabs to plates and garnish with dill sprigs.

REMARKS If using bamboo skewers, remember to soak them in water for at least 30 minutes before using.

Grilled Scallops with Mango and Jicama Salad

Mangoes and scallops are a wonderful combination and they are in perfect harmony in this rather sweet and spicy salad, which I like to serve with a side dish of grilled corn on the cob. Start by making the mango salad, then let it chill while you prepare the scallops.

SERVES 4 TO 5

1½ pounds large sea scallops

1 tablespoon grated lime zest

Juice of 1 lime

Juice of 1 orange

¼ cup grapeseed oil

2 tablespoons Thai fish sauce

2 teaspoons Thai chili sauce

2 large garlic cloves, crushed

Mango and Jicama Salad (recipe follows)

Whole mint leaves, cilantro leaves, or whole chives

I. Combine the scallops with the lime zest, lime juice, orange juice, grapeseed oil, fish sauce, chili sauce, and garlic. Toss to mix. Cover and refrigerate for 45 to 60 minutes.

2. Preheat a gas grill. Remove the scallops from the marinade and grill for 3 minutes on one side. Turn over and grill for 2 minutes on the other side. Do not overcook. Remove to a platter and season lightly with salt.

3. Place a mound of mango salad on individual serving plates and top with 3 to 4 scallops. Garnish with mint or cilantro leaves or whole chives.

Mango and Jicama Salad

SERVES 4 TO 5

2 ripe mangoes, peeled and cubed

2 cups finely diced jicama

Juice of 1 orange

1 fresh hot red chili pepper, finely diced (about 1 tablespoon)

3 tablespoons minced fresh mint

Salt and freshly ground black pepper
2 tablespoons minced cilantro, optional
3 tablespoons grapeseed oil

In a bowl, combine the mangoes, jicama, orange juice, hot pepper, and mint. Season very lightly with salt and a grinding of pepper. Add the cilantro and toss lightly. Taste and add more hot pepper to taste. Cover and chill until 20 minutes before serving.

Grilled Shrimp with Mushrooms and Bell Peppers

Come summer I start to seriously experiment with all kinds of kebabs. I find them appealing and very practical, since once the vegetables, meat, poultry, or shellfish is threaded onto the skewers, the main course is basically ready. All you need as an accompaniment is an interesting grain—be it rice, couscous, polenta, or bulgur.

SERVES 6

1 teaspoon whole coriander seeds

1 teaspoon whole cumin seeds

½ cup olive oil

¼ cup freshly squeezed lime juice

1 small yellow onion, minced

1 bay leaf

3 large garlic cloves, finely sliced

½ teaspoon coarse salt

Freshly ground black pepper

30 large shrimp, peeled and tails left attached

1 large red onion

1 large red bell pepper, seeded and cut into
   1-inch squares

1 green bell pepper, seeded and cut into
   1-inch squares

¾ pound cremini (brown mushrooms), cut
   into large cubes

3 tablespoons minced fresh cilantro or
   flat-leaf parsley

1. Make the marinade: In a dry heavy skillet, combine the coriander and cumin seeds and place over medium heat. Toast gently for 1 minute, or until the seeds are lightly brown and fragrant. Transfer the seeds to a mortar and pestle or a spice grinder and finely crush.

2. In a medium bowl, combine the crushed toasted spices, the olive oil, lime juice, minced onion, bay leaf, sliced garlic, salt, and pepper to taste. Whisk until well blended. Add the shrimp, stir to coat, cover with plastic wrap, and refrigerate for 30 to 45 minutes.

3. Prepare a hot fire in a charcoal or gas grill. Soak 6 long wooden skewers in water for at least 30 minutes.

4. Cut the red onion into eighths. Remove the shrimp from the marinade; reserve the marinade.

5. To assemble the kebabs, alternate the shrimp, onions, bell peppers, and mushrooms on the skewers, starting with a shrimp, then adding a piece of onion, pepper, and mushroom, ending with a shrimp. Use 5 shrimp per skewer. Sprinkle the kebabs with a little coarse salt and a grinding of pepper.

6. When the coals are very hot, place the shrimp kebabs on the grill directly over the hot coals and grill for about 2 minutes on each side, until the shrimp turn bright pink tinged with brown.

7. Remove the kebabs from the grill and transfer each to an individual serving plate. Sprinkle with minced cilantro or parsley and serve immediately.

Middle-Eastern Char-Grilled Skirt Steaks
in a Cumin and Cilantro Marinade

Skirt steak is an inexpensive cut of meat that is outstanding prepared on the grill. It is best when marinated in a zesty marinade such as this one and served with the Chickpea, Tomato, and Cilantro Salad (page 287) or the warm Lentil Salad (page 288). Double the recipe if you can because leftover skirt steak makes wonderful sandwiches.

SERVES 6

1 heaping tablespoon ground cumin
  seeds

3 bunches fresh cilantro, washed
  thoroughly and dried

4 large garlic cloves

2 tablespoons cracked black pepper

2 chipotle peppers in adobo sauce,
  or more to taste

$^{3}/_{4}$ cup olive oil

Juice of 2 limes

Coarse salt

3 pounds skirt steak

Sprigs of fresh cilantro

1. In a blender or food processor, combine the cumin seeds, cilantro, garlic, black pepper, hot peppers, olive oil, and lime juice. Season lightly with salt and process until smooth.

2. Cut the skirt steak into $^{1}/_{2}$-pound pieces and place in a large zippered plastic bag. Pour the marinade over the pieces and seal the bag. Set the bag in a shallow dish and refrigerate for 24 hours, turning the steaks in the marinade once or twice.

3. Prepare a hot fire in a charcoal grill. Remove the steaks from the bag and wipe off the excess marinade.

4. When the coals are red hot, sprinkle each side of the skirt steaks with a little coarse salt and set the steaks over the hot coals. Grill 2 to 3 minutes per side, until nicely browned for medium-rare, 130° to 135°F internal temperature on a meat thermometer.

5. Remove the steaks from the grill, transfer to a cutting board, and let sit for a few minutes before slicing. Cut the meat across the grain on the bias into thin slices. Garnish with cilantro.

REMARKS For a more intense cumin flavor, toast 2 tablespoons whole cumin seeds in a small skillet until fragrant and crush in either a mortar and pestle or a spice grinder.

Grilled Marinated Cremini Mushrooms

I am always looking for ways to use the fire after the main course is done and these mushrooms are ideal for this use, since they only take 3 to 4 minutes to cook, and the dressing can be made well ahead of time. I like to serve these mushrooms as an appetizer over young greens or as a side dish for grilled veal chops, chicken, or a sirloin steak. It is a good idea to double or even triple the recipe and let some of the mushrooms marinate for a day or two.

SERVES 4

¼ cup plus 2 tablespoons extra virgin olive oil

2 tablespoons lemon juice

1 tablespoon balsamic vinegar

1½ teaspoons Dijon mustard

1 large garlic clove, mashed

Coarse salt and freshly ground black pepper

1 pound cremini mushrooms, stems removed

2 tablespoons minced fresh thyme, oregano, or marjoram

1. In a bowl combine the ¼ cup olive oil, the lemon juice, balsamic vinegar, Dijon mustard, and garlic. Whisk the vinaigrette until well blended. Season with salt and pepper.

2. Brush the mushrooms with a little of the remaining olive oil. Season with salt and pepper.

3. Place the mushroom on a rack over medium-hot coals and grill for 2 minutes on each side. Remove to a serving dish. Drizzle the vinaigrette over the hot mushrooms and let them stand at room temperature until cooled before serving.

Grilled Eggplant

Grilling eggplants is a wonderful way to use a hot fire. The intensely flavored, smoky pulp of grilled eggplant can be used in many delicious ways. It is the base for the popular baba ghanoush in which the eggplant flesh is combined with tahini (sesame paste), lemon juice, and garlic. I often substitute mayonnaise or yogurt for the tahini which makes for a lighter dip.

I also use the grilled eggplant pulp as a base for soup and in spicy eggplant fritters. Be sure to choose eggplants that are light for their size. Heavy eggplants are usually seedier and may have a bitter flavor.

MAKES ABOUT 2 CUPS

2 medium eggplants, unpeeled

1. Prepare a charcoal grill.

2. When the coals are very hot, place the eggplants directly on the coals. Grill, turning often, until the skin is charred on all sides and the eggplants are quite tender. Be careful not to char beneath the skin.

3. Remove the eggplants carefully from the grill and transfer to a cutting surface. Scoop out the pulp and use as directed in your recipe (see headnote for suggestions).

Grilled Green Tomatoes in Basil Vinaigrette

I love the crunchy refreshing texture of green tomatoes and often use the hot fire to grill a few slices, which I marinate in a variety of vinaigrettes. You can vary this simple preparation by using cilantro or parsley instead of basil or use a combination of two of your favorite herbs. You can serve the tomatoes as an appetizer sprinkled with some aged goat cheese and diced oil-cured black olives or diced smoked mozzarella and tiny capers.

SERVES 6

4 to 6 medium-sized green tomatoes
½ cup plus 2 tablespoons extra virgin olive oil
Coarse salt and freshly ground black pepper
2 tablespoons sherry vinegar
1 to 2 large garlic cloves, mashed
½ cup basil leaves
2 tablespoons minced shallots or red onion

1. Prepare a charcoal or gas grill.

2. Cut the tomatoes crosswise into ⅜-inch slices. Brush with 2 tablespoons olive oil. Season with salt and pepper. Grill the slices over a hot fire for 2 minutes on each side, or until nicely browned. Transfer to a shallow serving dish and reserve.

3. In a blender, combine the vinegar, 1 clove of the garlic, the basil leaves, and remaining ½ cup olive oil. Puree until smooth. Season with salt to taste. Add a little more garlic, if desired.

4. Spoon the vinaigrette over the tomatoes and sprinkle with shallots or red onions and a generous grinding of black pepper. Marinate for 3 to 6 hours before serving.

Roasted Red Bell Peppers

I still remember a time when red bell peppers were only available in the fall. Now that we can get Holland peppers year-round, it is fun to make a batch of roasted peppers whenever you plan to cook on the grill. They will keep for several days in the refrigerator, covered with olive oil, in a tightly covered jar.

At different times of the year, many grocery stores carry both the Holland peppers and domestic, or Mexican, peppers, which have thinner skins and are more unevenly shaped. These peppers are usually less expensive and very flavorful but are harder to peel evenly.

1. *Charring the peppers outdoors:* Prepare a charcoal grill.

2. When the coals are red hot, place the peppers directly on top of the coals and grill until the skins are blackened and somewhat charred on all sides.

3. As soon as the peppers are done, remove them from the grill and wrap each pepper in a damp paper towel. Set aside to cool completely.

4. When the peppers are cool enough to handle, peel off the charred skin, core, and remove all seeds. The peppers are now ready to be used in a recipe.

5. *Charring the peppers indoors:* You may also roast the peppers indoors on either an electric or gas stove. For an electric stove, place the peppers directly on the coils of the burner over medium-high heat to char on all sides. For a gas stove, pierce the peppers with the tines of a long fork through the stem end. Set over a medium-high flame and char on all sides. In both cases remove from the burner, wrap in a damp paper towel, cool, and peel.

REMARKS You may also roast green bell peppers, the variety peppers (jalapeños, serranos, yellow, and orange), and fresh tomatoes in the same manner. Tomatoes do not need to be wrapped in a damp towel; just set aside to peel.

Grilled Tomato Salsa

The slightly smoky taste of charcoal-grilled tomatoes adds a wonderful dimension to this classic salsa. I often combine the salsa with some yogurt and a little mayonnaise and serve it as a sauce with grilled fish steaks. For a variation substitute cilantro for the rosemary and add 8 to 10 diced pitted black olives to the salsa.

SERVES 4 TO 5

4 to 6 medium-ripe large tomatoes

2 jalapeño peppers

3 tablespoons red onion, minced

1 large garlic clove, mashed

⅓ cup extra virgin olive oil

Juice of 1 lime

2 to 3 tablespoons minced cilantro

Coarse salt and freshly ground black pepper

2 tablespoons minced fresh basil, optional

1. Heat a small charcoal grill. Add a handful of wet wood chips and wait until the fire exudes a smoky aroma. Place the tomatoes and jalapeño peppers on a rack directly over the coals. Cover the grill and roast the tomatoes and peppers for 3 to 4 minutes, or until lightly charred. Remove from the grill and let stand until cool enough to handle. Peel the tomatoes and peppers and remove the seeds. Finely dice both vegetables. Transfer to a bowl.

2. Add the red onion, garlic, olive oil, lime juice, cilantro, salt and pepper to taste, and basil. Toss the salsa gently to mix. Taste and correct the seasoning. Serve at room temperature.

Beurre Manié

A *beurre mani*é is used in both classic and peasant cooking to thicken sauces. It is a flour-and-butter paste that can be formed into a ball and held successfully for several weeks. You will rarely need an entire beurre manié in any recipe in this book, since it is preferable to reduce the sauce naturally before thickening it so as to intensify the flavor.

MAKES 8 PORTIONS

> 8 tablespoons unsalted butter (1 stick),
>   slightly softened
> ½ cup all-purpose flour

1. Combine the butter and flour in a food processor and process until smooth.

2. Refrigerate the mixture just long enough so that you can shape into balls with your hands. Divide the mixture into 8 equal parts and shape each into a ball.

3. Place the balls in a tightly covered jar and refrigerate until needed. The beurre manié can also be frozen for 2 to 3 months.

Clarified Butter

Clarifying butter is a simple technique that removes the milky residue and impurities that make butter burn quickly. It works best when done with at least 8 ounces of butter. Once clarified, the butter can be refrigerated in a tightly sealed jar for at least 2 weeks or frozen for several months. Clarified butter is used for sautéing delicate foods such as fish fillets, fritters, or anything that is breaded. You can also use it for sautéing in any recipe that calls for regular butter.

1. Melt any desired amount of the butter in a heavy saucepan over low heat. As soon as the butter is melted and very foamy, remove from the heat and carefully skim off all the foam.

2. Strain the clear yellow liquid through a fine sieve, discarding the milky residue on the bottom of the pan. The strained, clear yellow liquid is clarified butter. It can be stored in a covered jar in the refrigerator for 2 to 3 weeks.

Basic Tart Dough

MAKES ONE (10- TO 12-INCH) PASTRY ROUND

1½ cups all-purpose unbleached flour

¼ teaspoon salt

9 tablespoons unsalted butter, cut into
   12 pieces and chilled

3 to 5 tablespoons ice water

1. In a food processor, combine the flour, salt, and butter. Pulse quickly until the mixture resembles oatmeal. Add 3 tablespoons of the ice water and pulse quickly until the mixture begins to come together. Do not let it form a ball.

2. Transfer the mixture to a large bowl and gather it into a ball. If the dough is too crumbly, add the remaining ice water, 1 tablespoon at a time, and work it quickly into the ball.

3. Flatten the ball into a disk, wrap it in foil, and refrigerate for at least 30 minutes, or until firm enough to roll. The dough is now ready to be used.

Basic Tart Shell

2 cups all-purpose unbleached flour

¼ to ½ teaspoon salt

12 tablespoons unsalted butter, cut into 12
   pieces and chilled

4 to 6 tablespoons ice water

1. In a food processor, combine the flour, salt, and butter. Pulse quickly until the mixture resembles oatmeal. Add 3 tablespoons of the ice water and pulse quickly until the mixture begins to come together. Do not let it form a ball.

2. Transfer the mixture to a large bowl and gather it into a ball. If the dough is too crumbly, add the remaining ice water, 1 tablespoon at a time, and work it quickly into the ball.

3. Flatten the ball into a disk, wrap it in foil, and refrigerate for at least 30 minutes.

4. Roll out the dough on a lightly floured surface, into a round about ⅛ inch thick. Roll the dough around the rolling pin, then unroll it into a 9- or 10-inch tart pan with or without a removable bottom. Press the dough into the bottom and sides of the pan, being careful not to stretch the dough. Fold the excess overhang into the pan and press it firmly against the sides. This will create a double layer of dough, which will reinforce the sides of the shell. You now have an unbaked tart shell.

5. Prick the bottom of the shell with a fork, cover with aluminum foil, and place the shell in the freezer for 4 to 6 hours or overnight. At this point the dough can be wrapped tightly and frozen for up to 2 weeks.

6. Preheat the oven to 425°F. Remove the foil and line the frozen shell with parchment paper or buttered foil. Fill with pie weights or large dried beans and place it on a cookie sheet. Bake the shell in the center of the preheated oven for 12 minutes, or until the sides are set.

7. Remove the paper and beans and continue to bake for 4 to 6 minutes longer, until the shell is set but not browned. Remove the shell from the oven and place the pan on a wire rack to cool until needed. The tart shell is now partially baked. For a pre-baked shell, after removing the paper and beans, bake for 10 to 12 minutes, or until golden brown.

REMARKS For a dessert tart shell, use only a pinch of salt instead of ½ teaspoon. Add 2 tablespoons of confectioners' sugar along with the flour, salt, and butter to the food processor and proceed with Step 1.

Double-Poached Garlic Cloves

The garlic may be cooked days in advance. Simply place the poached garlic in a jar, cover with olive oil, seal tightly, and store in the refrigerator until needed. The garlic will keep for up to 3 months.

2 to 3 heads of garlic, separated into cloves
   and peeled

1. Bring plenty of water to a boil in a medium saucepan. Add the garlic and return the water to a boil. Cook for 1 minute.

2. Drain, discarding the poaching liquid. Return the garlic cloves to the saucepan, add fresh water to cover, and again bring to a boil. Simmer for 15 to 20 minutes or until the cloves are tender when pierced with the tip of a knife. Drain again. The garlic is now ready to be used in any recipe that calls for it.

Brown Chicken Stock

5 tablespoons corn or peanut oil

2 large onions, quartered and sliced

20 to 24 chicken wings

3 to 4 pounds beef shanks, meaty beef neck bones,
   or short ribs of beef, or a combination

3 small onions, skins on, cut in half crosswise

3 large carrots, peeled and diced

3 large celery stalks, diced

1 parsley root with greens attached, peeled,
   optional

1 teaspoon dried thyme

1 bay leaf, crumbled

6 whole black peppercorns

3 large sprigs of flat-leaf parsley

1. Preheat the broiler.

2. In a large heavy skillet, preferably cast iron, heat 3 tablespoons of the oil over medium-high heat. Add the sliced onions, and cook, stirring constantly, for 2 to 3 minutes, or until they begin to brown. Reduce the heat to low, partially cover, and cook for 25 to 30 minutes, or until the onions are soft and nicely caramelized; do not let them burn.

3. While the onions are browning, prepare the chicken wings and beef: Cut each chicken wing at its joints into 3 pieces. Place the chicken pieces in a single layer in a roasting pan, set under the broiler 4 to 6 inches from the source of heat, and broil until nicely browned on all sides; be careful not to burn them. Transfer the wings to an 8- to 10-quart stockpot and reserve.

4. Place the beef shanks, bones, and/or ribs in the roasting pan and broil until nicely browned on all sides, again being careful not to burn them. Transfer to the stockpot.

5. When the onions are done, transfer them also to the stockpot and add the remaining 2 tablespoons oil to the skillet. Add the unpeeled onions, cut sides down, and cook for 5 to 8 minutes, or until very brown. Add them to the stockpot.

6. Add the carrots and celery to the skillet and cook, stirring often, for 10 to 15 minutes, until nicely browned; they will not brown evenly. Transfer to the stockpot together with the parsley root, if using, thyme, bay leaf, peppercorns, and parsley sprigs. Add enough water to cover by 2 inches, 14 to 16 cups. Bring to a boil, reduce the heat, and simmer, partially covered, for 3 to 4 hours, skimming often, until the liquid becomes a deep hazelnut brown.

7. When the stock is done, strain it through cheesecloth into a large bowl and let it cool completely. Refrigerate, uncovered, overnight.

8. The next day, thoroughly degrease the stock, place it in a large casserole, and bring slowly to a boil. Remove from the heat and again let cool completely. Degrease again if necessary. Transfer to containers or jars, cover tightly, and refrigerate or freeze.

REMARKS The stock will keep for several months in the freezer. If refrigerated, it will keep for up to 10 days and must be brought back to a boil every 2 to 3 days.

White Stock

MAKES 2 QUARTS

4 to 5 pounds meaty beef bones, preferably
beef shanks or beef short ribs

2 large carrots, peeled and cut in half

2 to 3 celery stalks with leaves, cut in half

2 leeks, trimmed and washed

2 medium onions, peeled

6 whole black peppercorns

1 parsley root, optional

1 large sprig of fresh thyme

2 large sprigs of fresh flat-leaf parsley

1½ teaspoon salt

1. Combine all the ingredients in a tall and large but narrow stockpot with 3 quarts water. Bring to a boil, reduce the heat, and simmer, partially covered, for 3 to 4 hours, skimming the surface several times.

2. Strain the stock through a double layer of cheesecloth into a large bowl and set aside at room temperature, uncovered, until completely cool. Place in the refrigerator overnight.

3. The next day, remove and discard all the fat from the surface. Pour the stock into a flameproof casserole or large saucepan. Bring to a boil, remove from the heat, and let cool completely. Refrigerate for up to 1 week, bringing the stock back to a boil every few days, or freeze in covered containers for up to 1 month.

Cooked Pinto or Red Kidney Beans

MAKES ABOUT 6 CUPS

1 pound dried pinto or red kidney beans

1 small onion, skin on

1 large sprig of fresh thyme

1 large sprig of fresh parsley

6 whole black peppercorns

½ pound smoked pork shoulder butt, quartered

Salt

You can cook beans by either of the following two methods.

METHOD #1

1. Place the dried beans in a large bowl with plenty of water to cover. Let soak overnight at room temperature.

2. The next day, preheat the oven to 325°F.

3. Drain the beans and place in a large, heavy flameproof casserole with a tight-fitting lid. Cover with water by 2 inches and add the onion, thyme, parsley, peppercorns, and pork butt.

4. Bring to a boil on top of the stove and cook for exactly 1 minute. Immediately cover tightly and place the casserole in the center of the oven. Cook the beans for 1 hour to 1 hour 15 minutes, or until just tender. Do not overcook and do not add salt until the beans are almost done. Remove the casserole from the oven and let the beans cool in their cooking liquid.

5. Discard the vegetables and herbs. Store the beans in their liquid. They will keep in the refrigerator in their cooking liquid for up to 5 days. You will need both the cooked beans and the bean cooking liquid in most recipes.

METHOD #2

1. Do not soak the beans at all. Instead, place them in a large, heavy flameproof casserole with a tight-fitting lid. Cover with water by 2 inches and add the onion, thyme, parsley, peppercorns, and pork butt.

2. Bring to a boil on top of the stove and cook for exactly 1 minute. Immediately remove the casserole from the heat, cover, and set aside for 2 hours at room temperature. Drain the beans, add fresh water to cover by 2 inches, and continue to braise the beans in the oven as in Method #1, Step 4.

REMARKS Smoked pork shoulder butt is available in all supermarkets. It is often called a daisy ham or porkette.

Also use either of these two methods to cook white beans, kidney beans, black beans, and flageolets. Cooking times for each will vary.

Cooked White Beans

MAKES ABOUT 6 CUPS

 1 pound dried white beans

 1 small onion, skin on

 1 carrot, cut in half

 1 celery stalk with tops

 Pinch of salt

 4 to 6 whole black peppercorns

You can cook white beans by either of the following two methods.

METHOD #1

1. Place the beans in a bowl, cover with 2 inches of cold water, and let the beans soak overnight.

2. The next day, drain the beans. Place the beans in a large saucepan and cover with water by 2 inches. Add the onion, carrot, celery, salt, and peppercorns.

3. Bring the beans to a boil on top of the stove. Reduce the heat to medium-low and cook for 1½ hour or until tender. Do not overcook. The beans may be left in their cooking water for 3 to 4 days.

METHOD #2

Place the dried beans in a saucepan with 2 inches of water to cover. Bring to a boil on top of the stove for exactly 1 minute. Remove from the heat. Cover the saucepan and let the beans sit for 2 hours. Drain, add fresh water, and proceed with the recipe as above.

Strawberry Sauce

SERVES 6

2 packages (10 ounces each) frozen
   strawberries in syrup
¾ cup red currant jelly
1½ to 2 tablespoons lemon juice
2 tablespoons kirsch or Grand Marnier
Sugar, optional

1. Defrost the strawberries and drain well, reserving the juices. Place the berries with the juice of 1 package in a food processor and puree until smooth. (Reserve the remaining juice for another use or discard.)

2. Place the jelly in a small saucepan and set over low heat. Stir until the jelly is completely dissolved and add to the strawberry puree. Stir in 1½ tablespoons of the lemon juice, and the kirsch or Grand Marnier. Correct the sweetness of the sauce by adding either a little sugar or a little more lemon juice. Strain the sauce through a fine sieve into a bowl. Cover and chill until serving time.

KITCHENWARE

Broadway Panhandler

Excellent selection of knives, cookware, cookbooks, and bakeware

477 Broome Street

New York, NY 10013

1-866-COOKWARE or 212-966-3434

www.broadwaypanhandler.com

Sur La Table

Excellent assortment of cookware, gadgets, and small electrical appliances

800-243-0852

www.surlatable.com

Williams-Sonoma

Excellent selection of cookware and private-label spices

P. O. Box 7456

San Francisco, CA 94120-7456

800-541-2233

www.williams-sonoma.com

SPECIALTY FOODS

Aidell's Sausage Company

Huge variety of all-natural sausages

1625 Alvarado Street

San Leandro, CA 94577

Tel: 800-AIDELLS

Fax: 510-614-2846

www.aidells.com

E-mail: info@aidells.com

Asian Pantry (part of chefshop.com)

Assortment of Asian ingredients, including a variety of soy sauces, rice and curry pastes

Tel: 877-337-2491

Fax: 206-282-5607

www.chefshop.com

E-mail: shopkeeper@chefshop.com

Atlantic Game Meats

Superb quality of venison, including marinated venison steaks and roasts

Tel: 207-862-4217

www.atlanticgamemeats.com

Bob's Red Mill

Organic flour, whole grains, excellent polenta

5209 SE International Way

Milwaukie, OR 97222

Tel: 800-349-2173

Fax: 503-653-1339

www.bobsredmill.com

chefshop.com

Excellent choice of dried beans, including Arrocina rice beans from Spain, organic cannellini beans, porcini mushrooms, Italian canned albacore tuna in olive oil, and various types of capers

Tel: 877-337-2491

Fax: 206-282-5607

www.chefshop.com

D'Artagnan

The best source for game, rabbit, squab, poussins (baby chickens), quail, duck fat, duck breasts, duck foie gras, and chorizo sausage

280 Wilson Avenue

Newark, NJ 07105

Tel: 800-327-8246

Fax: 973-465-1870

www.dartagnan.com

Dean & DeLuca

Produce, grains, oils, vinegars, mustards, teas, and spices

560 Broadway

New York, NY 11101

Tel: 877-826-9246

Fax: 800-781-4050

www.deandeluca.com

Earthy Delights

Excellent source for dried beans and lentils

1161 E. Clark Road, Suite 260

DeWitt, MI 48820

Tel: 800-367-4709

Fax: 517-668-1213

www.earthy.com

E-mail: info@earthy.com

El Paso Chile Company

Dried chiles, southwestern spices, etc.

Tel: 888-472-5727

Fax: 915-544-7552

www.elpasochile.com

Kalustyan's

Large international selection of grains, rice, unusual spices, and nuts

123 Lexington Avenue

New York, NY 10016

Tel: 212-685-3451

Fax: 212-683-8458

www.kalustyans.com

Leech Lake Wild Rice Co.

Organic wild rice that is hand harvested and packaged by Leech Lake Indian Reservation

Tel: 877-246-0620

Mozzarella Company

Wonderful ricotta, cacciota, and fresh and smoked mozzarella

2944 Elm Street

Dallas, TX 75226

800-798-2954

www.mozzco.com

Penzeys Spices

Great selection of spices and spice blends, including Mexican spices such as achiote and Mexican oregano

Tel: 800-741-7787

Fax: 262-785-7678

www.penzeys.com

The Spanish Table

Spanish imports: rice, spices, beans, oils and vinegars

1427 Western Avenue

Seattle, WA 98101

Tel: 206-682-2827

Fax: 206-682-2814

E-mail: tablespan@aol.com

Spice Island

Top-quality dried herbs and spices

Tel: 800-635-6278

Todaro Bros.

Italian imports, pasta, rice, oils, and cheeses

555 Second Avenue

New York, NY 10016

Tel: 877-472-2767

Fax: 212-698-1679

www.todarobros-specialty-foods.com

Zingerman's

Quality foods including cheeses, aged balsamic vinegar, large selection of olive oils

422 Detroit Street

Ann Arbor, MI 48104-1118

Tel: 888-636-8162

Fax: 734-477-6988

www.zingermans.com

E-mail: toni@zingermans.com

Celery
    nutrients in, 71
    and Stilton Cheese Soup,
        Creamy, 71, 118–119
    in stock, 70, 191, 389–390,
        391
    storage of, 71
    varieties of, 71
Celery Root
    appearance of, 71–72
    freshness of, 72
    Potatoes, and Sweet Garlic,
        Puree of, 117
    rémoulade, 72
    storage of, 72
Chanterelle Mushrooms, 91,
    92
    Acorn Squash, Apple, and
        Wild Mushroom Soup,
        147–148
Charcoal grilling
    amount of charcoal, 349
    briquette safety, 348–349
    burying food in ashes, 355
    cleaning, 355
    direct and indirect method,
        346, 347, 350
    flare-ups, 353
    vs gas grilling, 346, 347
    lighting fire, 349
    mesquite, 349
    readiness of coals, 350, 353
    selecting grill, 347–348
    with wood chips, 351–352
    See also Grilling, Grilled
Charentais melon, 310, 311
Chateaubriand, 223
Cheese
    Gruyère, Wild Mushroom,
        and Scallion Bread
        Pudding, 133–134
    Mozzarella, Smoked, Penne
        with Broccoli, Peppers,
        Tomatoes and, 271–
        272

Mozzarella, in Spaghettini
    with Tuna, Capers, and
    Black Olives, 273
Stilton, and Celery Soup,
    Creamy, 118–119
Stilton, and Leek Risotto
    with Mascarpone, 280
varieties of, 46–48
See also Goat Cheese; Mascar-
    pone; Parmesan
Chef's knife, 8
Cherry(ies)
    Clafoutis, Classic, 327–328
    dried, 52
    pitting, 304, 328
    in season, 303
    tart, 304
    varieties of, 303–304
Cherrystone clams, 162
Cherry tomatoes, 104, 105
Chervil, 84, 87
Chestnuts, prepared, 54
Chicken
    Bouillabaisse of, 202–203
    Breasts
        on bone vs boneless, 190
        boning, 191
        cooking methods for,
            194–195
        cutlets, 193–194
        Slow-Braised, with Peas
            and Lemon-Dill
            Sauce, 204–205
    brining, 192
    broilers and fryers, 190
    cuts of, 193
    European vs U.S., 187–189
    free-range, 189–190
    freshness of, 189
    Grilled, Lemon-Herb, "Under
        a Brick," 356–357
    grilling vs broiling, 193
    grilling whole and cut-up,
        354
    Kebabs, Lime-Marinated, 358

kosher, 190
Legs, Broiled, with Herb
    Butter, 195, 201
Legs with Fennel Sausage,
    Ragout of, 208–209
marinating, 195
organic, 189, 190
Paella, Catalan, 275–276
Roasted, à la Flamande, 210
roasting, 192–193
rotisserie style, 193
safety measures in preparing,
    192
salad, 195
with Sherry Vinegar-Garlic
    Essense and Concassé of
    Tomatoes, Provençal,
    206–207
skin color, 190
stir-fry, 195
stock, 190–191
Stock, Brown, 389–390
storage of, 191–192
wings, cooking methods for,
    195
Wings with Spicy Peanut
    Sauce, 359–360
wings, in stock, 22, 191,
    389–390
Chicken liver, sautéed, 190
Chickpea(s)
    canned, 262
    names for, 262
    soaking, 262
    Tomato, and Cilantro Salad,
        287
Chiles
    bottled and canned, 73
    dried whole, 29, 73
    ground vs powder, 32, 73
    handling precautions, 74
    heat of, 72–73
    reducing heat, 74
    substitutions, 73
    See also Jalapeño